How to
Feel
Loved

Also by Sonja Lyubomirsky

*The How of Happiness: A New Approach
to Getting the Life You Want*

*The Myths of Happiness: What Should
Make You Happy, but Doesn't, What
Shouldn't Make You Happy, but Does*

Also by Harry Reis

*Relationships, Well-Being and Behaviour:
Selected Works of Harry T. Reis*

How to
Feel
Loved

THE FIVE MINDSETS
THAT GET YOU MORE OF
WHAT MATTERS MOST

SONJA LYUBOMIRSKY
AND HARRY REIS

HARPER

An Imprint of HarperCollins*Publishers*

HarperCollins books may be purchased for educational, business, or sales promotional use. For information, please email the Special Markets Department at SPsales@harpercollins.com.

hc.com

FIRST EDITION

Designed by Bonni Leon-Berman

Library of Congress Cataloging-in-Publication Data has been applied for.

ISBN 978-0-06-342666-5

Printed in the United States of America

25 26 27 28 29 LBC 5 4 3 2 1

For Olivia, who makes me feel loved,
every moment and every day.

—*Sonja*

For Ellen and Lianna, who showed me what
it means to love and be loved.

—*Harry*

There is only one happiness in life, to love and be loved.

—*George Sand*

Contents

Introduction: Do You Want to Feel More Loved?   1

PART I: WHY FEELING LOVED MATTERS

1 Hardwired to Feel Loved   19

2 The Cost of Not Feeling Loved   32

3 Revisiting Popular Beliefs About What Makes You Feel Loved   52

PART II: A NEW PARADIGM

4 The Relationship Sea-Saw   75

PART III: PUTTING THE SEA-SAW INTO PRACTICE— THE FIVE MINDSETS

5 Sharing Mindset   97

6 Listening-to-Learn Mindset   124

7 Radical-Curiosity Mindset   155

8 Open-Heart Mindset   181

9 Multiplicity Mindset   221

PART IV: APPLYING THE FIVE MINDSETS TO MODERN LIFE

10 Feeling Loved in Different Kinds of Relationships   245

11 What If One Size Doesn't Fit All? Diagnosing the
Personal Qualities That Make Feeling Loved Easier or Harder   274

12 Can You Feel Loved by an AI Chatbot?
How About a Throuple? And Other Questions for
the New Age   291

Conclusion: Why All Five Mindsets Are Essential . . .
and Why You Have to Go First   315

Epilogue   319

A Note from the Authors: The Five Mindsets Diagnostic   321

Acknowledgments   323

Notes   329

Index   381

Do You Want to Feel More Loved?

When Sonja Met Harry

Twenty years ago, Sonja was booked to speak about the science of happiness on a TV talk show with a popular host. It was only her second television appearance, and she was nervous. She'd spent several weeks emailing back and forth with the producers about the questions and her proposed responses. She's very conscientious and has a low tolerance for uncertainty, so this preparation eased her anxiety. Finally, it was happening. She flew to New York, had her makeup done, and waited in the greenroom for her turn, heart racing. Abruptly, a mere few minutes before she was to walk backstage, the senior producer burst in. "The host decided to go in a different direction," he said. [Translation: The host threw out the script we'd all worked so diligently on.] "When you go on, she is going to ask you this: 'Tell me the secret to happiness.'"

Being a happiness expert means being asked over and over again, "What is the secret to happiness?" Sonja has always dreaded that question. It's ridiculous, it's reductive, and it's restrictive. But mostly she has dreaded it because she has never had a solid, science-based answer that she could offer with any confidence.

There is no secret to happiness. But there are huge contributors to happiness, and some of them are more powerful than others. Sonja resists being pinned down to just one. But if she were pressed to give an answer, she now has one.

She found it when she met one of the world's leading experts on the science of relationships, her coauthor, Harry. They were standing around at a conference in Washington, DC, and she told him the story about the TV host. He said, "I don't know the secret to happiness either, but I do know people who are happy, and I know people who are unhappy, and I can tell you the main difference between them: Happy people feel loved."

The secret to happiness is feeling loved.

Harry also said, "Isn't it odd that happiness researchers and relationship researchers don't talk with each other?" So here we are.

Do you want to feel *more* loved? Or to feel loved more *often*?

For months, we had been asking this question—again and again—to anyone willing to listen. Not all were comfortable sharing, but those who did spoke with striking candor. The more we asked, the more it became clear that many people struggle with feeling truly loved. Some of our friends worried that the love they received was conditional—that if their family, friends, or partners saw their flaws too clearly, that love may disappear. Others understood, logically, that they *were* loved, yet they didn't always *feel* it, or at least not as often as they wished. Just as you can be beautiful without *feeling* beautiful, you can be loved without *feeling* loved. And some simply wanted to better understand what brings them the love they already feel.

If one of these feelings resonates with you—if there are times when you want to feel more loved—you're not alone. Human beings are social animals, driven by a deep need for connection and belonging, whose way of being is profoundly communal. As a result, one of the most important things that you likely want from your relationships—probably *the* most important thing—is to feel loved, appreciated, and understood. To feel that the people in your life truly get you, value you, and love you is what makes life worth living. This is what makes people happy. And this is the science-backed conclusion that Harry's career-long research program landed on.

Of course, not everyone is walking around feeling unloved. Many people do feel loved—but they're not always sure what they're doing right or how to make that feeling last. Others feel loved and want to feel it even more. (Love is like happiness—there's always room to feel more.) And then there's a pattern therapists know all too well:

You're doing your best to love someone—your partner, a parent, a close friend—but that person never seems to *feel* loved, no matter what you do. This book will help you understand why that happens and how you can help bridge that gap.

Despite being frequently surrounded by others or constantly connected through devices, it's common to still grapple with not feeling loved, either not feeling loved as deeply, or as often, as one would like or not feeling loved for the right reasons. Despite sharing many fun activities with friends or experiencing passion with lovers, many people still don't feel loved in the way they want to feel loved. Furthermore, in order to feel more loved, many turn to strategies that seem intuitive and yet, as this book will argue, don't lead to the results they hope for.

As researchers who have spent our entire careers studying happiness and connection, respectively, we came together to write *How to Feel Loved* to explain why feeling loved can seem so difficult, eluding even one's most sincere efforts, and how to attain it. Drawing on a wealth of empirical studies, established psychological theory, personal stories, and ancient wisdom, we will challenge your preconceived notions and show you (1) how to *think differently* about the people you care about and (2) how to *approach differently* your next opportunity to feel loved.

In other words, we will show you how to embrace new mindsets and change your conversations.

What It's Like to Feel Loved

Think about the moments when you've felt truly loved. Maybe it was a quiet instant, when a friend remembered something deeply important to you without being prompted. Maybe it was the way a partner looked at you—really looked at you—when you were speaking, as though they were hanging on every word. Or maybe it was the way a mentor encouraged you at a pivotal moment, showing you that they saw something in you that you hadn't yet seen in yourself. These moments stand out because they make you feel deeply known, understood, and valued. You carry them with you long after they happen.

Are there times you've felt loved this way? And if not as often as you'd like—why?

What Not to Do

Consider this: You're on a first date where the other person is clearly eager to impress you. They talk animatedly about their latest promotion, their workout routine, the exotic places they've traveled—barely pausing for breath. You get the sense that they want you to like them, but something feels off. There's no back-and-forth, no real connection—just them, performing. By the end of the date, you realize that despite learning plenty about them, you don't actually feel closer to them. You didn't get a glimpse of their real thoughts, struggles, or quirks—only a polished highlight reel. And because they were so focused on impressing you, they never really saw you either. The problem isn't that they lacked interesting qualities—they actually had lots of them. It's that they weren't truly sharing themselves in a meaningful way. Instead of inviting a sense of being known and loved, they were curating an image—leaving no space for you to be seen or known in return. Real connection depends on reciprocity—on a mutual willingness to reveal, to witness, and to engage. Without that, no amount of charm or achievement can bridge the emotional gap.

This example offers a clue about how to start thinking differently: Feeling more loved is not about making yourself more lovable. It's not about trying to mold yourself into someone more interesting, better looking, funnier, smarter, wealthier, or more successful. It's not about getting the other person to think you're wonderful. It's not about trying to figure out what their love language is or what they want and forging yourself into that image. It's not about fixing yourself. It's not about emphasizing, exaggerating, or selectively showing the parts of you that you think the other person will approve of while hiding the less desirable parts.

Yeah, we know: That's a lot of *not*s. In this book, we will show that doing all those things might (sometimes) lead you to be *admired* but won't lead you to *feel loved*.

There are a few reasons why. How can you truly feel loved when your loved ones only know the rosy side of you—more audition-tape than real-life? How can you truly feel loved when you worry that unveiling your raw, full, imperfect, innermost self might cost you their love and respect? How can you truly feel the love coming *from* them when your attention is focused on how you are coming across *to* them? How can you truly feel loved by them when you're not doing anything to help them feel loved by you?

Imagine the other person's love as a radiant sun shining on you. If it shines on and warms only the outer surface or only the parts that are unimportant or even untrue, you won't feel illuminated or warmed to your core. You can't and won't feel loved.

The Good News Starts with a Cliché

"Just be yourself." It's a cliché we've all heard before, maybe even rolled our eyes at. But when you're in a relationship or friendship where you're not feeling as loved as you'd like to feel, what does that expression actually mean? We've suggested that many people aren't being themselves: Instead of showing themselves, they show off themselves. Yet herein lies both a paradox and a blessing. The paradox is that feeling loved is earned not through achieving perfection but through presenting more of your full self—your values, experiences, quirks, and dreams, even the small unpolished details of your daily life. Sharing your struggles and imperfections can build connection, too, but feeling loved isn't just about revealing your flawed, imperfect self—it's about revealing what truly matters to you.

To be clear, feeling loved doesn't hinge on oversharing or baring your soul to just anyone. It doesn't mean unloading your trials and tribulations in the first five minutes after meeting. It means selectively and progressively revealing parts of yourself in a way that fosters genuine connection.

The blessing is that showing your full self is fully within your control. In fact, it's a lot easier than contorting yourself into someone else's ideal image. Many people believe that in order to feel more loved, they must *persuade* others to love them more—as if they were trying to sell someone a new car. Years of empirical studies and observation suggest that this approach is ineffective. That's why our message is different: Feeling loved is more—much more—about *you* (and your mindset) than about trying to persuade the other person that you are worthy.

Yet people often behave in ways that work against feeling loved: They hide their deepest thoughts, emotions, flaws, and past misbehaviors because they are afraid of what others might think, or they fear being embarrassed or exploited. This tendency is so widespread that it directly ties to two of the most common deathbed regrets: "I wish I'd had the courage to live a life true to myself" and "I wish I'd had the courage to express my feelings." Yet, as we described above, paradoxically, the more you hide your innermost self and the less of yourself you reveal to others, the harder it is to feel truly loved and valued by the significant people in your life. This is a principle strongly supported not only by anecdotal evidence but also by relationship science. (If you've seen the television series *Ted Lasso*, where characters form deep bonds only after they reveal their insecurities and imperfections, you'll know what we mean. Or consider classic literature, such as *Pride and Prejudice*, where love becomes possible only after characters let go of their pride, masks, and mistaken impressions to reveal their more authentic selves.)

Moreover, when you focus on how you are coming across to others, your attention is drawn to what *you* are doing—for instance, trying to say just the right thing, while doing your best to make sure your shortcomings are hidden, so that you are seen as witty or attractive or brilliant. Ironically, this approach to relationships puts your attention in exactly the wrong place. As we explain later, you'll make the best impression when you focus your attention on the other person.

It's worth noting that unveiling the complexity of your multifaceted "true" self will almost always leave you feeling vulnerable because you are exhibiting your true colors and risking losing the other person's regard. However, vulnerability is not the goal; it is simply a necessary preliminary step. Ironically, showing weakness will make room for you to feel genuinely loved because you'll finally be confident that the other person is appreciating and loving the real you. (Otherwise, whatever love or admiration they express will ring hollow.) To paraphrase Nobel Prize winner André Gide: It is better to be known for what you are than to be loved for what you are not. Humility and authenticity and a caring interest in others create the conditions for you to feel fully *known*.

Approach Your Next Conversation Differently: The Relationship Sea-Saw

"You Get What You Give"

—*title of song by New Radicals*

In summary, then, three things have to happen for you to feel loved:

1. You have to **share** the complexity of your full, multifaceted self—both your strengths and your contradictions—with the other person. (No, this isn't as simple as saying, "Let me tell you everything.")
2. The other person has to **notice** what you've shared.
3. The other person has to **care** about what you've shared.

How do you increase the chances that the other person will *notice* and *care*? The answer is simple—you go first! That means you first need to notice and care—to show curiosity—about *their* multifaceted self. It may seem counterintuitive initially, but in order to create a context for sharing more of yourself, you need to focus not on yourself but on your conversation partner. You encourage them to notice and care about your full self by first noticing and caring about *their* full self. To feel loved by them, you begin by making them feel loved by you.

This step begins a back-and-forth process that we call the Relationship Sea-Saw, and we devote a whole chapter to it (chapter 4). Here's a preview: Imagine yourself and the person you wish to feel more loved by sitting on a seesaw submerged under water (hence, the deliberate spelling of *Sea-Saw*). Only parts of your multilayered selves are visible above the surface—these are the aspects you feel safe to share, the parts that the other person sees and loves when they tell you that they love you.

However, consider what happens when you give the other person your undivided attention—when you approach them with curiosity, listen deeply to their response, and bring to the interaction genuine warmth and an appreciation for their multidimensional self. By doing so, you help lift their self a bit higher out of the water, making more of their true self visible. When they feel truly seen, valued, and accepted—not just for their best qualities but for their whole richly textured self—they will also feel more *loved* by you than ever before.

Continuing with this metaphor, by pressing down, you are placing the full weight of your attention on the other person, lifting them up. As the focus shifts to them, your own self becomes temporarily more submerged. Essentially, you're holding them up and providing them support. You're creating the conditions that make it possible for them to open up, to be fully known, and to feel safe in revealing more of who they truly are.

Importantly, this step of lifting the other person higher isn't a sacrifice—it's simply a stage in a cycle. When the other person experiences the security of being deeply understood and accepted, they're likely to reciprocate. They, too, may express curiosity in you and listen to you more attentively and warmly, embracing your full complexity with an open heart. In doing so, they help lift more of your full self above the surface, enabling more of *you* to be seen, understood, and valued. In this way, the act of truly knowing and loving someone else becomes the very thing that opens the door for *you* to feel truly known and loved in return. It's a virtuous cycle of connection: The more connection is experienced, the more love, as well as the greater curiosity about and care for each other, is felt.

This reciprocal Relationship Sea-Saw is the cornerstone of feeling loved. When you express *genuine* interest in another person—not just going through the motions but truly listening, engaging with curiosity, and appreciating their many sides—you create mutual understanding and trust. And in doing so, you invite them to reciprocate. When someone feels deeply seen, valued, and understood by you, they become more willing, motivated, and even eager to do the same for you.

By contrast, even if someone initially wants to love you, if you don't help *them* feel loved by you, they may not be fully willing, motivated, or enthusiastic to listen curiously, nonjudgmentally, and warmly to you—and to see and know you. But when you help them feel loved, they will instinctively hold space for you to open up—lift your heart—a bit more and a bit more and a bit more. In these ways, the Relationship Sea-Saw empowers you to lift, then be lifted, and then lift again and be lifted again.

The Relationship Sea-Saw represents a new paradigm for how to think about relationships—and especially for how to think about your next conversation. Turn to chapter 4 to learn more.

Imagine you're catching up with a close friend over coffee. You've been feeling a little distant from them lately, so you're hoping for a real conversation, one where you both walk away feeling a little more connected. At first, though, the chat stays surface-level—weekend plans, parenting updates, funny anecdotes. Then, your friend shares something more personal: a recent struggle with self-doubt at work. This is your moment to engage the Sea-Saw. Instead of jumping in with your own similar experience or offering quick reassurance, you lean in, ask thoughtful questions, and really listen. You show them, through your curiosity and care, that they are safe to open up further. As they do, something shifts—you can almost feel them lifting on the Sea-Saw, revealing more of their true self.

Later, when they turn the focus back to you and ask how you're doing, it feels different. More natural. More meaningful. And because you made them feel seen and understood, they are now fully present, ready to do the same for you. You begin to share—not just the polished version of your life but your real thoughts and feelings. And just like that, the Sea-Saw tilts back in your direction. By first making space for them, you've created the conditions for a reciprocal exchange of openness and connection—one that leaves you both feeling more known, valued, and loved.

How to Know and to Be Known: Five Mindsets That Will Help You Think About Your Next Conversation Differently

Each person's life is lived as a series of conversations.

—*Deborah Tannen,* You Just Don't Understand

The Relationship Sea-Saw metaphor captures how the process of feeling loved unfolds, but to operate the Sea-Saw together with someone you wish to feel more loved by, you'll need to adjust your mindsets about both sides of the equation:

- **seeking to truly *know* the other**—by showing curiosity in them and listening to them with acceptance and an open heart (which invites *them* to open up)
- **inviting yourself to *be known***—by opening up (which invites *them* to reciprocate with curiosity, listening, acceptance, and warmth)

Only by embracing both perspectives can you create the reciprocal flow that lifts each of you higher.

Here's a point we can't stress enough: This isn't a step-by-step manual where you follow three simple rules and magically feel more loved. Instead, this book offers a mental shift in how you approach connection with the people who matter most. Accordingly, the heart of our book is reserved for describing five essential mindsets: (1) Sharing, (2) Listening to Learn, (3) Radical Curiosity, (4) Open Heart, and

(5) Multiplicity. Think of a mindset as a lens through which you see the other person, engage with them, and show up for them. Mindsets can be turned on and off, like a switch: They are under your control.

Sharing Mindset

The Sharing mindset encourages you to open up about your experiences and private thoughts, as well as your failings and insecurities, in a way that is *thoughtful, selective, incremental, and intentional*—choosing *whom* to share with, *how much* to share, *when* to share, *where* to share, *how* to share, and *why* to share. Consider the paradox of vulnerability, which highlights how revealing one's authentic self, despite fears of judgment or rejection, is essential to creating true intimacy. Drawing on relationship science, we'll give you a strategy for overcoming common barriers to self-disclosure, such as fear of negative evaluation and the impostor syndrome, and shift your focus from *finding* chemistry to *building* it.

Listening-to-Learn Mindset

As you already know, feeling loved doesn't start with sharing—it starts with listening. Specifically, it begins by rotating the process a full 180 degrees—and creating the conditions that help others feel loved by *you*. In other words, you cannot share and become fully known without also striving to fully know the other person. You accomplish this by giving them your undivided attention, patiently and fully attuning to them, and listening to what they have to say. The easiest way to begin is to embrace what we call the Listening-to-Learn mindset. To practice it, you should approach your next conversation by thinking of yourself as a listener, not a speaker—that is, listen and ask questions that clarify and yield insights about the other person's story, and do it as if you'll be quizzed on their story tomorrow.

Radical-Curiosity Mindset

It's possible to practice the tools of great listening without being genuinely interested and intrigued. Taking listening to the next level requires you to leverage as much enthusiastic—even radical—curiosity as you can muster. Both advice bloggers and psychological scientists have come to the same conclusion: It's critical to show strong, genuine interest and curiosity in the other person. Radical curiosity extends beyond learning the surface facts about the other person or focusing only on the most interesting or impressive parts of their story. It involves digging deeper—excavating not only their fears and flaws but also their deeply held beliefs, their eccentricities, their creative outlets, and the small details that shape their world—to truly understand what it's like to live inside their skin. By displaying this radical, enthusiastic curiosity, you encourage, empower, and hold space for your conversation partner to unfurl *their* true self.

Open-Heart Mindset

No matter how skilled you are at listening or how deeply curious you may be, if your heart is closed off, you won't help your conversation partner feel truly loved. Fundamentally, the Open-Heart mindset entails expressing genuine care and concern for their well-being, much as would a lifelong best friend—though in a broader, more fundamental way of seeing and supporting them. Embracing the Open-Heart mindset means more than just offering kindness and compassion (although it begins there); it's about truly believing in the other person and their potential. Think of Michelangelo, the Italian Renaissance artist, who is said to have had the ability to see a figure trapped in a block of stone and carve away until that figure was released and came to life. Similarly, adopting the Open-Heart mindset means seeing the best in others and helping them grow into that version of themselves, with solicitude and prosocial intent—whether through tangible acts of assistance or through encouragement and validation that strengthens their confidence and resolve.

Multiplicity Mindset

In some respects, the Multiplicity mindset may be the most challenging one to fully embrace. This mindset holds particular significance not only when you are listening to the other person's vulnerable disclosures but also when you are making vulnerable disclosures yourself. All too often, people think about others in absolute, one-dimensional terms: *This person is outgoing, but that person is obnoxious.* But people are many things: Alongside their difficulties and regrets are their virtues and generosities of soul. The Multiplicity mindset welcomes revelations of another person's complex and multifarious self and responds not by rushing to judgment but with acceptance, empathy, flexibility, and charitable attributions. All these responses come more naturally when you acknowledge the many varied facets that describe all humans.

Now turn the tables and apply the Multiplicity mindset—along with the Open-Heart mindset—to yourself. Viewing yourself as complex and multifaceted helps you treat yourself with sensitivity and a warm heart (much as a kind friend might), or with what psychologists call *self-compassion.* In these ways, the Multiplicity mindset helps you appreciate that no single attribute (good or bad) needs to define you—this mindset encourages you to feel forgivable, and makes it easier to share more of your full self and receive your partner's appreciation.

Applying the Mindsets

Each of the five mindsets represents a critical tool for engaging the Relationship Sea-Saw. When you express curiosity in your conversation partner—and listen thoughtfully, compassionately, and encouragingly when they open up—you set in motion cycles of mutual openness, understanding, connectedness, and responsiveness that create moments of feeling loved. Thus, by leveraging these five mindsets, you become more positive, more proactive, and more effective at obtaining the results you want. Again, the good news is that the power to feel loved resides within you, not within your partner. Specifically, you have control over three critical pieces: (1) the appropriate person—that is, *by whom* you wish to feel more loved (whether it be a colleague, friend, family member, or romantic partner); (2) *when, what, and how* you choose to show authentic interest in and respond to this person's full, vulnerable self; and (3) *when, what, and how* you choose to show your own full, vulnerable self to them.

We're certainly not suggesting that you inhabit these mindsets all the time or with everyone you meet—selectivity is critical to making them work. Rather, regard them as tools to help you lay the foundation for a relationship in which you can feel connected and loved. It won't happen overnight—feeling connected and loved is built by accumulating meaningful experiences over time. When the Relationship Sea-Saw operates successfully, both you and your conversation partner will respond to each other's ideas, revelations, and distinctive personalities in ways that lead both of you to feel more and more loved. But if the other person fails to take advantage of the opportunity to truly listen to and see the real you, if they don't lift you on the Sea-Saw, it may be a signal that either they are not an appropriate partner or the timing isn't ideal. Throughout this book, and especially in chapter 10, we discuss the importance of being discerning about your Sea-Saw partner.

Don't Change Yourself— Change the Conversation

According to our surveys, the reason some people don't feel as loved as they want or as much as they think they "deserve" is because they believe they're fundamentally unlovable. They suspect that if the person who is trying to love them ever discovered who they truly are inside—rather than the idealized or polished version they have presented to the outside world—that person will love them less or love them differently. Others do feel loved—at least in some of their relationships—but would welcome more love in their lives.

If you don't feel loved enough, we have a profound and empowering message for you: Feeling loved is not out of your control. For some, it will require a radical shift in how you orient toward conversations with loved ones. For others, it will simply call for more practice of that muscle that enables you to deeply know another person and become deeply known by them.

We've been conducting behavioral-science research since the Richard Nixon and George H. W. Bush administrations, respectively. We've won awards for our research on happiness (Sonja) and close relationships (Harry). Over the years, drawing from different perspectives, we've both come to the same conclusion: People feel happiest in moments when they believe that others understand and respect them for who they truly are—for their deepest, unvarnished self.

This book is our attempt to bring together well-being science and relationship science in a way that no one has quite done before. By putting our heads together, we offer a new perspective on the ingredients that make life worth living. *How to Feel Loved* presents these insights, backed by a feast of cutting-edge empirical research. What we offer is less a self-help instruction manual and more a new way of seeing and relating.

Because the secret to feeling more loved is not about changing yourself or about changing the other person—it's about changing the conversation.

PART I

Why
Feeling Loved
Matters

1
Hardwired to Feel Loved

You're gazing out the window, bracing for the long, stressful day ahead.
"Here, Elena."

Without asking, your sister hands you a cup of tea just the way you like it—cardamom, cinnamon, and the right amount of honey. She doesn't make a fuss; she just knows. And in that small unspoken act, you feel loved. Not because of grand declarations or dramatic gestures, but because someone sees you, remembers you, and cares about the details that make you, you.

Feeling loved often happens in quiet moments like that one.

Or this one:

He didn't say, "Let me know if you need anything." He just showed up.

When Kayla's father died, the texts and emails flooded in. But it was her best friend, Mateo, who knocked on her door the next morning, holding a bag of groceries and a soft blanket. "You don't have to talk," he said. "I'm just here." And he was. Sitting with her in silence. Making sure she ate. Letting her be messy, exhausted, and utterly unfiltered—without the need to put on a brave face. Mateo had seen Kayla at her best and at her lowest, and he stayed.

And sometimes people feel most loved when they feel truly understood:

When Ravi got the promotion he'd worked toward for a decade, he expected to feel on top of the world. He celebrated with his colleagues, accepted the congratulations, and smiled through it all. But that night, when he sat across from his wife, Maya, she studied his face.

"You're not as happy as you thought you'd be," she said softly.

His throat tightened. "No," he admitted. "I thought this would make me feel . . . enough."

Maya reached for his hand. "You already are."

She knew. Not because he had ever voiced that exact thought to her, but because she had witnessed every part of him—his drive, his self-doubt, the way he sometimes mistook achievement for worth. And that's why, right there, he felt loved. Not because his wife was celebrating his successes, but because she knew his struggles, his fears, and even the things he rarely admitted to himself.

Perhaps one of these stories brings to mind a time when you felt the same. Or perhaps it reminds you of a person with whom you similarly experienced feeling loved. Now consider our colleague Vivian's story.

I remember sitting across from a friend I'd known for years—someone I had confided in, supported, and shared countless memories with. We were at a quiet coffee shop, the kind of place where people linger over half-empty mugs, wrapped in conversation. Outside, the rain tapped against the windows.

For months I had felt a growing distance between us, though I couldn't quite name why. That night I decided to be honest. I told him I missed the way we used to talk, that something felt different, and I wondered if I had done something wrong. I tried to sound casual, not wanting to sound needy, but my voice cracked just a little at the end.

He looked at me, stirred his coffee, and shrugged.

"I don't know, Vivian," he said. "I guess I've just been busy."

That was it. No reassurance, no curiosity, no follow-up question. Just . . . indifference. Maybe I hadn't shared enough of what had been weighing on me. Maybe he hadn't noticed, or maybe he hadn't wanted to ask. Either way, the conversation ended before it ever really began.

I nodded, pretending that answer was enough. But inside, something in me sank—a heavy feeling, like I had been reaching for something solid that wasn't there. I had thought that if I just tried hard enough, showed up enough, cared enough, I would be met with warmth. Instead, we sat there, side by side, yet the space between us felt vast.

We finished our coffees, exchanged small talk, and said goodbye. I walked home by myself, feeling lonelier than if I had been alone the whole evening.

We (Sonja and Harry) have both known what it's like to feel deeply understood and loved—and what it's like to feel unseen and unloved. You might recognize parts of yourself in any of the stories above, at different moments in time or in different relationships. When was the last time you truly felt loved? When was the last time you knew you *were* loved but couldn't quite feel it? This book is about creating the conditions to experience the kind of love that Elena, Kayla, and Ravi felt—and understanding what to do when you find yourself in a moment like Vivian's.

But before we explore how to approach conversations in ways that will open the door for you and your partners to feel loved, we need to take a step back and ask: What exactly do we mean by *love* and *feeling loved*?

More Than a Feeling: What *Is* Love?

Love is one of the most versatile words in the English language. People use it to describe their feelings about a romantic partner, their children, sleeping in on a lazy Saturday, their favorite music, the city they live in, or even mint chocolate chip ice cream. None of these examples, however, reflect what people mean when they say they want to *feel* loved. That's the kind of love this book is about—the kind that happens *between* people.

What does that kind of love look like? It takes on many shapes. Yet for most, the word *love* is most commonly associated with romantic relationships. So let's begin there. Relationship scientists who study couples have long distinguished between two major types of love: passionate (the "hot" kind) and companionate (the "warm" kind).

- **Passionate love**, often called *romantic love* or *limerence*, feels all-consuming, intense, urgent, and exhilarating. It often comes

with deep longing, excitement, and physiological arousal—
racing heartbeat, butterflies in the stomach, and an emotional
preoccupation with the beloved—as well as lust, if it's also a
sexual relationship. Passionate love may fuel the early stages of a
romance, but over time, its intensity often wanes.

- **Companionate love**, on the other hand, is steadier, characterized
  by warmth, trust, emotional intimacy, and a deep sense of
  commitment. Rather than igniting like a spark, it grows over time
  and can sustain long-term partnerships. Notably, companionate
  love is used to describe nonromantic relationships as well, with
  its deep attachment and mutual care reinforcing bonds between
  family, colleagues, and friends.

It's striking that many languages use one word, *love*, to describe
these two very disparate experiences. Yet even though a single word
is used, love is not a singular experience—it comes in many different
forms. The particular kind of love that we write about in this book is
broader than either of these definitions. It's best described like this:

Love is a powerful and embodied feeling of deep affection,
caring, and warmth for others when your life, activities, or goals
are gratifyingly intertwined with theirs. It is the sense that
another person makes a difference in your life—that they matter.

As you can tell from this definition, not all relationships involve
love, nor would it be desirable if they did. We focus here on those
special relationships in your life where love is present, as we define it
above. Psychologists call these *communal relationships*, and they can
be found within many different kinds of connections. In a communal relationship, people are responsive to each other's needs and are
concerned about each other's well-being. Relationships vary in the
degree to which they are communal, such that some relationships—
for example, between romantic partners, best friends, and parents and
children—are strongly communal, whereas others show communal
features but less robustly so.

Although the above definition may evoke love as a grand emotion, it doesn't have to be. Love isn't only about profound, life-changing bonds—it can also be found in a friend who gets you, a colleague who shares a deep intellectual connection, or a neighbor who always checks in. Thus, it bears repeating that love is not limited to romantic partners—it is felt in friendships, family bonds, workplace connections, and shared social or religious communities. Both the heat of passionate love and the warmth of companionate love, along with the many other ways that love manifests in people's lives, are explored in this book (and particularly in chapter 10).

Before we go any further, it's crucial to highlight something important. Most research on love focuses on the love people *feel for others*. That's why our definition of love, drawn from the literature on relationship science, does too. But this book flips the script. It's not about how much love you *feel* for someone else. It's about how much love you *feel coming to you*.

Love in a Moment

Now let's add a twist to this idea: You can feel loved within a communal relationship, and you can feel loved continuously for weeks, months, or even a lifetime. But you can also feel loved—whether in a communal relationship, in a noncommunal one, or even by a stranger—for a moment. Is that really possible? If you're skeptical, try to recall a time that you felt loved during a brief but meaningful experience—perhaps sitting in a pew, attending a ceremony, or listening to a speech? While singing or enjoying a song? In the presence of a valued community or in the company of the divine? While joining hands in a protest? While listening or being listened to? Such moments can be spontaneous and serendipitous—they can happen anywhere and at any time. They often involve words, but sometimes just a meaningful glance, or touch, or even collective silence can communicate love. It's possible that sometimes you might even overlook such brief but potentially meaningful opportunities to feel loved.

When we asked survey respondents to recall a time they felt truly loved (more on the survey later), we expected to hear about profound moments—deep connections, life-changing experiences, and major family milestones. And, sure enough, we did. People described feeling loved when friends stayed by their bedside during an illness, when loved ones threw them a surprise birthday celebration, or when they held their child for the first time. But surprisingly, many experiences of feeling loved occurred not in response to grand gestures but during smaller, everyday moments, such as when someone was attentive, considerate, or supportive, echoing Elena's story from the beginning of the chapter. For example:

- "I feel most loved when my partner makes my morning coffee just the way I like it."
- "They remembered the exact book I wanted and got it for me 'just because.'"

These small everyday moments of feeling loved are far from trivial. In a set of studies conducted in Canada and China, researchers asked university students to recall a time that someone close to them made them feel loved. Simply reflecting on feeling loved had powerful ripple effects on memories and judgments—for example, it led participants to view their relationship with that person as more satisfying, made them more willing to support that person during stressful times, and even increased their willingness to forgive that person for past mistakes (like lying).

As we noted earlier, love—especially the passionate kind—is often described as a big, fierce, lasting emotion, frequently tied to a long-term bond. Emotion scientists, however, have shown that love sometimes comes in "momentary surges." You might feel loved during one moment in everyday life and not the next. In her book *Love 2.0*, Barbara Fredrickson labels these moments with the lovely name "positivity resonance," describing them as being typically characterized by:

- **shared positive emotion**—you laugh together or experience a feeling of mutual gratitude

- **biobehavioral synchrony**—your heart rate, breathing, or even neural activity aligns
- **mutual care**—you are invested in each other's happiness

Furthermore, Fredrickson and her colleagues have shown that frequent moments of love are associated with health benefits (e.g., lower levels of inflammation, stronger cardiovascular functioning, and even longer life), relationship benefits (e.g., longer marriages and more generosity), and improved well-being overall, including less loneliness and greater resilience and satisfaction. Parallel moments experienced at work—what behavioral scientists call "high-quality connections"—have also been found to produce increased well-being, psychological safety, and resilience, while enhancing physical health, belonging, and productivity.

The Neurobiology of Love

Part of the story of love is biological. For centuries, poets and philosophers have located love in the heart—which is why one uses a heart emoji to communicate love when texting. But, in fact, the most important organ for experiencing love is the brain. This is a topic where the distinction between passionate love and companionate love matters a great deal.

Let's start with passion. During the early stages of romantic love, the brain releases dopamine—the neurotransmitter associated with reward and pleasure—contributing to feelings of euphoria and excitement. Brain-scanning studies have shown that feelings of intense romantic love activate regions of the brain rich in dopamine receptors, such as the ventral tegmental area and the caudate nucleus. For example, in one study, participants viewed photos of either a romantic partner or a familiar but emotionally neutral person while in an fMRI scanner. Only when looking at their partner's face was there activation in these dopamine-sensitive regions. Notably, these same brain regions are also involved in the abuse of addictive substances such as cocaine—which would seem to lend scientific weight to the metaphor in the title to Roxy Music's song "Love Is the Drug."

These neural underpinnings help explain many of the intense feelings and behaviors associated with passionate love: the elation of being near the loved one, a powerful desire for their presence, a rush of longing when seeing or thinking about them, occasional obsessive cravings for connection, and even signs of withdrawal when they're absent. Although these feelings often mellow as romantic relationships stabilize over time, brief moments of passion can still trigger similar, albeit somewhat muted, activation of the dopamine receptors in the brain.

By contrast, companionate love has been consistently linked to the neuropeptide oxytocin—sometimes referred to as the *cuddle hormone*. Secreted by the pituitary gland at the base of the brain, oxytocin stimulates feelings of love, trust, and attachment, as well as reduces anxiety and stress. Some of the earliest studies of oxytocin compared two genetically similar species of voles that notably differ in their social behavior: monogamous prairie voles, who typically pair bond for life, and polygamous montane voles, who are less socially affiliative. Interestingly, relative to montane voles, prairie voles have more oxytocin receptors in the brain's reward system, which makes them more likely to respond when given a dose of oxytocin. Thus, researchers have found that when prairie voles are injected with oxytocin, they show a strong preference to cohabit with a familiar partner rather than a stranger.

In humans, oxytocin has demonstrated a range of effects, all linked to caring and trust. For example, mothers with higher levels of plasma oxytocin after childbirth show stronger maternal bonding behaviors—such as gazing, vocalizing, affectionately touching, and frequently checking on their infants. Similarly, fathers administered a dose of intranasal oxytocin become more behaviorally affectionate when interacting with their five-month-olds. Among romantic couples, higher levels of oxytocin have been associated with more frequent hugging and lower physiological reactions to stress. In other studies, oxytocin has increased the ability to read others' emotions and produced greater levels of trust in economic games. (Sometimes, however, oxytocin leads people to favor friends and family over strangers or dissimilar others.) Perhaps most compelling is the finding that orgasm stimulates the production of oxytocin—offering a biological explanation for the "warm glow of connection" many people feel after sex.

In sum, this and other research has led scientists to propose a broad role for oxytocin in social behavior and bonding—namely, that it's responsible for increasing people's sensitivity to social cues while simultaneously enhancing their desire to affiliate and connect across a wide variety of relationships.

That the story of love is situated in the human brain should come as no surprise. The brain is where most evolutionarily significant behaviors are regulated, and, as we explore in more detail next, love plays a central role in many of them—from procreation and parental care to the functioning of romantic bonds, families, kin networks, and group alliances. As you consider the behaviors explored in the chapters ahead, it may be useful to remember their neural underpinnings.

Why Humans Crave Feeling Loved

No [person] is an island.

—*John Donne*

If you've picked up this book, chances are you want to feel more loved—or perhaps, deep down, you recognize how much of your happiness is tied to feeling loved. But why is this need so fundamental? This may sound like a bold claim, but the answer lies in your biology, your psychology, and the very essence of what it means to be human. One seminal idea came not from a lab experiment but from a conversation at a beachside conference.

A Need to Belong

In the 1980s, in springtime, a group of psychological scientists gathered for a small conference at Nags Head, a thin stretch of island off the coast of North Carolina, to explore pressing research questions about human behavior. One of these meetings centered around anxiety, and several scholars argued that the root of human anxiety was the fear of death. Roy Baumeister, our colleague and good friend, sat in the audience, skeptical. Most people, he thought, don't spend their days pondering their mortality. What preoccupies them, what keeps them up at night, are social fears—being rejected, excluded, ignored, made fun of, left behind, unloved.

Baumeister wasn't alone in this thinking. His late-night conversations with fellow psychologist Mark Leary sparked an idea for a paper that would reshape the field. In 1995, they published "The Need to Belong," a landmark work arguing that human beings evolved with a fundamental drive to form lasting social bonds. Throughout history, survival and thriving in harsh environments depended on finding mates and forming alliances to secure food, protection, exploration, and care (see the long-running reality show *Survivor* for a vivid illustration).

Fast-forward two hundred thousand years, and even today, as psychologist Esther Perel famously put it, "the quality of your relationships determines the quality of your life." In other words, humans are profoundly social creatures who are evolutionarily programmed to value belonging to tribes and to derive happiness from connecting, building bonds within communities, and falling in love with other humans.

Baumeister and Leary put it more formally: Humans are evolutionarily designed to form strong, enduring attachments with others and to resist their dissolution. Across cultures and historical eras, from cradle to grave, people are strongly motivated to cooperate, to fit in, and to feel accepted, included, and cared for. And when attachments are threatened, the consequences ripple through physical health, psychological adjustment, and overall well-being. (Interestingly, while many nonhuman species—parrots, elephants, dolphins—also bond in social groups, humans are the only species to reflect consciously on their social standing, asking questions such as *Does this group value me?* and *Do I feel loved?*)

Furthermore, the need to belong isn't just about emotional support and social standing—it's also about reproduction. Access to potential mates, cooperative child-rearing, and the successful raising of offspring to maturity all depend on social bonds. Evolution favored individuals who were embedded in networks of mutual support—not just romantic partners but extended kin and community. In short, it really does take a village of relational cooperation.

A Need to Feel Loved

Why does this matter? Because the need to belong is deeply inter-twined with the need to feel loved. When defined broadly, they are more or less the same thing. Relationship scientists describe the feeling of being loved in terms of the internal sensations of safety and security. In other words, when you feel loved, you feel *at home*—you feel *safe*. You feel *secure* when you have a place to belong. By contrast, when you don't feel loved, you question whether you belong, feeling lost and worried about acceptance. Hence, feeling loved isn't just comforting—it's critical. It's the mental and emotional glue that keeps you connected with your caregivers and your social group, even during difficult times. It also reinforces your sense of belonging within your larger commu-nity or tribe. In many ways, feeling loved can be seen as the ultimate barometer of evolutionary fitness—a signal that one is socially connected and supported.

We would go so far as to postulate that humans wouldn't have survived as a species without feeling loved, because feeling loved is grounded in a process that's deeply embedded in the most ancient parts of your mammalian brain. And that process is one of the most important influences on survival and reproduction—the key elements of human evolution.

Our need to belong explains why feeling lonely and unloved can be so painful. In ancestral times, not having mates or friends you could rely on could mean the difference between life and death. Today, the same situation just *feels* as if you're dying inside. Neuroscientist Jaak Panksepp, for instance, has shown that the brain processes separation from a loved one as a threat to survival, underscoring why social dis-connection can feel profoundly difficult—if not unbearable.

Another piece of the puzzle that explains why social disconnection can feel so difficult comes from Social Baseline theory. Taking the Need to Belong theory a step further, James Coan and his colleagues proposed that human connection—feeling loved—is not just emotionally rewarding, but a built-in default state. In other words, feeling loved is so important because it serves as *baseline* (a necessary foundation or "default setting") for optimal human functioning—the ultimate starting point for effective action and happiness. The implication of this theory is that when you feel close and connected to a relational partner, you are ready to share the load of living in a dangerous world. You take up each other's burdens that weigh you down. When you have strong bonds with others, you perceive fewer threats (you feel *safer*), and your brain literally requires less metabolic energy to respond to threats and ordeals, showing reduced neural activity in response to danger and muting your body's stress response. For instance, in one classic study, women administered an electric shock found it less painful when they were holding their spouse's hand, but not the hand of a stranger. In simple terms, love lightens the cognitive and emotional load of everyday life.

This isn't just a theory—it's a process that plays out in real relationships: Feeling loved doesn't just provide a personal benefit; it provides a resource for the people around you. In a series of studies conducted across four different countries, a research team that included Harry found that as long as *one* partner in a dating or married couple felt loved, both partners were less likely to react with hostility or blame—whether in an argument with each other or while parenting their child. In a sense, feeling loved creates a buffer, making relationships more resilient.

Where This Leads Us

If there's one takeaway we hope you remember from this chapter, it's this: Feeling loved isn't a luxury—it's what human beings are built for. Across disciplines, from neuroscience to relationship science, research and theory reveal that feeling loved calms the nervous system, strengthens connections, builds resilience, and reminds you that you belong. The Jersey Shore rocker Southside Johnny echoes this point in his song "Without Love," when he points out that it's feeling loved that makes us who we are. And yet, if it's so essential, why do people sometimes feel less loved or lonelier than they expect? In the next chapter, we turn to the science—and the stories—behind those moments. Indeed, understanding the prevalence and roots of disconnection will help you understand how to avoid it.

2

The Cost of Not Feeling Loved

Our friend Erika would be dumbfounded to find herself in this chapter—let alone as someone who would relate to its message. If you asked her, she'd say she's a pretty happy person, and our observations over the years would confirm this. She's been married for more than eleven years to a husband she describes to girlfriends as "pretty much perfect." She has an eight-year-old daughter and a twenty-year-old stepdaughter. She loves her work as a graphic designer and has close colleagues she enjoys collaborating with. She's also stayed connected to at least a dozen friends from high school, college, and beyond—people she knows she can count on.

And yet some nights Erika can't sleep, feeling lonely. She knows, logically, that her stepdaughter loves her, but she seldom feels loved by her. Erika often walks away from conversations with her mom feeling misunderstood and from meetings with her manager feeling undervalued—despite how tirelessly she works. Even her eight-year-old seems more excited to be with her friends than with Erika. And as much as she adores her "perfect" husband, she can't shake the feeling that he takes her for granted—rarely offering a compliment, often too distracted by his own world to truly see her.

Do You Feel Loved?

Is Erika's experience uncommon? When we told our friends and colleagues that we were writing a book about feeling loved and asked them for personal reflections, a few of them didn't hold back. Here are six direct quotes that stayed with us:

- "I know my husband loves me, but sometimes I just don't *feel* it. It's like . . . I know it intellectually and have to remind myself."
- "I have plenty of friends, and I spend a lot of time socializing. But honestly? I don't know if anyone deeply loves me."
- "I worry that if people really knew me—the good *and* the bad, all my many flaws too—they might love me less. Like their love is conditional on my being a certain way."
- "I think when I don't feel loved, it's because, deep down, I wonder if I deserve to be loved."
- "Sometimes, I feel like I'm the one always giving love—spending time and effort on my friends, my family—but they don't love me back in the same way."
- "All of my friends planned a trip to visit another friend and didn't include me. I felt alone and abandoned. It was sad."

If these accounts are representative, many people have moments or days or even years in which they don't feel loved—or loved enough—by a particular person in their lives or by their family, friends, or community more broadly. But personal stories can only tell us so much. We wanted hard, empirical data. So, in 2024, we designed a survey expressly for this book, reaching out to a large and representative sample of American adults, and obtaining responses from 1,998 individuals.

We asked participants how much they currently felt loved in various relationships and whether they wanted to feel more loved by these individuals. We also invited participants to describe a time when they felt truly loved and another when they did not. Their insights and reflections appear throughout this book.

In our survey, roughly two-thirds of respondents expressed a desire to feel more loved or loved more often by people in their lives. More than half specifically wished to feel more loved by their communities, their close or best friends, their family members, their parents, and their romantic partners. Over a third also longed to feel more loved by their children, colleagues, and even by God. Which category earned the most votes for desires to feel more loved? Romantic partners. Interestingly, although partnered individuals reported feeling the *most* loved by their romantic partners (with 78 percent reporting feeling loved *a lot*), romantic relationships also showed the greatest gap between feeling loved and wanting more—a full 40 percent of the sample said that they wanted to feel more loved by their romantic partner. In other words, many partnered individuals felt loved but not enough.

When asked to vividly describe moments when they didn't feel loved, our respondents shared experiences across various kinds of relationships, such as:

* their partner just going through the motions
* feeling used for their money
* not being appreciated at work or valued for their contributions
* their friends forgetting their birthdays, not replying to messages, or leaving them out of gatherings
* their family members not checking up on them when they were sick or suffering
* people in their lives not listening or remembering what they said or failing to understand something deeply important to them
* their partner not believing their experiences
* not being seen for who they really are

A common thread in these survey responses was that not feeling loved felt a lot like loneliness. (Indeed, the correlation between loneliness and feeling loved was strikingly high at -.55; for context, most psychological correlations hover around +/-.30.) Again and again, respondents described moments of feeling lonely—for example, "deeply alone living on their own" or "walking through the crowded streets surrounded by people yet feeling utterly alone." Many equated the absence of feeling loved with feeling invisible, misunderstood, overlooked, or left out.

If any of this resonates with you, take heart—we'll show how shifting your approach to conversations, using the five mindsets, and engaging with the right people can help replace moments of feeling lonely and unseen with moments of feeling loved and seen. But if the rest of this book is about what's possible, this chapter is about what's at stake when you don't feel loved.

All the Lonely People: What Lonely Moments Teach About Feeling Loved

The experience of not feeling loved is not the same thing as loneliness, but the two share several key ingredients. In fact, if we want to understand why so many people wish to feel more loved—and how to help fulfill that wish—a brief look at loneliness is a good place to start.

Understanding Trends in Loneliness

Our survey findings on not feeling loved echo what recent large-scale surveys on loneliness have been showing: Loneliness is widespread and increasing, not just in the United States but across the world— so much so that countries such as Britain, Sweden, and Japan have appointed Ministers of Loneliness. In Japan, for example, the Minister of Loneliness is tasked with developing policies to reduce social isolation, funding initiatives that build community, and tackling mental-health concerns linked to loneliness. The UK's Minister of Loneliness has pioneered social prescribing, where doctors refer patients to community activities such as gardening clubs or volunteer work to help people build meaningful relationships. Biologist E. O. Wilson even proposed renaming the current Anthropocene era as the Eremocene era (*eremos* for lonely place or person).

A review of data from 345 studies, spanning 124,855 participants, found that loneliness levels have been steadily rising since 1976. A 2023 Gallup/Meta study of 142 countries found that 24 percent of the global population—both men and women—reported being "very" or "fairly" lonely. In the United States, a highly cited 2018 Cigna study of over 20,000 Americans found that 46 percent felt alone or left out, and 27 percent didn't feel there are people who really understand them. Alarmed by such data, on May 3, 2023, Vivek Murthy, the US surgeon general at the time, declared loneliness an epidemic.

Although loneliness affects all age groups, it appears to be especially prevalent in younger generations. A 2023 survey found that two-thirds of men between ages 18 and 23 agreed with the statement "No one really knows me." Another found that loneliness rates were 10 percentage points higher in young adults (ages 19–29) compared to older adults (ages 65+). And in a study of more than 6,000 adults, conducted in September 2024, nearly a quarter of Americans under 30 reported feeling lonely most of the time—but that number decreased to 20 percent for people in their 30s and 40s, 11 percent for people ages 50 to 64, and only 6 percent for those over 65. Our own survey echoed this: The younger our participants, the lonelier they reported feeling. In fact, the rise in loneliness among people under 30 may explain why the United States dropped out of the top twenty happiest countries in the *World Happiness Report* for the first time in 2024—and why, in 2025, it fell to its lowest ranking yet (#24).

Although the causes of these age differences aren't fully understood, research suggests that they reflect broader shifts in cultural norms: For example, previous generations had more built-in social capital, greater self-reliance, and more face-to-face connection. The encouraging news is that understanding these differences helps inform interventions to reduce disconnection—for example, promoting community engagement and leveraging technology for meaningful connections. *How to Feel Loved* is essentially a guidebook for future interventions. Despite the alarming trends, loneliness is neither inevitable nor irreversible.

For years, Harry watched these statistics unfold—first with curiosity, then with concern. Could loneliness really be increasing so dramatically? Then he realized that without intending to track the trend over time, he had been collecting highly relevant loneliness data for over two decades.

Year after year, Harry has taught the same psychology course—

"The Science of Relationships"—at the University of Rochester. Primarily juniors and seniors, his seventy to one hundred students come from all different majors and from all around the globe. (Interest in relationships appears to be universal!) In 2002, Harry started administering a measure of loneliness to all his students, and this is what he found: For over a decade, the students' loneliness scores remained relatively steady, hovering around a 2.0 on a 4-point scale. But after 2016, a clear upward trend emerged, with the average rising to 2.4—a 20 percent increase.

When he shared these findings with his students, they weren't surprised. They were living it.

What Do Lonely Moments Mean?

Most loneliness surveys, including Harry's, make use of the UCLA Loneliness Scale, which presents statements such as:

- There is no one I can turn to.
- My interests and ideas are not shared by those around me.
- My social relationships are superficial.
- No one really knows me well.
- People are around me but not with me.

If any of these statements resonate—at least sometimes—then you belong in the company of three out of five Americans. Even people who seem "popular" and socially embedded—who have families, careers, and vibrant social circles—can feel unseen, misunderstood, or disconnected.

And yet, when one scrolls through social media, it appears as though everyone else is thriving socially—well-liked, surrounded by close friends, effortlessly connected. (Who really goes online to say that they feel lonely most of the time?) It may be heartening to learn that this is an illusion. Research from Harvard University shows that people tend to overestimate how socially connected, deeply loved, and understood other people are. In other words, you would have good reason to assume that you're the only one feeling disconnected—when in reality, many people around you are struggling with the exact same feelings.

Not feeling as loved as one would like isn't the only reason people feel lonely—but it's one of the biggest. For example, one study followed lonely individuals living in Switzerland and Germany across fourteen days—and also surveyed them several times over two years. The researchers found that what predicted loneliness wasn't rejection or criticism—it was the absence of affection and love. In other words, feeling lonely wasn't about experiencing negative interactions; it was about not experiencing enough positive ones. Although this study might sound discouraging at first, we actually find it empowering— because loneliness isn't just something that happens to you. Small intentional moments of warmth and connection can make a meaningful difference—and that's what the mindsets described in the chapters ahead are designed to create.

Even more strikingly, (lack of) loneliness and feeling loved can reinforce each other. The more love people feel, the less lonely they become. Conversely, the less love people feel, the lonelier they become. And the lonelier they become, the more likely they are to withdraw or hesitate in social situations—further preventing them from experiencing the very connections they crave—a process we examine in detail below.

That's why, before exploring how to feel more loved, we begin with loneliness—because an epidemic of loneliness indicates that there's an epidemic of not feeling loved.

Understanding Disconnection: Why Feeling Loved Matters

Loneliness isn't a lack of people. . . . [It] is a longing
for the company of one who understands you.
—*Bronnie Ware*, The Top Five Regrets of the Dying

Mother Teresa, who witnessed staggering economic poverty first-hand, referred to loneliness and feeling unloved as a different type of "the most terrible poverty." However, although loneliness is one of the most painful human conditions, it is not inevitable—nor is it permanent. In psychological research, loneliness is often defined as the absence of communal relationships in people's lives. As we discuss in this book, these are the very relationships—ones based on "sharing and caring" rather than on norms or obligations—that are essential to feeling loved.

Research by Harry and his team shows that when you feel understood, appreciated, and loved, loneliness is rare (or short-lived when it does occur). But when you are having a lonely moment, you feel misunderstood, ill-appreciated, and unloved. You may experience this even when you're around people every day—at home, at work, during your commute, at the coffee shop, on the street, at church. It's possible to be surrounded by adoring, kind, and interesting people and at the same time feel a sense of emotional distance. It's possible to engage with people who like you and yet not feel connected. It's even possible to laugh and enjoy social interactions and not feel loved. In fact, it's more than possible—it's common. In sum, feeling loved isn't just about being around people; it's about the quality of those connections.

How Disconnection Can Shape Social Interactions

Paradoxically, when people feel lonely, they sometimes act in ways that unintentionally heighten those feelings. In other words, lonely feelings may create a self-perpetuating (or "vicious") cycle, leading people to see the world as more threatening, unkind, and overwhelming. This, in turn, can lead them to withdraw or react with hesitation, skepticism, or even cynicism—responses that may further isolate them.

Consider Mariana, twenty-seven, a friend who gave us permission to share her story. She had always considered herself social, but a period of loneliness made even casual conversations feel difficult. One evening, she attended her friend Jack's annual Oscar-watching party and found herself talking with him at the end of the night. They spoke about the film that won Best Picture, funny moments from the ceremony, and their favorite dresses of the nominees. If you were eavesdropping, nothing about their interaction would seem out of the ordinary—except perhaps that Mariana seemed a little subdued. But inside, this was her internal dialogue:

- *I wonder if Jack is enjoying talking to me, or if he's being polite. He glanced away for a second—maybe he's ready to leave the conversation.*
- *I feel tense, second-guessing what I'm saying. Am I being interesting enough? Is this conversation engaging for him?*
- *I don't notice when Jack laughs at what I'm saying (even if his laugh seems genuine). And when I do, I can't tell if he really finds it funny or if he's just humoring me.*
- *I hesitate to share too much. What if he thinks my opinions are silly? What if he gossips about this conversation to someone else later?*
- *Part of me wants the conversation to end—as I don't foresee enjoying it if it continues; it's exhausting.*
- *I blame myself for feeling stuck in a loop of having this experience over and over.*

Mariana's experience highlights a common paradox: Even when people crave connection, fear of rejection or self-doubt can make them hold back. And when they hold back, they unintentionally make it harder for others to connect with them.

Breaking the Cycle: How to Shift Your Perspective

Research shows that thoughts like Mariana's—whether or not they reflect reality—can influence social interactions in ways that make disconnection more likely:

Simply *believing* that someone isn't interested in them can subtly change the way some people behave, making them more withdrawn or hesitant, which in turn makes them seem distant—potentially creating a self-fulfilling prophecy.

Focusing too much on how they come across can make people less present, causing them to speak less and ask fewer questions (thus appearing more disengaged than they really are), and to miss the genuine warmth others may be offering.

Loneliness can skew people's perceptions, making them notice rejection more than acceptance. Indeed, lonely people show weaker neural activation in the reward regions (ventral striatum) of their brains, suggesting that they experience less positivity and enjoyment even when social interactions are going well.

When people doubt their conversation partner's interest in them and are a bit suspicious of their partner's motives, they may avoid sharing anything meaningful or asking for social support, which results in the conversation partner's feeling like they don't really know them. As a result, relationships may remain surface-level rather than deepening into something fulfilling.

Finally, believing that social difficulties are unchangeable can prevent people from taking small steps to make their conversations work better. Adopting a growth perspective, which emphasizes the potential for development and learning, encourages embracing challenges and viewing failures and disappointments as opportunities to grow.

These patterns are not flaws—they are natural human responses (or "adaptations," in psychological jargon). And importantly, they are reversible. Understanding how loneliness shapes people's thinking is the first step in breaking free from it.

Loneliness, even when temporary, can take a toll—not just on emotions but on mental and physical health, and even longevity. A vast and remarkably consistent scientific literature has linked chronic loneliness to sleep and appetite difficulties; stress; poor work performance; weakened immune and cardiovascular function; and increased risk of depression, anxiety, substance abuse, cognitive decline, and even antisocial behavior. But just as loneliness can have cascading negative effects, meaningful connection—feeling truly loved—can have equally powerful benefits.

One of the most promising findings in social neuroscience is that connection doesn't just exist in your mind—it's something you *physically* experience. For example, neuroimaging studies reveal that the brains of people who feel relatively lonelier and more disconnected show more idiosyncratic responses. In one study, when lonely people were asked to make trait judgments about themselves, their friends, their acquaintances, and various celebrities (like that Best Actress winner), their reports and neural representations in the medial prefrontal cortex deviated more from the group consensus (e.g., that she's friendly or that she's funny) compared to those of nonlonely people. In other words, the lonelier people felt, the less their reports and neural representations resembled the reports and neural representations of other people.

The opposite was also true: The more connected people felt, the *more* similarly their brains processed social information. In another imaging study, the brains of undergraduates who felt connected responded to emotionally evocative situations relatively more similarly to one another, while disconnected people responded relatively less similarly to their peers.

Perhaps you are wondering why similar neural responses promote connection. It's because people who feel loved are more likely to share their understanding of the world with those around them—to be "in sync" with their peers—while people who feel lonely may be more out of step with their peers' perspectives. (The interesting upside is that this disconnect might occasionally give rise to unique, out-of-the-box ideas.) Notably, research consistently shows that such shared understandings—known as "shared reality"—are critical to building and maintaining strong relationships. This doesn't mean that everyone needs to see things identically. Rather, what matters is a shared sense of how the world works—a basic sense of alignment that makes interactions easier and cooperation more natural.

Indeed, when you and someone else see and interpret the world in similar ways, conversations flow more easily, inside jokes become more meaningful, coordinated action is more effective, and deep connections become possible. (Imagine how much harder it would be to work together as a team or to enjoy a casual conversation if everyone saw things idiosyncratically!) Shared reality also instills a sense of confidence in one's own beliefs and viewpoints—that you "get it." Fortunately, shared reality isn't just something you either have or don't—it's something you can build. As we explore throughout this book, by being curious about another person, listening thoughtfully to what they have to say, and sharing more of yourself, you create opportunities for deeper understanding, even in relationships that don't feel quite in sync yet.

It's much easier to feel loved when there is a sense of shared reality between you and the person you want to feel loved by. The good news is that creating this sense of shared reality—and hence the feeling of being loved—isn't just about luck or circumstances; it's something you can cultivate. This book is about how to do exactly that. The chapters ahead will explore how small shifts in your mindsets during your conversations can create the conditions for meaningful, reciprocal connection—helping you move from moments of distance to moments of feeling valued and loved.

Loneliness may be part of the human experience, but it doesn't have to be your story. No matter where you are in your relationships, it is never too late to take steps to feel more loved.

"Overdigital" and "Undersocial": Finding Balance in a Connected World

While working on this book, Sonja and Harry messaged constantly. Those communications were helpful, but no matter how often we texted or video-chatted, nothing matched the energy of being in the same room— throwing ideas around, connecting on every level, and repeatedly lifting and being lifted on the Relationship Sea-Saw.

If you've ever felt like modern life is making it harder to connect in a deep and meaningful way, you're not alone. While technology has made it easier than ever to stay in touch, many people still find themselves feeling less frequently loved than they'd like. Even if you don't technically score as "lonely" on the UCLA Loneliness Scale, you may be feeling more disconnected than your parents and grand-parents did at your current age. This isn't necessarily because you're isolated or lacking social interactions but because the nature of those interactions has shifted.

Concerns about dwindling social connection aren't new. Back in 1995, political scientist Robert Putnam warned that Americans were spending less time in community with others, opting to "bowl alone" rather than engage in the shared activities that foster close relation-ships. Nearly thirty years later, he conceded that that trend hasn't reversed and has maybe even worsened, likely contributing to the generational trends in loneliness we've described. Today, it's not just bowling alone; according to the restaurant-booking platform Open-Table, more people are dining alone as well.

But this trajectory isn't inevitable. Connection will always be im-portant, but the way people connect is changing. What follows isn't a rant about putting your phone down—we promise. Rather, it's an invitation to understand the moments when you don't feel loved—and a preview of what modality we recommend (hint: it's in person) when engaging with the Relationship Sea-Saw and the mindsets.

Are People Becoming Overdigital?

In his 2024 book *The Anxious Generation*, New York University pro-fessor Jonathan Haidt argues that rising disconnection and mental-health struggles in youth are not primarily driven by economic recessions or climate insecurity, but by excessive digital engagement, particularly on social media. While this remains an area of ongoing debate among researchers, and we—like most scientists—are cautious about drawing causal conclusions from correlational and longitudinal data, many scholars, including us, find the evidence compelling.

Consider just a few examples: An investigation of more than a hun-dred thousand young people in the United States and another one of more than a million adolescents in thirty-seven nations both found that rising loneliness is linked to increases in screen time and reduced face-to-face interactions. This pattern has been documented in adults as well—neighborhood and community engagement has declined at the same time that digital interactions have surged. For example, a 2024 study that followed nearly seven thousand Dutch adults over the course of nine years found that the more time they spent on social media, the lonelier they became, and vice versa.

Furthermore, since the introduction of smartphones around 2010, social interactions have become more text-based. Indeed, more than half of young people's social interactions involve texting or typing—which begs the question of whether they are really "social" or "interactions." Convenient and immediate as it may be, text-based communication leads people to miss nuance, sarcasm, and emotional tone—making misunderstanding, miscommunication, and disagreement more likely, while reducing the emotional depth of conversations. Although it's possible to engage on the Sea-Saw via texting, for all these reasons, we recommend limiting it to a bare minimum—say, 5 percent to 10 percent of your conversation time.

Furthermore, smartphones aren't just tools for communication; they are constant attention magnets, with the typical user exchanging an average of eighty-five texts a day. Indeed, the simple presence of a smartphone—even sitting unused on the table—has been shown to reduce the quality of face-to-face interactions. Even children report feeling more disconnected from their parents when their parents are absorbed in their screens.

Of course, digital interactions aren't inherently bad. Social media can be invaluable in finding meaningful communities. For many, digital connections help sustain relationships across cities, continents, and busy schedules and serve as a bridge for forming new ones. Yet, at the same time, research suggests that social-media use can also con-tribute to feelings of anxiety, loneliness, self-doubt, invidious social comparison, and FOMO—particularly when it replaces rather than enhances in-person interactions.

One of our favorite—and most nuanced—studies on this topic sheds light on why digital interactions can sometimes leave people feeling worse and sometimes not. Researchers followed more than two thousand adolescents in the United Kingdom between 2015 and 2019, tracking how they spent their time and how they felt. The key takeaway? It wasn't *how much time* they spent on screens that mattered—it's *what their screens were replacing*. Teens who spent excessive time on their devices, especially late at night, reported feeling worse about themselves, more distressed, and less satisfied with their lives. But screen time, even when extensive, wasn't inherently bad. Those who balanced digital interactions with in-person socializing, physical activity, and sleep were just fine.

The real problem wasn't just being overdigital—it was being less social. When digital interactions replace face-to-face interactions, rather than complement them, people miss out on deeper, more fulfilling experiences—and may even start losing the art of in-person connection. It's hard to feel truly loved when all you see is a heart emoji.

Are People Becoming Undersocial?

There are now two generations who grew up with smartphones and social media's "like" and "share" culture: Gen Z, who were between infancy and thirteen when the first iPhone was released, and Gen Alpha, the generation immediately following them. Notably, these youths appear to be showing patterns of disconnection (recall our friend Mariana from earlier), even when they're not technically lonely.

As behavioral scientist Nick Epley and his colleagues recently put it, humans are becoming "undersocial." Researchers have found, for example, that many people today view in-person social interactions, especially with strangers, as more effortful and even risky and thus try to avoid them. In experiments, when prompted to engage in actual face-to-face conversations, people tend to wrap them up too early, even when continuing to chat would have been enjoyable. They also show a preference for texting over speaking, and they gravitate toward small talk over more meaningful (and ultimately more entertaining) topics.

Sonja and her team conducted a study with more than five hundred employed adults to test whether in-person interactions were more connecting than were digital interactions. The answer was yes—but with some surprises. Participants were asked to report how connected they felt when they engaged with others—that is, what percent of the time during those interactions they felt in sync, a sense of warmth, and a sense of mutual trust. As expected, in-person interactions—which included activities such as planning an outing with a friend, bringing a cup of coffee to a colleague, or discussing a new podcast on their walk home—topped the list as the most connecting. However, an unexpected finding emerged: Phone calls and video calls were just as effective at fostering connection. Furthermore, the more connecting these experiences were, the more positive emotions the respondents avowed. By contrast, text-based communication—including messaging, social media, and email—was rated as significantly less socially connecting.

We don't need much persuasive skill to argue that there's something special about in-person interactions, where you and your partner are breathing the same air, catching subtle nonverbal signals, feeling auditory vibrations through your bones (yes, that actually happens), and not being distracted by seeing your own face on a Zoom screen. Yet, as Sonja's team found, even digital interactions can be deeply connecting—intimate even—when they involve real-time, voice-based communication. That's because humans are wired for spoken language and synchronous exchanges; hearing another person's voice in real time is more likely to activate social and emotional circuits in the brain than is text-based communication.

Because video conversations involve both voice and real-time communication, they can help people feel connected. When meeting in person is impossible, you can practice the five mindsets on a video call. However, there's an important caveat: Over time, video calls can become draining and can even impair communication. A 2023 study from *Imaging Neuroscience* illustrated these limitations. Researchers compared the brain activity of individuals engaged in face-to-face conversations to that of individuals communicating over Zoom. The results revealed that dyads involved in in-person conversations showed heightened brain activity and more coordinated (synced-up) neural responses, suggesting that the social systems of the human brain are more active during real-life encounters than during virtual ones.

Reclaiming Real-World Social Connection

If face-to-face connection is so powerful, why do so many struggle to prioritize it? One answer is simple: Life gets busy, and digital interactions feel almost effortless. However, despite the strong pull of technology, small intentional changes such as the following can help restore balance:

- Engage in more face-to-face interactions, even brief ones. We cannot emphasize enough how robust the evidence is that even small casual moments of in-person connection—chatting with a barista, exchanging a joke with a colleague—can boost well-being. Research from Sonja's lab shows that simply trying to act more extraverted in daily (nondigital) life has substantial benefits for well-being. Getting out of the house and doing things with people who like the same things you do is even better.
- Lay the groundwork for the more engaged and meaningful conversations that foster feeling understood and loved through brief real-world interactions. Because social contact tends to be pleasant more often than not, even transient interactions can create a foundation for deeper connections. (More on those in later chapters.) Indeed, we argue that you can fast-track feeling genuinely loved if you spend more time in real face-to-face contact with significant others.
- Don't underestimate the power of a voice call (with or without video). When text feels too impersonal but meeting in person isn't an option, research suggests that a voice call can be a surprisingly effective way to reconnect.
- Make space for deeper conversations. Simply taking time to chat—about substantive topics, not just small talk—is linked to greater well-being.

While the world has become more digital, humans haven't changed in one crucial way: We are hardwired for real, embodied connection—for synchronous, face-to-face, and voice contact. Yet, according to the American Time Use Survey, Americans spent 27 percent less time per day socializing and communicating in 2023 than they did in 2003. The evidence is strong that humans are failing to take advantage of the abundance of the social connections that surround them—like someone stranded on a lush desert island yet undernourished because they fail to take advantage of the bounty. Fortunately, whether or not you take advantage of this bounty is not a matter of chance—it's a matter of choice.

Now What? The High Price of Not Feeling Loved

So far, we've explored the cultural trends, the roots of loneliness, and the technology behind rising disconnection. Yet the decline in meaningful connection isn't just a cultural curiosity. Beneath the numbers is a story that we haven't yet addressed—namely, the wider personal and societal costs of not feeling loved.

When people don't feel loved, it shapes how they see themselves, how they relate to others, and even how society functions. To begin with, research has established that when individuals don't feel securely loved, their brains and bodies react as if they're in danger. A toddler who senses that their caregiver cannot be counted on becomes anxious and depressed. Similarly, when adults don't feel loved, they are triggered to feel *lost* and *at risk*, which provokes a self-protective orientation that can have far-reaching consequences.

These consequences include becoming paralyzed by despair, afraid of being cut off from others, limited in one's ability to be effective or to move forward, and defensively unwilling to take steps that could strengthen relationships. For example, a person who doesn't feel loved by their partner may become emotionally withdrawn, hesitant to express their needs, or even preemptively push others away to avoid potential rejection. Over time, these patterns can contribute to loneliness, self-doubt, and even behaviors that harm relationships rather than strengthen them.

At the extreme, a lack of felt love doesn't just cause distress—it can lead to destructive acts. Research shows that feeling disconnected can fuel not only personal struggles such as anxiety and withdrawal but also societal problems such as violence and hate. The modern crises of loneliness, mental-health struggles, and even rising racial harassment, hate crime, and school shootings likely have a common root: Too many people don't feel loved enough.

At the same time, these crises extend beyond individual actions or choices. A culture that rewards self-sufficiency over interdependence, consumerism over community, and digital convenience over in-person connection has contributed to rising disconnection. While this book offers tools to help you feel more loved in your personal relationships, larger systemic and cultural shifts—such as building community networks, creating more inclusive social spaces, and supporting policies that make connection accessible to everyone—are also important pieces of the puzzle.

Encouragingly, while large-scale change is necessary, you're not powerless in the meantime. Culture shapes connection, but, as we explore throughout, so do your daily choices—what you say, how you listen, and how you show up for your relationships, starting now.

Three Hopeful Takeaways
from This Chapter

The hopeful news? Embedded in the stories and the science explored in this chapter are three ways to reframe what it means when you don't feel loved.

First, a feeling of not being loved is not a personal failing—it's an evolutionarily hardwired signal that something is amiss and that you need to muster energy and resources to reconnect. Put another way, feelings of not being loved exist *precisely* because their unpleasantness motivates people to seek out and bond with others—for example, by repairing a fractured relationship or reaching out to an old friend. As Sonja's life coach Emilie likes to remind her, "Feelings are just data—like a light flashing on your dashboard to signal to you that something needs attention." *How to Feel Loved* focuses on how to right that thing that is amiss.

Second, a feeling of not being loved is harmful only when it persists. Presaging this idea, the world's leading expert on loneliness, John Cacioppo (1951–2018), argued that loneliness is only harmful when it's *chronic*. So instead of thinking, *I am unloved,* try reframing it from an indication of a personality trait to the description of a transient experience: *I am having a lonely moment* or *Right now, I don't feel loved by this person.*

Traits tend to be durable (long-lasting), immutable (difficult to change), and essentialist (tied to core aspects of your identity). Moments, on the other hand, are fleeting, changeable, and don't define you. They can stimulate you to pause and reflect and to make changes. When you start doing more of what leads you to feel loved and less of what doesn't (see next chapter), those not-loved moments will become fewer and farther between. Therein lies the heart of our message: Feeling loved is something you can actively work on. And—as we explore in future chapters—what you'll be working on has less to do with changing *who you are* and more to do with shifting the conversations you have.

Third, our reasoning in this chapter leads to a powerful conclusion: One of the key antidotes to feeling lonely, isolated, anxious, and depressed is *feeling loved.* Generalizing from the scientific literature, when people feel securely loved, they experience better mental health, are more openly loving toward others, are more productive and creative, and even discourage their partners from behaving badly. Just as loneliness and disconnection can ripple outward, feeling loved can ripple outward too.

3

Revisiting Popular Beliefs About What Makes You Feel Loved

What Do *You* Do to Feel More Loved?

When we asked nearly two thousand adults what they do to feel more loved, we were struck by how many seemed to find the question difficult to answer. Some weren't sure what steps to take, while others felt that love was something that either happened or didn't—something beyond their control. Here are some of their responses:

- "I don't feel there is anything I could do to make the people in my life love me more. [They] either love me or they don't."
- "I would like to feel more loved at work. I wish I knew how."
- "I don't know what steps I would take. I try to be the best person I can already, but it doesn't seem to make a difference."
- "I would like to feel more loved by a select few people, but there isn't really anything I can do about that."
- "I've already tried, and nothing has ever worked. It just blows up in my face."

Some respondents took an empowering view—proposing concrete steps they could take to cultivate love in their lives. They talked about being more present with others, expressing gratitude, opening up emotionally, and focusing on making their loved ones feel valued. These responses mirrored what research suggests actually helps people feel more loved—affirming that the mindsets we'll explore reflect the instincts and insights many people already carry within themselves.

So why does feeling loved feel elusive for so many people? The challenge often isn't a lack of love itself but rather the beliefs people hold about how love works. In this chapter, we'll examine some of the most common assumptions about feeling loved—some of which you might recognize from your own experiences. Our goal isn't to dismiss these beliefs outright, but rather to explore whether they're truly helping you feel as loved as you want to be. If not, we'll consider what you might do differently.

What People Think Makes Them Feel Loved—and What the Science Says

A myth is a widely held but misleading belief—an "if only" story we tell ourselves that often seems entirely reasonable at first. Myths gain traction because they tell plausible-sounding stories explaining how things are, and those stories resonate with people's hopes, fears, and intuitions. But when we examine those stories more closely, we sometimes find that they don't hold up.

The same is true for common beliefs about feeling loved. Many people instinctively follow certain ideas about what will make them feel valued, cherished, and secure in their relationships. And yet, what if some of those ideas aren't serving them as well as they think? In this chapter, we'll take a closer look at a few common beliefs (see figure 1) and explore whether they truly lead to lasting feelings of being loved. If some of these beliefs sound familiar, that's okay—almost everyone has embraced them at some point. But just as with nutrition, where some foods nourish you, while others leave you unsatisfied; some approaches to feeling loved sustain you, while others fall short. The good news? Once you recognize what isn't working, you can make space for the mindsets and skills that *do* bring happiness and connection into your life.

Figure 1. Common Beliefs About Feeling Loved

IF-ONLY BELIEF #1:

If only I were more attractive, powerful, or successful, I would feel more loved.

IF-ONLY BELIEF #2:

If only I could make sure others knew my positive qualities and successes, I would feel more loved.

IF-ONLY BELIEF #3:

If only I could hide my shortcomings, I would feel more loved.

IF-ONLY BELIEF #4:

If only my partner could speak my love language, I would feel more loved.

IF-ONLY BELIEF #5:

If only I could get my partner to love me more, I would feel more loved.

If-Only Belief #1: *If Only* I Were More Attractive, Powerful, or Successful, I Would Feel More Loved

Mike Prince (Corey Stoll): So I shouldn't have to worry about getting real love?

Andy Salter, his wife (Piper Perabo): I'm saying that the way to get it is to be a winner.

—*from* Billions, *season 7, episode 6*

Sonja met Sah D'Simone at a conference in California, in which he spoke about being a meditation teacher, artist, and healer. However, D'Simone was not always a spiritual seeker, as he describes in his book:

> When I left the fashion industry in 2012, I had been worshiping money-power-fame as my personal God for so long that I had no idea what I really cared about. My sense of self-worth came from my title, the money I could spend, and the contact I had with celebrities. . . . I leaned in to the character of the eccentric, over-the-top, high-powered fashion mogul: surrounded by "friends," always up for a good time, "the life of the party."

D'Simone's story may sound extreme, but many of us have felt, at one point or another, that success, beauty, and status would make us feel more loved. It's understandable—our culture constantly reinforces the idea that being admired will translate into feeling cherished. If you were wealthier, sexier, or had more renown, wouldn't the people in your life appreciate you more? Wouldn't you feel more loved? Yet research—and the lived experiences of many—suggests that this belief doesn't always hold up.

Through media, social norms, and the stories people tell each other, Western culture incessantly teaches that the secret to feeling loved is having more—more money, more beauty, more success. The modern dating landscape reflects this: Take a quick scroll through dating-app profiles or social media, and you'll see references to LMS (*looks-money-status*) as prized qualities. Many people, including us, at some point, have chased after things like A-list status, beauty, or success, hoping they would bring the best possible life. People strive to be influencers or to make as much money as possible to buy the latest tech, luxury vacations, or the hottest DJs for their parties. Others seek these qualities in their mates—one acquaintance insisted on only dating men with the "four sixes": six figures (salary), six-pack (abs), six feet (height), and six inches (for sex). She's still looking.

This instinct to optimize themselves—or seek the most "desirable" partner—is completely natural. But does achieving wealth, power, fame, or physical perfection actually lead to feeling loved? Research suggests that while these things may bring attention and celebration, they don't necessarily translate into feelings of being truly valued and known. Why, then, do people chase these goals? Although many tell themselves that they're doing it purely for their own fulfillment, deep down, they likely pursue them in hope of being seen as more appealing—more *worthy* of love. Indeed, "Significance-Quest Theory" states that humans have a drive or "quest" for significance, sometimes manifested in good works or humanitarian endeavors, but at other times reflected in efforts to bolster their sense of worth by achieving looks, money, or status, or by attracting socially desirable "trophy" partners. Some people even go so far as to have children in hope of experiencing pure unconditional love. But relying on external achievements to generate feelings of love can backfire.

Consider Madame Bovary, the iconic character from Gustave Flaubert's nineteenth-century novel. She hopes that having a child will bring the fulfillment she craves, only to realize that no external source—whether a child, a lover, or social status—can fill that void. While her story is fictional, it reflects a timeless human experience: Looking outside oneself for validation often leaves people feeling empty.

Hidden Costs of Relying on External Validation—and What Works Better

One reason that striving for extrinsic goals doesn't always lead to feeling loved is that people want to be loved for *who they are* rather than *what they have*—for their compassion, integrity, willingness to work hard, sense of humor, and so on and not for "surface" characteristics, such as money, status, fame, and beauty. Emphasizing your extrinsic virtues creates what social psychologists call *attributional ambiguity*—the unsettling doubt about whether others love you for the "right" reasons. For example, a beautiful person who has always received compliments on their looks might secretly fear that their desirability is the only reason people are drawn to them, rather than their kindness or character.

A classic experiment conducted at the University at Buffalo illustrated this phenomenon. Highly attractive women wrote an essay and then received praise from a hidden male evaluator. When the women believed that the evaluator couldn't see them, they took the praise to heart. But when they thought that the evaluator *had* seen them, they were more likely to dismiss the praise—believing it was based on their looks rather than their writing skills. The same pattern emerged for highly attractive men.

A similar dynamic plays out in relationships. Someone who is admired for their wealth or beauty may quietly wonder, *Do they love me for who I am—or for what I have? And would they still love me if I lost my money or my looks as I grew older?* This uncertainty can undermine trust, making it harder to truly feel loved. Perhaps this helps explain why celebrities and the ultrawealthy are often skeptical when they receive love and admiration from others. When you're unsure whether others appreciate you for who you are rather than what you bring to the table, that attributional ambiguity can erode relationship trust.

Another reason chasing extrinsic goals can be unfulfilling is known as the "hedonic treadmill"—the tendency for achievements to bring only a temporary spell of satisfaction before one again feels the pressure to accumulate more. Instead, such striving seems to never satiate, thus rendering a person ever more dissatisfied and lonelier. To paraphrase an oft-quoted commencement speech by the American writer George Saunders, the problem with succeeding is that the need to do so constantly renews itself—like a mountain that keeps growing ahead of you as you climb it.

Research shows that pursuing extrinsic goals—such as wealth and status—undermines, rather than bolsters, feelings of happiness and connection. In one longitudinal study of 12,894 US undergraduates, those who, during college, rated being very well-off financially as "essential" or "very important" were less satisfied with their lives two decades later compared to those who had placed less importance on wealth. (Notably, only respondents who ultimately achieved very high annual incomes—more than half a million in 2020 dollars—didn't show this effect.) Similarly, anecdotal evidence from megalottery winners suggests that sudden wealth doesn't always lead to greater happiness; in some cases, it creates distance and *dis*connection, as newfound riches make it harder to trust the intentions of friends and loved ones.

So what does lead to feeling loved? If external markers of success won't secure your feeling loved, what will? Research suggests an alternative approach—to focus on *intrinsic* goals rather than extrinsic ones. Intrinsic goals center on:

- **Personal growth**—learning a new language, exploring a creative passion, spending time in nature or in spiritual reflection
- **Connecting to close others and community**—reaching out to friends; being a joiner, not a watcher
- **Contributing your time, energy, and money**—caring for a sick friend, mentoring someone, volunteering for a cause

These activities are ones in which you "cultivate your roots rather than shine your leaves." Not only will they improve happiness, belonging, and self-worth, they will make you a psychologically "richer" person—more well-rounded, more interesting, and with almost infinite fuel and fodder for conversation and connection. (A lot more on the importance of conversations in the chapters to follow.)

At the end of the day, the question you might ask yourself is this: *Which epitaph would I rather have on my gravestone—"I Was Loved" or "I Owned Fancy Cars"?*

If-Only Belief #2: *If Only* I Could Make Sure Others Knew My Positive Qualities and Successes, I Would Feel More Loved

Many readers of this book have worked hard to achieve success—whether in their careers, social lives, or personal growth. And it's true that success can contribute to happiness, at least for a while. For example, happier people earn more and are better liked. But when it comes to *feeling loved*, there's a common instinct that can lead people astray. It's the belief that feeling loved comes from making sure other people recognize your strengths, talents, or successes: *If only they knew.* This belief may seem logical, but research suggests it doesn't quite work that way.

We live in a culture that celebrates visibility. Society lionizes confident, charismatic individuals who openly showcase their accomplishments—CEOs, influencers, entertainers, and top athletes. Social media has amplified this tendency, encouraging people to highlight their best moments and craft an image of success. Given this cultural backdrop, it makes sense that many people feel the need to broadcast their strengths—whether through direct boasting or carefully curated social-media updates. But, as you already know from If-Only Belief #1, there's a catch: While people may admire you for your achievements, admiration doesn't lead to feeling loved.

Let's return for a moment to the costs of digital self-presentation. Many people marvel at the extraordinary capabilities of modern technology. From near-human intelligence to the ability to instantly connect with loved ones across the globe, devices offer unprecedented access to potential friends, business partners, and romantic relationships. It's no wonder that 54 percent of US adults believe these technologies help them to connect—rather than hinder them from connecting—with others.

And in many ways, they're right. Digital tools can sustain long-distance relationships, introduce you to communities you might never have found otherwise, and give you opportunities to express yourself. But at the same time, as we explored in the previous chapter, they can also subtly reshape the way people interact—sometimes in ways that leave them feeling less, rather than more, connected.

One of the most profound shifts in social life over the past two decades is the emphasis on accumulating "followers" on screens rather than deepening friendships in real life. It's easier than ever to present a curated version of yourself—one that highlights your best moments, your most flattering angles, your biggest wins. And while there's nothing inherently wrong with wanting to put your best foot forward, the unintended consequence is that many people find themselves performing connection rather than experiencing it.

Consider a moment from Sonja's travels: One day, she found herself waiting an hour for a delayed flight in a crowded airport-gate area. Sitting next to her was a striking young woman with long black hair, and Sonja couldn't help but watch with fascination as the woman spent the entire hour meticulously taking selfies, carefully editing and retouching each one before taking more, and finally posting the best results on Instagram. Was she hoping for a certain number of likes, to get attention from someone special, or did she believe that a particular beautiful photo would win her love?

The impulse to showcase one's life online—through updates, snaps, tags, and posts—is often driven by a natural desire to be seen, appreciated, and valued. But being noticed isn't the same as being known. A carefully crafted showreel might impress others, but it doesn't foster the kind of deep, reciprocal understanding that makes people feel truly loved. Furthermore, research suggests that focusing too much on *how one is perceived*—on *making a good impression*—can actually make one feel *less* connected.

The Catch Behind Impressing Others— and What Works Better

At first glance, the ability to craft and control how one appears to others seems like a good thing. After all, why wouldn't you want to present the most polished version of yourself? For example, when it comes to people outside your inner circle, displaying your strengths, triumphs, and best qualities can certainly make an impression—it may open doors, attract dates, or even command respect. (Such displays can be good gatekeepers, after all.) And in some ways, that's completely natural—first impressions matter, and everyone wants to put their best foot forward. But when self-presentation takes priority over expressing what lies beneath the surface, one loses opportunities to truly know and be known to others.

Consider several familiar rituals of modern life:

- Carefully tweaking a dating profile to appear more appealing (perhaps even stretching the truth)
- Exchanging quick, surface-level text messages or engaging in small talk instead of meaningful conversations
- Collecting likes that momentarily boost confidence but rarely lead to deeper connection
- Humblebragging, or boasting masked by a complaint or false humility—e.g., "It's exhausting being the only person my boss trusts with our big client." (Studies show that this more subtle approach renders people less likable, not more.)

Each of these behaviors is understandable, even instinctive in a world where visibility feels like social currency. The irony is that the very tools designed to bring people closer together can unintentionally create distance instead. When people focus too much on how they appear to others, they risk missing out on the richness of real, unfiltered connection and end up feeling unseen. Also, at the same time that broadcasting strengths may inspire admiration, they may breed comparison, envy, and even resentment—pushing people *away* rather than drawing them in. Once again: You cannot feel loved if you're not known. Indeed, you cannot even feel fully satisfied with your accomplishments—there's always someone more beautiful, wealthy, or successful.

Recently, Sonja was hiking with a group of friends when one couple pushed back on this idea. "What's wrong with being proud of our accomplishments? People prefer winners to losers, stars over nobodies! Our friends and partners and acquaintances should be happy for us!" In some ways, they're right. Your successes—and the hard journey to achieve them—deserve recognition. The people who care about you *want* to see you thrive. They may even bask in your reflected glory, celebrating alongside you. But when it comes to sharing those accomplishments, the key is balance.

Talking about your successes in the right context—with the right people, at the right time—can deepen connections. When successes are related naturally—without an agenda to impress or obtain approval—others share in your joy, and your connection with them is deepened. But when success becomes something you *broadcast* rather than something you *share*, it can have the opposite effect. If the goal is to feel loved, then simply announcing achievements—especially as a way to seek validation—rarely brings what you're hoping for.

The good news? The people who truly care about you will notice your wins, whether or not you announce them. And when you share them in a way that invites connection rather than admiration, you're far more likely to experience the sense of being valued—not just for what you've accomplished, but for who you are.

Overfocusing on Self

Consider a common scenario: You're opening up to a friend about a painful problem—say, a tough breakup—when they swiftly turn the conversation to themselves.

Oh, I totally get it. When I broke up with Alex, it was even worse. Let me tell you what happened . . .

Suddenly, the focus shifts entirely to them, leaving you feeling unheard and unsupported. Scientists call this pattern of turning every discussion back to oneself "conversational self-focus," and research shows that it can strain relationships. In fact, when adolescents engage in conversational self-focus, their friends tend to view the relationship less favorably, which can contribute to unhappiness.

Ironically, self-focus in general, and a concern with making a great impression, is more likely to be seen in people who are less happy and secure to begin with. Studies show that those with relatively low self-esteem (whether situational or chronic) are the ones most fixated on being perceived favorably and approvingly. Research also finds that individuals who are relatively more depressed or relatively young are most likely to be self-focused.

Our takeaway is that self-focus, whether in conversation or in self-presentation, is often a response to a very common and human feeling—uncertainty about whether one is truly valued. Fortunately, overfocus on the self is easy to shift outward.

Turning Attention Outward to Feel More Loved

The logic here doesn't suggest that you should avoid reflecting on your successes, nor should you hide them when talking to others. But if the goal is to feel loved, the answer is not to work harder to impress your conversation partners but to engage with them. Instead of focusing on how you're coming across to others (which keeps the spotlight on you), focus on coming forward to fully know others (which strengthens connection and makes them feel valued).

Throughout the book, we'll explore exactly how to go about accomplishing that. But first it's worth acknowledging that shifting focus outward to get to know others can initially feel uncomfortable. If striking up deep conversations or drawing out people's stories feels awkward or intimidating, you're not alone. Here are four common barriers—and how they can all be overcome:

1. **Lack of practice.** Most people *want* to connect—they just haven't had much experience stepping into someone else's skin in a sustained way. The good news? Like any skill, this gets easier with practice. You'll find plenty of concrete suggestions in chapter 4 (on the Relationship Sea-Saw) and chapter 6 (on the Listening-to-Learn mindset).

2. **Worry about being intrusive.** Many people hesitate to ask deeper questions because they fear coming across as nosy. But studies show that this fear is misplaced: Asking questions—even seemingly sensitive or personal ones—actually leads the other person to like you more, not less. People yearn to be asked about themselves, especially when the listener is genuinely curious. If you're still skeptical, think about the last time someone asked *you* a thoughtful question about your lived experience. How did it make you feel? (We dive deeper into this in chapter 7, on the Radical-Curiosity mindset.)

3. **Fear of having to open up in return.** Some people are reluctant to engage deeply with others because they worry it will require them to be equally vulnerable. But sharing doesn't have to be all-or-nothing. You can create space for others to share openly without immediately revealing everything about yourself. And when you do choose to open up, you can do so at your own pace. Strategies for this are explored in chapter 5 (on the Sharing mindset).

4. **Being caught up in one's own world.** It's easy to get absorbed in one's own routines, worries, and to-do lists. As writer G. K. Chesterton beautifully observed, we are all guilty of inhabiting a "tiny and tawdry theater in which [our] own little plot is always being played." (Indeed, one could argue that the aim of much of psychotherapy, coaching, and personal development is to make a dent in humanity's self-absorption.) Yet imagine how differently your life would feel if you stepped off that small stage and into the richness of others' experiences. To return to Chesterton:

> How much larger your life would be if your self could become smaller in it; if you could really look at [others] with common curiosity and pleasure; if you could see them walking as they are in their sunny selfishness and their virile indifference! You would begin to be interested in them, because they were not interested in you.

The irony is that the more you shift your attention outward, the more loved you'll feel in return. Instead of focusing on how you're being perceived, focus on listening. Instead of talking about yourself, ask about the other person's experiences. Instead of crafting a flawless image, share something vulnerable and true. By doing these things, you create the very conditions that make feeling loved possible. Because ultimately, as numerous studies have shown, people don't feel drawn to perfection—they feel drawn to authenticity and reciprocity.

If-Only Belief #3: *If Only* I Could Hide My Shortcomings, I Would Feel More Loved

So far, we've explored how chasing success or carefully curating an image doesn't necessarily lead to feeling more loved. But what about the parts of yourself you don't want to showcase—the imperfections, struggles, and vulnerabilities. Everyone has flaws, faces setbacks, and experiences moments of self-doubt. Everyone is a work in progress. Yet a common belief persists: that to be loved, you must keep your weaknesses well-hidden and present only your best self. If-Only Belief #3 suggests that revealing anything "less than perfect" will push people away.

At first glance, this belief makes sense. After all, who doesn't want to be seen in the best possible light? But research—and real-life experience—suggests that molding yourself into someone you're not can push others away instead of bringing them closer.

The instinct to manage impressions is natural. As highlighted by If-Only Belief #2, many shape their self-presentations in ways that invite interest—and will be attractive and compelling to others. But studies show that people don't always know what will actually make them more appealing in relationships. Sometimes, the very traits you downplay—your quirks, challenges, or even past failures—are what draw people in. And even when you do manage to "get it right," molding yourself into what someone else wants (e.g., dressing like a rock star because your romantic partner prefers that look) can leave you feeling uncomfortable, inauthentic, or even like an impostor.

Consider the story of Cyrano de Bergerac, the seventeenth-century nobleman who ghostwrote poetic love letters on behalf of his inarticulate friend, Christian, helping him win his beloved Roxane's heart. The words that Christian sent were beautiful, but he didn't write them—so no matter how much those words moved Roxane, he couldn't feel truly known, valued, and loved. In the twenty-first century, many people do something similar—hiding who they are, carefully curating what they reveal, and hoping that others will love them for the version that others presumably want. But, as we've repeated before, how can you feel truly loved if the version of you being loved isn't you?

Furthermore, if you believe your flaws will push people away, you may instinctively reveal only "safe" imperfections—for example, that you never make your bed—or keep parts of yourself completely out of sight. But ironically, secret-keeping, which we explore in more detail in chapter 5, makes it hard to feel understood. Imagine someone who reveals little of importance to their close friends. They feel misunderstood, but at the same time, they share almost nothing of what truly matters to them. How could their friends possibly understand them if they never get to see the full picture? This same dynamic plays out with family members, partners, and colleagues—when you don't let others in, you deprive them of the chance to truly know you.

Of course, being open doesn't mean oversharing. Some people, recognizing the value of honesty and vulnerability, swing too far in the other direction—disclosing too much too quickly, emotionally unloading, or "trauma dumping" before the other person is ready to receive it. The key isn't to lay everything bare all at once—it's to share in a way that invites interest, receptivity, and concern. Instead of testing relationships with a flood of unfiltered disclosures, think of vulnerability as an invitation, one that allows space for your conversation partner to reciprocate, listen, and support. We explore exactly how to strike this balance—what to share, when to share it, and how to create emotional intimacy without overwhelming others—in chapter 5 (on the Sharing mindset).

When you give other people the chance to observe both your strengths and your struggles, something powerful happens: They don't just admire you—they grow to know and understand you. And being known is an absolute prerequisite to feeling loved.

If-Only Belief #4: *If Only* My Partner Could Speak My Love Language, I Would Feel More Loved

The next if-only belief is especially easy to embrace—and just as critical to examine. You'll recognize it instantly—the idea that you'll only feel loved if the other person speaks your love language. Introduced by pastoral counselor Gary Chapman in 2015, the idea that everyone has a preferred love language has become wildly popular, popping up everywhere you look, from song titles (SZA's "Love Language") to marketing taglines (Venmo's "Security is our love language"). Even present-day dating apps prompt users to declare their top-rated love language from Chapman's list of five—gifts, acts of service, quality time, physical touch, or verbal affirmation—in hope of finding a match that enhances their chances of relationship success.

There's a reason this idea resonates so deeply with people—it's a relatable and intuitive metaphor that offers a simple, straightforward framework for finding appropriate partners and improving relationships. It also suggests an easy complaint when you're unhappy with your romantic partner—"They're not speaking my love language!" Indeed, Sonja confesses that she mentions love languages in conversation at least once a week.

However, while the love-languages concept has captured the public imagination, recent research shows that it's not as scientifically sound as many believe. Yet, rather than viewing this as disappointing news, think of it as an opportunity—because what the research actually reveals is that love can be expressed and received in far more varied and flexible ways than a choice from a simple five-category system implies.

Consider these three key findings from recent studies that serve as nails in the coffin of the love-languages hypothesis:

- First, most people report appreciating all five languages, not just their single primary one. Indeed, in three studies of more than two hundred thousand participants, between 39 percent and 54 percent did not identify a single dominant love language.
- Second, the idea of five distinct love languages doesn't hold up statistically. A type of statistical analysis called *factor analysis* has failed to identify five separate categories, suggesting that these "languages" overlap and mush together. And, as many of you have already probably realized, love can be expressed in countless other

ways—such as through humor, intellectual chemistry, spiritual connection, creativity, supporting a partner's family and friends, sending flowers, or simply giving your partner space when they need it.

- Finally, having a partner who expresses love in your unique identified love language doesn't actually predict whether your relationship will be relatively more satisfying or long-lasting. Not surprisingly, research shows that couples tend to be happiest when love is expressed and received in multiple ways, not just one. In a study of 696 individuals in committed relationships, those whose partners used their "top" love language didn't feel any more loved than those whose partners used their four lower-ranked love languages. This finding even held true for people who reported strongly preferring a particular love language, such as quality time or touch, and it even held true for people in distressed relationships.

Rather than limiting yourself to one "right" way to embrace love, these findings suggest that expanding your perspective can open up even more opportunities to feel loved. Instead of waiting for someone to speak your preferred love language, what if you became fluent in recognizing and appreciating all the ways love is already being expressed in your life? Indeed, focusing too much on just one love language might actually mean missing out on important love experiences.

In fact, recent research uncovered something that took even us by surprise. Three hot-off-the-presses studies revealed that two particular love languages—no matter whether people favor them or not—are the strongest predictors of happy relationships and feeling loved by one's romantic partner. Can you guess which two they are?

Our main recommendation is that rather than focus on a single love language, think of them as ingredients in a well-balanced diet of connection. Different times and circumstances call for emphasizing one love language over another—affectionate touch during a stressful situation, words of affirmation when feeling insecure, or simply quality time when life feels chaotic. Most humans need to express and feel love in multiple ways. Instead of seeing love languages as rigid categories, our perspective instead emphasizes viewing them as concrete tools for building the feeling that your authentic, true self is known and embraced by the other. A well-titrated balance of different love experiences, which enables you and your partner to express your love for each other *more* and to express it more *naturally*, is more likely to help both of you to feel more loved.

So which two love languages matter most? The strongest predictors—for everyone—of happy relationships and feeling loved are quality time and words of affirmation.

Thus, our evidence-based suggestion is to practice these two "languages" more often in daily life. Prioritize quality time by putting away distractions during conversations, sharing activities you both enjoy, and scheduling intentional check-ins to reconnect. And don't underestimate the power of words—voice to your partner the qualities you love about them, offer encouraging messages, and express gratitude for little things.

If-Only Belief #5: *If Only* I Could Get My Partner to Love Me More, I Would Feel More Loved

At the beginning of this book, we mentioned an often-overlooked truth about feeling loved—one that can challenge even the best of intentions: You can *be* loved and still not *feel* loved. Even if your partner expresses love consistently and generously—offering compliments, warmth, and reassurance—feeling loved isn't guaranteed. The same goes for love from a parent, sibling, friend, colleague, or even a child. This brings us to the final, and perhaps most important, misconception about feeling loved: the belief that the key to feeling loved is *getting* the other person to change—specifically, *getting* them to love you more. But is that really the answer?

Before we go any further, an important reality check: If you've made genuine, consistent efforts—sharing vulnerably, listening with curiosity, showing compassion—and the love you're offering is still not requited, then it may be time to shift your focus. Sometimes, no amount of effort and patience can change how someone feels, and in those cases, the healthiest choice is to redirect your energy toward relationships that can truly nourish you. Or as the incomparable Bonnie Raitt famously sang in her moving hit song "I Can't Make You Love Me," you can't make someone feel love if it's not in their heart.

That said, if your love is reciprocated, but you still don't often *feel* loved, there's good news: This book can help.

Yet, If-Only Belief #5 is particularly tricky—because, in some ways, it contains a grain of truth. If your partner suddenly started expressing their love in a dramatically different way tomorrow, you'd probably notice. You'd likely feel more loved—at least for a little while. But here's why this belief can mislead: That initial boost doesn't last. Just like a salary raise feels exciting at first but soon becomes the new normal, an increase in your partner's expressions of love, without a shift in your own approach, is unlikely to lead to a lasting change in how loved you feel.

There are other reasons this if-only belief doesn't hold up:

- If you struggle with anxious or avoidant attachment, no amount of "additional" love will fully sink in or penetrate inside your heart (see chapter 11 for more details)—until you shift how you process and receive it. The love is there, but it may not feel like enough.
- Trying to get your partner to love you more by focusing solely on their needs tends to backfire. Overfocusing on the other person while neglecting your own needs and boundaries often leads to resentment, not deeper connection.
- If a relationship already feels empty or unfulfilling, more words of affirmation won't fix what's missing. Even if your partner repeatedly tells you they love you, it won't feel satisfying if the relationship itself lacks meaning or emotional depth.

That's why If-Only Belief #5 is one that resurfaces in different ways throughout this book: If your person loves you on some level but you still yearn to *feel* more loved, the shift that needs to happen is not in trying to get them to change—but in the mindsets that you engage with them.

In this chapter, we reviewed some of the most common if-only beliefs that get in the way of feeling loved. In the remaining chapters, we'll take a more positive approach, describing more constructive ways of thinking and acting that can help you cultivate the feeling of being loved that makes life worthwhile. To reiterate: It's not about changing something about the other person—getting your romantic partners, friends, family, coworkers, or neighbors to notice you more, to behave differently, or to love you more. It's about changing the conversation—so that feeling loved emerges naturally.

PART II

A New Paradigm

4

The Relationship Sea-Saw

A friend is one that knows you as you
are, understands where you have
been, accepts what you have become,
and still, gently allows you to grow.

—*Anonymous*

This chapter explores the process by which another person can truly *see* you and *know* you, creating the foundation that allows you to feel loved. How do you build this foundation? You already know part of the answer: Counterintuitively, it begins not by revealing more of yourself but by fully seeing, embracing, and accepting the *other* person—their true, vulnerable, and imperfect self. Consider Ed Koch, the mayor of New York City back in the 1980s, who famously walked around the city asking his constituents, "How'm I doing?" This approach—focused on how others see you—is exactly the opposite of what we suggest will be effective. Instead, if you want to be known and loved, start by shifting your attention outward, toward your conversation partner.

Why does this work? Because true connection is never one-sided—at least, not when it comes to genuine caring. Instead, true connection unfolds as a delicate ballet of mutual honesty, authentic curiosity about each other, and deep listening with acceptance and warmth. Like any intricate dance, true connection takes skill, effort, and time. And like any intricate dance, it can be learned by anyone, but it takes practice. While meaningful exchanges can take place in a single conversation, the strongest bonds will emerge gradually, across many interactions, sometimes involving weeks or even months, as trust and understanding deepen. Ideally, these interactions will take place in person, face-to-face—it's far more difficult to enact the Sea-Saw remotely, for reasons we explored in chapter 2. A foundation built in this way is not only more authentic but also more likely to be enduring.

Consider the following example, which illustrates the Relationship Sea-Saw and includes elements of all five mindsets:

In the 1985 coming-of-age classic The Breakfast Club, *five teenagers from vastly different high school social groups find themselves forced to spend an entire Saturday together in detention. Each is there for a different reason, and each is troubled in a unique and personal way. As one might expect, they begin their day by arguing and mocking each other. Gradually, though, they begin to recognize similarities in their private struggles, and they open up to one another, alternating between revealing their inner selves with providing responsive, even loving support.*

Ally Sheedy's Allison divulges her wish to run away from home but initially refuses to explain why. Andrew, played by Emilio Estevez, presses her with questions and curiosity, eventually leading Allison to describe how her parents ignore her, an admission that kindles heartfelt empathy in Andrew. Later, Andrew confesses the distress he feels in striving to live up to the hypermasculine image his father's approval depends on. He and Allison bond over the frustration they share relating to their parents.

Meanwhile, after first boasting about their sexual experiences, socially awkward Brian (played by Anthony Michael Hall) and cliquish Claire (played by Molly Ringwald) admit their lies and share their anxieties about being virgins. Rebellious delinquent Bender (played by Judd Nelson), initially detached and defiant, comes to feel supported by the group and reveals his father's physical abuse. The film ends with all five Breakfast Club members feeling connected and empowered—and, we propose, feeling loved.

The metaphor we use is an underwater seesaw—we call it the Relationship Sea-Saw. The Sea-Saw illustrates how a delicate interplay of mutual responsiveness and personal sharing can develop into an

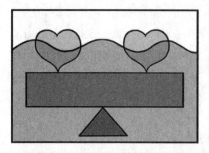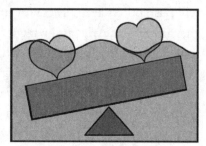

Figure 2. The Relationship Sea-Saw

authentic, loving connection. Let's revisit and extend our description from the introduction.

Imagine that you and the person with whom you wish to feel more love are seated on opposite sides of the Sea-Saw (see left panel of figure 2). The hearts in the illustration represent each of your full, complex, and multifaceted selves. But much of that fullness is hidden. The hearts are partially submerged, with only their tops visible above the waterline. What's above the surface represents the parts of you that you openly share—the traits, experiences, and emotions you allow others to see. When a new person in your life says they love you, they are often responding to this visible part, the version you present to the world. But below the waterline, concealed beneath the surface, lie your deeper and more vulnerable layers—your closely held opinions, private thoughts, insecurities, unspoken fears, and unfiltered emotions. These are the parts that even your closest confidants may not see.

The key to deepening a connection—and allowing yourself to feel truly loved—is the movement of the Relationship Sea-Saw. Four principles explain how it operates.

(1) **Much of what truly matters lies hidden beneath the surface.** Most people long to be understood and to feel loved for who they believe they really are—their truest, deepest self. Yet, as we explored in the previous chapter, at the same time, they instinctively conceal key aspects of that self, especially their shortcomings, their regrets, the experiences they wish hadn't happened, and the traits they fear

will push others away. These features aren't always negative—perhaps they involve an early family memory that touches your heart. The unspoken logic is self-protective—why reveal something that gives others the power to hurt or reject you? (As a musical artist once quipped to us, intimacy is a scary word, because it means "into me see.") Ironically, however, true intimacy isn't built on the polished version of yourself that you present to the world. Instead, it comes from being seen and loved in your entirety—vulnerable parts and all. When you allow others—even neighbors, colleagues, and acquaintances—to witness your authentic, unguarded self, you create the conditions for deep, lasting closeness. In chapter 5, we explore why adopting a Sharing mindset is essential to operating the Relationship Sea-Saw.

(2) With each downward push of the Sea-Saw, you lift a part of the other person into view. By showing warmly attentive interest in, curiosity about, and appreciation for their full self—not just the parts they initially share—you help bring more of your partner above the surface (see right panel of figure 2). As more of their true self becomes visible, you gain a deeper understanding of who they really are, which allows you to appreciate and love them more fully. Just as important, they experience the profound feeling of being truly seen and valued by you. Continuing with this metaphor: Pressing down on the Sea-Saw represents the full weight of your attention and care, lifting them higher. Meanwhile, as the focus shifts mostly to them, your own self may momentarily sink beneath the waterline, becoming less visible. But this doesn't mean that you've disappeared. On the contrary, you are the foundation holding them up, creating a safe and steady space for them to be known.

(3) Being lifted up motivates the other person to lift you up in return. The beauty of the movement of the Sea-Saw is that it's not one-sided. Once you have lifted the other person, they are likely to reciprocate, creating a natural rhythm of mutual curiosity, acceptance, and care. Your genuine interest in and concern for them invites their genuine interest in and concern for you. This reciprocity isn't just a hopeful outcome—as we explore later in the chapter, it's a rule that guides nearly all human social interactions. Social psychology

research shows that when someone invests in us with attention and care, we feel motivated to return that investment. By showing genuine interest in, curiosity about, and compassion and appreciation for *your* full self, they help lift your full, complex, multifaceted self a bit higher above the waterline. This reveals more of your deeper, more private layers—the parts that, when truly seen and valued, foster real intimacy and the feeling of being loved.

(4) **The Relationship Sea-Saw is a delicate dance of alternately lifting and being lifted.** With each back-and-forth movement—each moment you elevate someone else and each moment they elevate you—the connection between you strengthens. Psychologists call this an *upward spiral* or a *virtuous cycle*, in which positive experiences build upon each other, reinforcing and continuously increasing intimacy and trust. Of course, like any ballet pas de deux, this dance only works when both partners participate. (By partners, we mean two people engaging in the Sea-Saw, whether they're romantic partners, siblings, friends, neighbors, coworkers, or even strangers.) Clinical psychologist David Schnarch describes this dance of intimacy as *knowing* and *being known*—to which we add an essential ingredient: helping the other person know that they are known and loved. It's not enough to simply understand someone deeply; they must also experience that understanding. When you actively show another person that they are seen, valued, and cared for, you initiate a cycle that naturally leads you to feel more known and cared for yourself. Ultimately, the Relationship Sea-Saw is about balancing roles—the ongoing dynamic exchange of supporting and lifting, sharing and being lifted.

The Relationship Sea-Saw is a powerful metaphor for how you create the conditions that enable you to feel truly loved by another person. To fully engage in this delicate ballet with the person you wish to feel more loved by, you must rethink both sides of the experience: the sharing side (being known) and the responding side (knowing the other). We emphasize this crucial point—both sides matter. If you find yourself doing all the lifting, constantly supporting your partner without feeling the same in return, or if your efforts to elevate them seem to go unnoticed, it may be time to consider moving on from the relationship.

The Sea-Saw is effective only when you and your interaction partner achieve an equal balance of lifting and being lifted.

The Relationship Sea-Saw in Operation

> The meeting of two personalities is like the
> contact of two chemical substances: if there
> is any reaction, both are transformed.
> —*Carl Jung,* Modern Man in Search of a Soul

When we asked our survey participants to describe a time they felt truly loved, many of them described an interaction in which their partner responded to their vulnerable expressions in a generous, loving manner. Here are three examples:

- "A time that I felt most loved was when I was feeling very frustrated and hopeless due to a pattern with someone in my life ... which made me wonder if there was something wrong with me. ... I posted to my friend group, just to vent, and someone who I haven't seen since I was fourteen responded unexpectedly. She reassured me and told me that she had learned so much from me and that I helped her be a better person. ... It gave me so much hope that ... there were good aspects of myself which others noticed even when I didn't."
- "I think the time I felt most loved during my adult life was one night when I was hanging out with my two best friends. ... I've known both of them for many, many years, but I'm an incredibly reserved person emotionally. I don't open up very often. But we were all opening up that night. I let myself be vulnerable and talked about things that hurt me in the past, things I never told them about or never divulged the details of. They both made me feel so loved that night. They didn't judge me for anything I told them, and they didn't point out the fact that I was crying. I felt

such a heavy weight lifted off me after that experience, and it
brought us all even closer together."

- "The times I felt most loved were the times I was vulnerable. . . .
  Once I spilled my heart out to my mother about my real sexual
  orientation. Considering how we were both from a conservative
  background, it took a lot of strength on both of our ends. Her,
  to accept me, and for me to actually say it. . . . Being able to be
  vulnerable, spill your heart out, and let someone else know feels
  like love to me."

These quotes embody a process that Harry introduced to the
relationship-science literature called "responsiveness." Responsiveness
is more than just listening or being kind—it's about the dynamic
back-and-forth in which each person adjusts to the other, creating a
sense of shared understanding and appreciation. It unfolds sequen-
tially, in a series of self-disclosures and responses that foster a feeling
of togetherness, a whole that feels greater than the sum of its parts.
Imagine responsiveness with the metaphor used earlier—each partner's
movement only makes sense in relation to the other's. When both are
attuned, the interaction flows smoothly, deepening the bond between
them as they coordinate their steps. Furthermore, responsiveness has
benefits that extend beyond the interpersonal relationship. In numerous experiments, Harry and his collaborators have shown that when
people feel well responded to, they become less defensive, more open-
minded and humble, less prejudiced, and better able to cope with
negative emotions, such as anxiety.

When responsive interaction works well—as it does when people
feel loved—it sometimes feels like having "chemistry." Chemistry
seems like something reserved for naturally charismatic, beautiful,
popular, or extraverted people. But, as Harry and Sonja argued in a
scholarly article about interpersonal chemistry, that's a myth. Anyone
can create that sense of attunement with another person, and doing
so brings myriad benefits: greater happiness, stronger mental (and
maybe even physical) health, more satisfying relationships at home
and the office, and greater success in teamwork and collaborative

projects. These momentary experiences of chemistry and connection are building blocks for feeling loved. Even brief moments of attunement in a conversation can accumulate to create more meaningful connections. And the more connected you feel, the easier it becomes to both offer and experience that sense of being seen and understood. In this way, chemistry is what makes the Relationship Sea-Saw move smoothly and evenly.

Now we'll examine each stage of the Sea-Saw in detail.

Stage 1: Showing Curiosity Encourages Your Partner to Open Up

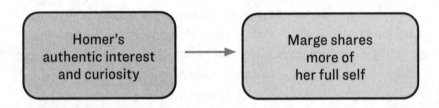

People love to talk about themselves—it's central to the powerful motive to be known and understood by others. Yet, paradoxically, many assume that their inner thoughts, emotions, and virtues are more apparent to others than they actually are, thus feeling that it's unnecessary to express them. Researchers call this the "illusion of transparency," and it often keeps people from sharing, believing that they don't need to spell things out. At other times, they hold back because they assume no one is truly interested in what they have to say—a belief that's only reinforced when listeners look around the room or check their phones. Add to this the natural reluctance many feel about being vulnerable—even with those closest to them—and the fact that many people keep their guard up, rarely letting anyone in, and it's easy to see why meaningful self-disclosure can be uncommon.

That's where you come into the picture as a curious listener. Using our illustration with Homer and Marge: By showing authentic interest in Marge, Homer creates the conditions that encourage her to open up. Hailey Magee, a personal-development coach, describes this as her preferred love language: "I show others I care for them by asking questions, learning their experiences, and being hungry for the *essence of them* beneath the small talk and the pleasantries. I want to see them for who they are and know what makes them tick."

How might you do this? The key is to find something genuinely intriguing in the other person's experience and inquire about it. It could be as simple as their collection of rare baseball cards, their cat's latest misadventure, or their passion for photography—or something more deeply personal, such as their feelings about a recent divorce or their worries about retirement. By expressing real curiosity about them as an individual, you create an invitation for opening up.

The country singer Dolly Parton captured what a genuinely curious listener feels like, in describing how she met her husband of over sixty years at the Wishy Washy Laundromat. "I was surprised and delighted that while he talked to me, he looked at my face (a rare thing for me)," Parton said of their meeting. "He seemed to be genuinely interested in finding out who I was and what I was about."

Stage 2: Listening Responsively

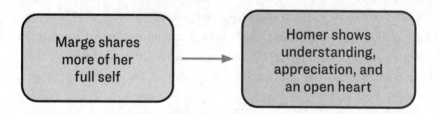

Opening up, by itself, isn't enough to set the Relationship Sea-Saw into smooth motion. What happens next—how the other person responds—determines whether the interaction deepens or stalls. Suppose Marge has revealed something personal—perhaps a difficult conversation she recently had with her adult daughter. Homer has a choice in how he responds. He could be a good listener, leaning in, asking questions about the conversation and how Marge feels about it. Alternatively, he might say, "Sorry to hear that," and quickly change the subject. The difference is profound. By being an attentive listener,

Homer encourages Marge to elaborate while also supporting her at a difficult time. By changing the subject, in contrast, he shuts down the moment, denying Marge the chance to receive empathy, advice, and connection.

This kind of attuned, engaged reaction is a perfect example of responsiveness. Responsive partners aren't just smiling head-nodders; they are active participants in the conversation, responding attentively, encouragingly, and supportively when someone opens up. They listen not only with their ears but also with their minds and an open heart, allowing themselves to react insightfully and to be moved by what the other shares. These moments of responsiveness build closeness, trust, openness, and safety. At its core, a responsive partner makes the other person:

- **feel valued**—or appreciated, validated, and respected
- **feel cared for**—or nurtured, as the recipient of compassion
- **feel understood**—or truly known

Being a responsive conversation partner involves many elements, which we explore in more depth throughout this book, and especially in chapter 6. In brief, responsiveness is conveyed with words; with nonverbal expressions; and, somewhat less commonly, with actions. With their words, responsive listeners show that they understand the nuances of what the speaker is saying, respect the speaker's unique experiences and perspectives, and genuinely want to know more. Thoughtful reflections, questions, and affirmations help accomplish this.

Connection is also built through what you don't say but do. Nonverbally, attentive body language includes steady eye contact, leaning in, and mirroring the speaker's facial expressions (e.g., smiling or showing concern) and tone of voice (e.g., excited or subdued). Most important of all is staying present and tuning out distractions. Finally, actions can communicate responsiveness—such as by giving a warm hug; an invitation to dinner; or, in the case of ongoing relationships, a small but special gift.

There's a deeper layer to what a responsive listener accomplishes. Sophie Wohltjen and Thalia Wheatley, social neuroscientists at Dartmouth University, describe conversation as a "mental road trip we collectively steer," with the aim of exchanging ideas and thereby building bonds. When we engage with each other openly, personally, generously, and empathically, we recognize that social connections don't just happen by accident when two people cross paths by chance. Rather, connections emerge through shared effort—by establishing rapport, assuming the best in the other person, finding common ground (no matter the topic), and being truly present. Responsiveness is what warmhearted, engaged, curious, and nonjudgmental listeners contribute to this process.

Stage 3: Receiving Responsiveness Leads to Feeling Loved

The longer I live, the more deeply I learn that love— whether we call it friendship or family or romance—is the work of mirroring and magnifying each other's light.

—*James Baldwin,* Nothing Personal

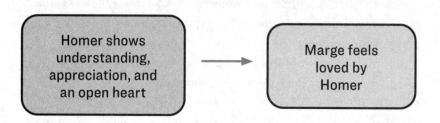

Homer shows understanding, appreciation, and an open heart → Marge feels loved by Homer

Feeling loved is like feeling the sun on your face. Sometimes your shades are drawn, blocking the warmth. The question is, What raises the shades to let the sun in? You create an opening by revealing your full self to your partner. But you will feel the warmth only if the sun is actually shining. Feeling loved works similarly. Sharing yourself doesn't automatically lead to feeling loved. When you let your partner see the real you, it's their responsiveness that makes it possible to feel loved.

Scores of studies highlight a subtle yet crucial truth: What one partner does, or intends to do, and what the other partner actually perceives can be two very different things. In close relationships, intimate connection develops only when the listener's reaction is experienced as responsive—that is, when the speaker *feels* understood, valued, and cared for. For example, in one study conducted by Harry and his then-graduate student David de Jong, simply knowing a partner's sexual likes and dislikes didn't necessarily lead to a happier romantic relationship. What mattered more was whether the partner felt that their preferences were *understood*. In another study, one partner's appreciation predicted greater relationship satisfaction—but only when the other partner also felt that appreciation. The takeaway message here is that it's not enough to believe that you are behaving responsively—you have to make sure your partner truly feels it.

The role that responsiveness plays in feeling loved is also underscored by research from the University of Alabama, where a sample of 468 undergraduate students were asked to describe, in their own words, what makes them feel loved in their family, romantic, and friend relationships. The most common theme to emerge from these answers was responsiveness—specifically, the students pointed to moments when their friends, family members, and significant others demonstrated affection, acknowledged their uniqueness and importance, and provided support.

Ultimately, your conversation partners don't simply make you feel loved—they help create the kind of interaction where feeling loved naturally develops. When you lift up your partner on the Relationship Sea-Saw—by letting them know that you see, value, and support them—you make that feeling possible.

Stage 4: Feeling Loved Sparks Curiosity, Starting the Cycle Anew

| Marge feels loved by Homer | → | Marge's authentic interest and curiosity |

When people feel loved, they become curious. This isn't just a coincidence—it's backed by well-established research. Studies show that when people feel accepted and safe, they become more open-minded, more willing to explore new ideas, and more eager to try new things. But in the context of the Relationship Sea-Saw, there's something even deeper in play. When you feel loved by someone, your curiosity turns toward them. You want to know more about them— their experiences, their values, the ideas they hold sacred, and what makes their lives meaningful. Simply by feeling seen and valued, you begin to seek deeper truths.

Self-Expansion theory helps explain this idea. Developed by married psychologists Arthur and Elaine Aron, this prominent theory proposes that people are motivated to broaden their sense of self by acquiring new perspectives, skills, and resources. One of the most powerful ways people do this is by investing in close relationships, particularly loving relationships. When people fall in love, the Arons' research shows, they begin to "include the other in the self"—in effect, their partner's attributes and viewpoints become part of their own identity. For example, Harry's wife has Armenian roots, and over time Harry has come to see himself as partly Armenian too. Sonja's three daughters share a passion and eye for visual art, and over time Sonja has come to identify art as central to her own sense of self. It's not surprising, then, that feeling loved would lead to curiosity: Learning about the other person—their world, their passions, their beliefs—is the first step toward self-expanding.

Another reason why feeling loved triggers curiosity is reciprocity. Think back to the first push of the Relationship Sea-Saw—Homer's conveying curiosity about Marge. By expressing genuine interest in Marge and then listening responsively, Homer invites Marge to reciprocate. The ancient Roman philosopher Cicero noted that "there is no duty more indispensable than that of returning a kindness." When you direct generous thoughts, energy, and actions toward others, they are naturally motivated to respond in kind. Dozens of studies have documented this principle across a variety of topics. For example, people tend to like those who like them; they generally compliment those who compliment them; and they respond with care and kindness to those who treat them the same. Although research shows that people sometimes underestimate the likelihood of reciprocity, it's actually one of the most powerful principles of social behavior. And, we propose, it applies directly to curiosity: When you show curiosity about another person, you not only invite them to open up but also encourage—perhaps even solicit—their curiosity about you.

Assembling the Pieces of the Relationship Sea-Saw

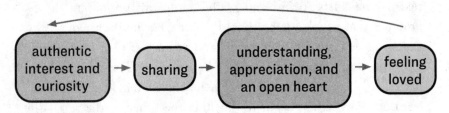

We've now come full circle, having explored all the elements of the Relationship Sea-Saw. Bringing them together, we argue, is the cornerstone of feeling loved, echoing a timeless idea familiar to anyone who remembers the closing lines of the classic 1969 Beatles song "The End"—that the love you get equals the love you give. If you want to feel more loved, the best place to begin is by making others feel more loved. When someone feels deeply valued and loved by you, they are more likely to reciprocate—to want to understand you, see you fully, and appreciate the complexity of who you are. By contrast, if you don't help *them* to feel loved by you, they probably will lack the willingness, motivation, or enthusiasm to truly listen and connect. But when you help them feel loved, they likely will create space for you to open up—lift your part of the Sea-Saw—gradually allowing you to feel known and valued. In this way, the Relationship Sea-Saw empowers you to lead and be led in turn, deepening connection with each cycle—one moment of feeling loved making room for the next.

As we've discussed, each push-and-lift of the Relationship Sea-Saw fuels an upward spiral of positive experiences—a virtuous cycle. When you respond warmly, openly, and attentively to your conversation partner, that response inspires them to be warm, open, and attentive in return, strengthening your connection. This deepened connection encourages you to be even more responsive to them, creating a reinforcing loop of intimacy, a process that the earlier *Breakfast Club* example poignantly illustrates. Responsiveness begets more responsiveness.

Our esteemed late colleague Caryl Rusbult laid the groundwork for this idea in her concept of "mutual cyclical growth." She argued that supportive interactions—particularly those that prioritize a partner's well-being over one's own preferences—are both the cause and the result of commitment and trust. In other words,

- commitment and trust foster supportive interactions, which, in turn,
- reinforce trust and commitment,
- engender further supportive interactions, and
- fuel an ongoing cycle of relationship growth.

Rusbult and her students conducted extensive research demonstrating how these reciprocal exchanges sustain and deepen relationships over time.

With each cycle—each lift of the Relationship Sea-Saw—the experience of feeling loved grows, as does the curiosity, appreciation, and care partners have for each other. This process is not just a matter of fleeting thoughts and feelings—the behavior of two partners actually synchronizes across multiple modalities. For instance, various studies show that in positive, supportive contexts, interaction partners tend to mirror each others' movements, facial expressions, eye contact, and moods. Their conversations become more attuned and spontaneous. A particularly striking study analyzed over a million emotional-support exchanges among strangers who were conversing online via text messages. The findings revealed that people felt more understood when their conversation partners used similar language styles—mirroring each other in subtle ways, such as using the same negations, quantifiers, prepositions, adverbs, and other subtle linguistic markers, as well as the same emotional tone and meaning.

It's useful to recognize that the Relationship Sea-Saw isn't just simple turn-taking, where conversation partners alternate speaking about themselves with passively waiting for their turn to talk. Instead, it's more like an intricate dance—one that requires coordination, attunement, thoughtfulness, and genuine responsiveness. Partners don't just shift between the roles of speaker and listener; they actively shape each other's experience by offering curiosity, openness, thoughtful questions, and affirming comments that deepen understanding and connection. It's almost like a process of spontaneous combustion, where each partner's response kindles the other's experience. Sometimes, this ignition happens instantly, sparking an immediate sense of closeness. Other times, it's a slow-simmering warmth that builds over time. Either way, the key is cocreating a rhythm of mutual engagement.

The Sea-Saw and the Brain

The process described by the Relationship Sea-Saw isn't just a matter of fleeting thoughts and feelings—brain-imaging research has found that two individuals show neural synchrony during such moments of connection. Specifically, functional MRI studies demonstrate that when one person speaks and another listens, their brain-activity patterns align, with the listener's neural responses often mirroring the speaker's, with a slight delay. This synchronization extends beyond simple hearing (auditory processing) to areas of the brain involved in meaning-making and interpreting social cues, indicating shared understanding. Remarkably, the stronger this neural coupling, the greater the listener's comprehension—suggesting that feeling deeply connected and understood by someone is, quite literally, a meeting of the minds.

Building on this idea, other brain-imaging studies have found that partners in a close relationship show neural synchrony during emotional experiences. For example, a study conducted in China showed synchronized patterns of neural activation in a pair of friends, one of whom received a painful electric shock to her finger while the other observed. Another investigation showed a similar synchronization of brain activity while one friend watched the other receiving favorable or critical evaluations from a group of peers.

Close friends can even exhibit neural synchrony when they are physically apart. In one of our favorite studies, researchers asked pairs of friends to sit in separate rooms while watching the same series of video clips—for instance, a soccer match, a comedy skit, and an interview with President Obama. Remarkably, across eighty different brain regions, close friends displayed similar patterns of neural activation in response to these videos. More-remote contacts, such as friends of friends, and especially more-distant acquaintances, showed far less similarity. This finding suggests that deep connection not only is something that happens during shared activities and conversations—it extends to the way people process the world. Similar findings were obtained in a study of romantic partners.

Balance Is a Recurring Theme in Nature

The Relationship Sea-Saw is a powerful example of how a relationship can be more than the sum of its parts—that is, more than just you and your partner as individuals. When two people take turns lifting and being lifted—through personal sharing, caring acceptance, curiosity, and responsive listening—their connection deepens. Balance is the essential key to this dynamic and is a principle reflected throughout the natural world. For example:

- **Physics**: Two tuning forks vibrating at the same frequency amplify each other. Likewise, when two people engage in the Sea-Saw by sharing vulnerabilities, listening with curiosity, or tenderly embracing each other's complexity, their "emotional frequencies" align, intensifying the feeling of being loved.
- **Apiculture**: Bees and flowers thrive in a symbiotic relationship, each offering something valuable to the other. Similarly, the Sea-Saw dynamic only works when both parties contribute to giving and receiving in a way that enriches the relationship.

- **Engineering**: An unbalanced system leads to inefficiency or failure. In the same way, the Sea-Saw falters if one person does all the emotional labor—whether it's sharing, listening, or showing openheartedness—while the other remains passive. Balance prevents either partner from feeling overwhelmed or neglected.
- **Music**: The call-and-response pattern in music—where one person calls and another responds—mirrors the conversational rhythm of the Sea-Saw, where alternately sharing and listening attentively creates a harmonious back-and-forth of connection.

In each of these examples, the interplay between individual elements creates a dynamic that is simultaneously more complex, more intricate, and ultimately more successful than what could be accomplished individually. Just as in nature, relationships flourish when both sides contribute and remain in balance. And that's exactly what makes the Relationship Sea-Saw special.

Five Mindsets for Putting the Relationship Sea-Saw into Motion

There's a term we love—*ubuntu*—from the Bantu languages of sub-Saharan Africa. It translates to "I find my worth in you, and you find your worth in me." This idea captures the human essence of connection and bonding. At its core, the Relationship Sea-Saw is about ubuntu—the mutual exchange of presence, care, and understanding that people seek, especially in their closest relationships.

Even if the stages of the Relationship Sea-Saw described in this chapter seem clear, you may be wondering, *Yes, but how do I make them happen?* The Sea-Saw is the conversation—what actually happens in the back-and-forth between you and your partner. But how you approach that conversation is critical. That's where the five mindsets we describe in the following chapters come in. These are not just techniques, but ways of thinking—mental shifts that help you enter and maintain interactions with an attitude and an approach that can create the loving connection you seek.

Here's another way to think about how the five mindsets contribute to the Relationship Sea-Saw. Imagine feeling loved as if it were a thriving garden—lush, colorful, growing, full of life. But no garden gets that way on its own; it needs care, nourishment, and the right conditions to flourish. The Sea-Saw is found in that garden, and you nurture it with the loving attention that it needs to thrive, all the while experiencing its beauty. The five mindsets are the essential elements of that care, each playing an important role in cultivating a strong, loving relationship. We extend the gardening metaphor to help better visualize the necessary elements:

- **Radical Curiosity**: the soil preparation—establishing a fertile environment in which openness can germinate
- **Sharing**: the seeds—sowing the source of connection through authenticity and vulnerability
- **Listening to Learn**: the water and the sunlight—stimulating growth and providing the essential ingredients for deep connection through active, responsive listening
- **Open Heart**: the nurturant caretaking—staking seedlings, pulling weeds, and adding nutrients to the soil with support and generosity so the relationship can reach its full potential
- **Multiplicity**: the biodiversity—embracing the full diversity of your partner's strengths and shortcomings, rather than expecting a one-dimensional version of them

Just like a thriving garden, a loving relationship requires ongoing care. When you apply these mindsets, you're not just maintaining the status quo of your connection—you're helping it grow into something stronger, more vibrant, and more deeply fulfilling.

Some claim that finding love is largely a matter of choosing the right partner. Choosing wisely is undoubtedly important—the Sea-Saw won't balance with just anyone. Yet making that choice is only the beginning. Loving is what you do to feel loved.

Of course, all of this takes effort. You don't grow a thriving garden by simply picking out a few nice-looking plants at the garden center and sticking them into the ground. A flourishing garden requires care, patience, and commitment. The same is true for successful relationships. Like any garden, a thriving relationship isn't about forcing love to grow—it's about creating the right conditions for love to flourish naturally. The five mindsets offer a new, research-backed approach to doing just that—using the tools to help both people to feel loved.

PART III

Putting the Sea-Saw into Practice— The Five Mindsets

5

Sharing Mindset

The real gift of love is self-disclosure.

—*John Powell*

Authenticity means erasing the gap
between what you firmly believe inside
and what you reveal to the outside world.

—*Adam Grant*

For many years, Harry's interactions with Trevor were limited to academic conferences, where they'd attend research symposia together and gossip about the state of social psychology. Harry never felt comfortable sharing personal details or feelings with Trevor, because their relationship hadn't evolved in that way and because of some vague sense that they were competitors in the academic marketplace. However, an unexpected shift occurred when a weather mishap left them both stranded for two days in a distant city. Over dinner and more than a few drinks, the barriers began to dissolve. Trevor and Harry gradually started opening up about their lives, upbringing, lovers, and hopes for and worries about their academic careers. That initial opening paved the way to more conversations, many of them vulnerable and deeply intimate, and their friendship continued to blossom. Today, Trevor and Harry consider each other close confidants and friends.

Sidney Jourard, born and raised in Canada, received his PhD in clinical psychology from the University at Buffalo in 1953. Trained in the orthodox psychotherapy techniques of that era, Jourard quickly rejected these approaches. "When I was faced by someone who behaved toward me like a client-centered counselor or a psychoanalyst," he remarked, adding somewhat vividly, "it would almost make me vomit." In his subsequent two-decade-long academic career spent in the American South, Jourard instead came to believe that any successful relationship—be it with your friend, spouse, or therapist—depends on how you open up about yourself.

Jourard was an early pioneer of research on the ways in which people reveal themselves to others—a behavior he called "self-disclosure." Although the majority of his work was conducted in the 1960s and early 1970s, it served as a springboard for research that continues to receive healthy interest among relationship scientists. At the core of his thinking, Jourard felt that an unhealthy person is someone who misrepresents themselves to or conceals themselves from others. To Jourard, this kind of deception is harmful in two distinct ways. First, he believed that you come to know yourself both by observing the words and behaviors you choose to show others and (especially) by observing their reactions to these self-disclosures. As a result, holding back impairs self-understanding. Jourard saw openness as the primary means by which humans—social beings that they are—gain insight into who they are (into their core being). In other words, self-disclosure is essential to creating a sense of authenticity in one's dealings with the world. More on this later.

Second, Jourard felt that an inability or unwillingness to be open with others damages existing relationships and hinders the development of new relationships. This is because self-disclosure establishes a foundation for liking, trust, and love. Jourard put it this way: "My aim, in disclosing myself, is to be known, *to be perceived by the other as the one I know myself to be*" (italics in the original). In essence, Jourard asked, How can others know who I know myself to be if I don't tell them? Being open and genuine lets others see your core self, creating an opportunity for supportive responses, as we described in chapter 4. This isn't easy—Jourard himself admitted that disclosing to significant others can be "terrifying," which helps explain why people often hesitate to become known by others. Authentic sharing also strengthens relationships by empowering partners to feel free to do the same, as the Sea-Saw of chapter 4 describes.

We sometimes wonder what other insights the psychology world would have gained if Jourard's life had not been tragically and prematurely cut short by an accident at the age of forty-eight. Although his research methods may not hold up to modern scientific scrutiny, Jourard's keen observations remain highly relevant, such that one can readily appreciate how his analysis applies to Harry's conversation with Trevor. With this foundation in mind, let's take a closer look at what contemporary theory and research reveal about the role of a Sharing mindset in building relationships and contributing to a sense of feeling loved.

People feel happiest during moments when they believe that others understand and respect them as they really are, in their core self. Yet this isn't easy to achieve. You may hide your deepest thoughts and emotions because you're afraid of what others might think or because you fear being embarrassed or exploited—which reflects the dynamic described in If-Only Belief #3 from chapter 3. This hiding is so common that it's actually the third most frequently expressed deathbed regret. Yet, paradoxically, the more you hide your innermost self, and the less of yourself you reveal to others, the harder it is to feel truly understood and valued by the people around you. This is a principle that has been recognized and codified throughout human history and, more recently, supported by relationship science.

On the one hand, disclosing information about yourself is intrinsically satisfying. You likely value opportunities to tell other people in your life what you're all about, so much so that one study estimated that 30–40 percent of individuals' speech output is devoted to informing others about what the authors called "subjective experiences"—their personal thoughts, their feelings, and their life stories. On the other hand, and perhaps ironically, you often fail to let others know who you are and what you stand for deep inside. This is the paradox of vulnerability—you yearn for authenticity and deeply want to be recognized for who you are, yet at the same time you are reluctant to let go of your polished public image and expose your true self, complete with your insecurities and short-comings, to others. It takes courage to expose who you are in your heart of hearts—*courage* being a word derived from the French word *coeur*, for heart. Yet the only way to let others show appreciation and warmth for the real, authentic you is to invite them in—to let them know who you are and what matters to you. In this way, you begin to create the conditions for connecting moments—and the feeling of being understood and valued by others—to happen spontaneously.

The Importance of Feeling Understood

"Don't Let Me Be Misunderstood"
—*title of song by the Animals*

One of the most common themes in human psychology is the desire to be understood. People want others to understand them for who they genuinely are. In plain language, you want others to "get" you. What this means is that you want your friends, partners, families, and acquaintances to understand your needs, emotions, and beliefs; your hopes and fears, your strengths and shortcomings; how you feel about your life and circumstances; and how you came to be the person you are. This desire to be known and recognized—to be deeply seen—is, as we will explore, a precondition to feeling appreciated and loved. Just think: If you believe that others do not know who you are, how can you take to heart their expressions of affection and admiration?

Imagine being in a conversation in which someone praises you for your taste in music or for writing incredibly funny holiday letters—only you picked your music choices from a list of popular songs on the internet and didn't intend your letters to be funny. Would you feel understood by that person? Or imagine that you are part of a work team in which each member has a specific assignment. You feel overwhelmed by your part and secretly pay an online gig worker to complete it. Later, that work receives a commendation for excellence. Would the praise lead you to feel proud?

Feeling understood makes it easier to connect with other people and join with them in various life activities. When you are confident that your partners see you accurately, you feel closer to and more accepted by them. You are more likely to trust what they say and do; it is simpler to cooperate with them to achieve common goals; and you feel more open toward them. By contrast, misunderstanding increases the chances that you'll feel distant and self-protective, wary when the other person tries to influence you, and hesitant to reach out with a favor or kind word. Sometimes, you simply accept these misunderstandings and the distance they engender—it might be too difficult, uncomfortable, or inconvenient to correct the other person. At other times, though, the desire to be seen accurately is so strong that you endeavor to correct the mistaken beliefs. The singer Amy Winehouse expresses this wish in "A Song for You," when she quietly pleads for her love not to just see her but *to see through* her.

Research bears out these ideas. In a series of studies, relationship scientists Amie Gordon and Serena Chen wanted to see how conflict might play out differently when romantic partners feel understood by each other. Conflict, after all, is inevitable in close relationships, and mutual understanding might be an effective tool for minimizing its harm. Gordon and Chen's work demonstrated that when relationship partners felt understood by one another, conflict was less likely to create emotional turmoil and dissatisfaction. Other research has shown that romantic partners who feel known by each other communicate more constructively, anticipate higher levels of support from each other, feel more bonded within their relationships, and are more compassionate. This tendency is particularly true for communication about sex—likes and dislikes, personal difficulties; and past experiences.

Presumably, feeling understood has these beneficial effects because it creates an underlying foundation of strength in a romantic relationship— that is, the thought that "you know and value me, no matter what we happen to be disagreeing about right now." Not surprisingly, these effects register in the brain. Feeling understood activates neural regions associated with reward and social connection (i.e., the ventral striatum and middle insula), whereas feeling misunderstood activates regions linked to negative affect and social disconnection (i.e., the anterior insula).

The positives that accrue from feeling understood extend beyond your relationship with the person by whom you feel understood. Research conducted by Harry and others shows that when people believe that their friends and partners generally understand them as they see themselves (indicated by endorsing survey items such as "My partner not only listens to what I am saying but really understands and seems to know where I am coming from"), they feel happier and more appreciated in general, become more open-minded in their attitudes, sleep better, and even experience less physical pain. For example, in one line of research, Harry asked participants to remember a time when they felt that a close friend or partner "knew the real you" and was "interested in what you are thinking and feeling." He then asked them to imagine that person sitting right next to them at this very moment and to consider what they might talk about. In one experiment, this simple exercise, designed to evoke an immediate feeling of being seen and heard, led the participants to be more open to information that differed from their opinions. In another experiment, it led majority-group individuals to be less prejudiced toward outgroups, such as LGBTQ+ individuals and immigrants.

It is important to acknowledge the advantages of feeling understood in relationships beyond romance and friendship. For instance, students have more success in school when they feel understood by their teachers. In business, organizational climate improves when managers convey a genuine understanding of their workers' experiences. When it comes to health care, patients who believe that their providers truly understand their symptoms and concerns are more likely to comply with treatment and medication plans than are patients who feel misunderstood. In psychotherapy, the effectiveness of the "therapeutic alliance"—the all-important working relationship between therapist and client—is in large part shaped by the extent to which the client feels understood by the therapist. Even the political arena has shown the impact of feeling understood. Voters are more likely to support politicians who can convince the electorate that they understand its needs and priorities. In the words of one British interviewee quoted in *The Guardian*, "If you want to win my vote, you need to show me that you understand our reality."

Do *You* Understand How *They* See You?

> You don't have to be perfect to be worthy
> of love. You just have to be seen.
> —*Anonymous*

> Perhaps one did not want to be loved
> so much as to be understood.
> —*George Orwell*, 1984

When people wonder whether they are being understood, they usually begin by considering what others think of them. Do your friends believe you are a kind person? Does your boss or coach feel that you have talent? Do your teachers think you are smart? Are you attractive to the people you would like to date? And, of course, the key question with which this book is concerned: Do the people in your life love you?

An essential element of social life involves forming impressions of how other people perceive you. This mental exercise underlies many of your choices. After all, whether and how you decide to approach another person hinges on the reaction you expect. If you think that a friend values your abilities and viewpoints, you can proceed confidently, anticipating a positive reaction. If, on the other hand, you foresee a more standoffish response, you might opt to be more cautious in your approach. This judgment relies on a mental construct that all people acquire as their cognitive skills develop during childhood, called *theory of mind*. Having a theory of mind involves recognizing that other people possess beliefs, needs, thoughts, and perspectives that differ from your own. You use your theory of mind every time you speculate about what another person is thinking and feeling— *Will he know the answer to my question? Is she pleased by this gift? Do they feel welcome at my house? Do they like my singing voice?* Indeed, such speculations constitute one of the most common everyday mental activities. And few subjects are more intrinsically intriguing than what the people in your life think about you.

Here's a vulnerable self-disclosure from one of your authors. Most of you likely keep your guesses about others' opinions of you to yourselves. Maybe you write them down in a journal or discuss them with a friend or therapist. When Harry was in middle school, he took a rather more graphic approach: Specifically, he kept charts to track how he thought his classmates were viewing him. Every week or so, he would estimate how he thought several of his friends had felt about him during the past week. When graphed—with varied color pens, of course—these ratings would illustrate whether his social standing was improving or declining, as adolescents often wonder. (His graphing project also clearly exposed Harry's budding talents as a data scientist.) In adulthood, however, these inferences are usually more detailed than simply going up or down. We mull over whether we are seen as generous, middling, or unkind; attractive or plain; socially capable or awkward; smart or ordinary thinkers; effective leaders or just barely adequate ones. These inferences aren't just a record-keeping habit—they matter. They matter because they provide a basis for choosing our friends and partners and for how we interact with them.

People's interest in knowing what others think of them was captured humorously in the 1988 movie *Beaches*. Bette Midler played C. C. Bloom, a cynical struggling entertainer who finally achieves stardom. After dominating a lengthy conversation, she offers her partner an opportunity to speak, saying, "But enough about me; let's talk about you. What do you think of me?" Of course, even when you ask explicitly, as C. C. Bloom did, some amount of interpretation and filling in the gaps is needed. Indeed, it's impossible to definitively determine what another person thinks of you. People hold back. They minimize. They exaggerate. They twist the truth. They outright lie.

And even when they are being sincere, their words may not tell the complete story. You do not have direct access to others' thoughts, of course. Instead, if you wish to arrive at a sensible answer to the question of what they think of you, you must rely on many different clues and cues—from thoughtful attention to their words and nonverbal actions, feedback other folks might offer, and your general social intelligence to your insights gleaned from prior experience with this and other partners, your own sense of yourself, and so on.

A large body of research has investigated how people put together these disparate pieces of information, which researchers call *metaperception*. *Meta* comes from the Greek for "about itself," thus indicating a person's "perception about itself." For simplicity, we will use the term "you-in-their-eyes." The concept of metaperception (you-in-their-eyes) underscores the critical importance of a Sharing mindset: If you keep your full self hidden from another person, you can't expect them to understand and appreciate you as the person that you believe you are at your core. Sharing your vulnerabilities (to pick one example) lets them know what you are all about, and, importantly, it also lets you know that *they* know. A Sharing mindset, in other words, helps you form metaperceptions (you-in-their-eyes) that are aligned with your authentic, genuine self. Without opening up and seeing the other's response to your truth, the you-in-their-eyes is very likely to be skewed. Thus, embracing a Sharing mindset sets the stage for interactions in which you feel truly understood.

Researchers once believed that people are not very accurate in knowing what others think of them. After all, knowing how you come across to others would seem to require some skill at mind reading (a skill the human species has yet to evolve). However, the recent development of sophisticated research tools has revealed that most people are not as socially oblivious as previously thought. Here are a few interesting insights about the accuracy of you-in-their-eyes that emerge from this research:

- People seem to do reasonably well at two kinds of you-in-their-eyes judgments: (1) knowing how others typically see them (what you might call your public social reputation—for example, "I am seen as the kind of person who will pitch in when a job needs to be done") and (2) knowing how particular individuals see them in general terms—for example, "My boss values the work I do". Of course, these judgments are far from perfect, with tons of room for error. But the more attention you pay to social cues, the better you will likely do. (By social cues, we mean the myriad ways that others react when they are in your presence. Some of these cues are overt—displays of affection or animosity, compliments or insults, a smile or scowl. Others are more subtle—a distracted glance, a steady gaze, an overheard remark.)

- People typically underestimate how much their conversational partners like them, a bias called "the liking gap." Similarly, people underestimate how much others in their groups like them. This isn't necessarily a bad thing—it encourages you to be mindful of your partners and to keep trying to be congenial and supportive, which can improve your partner's feelings of relationship satisfaction (as research conducted by Harry and his colleagues has shown). When these estimates of liking diverge too greatly from reality, however, they can undermine the development of relationships. This is especially true for people who struggle with social anxiety or low self-esteem, which helps explain why their social interactions often feel unsatisfying and why they tend to avoid intimate contact with others, despite their desire to have closer relationships.

- In some instances, people will *over*estimate how positively they are seen by others than is actually the case—not by a lot (which would be narcissistic and therefore not desirable) but by a little. When this happens, it helps you feel confident in social situations, which can benefit relationships.

- People are usually better at knowing how they are seen on relatively transparent traits, such as extraversion or popularity, than on qualities that tend to be more private, such as fantasy-proneness or anxiety. Of course, the more open you are about those private qualities, the more transparent your inner nature becomes. This is one important reason why self-disclosure matters. The less you reveal about yourself, the less your partners can know about you and the less known you can possibly feel.

- Degree of acquaintance matters a great deal too. It's not surprising that people close to you know you better than strangers do. But it's also true that you're much better at knowing how close others see you than you are at knowing how casual acquaintances and strangers see you.

Underlying these findings is the central idea that impressions about you-in-their-eyes require an inference about what another person is thinking and feeling. This judgment starts with what you observe and experience, but just as importantly, it also depends on your assumptions about what interaction partners are able to see—which aspects of yourself they can recognize and which are hidden from them. As mentioned earlier, many personal attributes are relatively transparent and easily observed by other people—your attractiveness, your strength, your musical ability, your outgoingness, and the emotions you openly display. It is a reasonable assumption that others are aware of these qualities. In contrast, the countless thoughts and feelings that you muse about all day tend to be relatively invisible—your self-doubts and hesitations, your worries about the future, your sexual fantasies, your internal commentary about your friends and colleagues, and the secrets that you keep. These thoughts and feelings—often fleeting but sometimes recurring—are accessible to outsiders only when you divulge them, whether deliberately or inadvertently.

This very general idea underscores the critical importance of a Sharing mindset: If you don't share who you are deep down with another person, you can't reasonably expect them to fully understand and appreciate the true you that you know yourself to be. Without conversations that involve opening up and seeing the other person's response, your perception of the you-in-their-eyes is very likely to be unreliable. In particular, you probably won't recognize their love for you when they actually are feeling it. Taylor Swift expresses this need touchingly in her song "Dress," when she sings about the lover who could see her true best self even during her lowest, most deceitful moments.

Moreover, when you can't trust your sense of the you-in-their-eyes, you will likely find it difficult to know how to engage with them in a way that feels comfortable and satisfying—and that means shying away from precisely the kinds of interactions in which you are most likely to feel loved. Nevertheless, even knowing this, people frequently opt to keep important parts of themselves under wraps. Let's look more closely at the consequences of maintaining such secrets.

Keeping Secrets

John William Damon passed away in Queensland, Australia, in 2010, at the age of sixty-nine, mourned by his wife and two children. By all accounts, he lived a good life there and was a loving husband and father. There was more to his story, however. In 2022, DNA testing led to the discovery that his real name was William Leslie Arnold, and he was an escaped inmate from Nebraska who, at the age of sixteen, had murdered his parents during a fight and buried them in their backyard. Living with this terrible secret apparently did not interfere with a life that, to all outward appearances, seemed unexceptional and satisfying. But that may not describe how John (a.k.a. William) felt all those years: Hiding his full, true self from his new family, did he feel loved by them?

We all harbor secrets, though few of us have ones as big and long-standing as John William Damon's. One study estimated that 97 percent of people keep secrets, and the average person holds thirteen. Secrets are information that we don't want others to know and deliberately conceal from them. People keep secrets for many reasons—for example, they may feel ashamed about a personal shortcoming, an imperfection, or a past misdeed; they may anticipate rejection or harm to their reputation if the secret came out; they may worry that the secret would be hurtful or disruptive to others; or they may even anticipate punishment if others knew. (John William Damon presumably experienced all of these.)

Popular media provide many examples of people hiding important aspects of themselves to avoid what they see as potential harm. For instance, in the 1999 film *The Talented Mr. Ripley*, Tom Ripley hides his true identity and lives a life of deceit, depriving himself of genuine human connection. In a Chinese folktale adapted into a classic Disney film, the eponymous character, Fa Mulan, sings about the sadness she feels wearing a mask that will "fool the world," all the while yearning to be loved for who she is "inside her heart." Dick Whitman, a nondescript Korean War soldier with a checkered life story, becomes Don Draper, the lead character in the hit television series *Mad Men*, by stealing Draper's identity to conceal his own past. This identity theft leads to a lifetime of despair, alcoholism, and broken relationships. Jay Gatsby, the tortured hero of F. Scott Fitzgerald's classic novel *The Great Gatsby*, similarly masks his impoverished beginnings, crafting an illusion of an extravagant and wealthy background.

"Nothing makes us so lonely as our secrets," noted Swiss physician Paul Tournier, and, indeed, as the above examples illustrate, keeping secrets is often isolating. When people conceal themselves from others, they feel less authentic and, as a consequence, less close to their partners. It's almost impossible to feel loved when you are hiding something important about yourself—for example, when you are afraid to "come out of the closet" about your sexual orientation to family members. Authenticity is critical to feeling understood by others, as we explain later in this chapter. Although authenticity can lead you to feel vulnerable, the desire to be authentic is powerful and familiar. Moreover, you also want your friends and family to be authentic with you. (How would you feel if you learned that your partner or close friend is "acting" around you or hiding an important secret?) Indeed, this is likely one reason that interactions with AI-powered chatbots and companions can sometimes be experienced as impersonal and even disagreeable.

Keeping secrets can be effortful and uncomfortable, so much so that people sometimes become preoccupied with them. Secrets intrude into your consciousness, requiring mental energy to actively monitor them, inhibit them, and sometimes even lie to others to ensure those secrets don't leak out. Ironically, these efforts can increase the likelihood of slipping up and accidentally revealing a secret. A clever set of experiments conducted by the late social psychologist Daniel Wegner demonstrated how this happens. His team asked their research participants to keep a secret. Sometimes the secret was a word, a memory, or the fact that they were playing footsie under the table with another participant. The research showed that the mere fact of keeping something secret increased the ease with which the secret was recalled, required more effort to suppress it, and made it more likely to intrude unexpectedly into the participants' thoughts.

It follows, therefore, that the desire to unburden yourself by divulging secrets can be quite strong. Some ways of doing this pose little risk. For example, an exercise called "expressive writing"—developed by our colleague Jamie Pennebaker at the University of Texas at Austin—involves writing in a private journal one's deepest thoughts and feelings about traumatic events or stressful experiences. Meta-analyses of numerous studies have shown that when people engage in such expressive writing with the goal of gaining insight into difficult experiences and a sense of coherence, they see improvements in emotional well-being and even physical health.

On the basis of this and other research, some thinkers have proposed the existence of a "drive to disclose," similar in its impact to other human drives such as hunger. Perhaps this drive can help explain why people occasionally overshare on social media: In one study, 21 percent of respondents reported regretting that they had posted something on Facebook. This drive can also shed light on why people gravitate to modern technology that provides an avenue for anonymously and safely confessing a secret, as is evident in the growing number of websites, apps, and online communities where users can share things incognito that they've never revealed to anyone before (e.g., Frank Warren's PostSecret website or the Whisper app).

When it comes to feeling loved, deciding what to do about a secret creates an inherent risk-reward dilemma. On the one hand, if you reveal a secret to a friend or partner, you risk their disapproval and perhaps even rejection. On the other hand, revealing a secret has the potential to be bonding and rewarding and may even lead to feeling loved. As one of our survey respondents wrote, "A time I felt most loved in my adult life was when I opened up about my past to my first love. He was very receptive to what I was saying, did not judge me, and I felt like he really cared."

This sentiment is confirmed in research. In one set of studies with more than eight hundred participants who kept more than ten thousand secrets, participants who confided a secret experienced not only greater happiness but also more social support from the person they told. In another study, sharing and receiving personal secrets were both robustly related to higher closeness. Secrets interfere with feeling loved for a simple reason: People want to be known and valued for their real self, but how can that happen if the real self is shrouded? Self-disclosure, in contrast, gives your partners an opportunity to communicate that they understand and accept who you are, shortcomings and all. That opportunity disappears if they sense that they are not seeing the real or complete you. Thus, self-disclosure helps your partners love you purely and unconditionally and gives you the chance to fully experience their love. In this manner, opening up about secrets is a necessary foundation for feeling truly and fully loved.

This point is poignantly illustrated in William Kent Krueger's novel *The River We Remember*. Brody, a highly decorated war hero, is overcome with feelings of guilt and shame about his actions during World War II and has not been able to speak about them. Instead, he carries "the crushing weight of all those memories" and fears that others will discover him as exactly the person he believes he is: "A liar. A coward. A murderer." Brody is dating Angie, a war widow, who has secrets of her own and is terrified that someone will expose her history as a sex worker. After Angie reveals her secret to Brody, he tells her about his experiences becoming a killing machine during the war. Each forgives the other, saying, "Now you know the worst about me, and I know the worst about you." Their mutual disclosures and forgiveness bring them closer, leading to a deeper, more committed, and more loving relationship. Imagine how much weaker and less durable their love might have been if they had only known the earlier, less complete and less authentic version of each other?

Holding on to secrets can be especially damaging in established intimate relationships. It's stressful to keep a secret in an intimate relationship, and it's risky too: Such secrets often surface in harmful ways or come to light at inopportune times. Moreover, even when a secret (say, an old resentment or a long-ago betrayal) stays hidden, it can fester, adding to relationship grievances without creating possibilities for resolution. In brand-new relationships, the most common unshared things are about you—for example, you might hide from your new partner a character flaw, a health problem, or an embarrassing past event. In long-term relationships, by contrast, many of the most common unshared things are about your relationship (e.g., feeling bored about spending too many nights at home watching TV) or your partner (e.g., you might hide your true feelings about their weight, their friends, or how they've changed). Furthermore, long-term couples often have relatively long-term secrets. If and when such secrets end up coming out, perhaps in couples therapy, their very longevity only worsens the impact (e.g., "How could you not have told me all these years that you wanted to try kinky sex?"). No wonder people say that "hiding secrets from a partner is like building a house on a shaky foundation; sooner or later it will collapse."

Opening Up:
The Right Way and the Wrong Way

Be weird. Be random. Be who you are. Because you never know who would love the person you hide.

—*Anonymous*

You might as well be yourself. Everyone else is already taken.

—*Oscar Wilde*

Now that we have made the case for opening up, the question becomes how, when, and with whom to do it. Once you identify a compatible partner, you may be tempted to share your world with them instantly. But opening up is not a matter of pouring out every thought, feeling, intimate detail, and story that constitute your life; rather, opening up requires exquisite timing and blending to get it just right. We discuss here the key steps in opening up appropriately and effectively—steps that will help you captivate the other and then create chemistry with them.

To repeat: Self-disclosure is essential to feeling loved. It lets other people see into the real you, and, more importantly, it lets you feel as if they know the real you. Self-disclosure opens the door for them to demonstrate care for and interest in the real you, and you'll find their gestures all the more meaningful precisely because they're responding to the real you. In this way, the Sharing mindset serves as a bridge between how you approach others and how they respond to you (as the previous chapter highlighted).

There's another reason self-disclosure helps build the kind of connections that lead to feeling loved. Storytelling is a traditional means of passing down family and cultural lore, as any anthropologist or historian will tell you. Like most people, you probably enjoy listening to stories, especially stories that involve people you know. When you self-disclose to another person, you are sharing a story about yourself. As a result, they are more likely to feel engaged with you, to listen to the details, and to feel attracted to you. One study even found that when people listen to a partner's personal stories, they and their partners show similar patterns of electrical activity in the brain (likely because they are experiencing some of the same emotions). Such sharing enables feeling as though you are "on the same wavelength." Of course, this only happens when your self-disclosures are timely and welcome, so it is necessary to attend to the guidelines that we review next.

Research on self-disclosure suggests a number of specific strategies that will maximize your chances of success.

- Choose your pacing carefully. There's a right time, a right place, and a right pace for opening up. Don't offer your innermost thoughts or private details immediately: Instead, forge intimacy—and build momentum—in slowly increasing increments over the course of getting to know a person. Create comfort by starting with an easy, safe topic that the other person can participate in, and grow slowly from there.

- Mix worries with humor, serious topics with lighthearted banter, and personal stories with material that piques the other person's interest. Don't be a Johnny One-Note.
- Gauge the other person's curiosity before deciding what to say and when to say it. Gear your comments to content that would interest your partner, and give them ample opportunity to "digest" your meaning—in this case, by letting them be responsive listeners (as we described in chapter 4).
- Remember the rule of reciprocity: Be sure to give your partners ample time to disclose their own thoughts and experiences, and show genuine interest when they do (as we cover in chapter 6). Live by the motto "See and be seen"—appearing on a road sign Harry once spotted on a trip through Ontario, Canada. It was a message encouraging drivers to keep their headlights on, but one that applies equally well to relationships.
- Choose topics that are likely to foster connection. On the less-disclosing side is information that most people know, that is superficial or fact-oriented, and that concerns the outside world. On the more-disclosing side are topics that are customarily private, that have more depth of feeling, and that reference the "here and now" of your interaction with the other person (e.g., how comfortable you're feeling at that moment).
- Match your disclosures to the situation. Opening up should be done not indiscriminately but rather in a way that is appropriate for the particular situation and the particular relationship. In other words, sharing yourself is always context dependent. Much like adjusting a radio to the right frequency and volume, calibrating your conversation to your partner and the setting is critical. Too much self-disclosure in the wrong circumstance or with the wrong person

can be more harmful than too little. When you "overshare"—
initiating a level of intimacy that your partner doesn't want—you
are more likely to create distance than closeness. There's a time
and a place for small talk, and there's a time and place for deep
talk. By paying attention, you will recognize the right situations and
the best candidates for opening up.

- Remember that some things are best left unsaid. Self-disclosure
doesn't mean "letting it all hang out." Vulnerability is the key to
bonding, but you shouldn't flood your conversational partner with
your deepest, darkest secrets. It's perfectly fine to hold back on
things that other people might find rude or objectionable, or that
might lead you or your listener to feel uncomfortable.

- Be mindful about going too far. Similar to what we wrote about
unloading secrets, appropriate self-disclosure doesn't mean
dumping all your woes and anxieties on an attentive listener—a
tendency sometimes called *trauma dumping*. When anxieties or
problems are disclosed too often, too early in a relationship (or too
early in an intimate conversation), too intensely, or at inappropriate
times and places, your listener may be overwhelmed with
discomfort or negativity and may even shut down. Indeed, research
shows that while venting and ruminating may feel cathartic and
even connecting in the moment ("They really heard me!"), these
behaviors are unlikely to foster a durable sense of feeling loved.
There is a fine line between courageously sharing your human
fallibilities and indiscriminately unloading all your shortcomings
and doubts.

- Expressing yourself is different than seeking a solution. Asking
your partner to solve your problems is also unlikely to land well:
The goal of self-disclosure is not to persuade other people to fix
things for you. Rather, it's to make your private self known to the
other. You do this by intermingling the positives with the negatives
in a delicate balance that will earn not only their attention but
also their interest, laughter, and delight. Of course, it's fine to
express concerns in a way that invites your partner to offer input

and encouragement and then to pause and truly listen to their suggestions and show appreciation for their support. Just don't ask for an immediate fix.

- Finally, never engage in "boomerasking"—exemplified by the caption of a recent *New Yorker* cartoon: "So, tell me what music you like, and make it quick because I really want to spend the next forty minutes telling you what music I like." Boomerasking is asking your partner a question as an excuse to talk about yourself, just as a boomerang returns to the person who throws it. Research shows that people are quick to perceive boomeraskers as insincere and self-centered.

The idea of having "boundaries" is sometimes offered as a defense or excuse for not opening up—that parts of yourself are so vulnerable that they must be kept walled off from others. Our analysis suggests that when boundaries preclude trust and sharing, they can undermine the possibility of being understood and prevent you from feeling loved. Indeed, the more you keep concealed, the harder it is to feel loved. Of course, this does not mean that you should divulge difficult matters and feelings to everyone in your life or at the drop of a hat. As we indicated earlier, self-disclosure should be discretionary, thoughtful, and aimed at the right partner at the right time.

One of the more fascinating topics in self-disclosure research is gender differences. In her enduringly popular book *You Just Don't Understand*, the sociolinguist Deborah Tannen argues that women are more likely to use "rapport talk," while men use "report talk." As these labels imply, rapport talk involves conversations that emphasize sharing feelings, matching experiences, and building connection, while report talk involves exchanging information in a manner that builds status and preserves autonomy.

Over the years, various explanations have been offered for this difference. One of the researchers studying gender differences in self-disclosure happens to be Harry. His research over the past forty years strongly points to the influence of socialization pressures: Men, especially men raised in Western cultures, are taught that emotional openness is a weakness that can profoundly damage their reputation, their social position, and even their desirability as a mate. It can also create vulnerability in competition with other men, which helps explain why Harry's research has revealed that the aforementioned gender differences are most evident in same-gender interactions—that is, in men's conversations with other men and in women's conversations with other women. We explore these and other related differences between men's and women's conversational styles in greater detail in chapter 11—as well as the research supporting them.

The principles highlighted above suggest why in certain situations you might be genuinely concerned about oversharing unpleasant aspects of yourself in unproductive ways. Ironically, however, it's far more common to undershare. People reveal too little of themselves, holding back for a variety of many reasons (discussed next). Nevertheless, it bears repeating that feeling loved *requires* that others see *into* you. If you desire to feel more loved, you must be ready to share more of your full self—both your proudest moments and the raw, more vulnerable parts that you fear might be unattractive and off-putting. Only by opening up can you feel confident that "yes, they really get me."

Why Do People Undershare?

I am afraid to show you who I really am, because if I show you who I really am, you might not like it—and that's all I got.

—*Sabrina Ward Harrison,* Spilling Open

As we were kicking off this book, Sonja had drinks with two friends who are brothers and brought up some of the ideas we had been brainstorming. As she was introducing the idea of a Sharing mindset, the brothers grew increasingly uncomfortable. Their strong reaction genuinely surprised her. "It's risky to share!" they pointed out. "It's dangerous. I could get hurt. Other people could get hurt." Since that evening, these remarks have struck a resonant chord with the many friends and colleagues we have talked with: When people think about the possibility of opening up to someone, they often worry about the harm that might result.

A common reason people resist opening up is elementary. They anticipate that others will be disinterested in the nitty-gritty of their lives, their feelings, and their perspectives. An ingenious series of studies exposed such expectations as being misguided—and showed that it's these very assumptions that often prevent people from having the kinds of deep conversations that they most desire. In this work, the research team asked their participants to have a relatively deep conversation with a stranger, discussing intimate topics—for example, to describe a time they cried in front of another person. But first, they were asked to estimate the extent to which the stranger would be interested in what they had to say. The results? The conversations invariably went much better than expected and also produced higher levels of care, concern, and closeness than expected. Other people are simply more interested in our stories than we think they are.

People may similarly mispredict the consequences of honesty, overestimating how negatively others will respond. In fact, another study showed that your listeners tend to be more charitable than you expect. "When we're thinking about conveying negative information about ourselves, we're focused on the content of the message," said study co-author Amit Kumar, assistant professor of marketing at the University of Texas's McCombs School of Business. "But the recipients are thinking about the positive traits required to reveal this secret, such as trust, honesty, and vulnerability."

Other reasons for undersharing have to do with the potential psychological or material costs that people expect (rightly or wrongly) from self-disclosure. You hold back to protect your reputation. You fear embarrassment, rejection, exploitation, or a loss of privacy. You foresee the possibility of hurting your friends and partners. You are apprehensive about creating distance or strain in your relationship if something became known. You hesitate because the topic is just too painful or difficult to discuss. You anticipate losing your partner's respect or creating awkwardness in your interaction. You are afraid that something you reveal will get back to others. You worry that the person you tell will mock or betray your confidence. Not surprisingly, then, opening up takes courage.

An irony inherent in undersharing for any reason is that it can lead you to feel inauthentic, even while you simultaneously crave authenticity. Sometimes, in the process of holding back your true self from others, you may even end up hiding yourself from yourself. A popular 1969 book by the Jesuit priest John Powell was titled *Why Am I Afraid to Tell You Who I Am?* Powell's thesis was based on the idea that personal growth requires communicating and interacting with others. However, people resist being emotionally open because honest interactions have the potential to create doubts and questions about their core self, the self that they believe they are. In other words, the self that might be revealed during a conversation may not be the self that you wish to see. By wearing masks in social situations, you block any possibility of receiving feedback that would challenge these self-views. We discuss a related idea in chapter 6—when describing people's attraction to listeners who confirm their self-views.

Putting on masks during social interaction can become automatic and reflexive—one of the "games people play" in their social lives, as the psychiatrist Eric Berne dubbed it. Of course, some people find it easy to open up, but others find it really challenging. For example, research links openness with personality traits such as extraversion, sociability, high self-esteem, femininity, and trust, whereas a reluctance to self-disclose is associated with traits such as loneliness, social anxiety, masculinity, and avoidant attachment. But don't put too much stock in these correlations; the much more important point is that self-disclosure hinges on your relationships with the people you engage with. Everyone is more open with the people they trust and care about and less open with those to whom they feel less close. This idea points directly to this book's central thesis: To build the sort of connection that leads to feeling loved, a Sharing mindset is a necessary first step.

The Impostor Syndrome and
Your Shortcomings

Rita Hayworth, nicknamed "The Love Goddess," was one of the most glamorous Hollywood stars of the 1940s. Her most famous role was as a femme fatale in the blockbuster film Gilda. *Hayworth was beautiful, charismatic, talented, and one of the most successful actresses of her era. Nonetheless, she struggled with emotional disorders and alcoholism and was married and divorced five times. When asked to explain her unhappy marriages, Hayworth is said to have replied, with evident bitterness, "Men go to bed with Gilda, but wake up with me."*

Sometimes, you wear a mask in social situations to shield yourself from the self-doubt that comes from assuming that if others knew the real you, they would recognize your unworthiness. A good example here is the "impostor syndrome"—the menacing anticipation of shame and ostracism once others discover, as you foresee they surely will, that you do not possess the ability or talent that you are presumed to have. Coined in 1978 by the clinical psychologists Pauline Rose Clance and Suzanne Imes, this concept was intended to describe people who feel less bright or less capable than others judge them to be; as a result, they experience anxiety, fear of not living up to others' expectations, and an internalized sense of inadequacy. Although not everyone feels like an impostor most or even some of the time, you can learn from this phenomenon without experiencing it. Thus, for our purposes here, we highlight a somewhat different consequence of the impostor syndrome—hiding your true self from others in the hope that they somehow will not notice your imperfections.

Unfortunately, this sort of self-hiding hampers feeling loved in at least two respects. First, as previously mentioned, if others don't have access to your true self, it is impossible for them to respond in ways that help you feel understood and valued. The self they see is not the self that you are, in your heart of hearts. As a result, whatever positive sentiments your friend or supervisor conveys will simply feel premature, because sooner or later, your true self will be apparent. We suspect this is how Rita Hayworth felt when men complimented her on her glamour.

Second, imagine what happens if your partner expresses appreciation for some skill or knowledge that you are known for—say, a talent for public speaking or erudition about the history of Christianity—but that you don't actually believe is true of you. Their praise likely would ring hollow or feel false. Even worse, because of the potentially impending need to live up to that skill or knowledge, the fear of exposure may lead you to avoid contact with that person. Interactions of this sort move you squarely in the direction of feeling *mis*understood and *not* genuinely valued. To paraphrase André Gide: It is better to be known for what you are than to be loved for what you are not.

The 2019 film *Yesterday* provides a striking example of this latter point. After a freaky storm, struggling musician Jack Malik (Himesh Patel) awakens to discover that no one besides himself has ever heard of the Beatles. Seizing the opportunity, he begins to perform their music widely, taking credit for writing their classic songs and becoming a celebrity in the process. Jack's success, however, does not bring him the fulfillment he has sought; he knows that he doesn't deserve credit for the music, and his celebrity life alienates him from the woman he loves and feels loved by, Ellie (Lily James). A pivotal moment arrives when, moments before a major concert, Jack encounters two people who do remember the Beatles and see through his fraud. Only when he confesses his piracy in front of a roaring crowd at Wembley Stadium does he begin to feel authentic, walking away from the limelight and instead reuniting with Ellie and working as a music teacher.

When you feel like an impostor, authenticity is impossible. And, as we've argued before, authenticity is critical for feeling understood. Feeling loved requires not only that others see into you, but that your experience of the you that they see matches your authentic self—the you that you really are. The only way this can happen is if you share your full self openly—the parts of yourself that you feel most proud of, the parts of yourself that you feel most unsure or vulnerable about, and the parts of yourself that you consider weaknesses. Feeling loved for these last two parts—vulnerabilities and weaknesses—may actually be more important than feeling loved for one's talents, no matter how counterintuitive this may seem. Why? Let's consider each of them in turn.

Sharing thoughts and feelings about the things that evoke vulnerability gives others an opportunity to provide positive feedback and perhaps even advice. Admit that you cringe when someone asks you to dance; that you worry about completing assignments, even though you've done them successfully a dozen times before; and that you rehearse before calling a new acquaintance on the phone. You may be surprised that other people view your vulnerability more positively than you do! Research indicates that flattery is most effective when it pertains to skills or attributes about which the recipient is uncertain. After all, telling a professional basketball player that he is an excellent athlete isn't newsworthy, but the same message to a high school student trying out for the junior-varsity basketball team is much more likely to land well. Of course, the message must be delivered honestly and convincingly—praise that seems false, disingenuous, or misleading is unlikely to succeed.

As for being open about weakness, in her book *It's Great to Suck at Something*, author (and our editor!) Karen Rinaldi describes the joy of being really bad—sucking—at something. Rinaldi recounts how people were usually reluctant to tell her what they sucked at. But as soon as she wrote a *New York Times* article in which she happily admitted that she sucked at surfing, suddenly the dam broke, and everyone started confessing to her—as was revealed in the online comments for the article and book. One commenter noted how sucking helps you enjoy "perseverance without the pressure of perfection." Sucking, Rinaldi explains, gives you the opportunity to develop grit and resilience, and inspires you to experience joy in an activity without concern about success or accomplishment. And when you open up about things you suck at, it enables your friends and acquaintances to let you know that this doesn't diminish their love for you—it may even increase it!

From the standpoint of feeling loved, research on the impostor syndrome suggests an alternative approach: Rather than concealing self-perceived vulnerabilities and shortcomings, opening up about them—selectively, with the right person and at the right time—might open the door to a more deeply felt connection. True, unveiling the complexity of your multifaceted true self can leave you feeling vulnerable because you are exhibiting your true colors and risking loss of the other person's regard. However, vulnerability is not the goal; it is simply a necessary preliminary step to feeling deeply confident that the other person appreciates and loves the real you.

If you embrace a Sharing mindset, you will ensure that your social partner, whether friend, lover, kin, or new acquaintance, knows the real you. Just as important, you will know that they know the real you. However, on its own, sharing is only one side of the Relationship Sea-Saw; your partner is not likely to feel understood and valued if the only person being raised up is you. One-sided sharing simply doesn't constitute the kind of back-and-forth reciprocation that leads to a mutual and lasting sense of connection for both of you. Thus, a Sharing mindset is only the first step on the path to feeling more love in your life. Chapter 6 describes the next step for moving forward on that path.

6

Listening-to-Learn Mindset

If we were supposed to talk more than we listen, we would have two tongues and one ear.

—*Mark Twain*

While researching this book, we (Sonja and Harry) realized that we needed to learn more about listening. So when two of the world's leading experts on listening, Avi Kluger (from Hebrew University) and Guy Itzchakov (from the University of Haifa), invited us to a workshop in Tel Aviv titled "Promoting Human Flourishing with Interpersonal Listening," we didn't hesitate to accept.

The workshop offered a mix of scholarly talks on listening and hands-on exercises, but the most revealing and memorable experience was a seventeen-minute exercise in which we were asked to interview a stranger about a meaningful life event. After the interview was concluded, our task was to retell every detail of their story aloud to them. It's incredibly challenging to keep track of all the narrative details, let alone to encourage the interviewee to elaborate by asking them questions and offering insights. Yet the most powerful step of this exercise involved not just repeating the story but recounting it to the entire group as if it were our own story, from a first-person perspective (e.g., "After my parents divorced, I was lost").

We had both long prided ourselves on being relatively attentive listeners, but this exercise was humbling. Indeed, we discovered that high-quality listening is far from being easy or instinctive—it demands thoughtful attention, skill, and a genuine desire to learn more about the other person. However, the listening exercise was also surprisingly compelling—by its end, we each felt a deep connection with someone who, just moments earlier, had been a stranger.

The irony of this exercise was not lost on us—here we were, listening to learn (about another person) while we were at a workshop to learn about listening. We came away convinced that feeling loved yourself starts with helping the *other* person feel loved by adopting a Listening-to-Learn mindset and authentically listening to them. In this chapter, we discuss why this is so critical. Most people know that "listening" is important, but all too often they listen with the wrong mindset. As Steven Covey famously put it in *The 7 Habits of Highly Effective People*, people typically listen to respond rather than listen to learn. When people claim to be listening, they are usually attending only distractedly to what the other person is saying—instead, they are mentally preparing what to say next or how to refute their conversation partner or how to dazzle them. This approach makes it difficult for the listener to properly craft a response that will help the speaker feel heard. In short, too often people treat a conversation like a tag-team performance, waiting for their turn with the mic to speak and to impress.

We propose that you flip the usual turn-taking conversational mindset—in other words, approach conversations intending to be a listener rather than a speaker. Listening, as we explain later in this chapter, is different from hearing. Listening involves being actively engaged in processing and encouraging the speaker's message. (Hearing is just passively receiving the words.)

Let's begin by describing just what active listening is.

What Is High-Quality Listening?

In the 1998 movie *Patch Adams*, Robin Williams plays the eponymous main character, a young man with suicidal thoughts who admits himself to a psychiatric institution. In an early therapy session, his doctor asks him, "When your father died, how did that make you feel?" Patch begins to answer meaningfully, but the doctor ignores him, instead focusing on putting milk and sugar in his own coffee. In response, Williams quickly shifts to silliness, commenting, "If I could light my own farts, I could fly to the moon, or at least Uranus." The therapist mindlessly informs him that his progress is fine, but the damage is done.

Contrast this scene with one from another Robin Williams movie, *Good Will Hunting* (1997). Matt Damon plays Will Hunting, a self-taught mathematical genius working as a school janitor after being paroled from jail. When Will assaults a police officer after being (falsely) accused of vandalizing school property, he avoids additional jail time by agreeing to see Dr. Sean Maguire (played by Robin Williams), an instructor at a local college. In one particularly moving scene, Will recounts how his father used to force him to choose the object he would use to beat him with. Sean, listening carefully and empathically, repeatedly tells him, "It's not your fault." Will's reaction is nonchalant at first and then denying, but eventually Will breaks down, sobbing like a baby as Dr. Maguire holds him tightly. Through high-quality listening and compassion, Dr. Maguire helps Will confront his indifference and inner demons, leading him to develop the self-confidence to pursue a more hopeful future.

Most readers will be familiar with stories like these; indeed, you likely have experienced them yourself. Research indicates that the type of active, high-quality listening shown by Robin Williams's character in *Good Will Hunting* communicates three powerful messages to the speaker: (1) attention, (2) comprehension and elaboration, and (3) positive intent. Before introducing specific high-quality listening behaviors that can be learned and enacted, we first describe what these three messages are. You'll want to grasp the big picture before diving into the details.

The first feature of high-quality listening involves paying steady *attention* to the speaker while disregarding external distractions, such as other people in the room, one's phone, or one's own mind-wandering. Conversationalists do not stare at each other continuously, of course, but they do frequently look back at each other to gauge whether their partner is involved or distracted—*Am I boring them? Are they interested in what I am saying?* Behavior that conveys the listener's interest and engagement provides the speaker with a sense of confidence and encourages them to elaborate.

The second feature of active, high-quality listening requires *comprehension* of and *elaboration* on the speaker's message and meaning. It's not sufficient for the listener to believe that they understand the speaker's point. The listener needs to convey this understanding to the speaker—letting them know that you, the listener, "get" what they are trying to communicate. This refers both to the surface content of what's being said and, if there is deeper meaning embedded in the message, its personal relevance for the speaker. Thus, comprehension is not a passive activity, because it involves elaboration too—to be sure, it is an effortful process that requires energy and action. For example, good listeners paraphrase what they have heard and ask questions that give speakers a chance to clarify points that might have been unclear. When a listener asks thoughtful questions, she makes her desire to understand crystal clear and provides a basis for the speaker to feel understood.

Yet attention, comprehension, and elaboration are not enough. The third feature of active, high-quality listening is conveying *positive, caring intent* or adopting a receptive, nonjudgmental stance toward the speaker. When a listener communicates concern and validation, speakers feel more confident about what they are saying and are more willing to be open and authentic, which leads to the kinds of conversations in which people feel loved. The psychologist Carl Rogers called this "unconditional positive regard," by which he meant a way of relating to other people with warmth and respect, with a receptiveness to their most vulnerable disclosures, and with a genuine willingness to try to understand how things appear from their perspective. We develop this important point more fully in chapter 8.

It is obvious that Patch Adams's doctor did not attend to his comments, nor did he exert any effort at comprehension or conveying positive, caring intent. In contrast, Robin Williams's character in *Good Will Hunting* displayed all the qualities of someone who is genuinely listening to learn. You probably recognize his generosity, but the more challenging question is, To what extent can you emulate him?

High-quality listening, as we learned the hard way in Tel Aviv, is a skill not easily acquired, but it *can* be learned. Critically, if you succeed in being a high-quality listener, you will experience the other person's story as *your* story, and you will endow the speaker with the motivation and courage to say more. You will also learn a great deal about the people you are talking with (which is why we emphasize the idea of listening to *learn*). Although some people are inherently good listeners, listening is fundamentally relational, depending on the specific connections between speaker and listener. In other words, you may be a wonderful listener to your best friend and a lousy one to your nosy neighbor. More important, even if high-quality listening does not come naturally to you, by practicing the suggestions described later in this chapter, you can markedly improve the effectiveness of your listening. In this way, you'll be able to launch the Relationship Sea-Saw and not fall off.

When Does Listening Matter?

Sometimes, people believe that listening only matters when friends and romantic partners talk about problems that one or both of them are having. In fact, listening applies to almost all of the interactions you engage in throughout life. For example, Avi Kluger and Guy Itzchakov, our hosts in Tel Aviv, have conducted many studies and trainings showing that listening is critical in business settings—such as in promoting the well-being of relationships between leaders and their supervisees, in smoothing the functioning of work teams, and in helping salespeople better serve their clients and customers. Dale Carnegie, in his masterwork *How to Win Friends and Influence People*, was an early champion of listening, providing principles that apply across assorted conversations and contexts. One of his prime maxims was "Ask questions that the other person will enjoy answering. Encourage them to talk about themselves and their accomplishments. Remember that the people you are talking to are a hundred times more interested in themselves . . . than they are in you." We agree, though we note that Carnegie was talking about one-sided relationships. The Relationship Sea-Saw builds on this observation and expands it to two-sided conversations.

Research has demonstrated the importance of listening, in a variety of contexts. Consider the relationship between parents and their children. Numerous studies show that when parents listen attentively and supportively to their children, both the parents and their children experience fewer and less intense conflicts and greater well-being in their relationship. Adolescents who feel well listened to are also more likely to be open about their concerns and problems with their parents. For example, in one recent survey, 62 percent of Gen Z adolescents said that they wanted their parents to just listen to them when they were upset—more than they wanted advice (28 percent). In the classroom, listening encourages students to be more responsive to their teachers' entreaties and helps teachers better understand what their students need. Listening to learn even works in idle chitchat, enabling new acquaintances to feel like potential friends.

Listening to learn is also relevant outside of one-to-one interactions. For example, listening is a key element of many interventions intended to bridge the damaging societal divides that exist across race, socioeconomic class, gender, political orientation, religion, and other social categories and identities. These interventions typically bring together groups of individuals from different backgrounds or with different beliefs, giving them an opportunity to share perspectives with one another. One pair of commentators addressed the increasing political polarization in the United States succinctly in a *USA Today* op-ed, titled "Let's Fight for America by Learning to Listen First." Listening even turns out to be a useful tool in spycraft. In a thoroughly engaging interview from the International Spy Museum (viewable on YouTube), Darrell Blocker, a former clandestine CIA officer, notes the effectiveness of listening, rather than speaking, in his experience developing assets in Afghanistan and Iraq.

Given that good listening is so highly valued, you may be tempted to think it is common. In fact, in our survey, nearly 93 percent of the respondents said that they listened attentively to their conversation partners "often," "very often," or "always." In another study, 71 percent of people said they were better than the average person of their age and sex at listening to someone who was struggling. Unfortunately, those estimates are not consistent with what most people report experiencing as speakers. All of us can recall conversations in which our partners were inattentive or distracted; interrupted or changed the topic; denied or misconstrued what we were saying; were selective in what they seemed to hear; or seemed just plain disinterested. These recollections mirror research findings. In one study conducted with nearly fourteen thousand employees on LinkedIn, only 8 percent said that their mid- and senior-level managers were listening "very well." A different investigation, conducted by Guy Itzchakov, found that 94 percent of people overestimated their ability to listen well in conversing with strangers. Perhaps Ernest Hemingway was right when he wrote, "Most people never listen."

Kate Murphy's 2020 book *You're Not Listening* described listening as a lost art (if it ever was a common talent). Murphy cites many reasons why people don't listen well. Some people may never have learned the skills involved in good listening, perhaps because those skills were not taught or perhaps because they habitually tuned out critical parents, teachers, and coaches. Or perhaps in some individuals, listening skills, once acquired, have become dormant, victims of the short and divided attention spans that the pace of modern life and the staccato format of text messaging have inculcated—a sort of "Just tell me the facts I need, and let's move on" mentality. Still others are so focused on their own perspective that they cannot wait to impress you with their own point of view or version of the same experience. Contemporary media, with its emphasis on monologuing and witty repartee, doesn't help—when was the last time you saw characters on *Friends* or guests on *The Tonight Show Starring Jimmy Fallon* truly listen to each other? Whatever the underlying cause, Murphy's book hit a resonant chord with many readers—as evidenced by the 90 percent positive ratings her book has received on Amazon. Patch Adams's experience may not be uncommon.

Charismatic Leaders Are Good Listeners

The art of conversation lies in listening.

—*Malcolm Forbes*

There's a secret that charismatic "good listeners" have long known. Consider the example of former US President Bill Clinton. Strangers talking to him for even a few moments often felt that he was laser-focused on them and undistracted by other things. Even in the most trivial conversations, he made them feel like they were the only person in the room. Through his subtle nonverbal behaviors (attentive and directed eye gaze, mirroring of posture and gestures, smiling, and so on), Clinton made conversation partners feel "seen" and listened to; they felt that they were important enough to get his full attention. In that single moment—or five minutes or two hours—the other person *felt* really listened to—that is, heard and valued in ways that they have probably rarely felt. At the same time, they felt alert and connected, completely comfortable and at ease.

Bill Clinton is not an isolated case. Many other transformational leaders established their reputations by listening well. Mahatma Gandhi, the inspirational torchbearer of the Indian independence movement in the 1940s, was known for his ability to listen actively to the needs and concerns of ordinary people. Nelson Mandela, the anti-apartheid revolutionary and subsequent president of South Africa, was celebrated for his insistence on listening not only to his followers but also to his adversaries. Mandela reportedly learned about the power of listening from his father, a tribal elder who would speak only after listening intently to what others had to say and asking questions so that he was sure he understood. Through these observations, Mandela developed his charismatic manner of patient and empathic listening, which served as a foundation for his commitment to dialogue and reconciliation.

Charismatic figures who are adept at implementing the skills of good listening can be found in many walks of life. Fred Rogers, the creator and host of the classic children's television show *Mister Rogers'* *Neighborhood*, created a safe and nurturing environment for children by attentively listening to and validating their concerns. In the literary world, the British novelist E. M. Forster was notoriously reserved but nonetheless a captivating listener. One of his biographers described him this way: "Forster instead chose to draw people inward, to reveal themselves to him as he remained enigmatic. To speak with him was to be seduced by an inverse charisma, a sense of being listened to with such intensity that you had to be your most honest, sharpest, and best self." One place where you might not expect listening to be highly valued is in the competitive, ultrahierarchical world of professional sports. Yet when asked what advice he would give to someone who wanted to be a football head coach, the first response of Mike Tomlin, the longtime coach of the NFL's Pittsburgh Steelers, was "Listening . . . is something we focus on and work at. . . . I come with a growth mentality. I come ready to grow and get better from anywhere and anyone."

Listening is a singularly critical skill for journalists and interviewers—after all, their job is to collect information, particularly the sort of information that their subjects might be reluctant to reveal. The media mogul Oprah Winfrey is known for her empathic interviewing style, creating a setting that encourages her guests to tell their stories openly. Walter Isaacson, writer of numerous bestselling biographies of creative thinkers (Leonardo da Vinci), politicians (Henry Kissinger), scientists (Albert Einstein), and inventors (Steve Jobs) is a master of getting his interview subjects to talk candidly to him. Isaacson's approach is built on the idea that people want to open up (as we described in chapter 5)—you just have to create the conditions for it to happen (i.e., mindful attention and long pauses). He describes first becoming aware of this principle in his earliest experience as a journalist covering a gruesome murder:

> To my surprise, [the parents of the perpetrator] invited me in. They pulled out photo albums. They told me stories as they wiped their tears. They wanted people to know. They wanted to

talk. It's another basic lesson I learned: The key to journalism is that people like to talk.

Shankar Vedantam, the founder and host of the immensely popular podcast *Hidden Brain*, is similarly skilled. Both of us (Sonja and Harry) have been interviewed for separate episodes of his show, as have quite a few of the researchers whose work appears in this book. Vedantam's approach exemplifies what researchers mean when they say that listening is an active, effortful, participatory activity. Both of us felt a palpable sense of connection with the *Hidden Brain* team, even though our contact with them was remote, limited to a couple of hours of prep and an hour-long interview. The show kicks off with the research itself but then digs deeper to uncover the personal story behind the research—how the scientist came to be interested in that topic. Vedantam pushes his guests to tell their story by showing genuine interest in what they have to say. He puts them at ease, asks thoughtful questions, and listens intently to their answers—as though he wasn't just collecting material for his podcast but rather was connecting with them on a human level. This talent is a large part of why episodes of *Hidden Brain* resonate deeply with their audience, receiving millions of downloads weekly. Vedantam and his team illuminate the way that an active Listening-to-Learn mindset shapes conversations and supports connection.

How Listening Differs from Hearing

Before we explain how to listen really well to your conversation partners, it may be useful to dispel a common misconception about listening. As we mentioned earlier, listening (being actively engaged in processing the message and responding to a speaker) is different than hearing (passively receiving a speaker's words).

Here's why: Taking in a speaker's words is a fine feat, as far as it goes. It may help you understand the speaker to some extent, but it doesn't get you very far. Instead, it's important for the listener to go beyond the speaker's words—as the aforementioned humanist Carl Rogers put it, to go "beyond the immediate message of the person"—by reflecting on the deeper meaning of what they are communicating. In other words, listeners must strive to recognize the personal significance of the speaker's words—what the speaker may be feeling, the experiences that the message reveals, how the speaker intends to come across, and where they would like the conversation to go. The psychoanalyst Theodor Reik called this "listening with the third ear." Actively and thoughtfully reflecting on a speaker's message is how one listens to learn—it naturally leads you to ask questions that encourage elaboration and openness.

A more important distinction between hearing and listening is that although passive hearing may enable you to understand the speaker, it does nothing to help the speaker feel understood. Have you ever had the experience of being asked a probing question and giving a fairly thorough response, only to have the listener nod their head and then change the subject? When this has happened to either one of us, we've felt awkward and shut down, as if our answer had been inappropriate, out of line, unwelcome, or boring. The purpose of listening to learn is to let the speaker know that you get the point of their message and that you appreciate its meaning. That only happens when you actively engage the speaker in a responsive and fully interactive dialogue—as the Relationship Sea-Saw of chapter 4 explains.

The fictional detective Sherlock Holmes exemplifies a reputedly good listener who might better be called a good hearer. Always paying close attention to his protagonist's words and actions, Holmes was able to pick up on the slightest clue or detail that would enable him to discern what a speaker was trying to hide. While Holmes's understanding was undoubtedly exquisite, it seems unlikely that his subjects felt listened to or understood by him. The same logic applies to poker players adept at seeing through another player's "tell," police interrogators skilled at separating truth from lies in a defendant's story, or manipulative salespersons who can read and thereby exploit a buyer's vulnerabilities. In none of these cases is the speaker likely to feel understood—that is, listened to. More importantly, the listener's understanding in these instances obviously would not create inter-actions that lead to feeling loved.

This is a principle well-appreciated by couples therapists. A typical couples' conflict might go something like this:

Partner A: "I was trying to—"

Partner B interrupts: "Yes, I know what you were trying to do, but—"

Partner A interrupts: "No, you don't know what I was trying to do—"

Partner B rejoins: "Yes, I do so know."

Each partner interrupts the other, confident in their belief about what the other thinks, feels, and was about to say. Conversations like this often snowball, with the result that frustrations mount, while little is resolved. To be sure, long-term partners generally know each other well, so that their anticipation about the other's thoughts and feelings may at times (and perhaps even often) be factually correct; however, this kind of accuracy, even when well-intentioned, hampers good-communication practice. Speakers want to fully express their sentiments and have listeners react to what has been said rather than hunches based on preexisting knowledge. In other words, accurate knowledge plays a much smaller role in resolving disagreements than does actively taking steps to help one's partner feel understood in the moment. (In chapter 5, we described the many beneficial outcomes that accrue to couples when they feel understood, as almost every episode of the Showtime series *Couples Therapy* demonstrates.)

A team of clinicians led by Howard Markman at the University of Denver has developed a technique designed to short-circuit such conflicts as part of the well-regarded Prevention and Relationship Education Program. Called the Speaker-Listener technique, this method provides a step-by-step structure to facilitate self-expression and promote effective listening. Imagine Olga and Travis sitting in front of two lights, one in front of each of them. Each has the floor and is permitted to speak, uninterrupted, only when their light is lit (a signal similar in meaning to the conch shell in the novel *Lord of the Flies* or the talking stick in the TV sitcom *The Big Bang Theory*). When Olga's light comes on, she begins to recount something of concern to her, emphasizing her own perspective—"I felt . . ." When she finishes, Travis's light comes on. His task is to paraphrase Olga's message back to her—not to interpret, rebut, or respond but rather simply to restate in his own words what he has heard. Olga is then given the opportunity to either confirm or clarify what Travis has said, after which Travis again paraphrases the new information. The process continues until both agree about Olga's message. They then reverse roles, so that Travis has an opportunity to express his concerns.

Yes, you can try this yourself at home. The technique is somewhat cumbersome for ordinary conversation, and, as we explain later in this chapter, paraphrasing is only part of what accomplishes good listening. However, the beauty of this technique is that it laser-focuses conversation on three critical components of being a good listener: paying close attention to what the other is saying; checking out, rather than just assuming, the accuracy of what one has heard; and ensuring that the speaker feels understood.

What Are Good Listeners Trying to Accomplish?

Only through the power of listening
can you truly know anything.
—*Victor Wooten,* The Music Lesson

Research indicates that listening to learn accomplishes several important goals. As the listening researchers Avi Kluger and Moran Mizrahi point out, high-quality listening is effective only when it results in the speaker feeling listened to. You can put into practice every skill you learn at a listening workshop, but if your conversation partner does not experience your attention and comprehension, your effortful listening is unlikely to yield its intended benefits. In point of fact, the phrase *feeling listened to* is in itself somewhat imprecise. We might therefore better ask, what are listeners trying to accomplish when they listen to a speaker?

Most obvious among these goals is acquiring information—that is, as the phrase *listening to learn* implies, gaining a deep comprehension of the other person's experience and viewpoint. We will say more about this goal in chapter 7 (on radical curiosity), but for now we note that many disagreements stem from erroneous or incomplete understanding of another person's position. As recent studies have shown, disagreements are often mistakenly assumed to be the result of poor listening. Have you ever had a heated conversation in which you strongly disagreed with someone, but instead of acknowledging that there's a genuine difference of opinion, that person blamed you for not listening ("If you would only listen, you'd see my point!"). Indeed, simply knowing more about another person—their history, their beliefs, the circumstances of their life, their strengths and weaknesses—builds bridges between people. It helps establish common ground and facilitates shared activities. Moreover, as we explained in chapter 5, the more familiar you are with another person, the more you will like them and—the key point here—the more they will feel liked by you. When you listen attentively to another person, you empower them to feel liked and appreciated by you.

A second reason for listening is to enable the other person to feel heard and to feel seen. Feeling heard matters a great deal to people in many different ways. In romance, you probably hope to "find a love that makes you feel heard." In politics, voters insist on being heard by their elected representatives, and for that reason, candidates actively endeavor to attend to their constituents (or at least to give that impression). Conflicts escalate when disagreeing parties do not feel heard. Workers and students ask and often demand to be heard by their employers and teachers. In medical care, patients may resist treatments when they do not feel "respected, heard, and known as a person" by their physicians and caregivers.

The profound impact that a person can have by assisting others to feel heard is illustrated by a recent experience of Harry's daughter. Lianna is a nurse in a rural North Carolina hospital. One of the hospital patients had just been diagnosed with an advanced and extremely aggressive cancer. He was angry and belligerent, refusing to cooperate with the hospital routine and his prescribed care, and antagonizing his caregivers. Lianna recognized that in their task focus, no one was listening to his profound distress at having received this life-threatening diagnosis. So she sat down with him and encouraged him to open up, expressing his feelings and worries about what lay ahead. He lamented that no one was listening to his concerns, even that a different nurse had called him a bad patient when some small problems arose. As Lianna patiently listened, he described his anger and frustration, the disruption to his plans and family, and his fear about becoming debilitated and dying. His anxieties heard, he quieted down, thanked her for listening to him, and accepted the hospital staff's care.

Like Lianna and her patient, most people have observed or experienced feeling heard, but what exactly does feeling heard mean? In one of our joint academic papers, we (Harry and Sonja) theorized that this quality emerges from interactions in which partners demonstrate understanding, appreciation, and support for each other's feelings and goals, all of which contribute to a sense of trust and compatibility. Another group of researchers has defined feeling heard as "the feeling that one's communication is received with undivided attention, empathy, respect, and in a spirit of mutual understanding." Yet others have characterized feeling heard in terms of voice and receptiveness: the perception that one's positions and priorities have been genuinely considered. Finally, some theorists simply offer the idea that we feel heard and seen when we feel that we have social worth—that we matter to others in our social network.

Elements of all these theories are represented in research focusing on the ways in which an active and encouraging listener can support an individual's beliefs, values, and even self-worth. When you believe that significant others appreciate your abilities and worldview, your confidence in these attributes is bolstered. This idea, which goes by the name *social validation*, has received a great deal of empirical attention. Indeed, together with Guy Itzchakov, Harry has conducted several relevant studies. In one example, they first instructed participants to vividly recall a time when they felt valued and respected by others (as opposed to times when they felt devalued or disrespected). Participants were then asked various questions about an attitude that differed from their own (e.g., about genetically engineered food) or a social group toward which they felt some animus (e.g., about homeless persons). Validating recollections were effective in increasing open-mindedness and tolerance for opposing points of view while also decreasing prejudice. Many other studies conducted by other researchers have shown related effects; for instance, that social validation helps people become more confident of their attitudes, less defensive, more tolerant of others, and more self-assured.

The social psychologist Mark Leary explains these and many other related findings as the by-product of an innate human drive for social inclusion: Humans evolved to experience safety in groups, and the respect of other people builds confidence that one's place in valued groups is secure. A complementary idea, proposed by William Swann at the University of Texas, suggests that validating feedback is useful because it reinforces people's existing views of themselves. That is, when others see you in the same way that you see yourself (e.g., that you are often absent-minded but are a loyal friend), it is easier to navigate the ebb and flow of everyday life because there is less risk of failing to live up to others' expectations or of facing situations whose demands cannot be met. Importantly, this principle suggests that a listener's validating feedback will hit home to you only when it is credible— that is, when you feel understood by the messenger. Swann's research shows that feedback that is discrepant from a person's self-concept, no matter how favorable it may be, tends to be dismissed as irrelevant, misguided, or false. This idea returns us to a key point stressed earlier— that to be effective, listening must impart a deeply felt sense of being seen.

What Are the Consequences of Listening? What the Research Says

In 1936, Dale Carnegie wrote *How to Win Friends and Influence People* with the goal of improving the effectiveness of salespersons. That book, which remains a bestseller to this day, offered a series of practical techniques that embody high-quality listening. Perhaps not coincidentally, many of the most impressive studies of listening to date have been conducted in the world of business and organizations. In 2022, Avi Kluger and Guy Itzchakov—the world's leading listening researchers whom we met in Tel Aviv—conducted a comprehensive review of this research, which they aptly titled "The Power of Listening at Work." Their review documented widespread benefits of experiencing good listening in the workplace. When workers feel listened to, their job performance improves (e.g., salespeople literally sell more); they offer more voluntary, cooperative contributions to their workplace (a concept known as *organizational citizenship behavior*); conflict and other counterproductive behaviors are reduced; harmful stress and burnout are minimized; and they evaluate their leaders as more trust-worthy and effective in their leadership roles. The authors conclude, as Carnegie doubtless would have anticipated, that "high-quality listening brings a cornucopia of positive outcomes for speakers, listeners, teams, and organizations."

Other research shows that listening reduces polarization during conflict. People often become entrenched in conflictual conversation, focused on defending their own position. In one series of experiments, researchers taught experimental confederates (members of the research team instructed to behave in a certain way) to engage in poor, moderate, or high-quality listening during a disagreement. When research participants spoke with a confederate who showed high-quality listening to them, they became more comfortable and open-minded; as a result, they were more willing to thoughtfully rather than defensively consider the thorny issues at hand. Thus, high-quality listening weakened polarization and increased the likelihood that two conversation partners would find common ground. In other experiments, good listening has been shown to reduce prejudice, again by a similar means; when people feel truly listened to, they are more open to others and more willing to genuinely consider alternative points of view.

The central idea of these experiments was poignantly illustrated in a *New York Times* essay about the death of a nonbinary Oklahoma teenager named Nex Benedict. Benedict had been bullied and harassed in school and committed suicide the day after a fight in a high school bathroom. Benedict became a tragic statistic—one more data point illustrating the rising impact of political polarization's and extreme speech's contributions to hate crimes throughout the United States. But more than merely a data point, the tragedy was brought home when we read about the anguish felt by Benedict's grandmother, who lamented the unwillingness of Benedict's peers and community of adults to simply listen, "to try to understand the world as [nonbinary young people] are experiencing it." Is it too much to hope that listening might foster a more harmonious future? Perhaps less polarization and fewer tragic statistics would happen "if every grandmother . . . would take the time to listen to children who are trying to explain—or just to understand—their own identity."

Research studies also document the value of listening for improving human relationships. Many studies establish that personal disclosures—for example, of concerns and anxieties, strong emotions, traumatic experiences, or private information—amplify trust and intimacy, but only when they are followed by responsive listening. (Imagine disclosing something deeply personal and your conversation partner's reacting with silence or by changing the subject.) As we described in chapter 4, responsive listening conveys the listener's interest and caring as well as signals that the speaker can share their emotions and experiences honestly and safely—both of which are essential to building closeness. Interestingly enough, even mundane conversations can have this effect. For example, a simple conversation in which partners ask each other "How was your day?" (and really mean it) can convey caring and build trust and closeness. Presumably, this works only when the partner listens.

In the 2013 book *The Art of Communicating*, the Vietnamese Buddhist monk Thich Nhat Hanh wrote: "Compassionate listening is crucial. We listen with the willingness to relieve the suffering of the other person, not to judge or argue." In other words, when we listen well, the speaker feels happier. Research bears him out. Many studies have shown that people who feel well listened to generally experience more positive emotions, fewer negative emotions, and a greater general sense of well-being. They are also less likely to feel lonely. In one particularly noteworthy experiment, the researchers asked participants to describe and reflect on an experience of social rejection. For example, one participant in this study wrote about feeling rejected after moving to a new school. In the key experimental condition, they then conversed for ten minutes with a confederate who had been trained to provide high-quality listening. After these conversations, participants felt closer to their listener—and more importantly, they also left the study feeling less lonely.

With so much research establishing the positive outcomes that result from being well listened to, you might expect that there is a parallel literature examining the *listener's* experience. Surprisingly, there isn't. Of course, many of the benefits described for the recipients of good listening likely accrue to the listener as well. For example, when an employee feels trust during a conversation with their manager or when one friend feels intimately connected after revealing a secret, both parties benefit.

We were curious if people who describe themselves as good listeners would also experience higher well-being than people less inclined to listen attentively, and so we included questions from a standard measure of listening in the survey described in chapter 2. Our curiosity was satiated: Self-described good listeners in all age groups and of either gender were less lonely and more satisfied with their lives. Furthermore, they reported feeling more loved in all the categories included in our survey—by their romantic partners, by their friends, by their parents and children, by their community, at work, and by God (if they were religious). Thus, it's not just *receiving* good listening that leads people to feel loved; as the metaphor of the Sea-Saw suggests, *being* a good listener promotes feeling loved too.

"Attention. Comprehension. Elaboration. Positive Intent . . . Action!": The Nuts and Bolts of Being a Good Listener

We hope that by now we've convinced you that being a good listener is a key piece of feeling loved. If so, you're probably either curious about the how-to question (*How can I become a better listener?*) or maybe dubious about the whole endeavor (*Isn't good listening obvious?*). Alas, there's no set formula, no checklist of magic words to utter, and no established behaviors to display that guarantee success as a listener. That's because the effectiveness of particular listening behaviors depends on the way they are put into action, the context and manner in which they are used, and your relationship with the speaker. A better way to begin is with the mindset with which you approach listening. Instead of marking off a mental catalog of dos and don'ts as you converse, we suggest that you focus on what you are trying to accomplish—the way you want your presence to be experienced by the person you are listening to. What do *you* look for in a listener? Now embody it.

As we noted earlier, effective listening involves communicating three core messages: attention, comprehension and elaboration, and positive intention. The more that you, the listener, show that you are (1) paying attention, (2) understanding the speaker's meaning and helping them clarify and deepen their ideas, and (3) displaying genuine interest and warmth, the more a sense of togetherness is likely to be established. Conversely, connections are likely to fail when a listener appears inattentive, inaccurate, unhelpful, cool, and aloof. In the next section, we describe specific behaviors that can convey each of these three core elements, relying on several sources, some of which we have touched on already: the research literature, the behavior of charismatic people who know how to galvanize an audience, and our own observations. But keep in mind that there is no checklist. Thus, because a variety of behaviors can accomplish the same ends, our sampling is not exhaustive. Rather, we list behaviors that are amenable to being put into practice with the appropriate mindset.

Attention

To be a good listener, you need to show with your words and body language that you are truly engaged and attentive, ignoring everything else (e.g., not looking at your phone or scanning the room to see who else is around or what others are doing). This can involve eye contact (steady, but not staring, looking away briefly now and then), orienting body posture toward the speaker (e.g., a slight lean forward, without crowding the speaker), nodding or offering utterances (e.g., "hmm" or "uh-huh") that encourage the speaker to continue without interrupting their speech, and keeping silent when the speaker seems to be focusing on an important point. Yet staring at the speaker in silence for a period is not your goal. Instead, these behaviors should be displayed with a situationally appropriate level of engagement and energy—nothing deadens a conversation more than a sense that one's partner is disinterested!

One of the more intriguing ways of establishing attention involves mirroring nonverbal signals and language styles to the speaker. In a fascinating experiment, Yale University social psychologists trained an experimental confederate to display language and gestures that subtly matched the behavior of a research participant—for example, rubbing her cheek or smiling whenever the participant did so. This kind of understated mirroring led the participant to like the confederate more and to feel more comfortable during the conversation.

Shared nonverbal behaviors are one way that people signal their attentiveness to partners. Most of the time, we do this unconsciously, as a way of building rapport. But sometimes mimicry can be used strategically or manipulatively to gain trust or appear more likable. In these cases, if detected, the mimicry is likely to seem inauthentic and self-serving, perhaps even foolish, rather than relational. So be careful if you try this—people may think that you're trying to take advantage of them. Mimicry only works if it is subtle enough to be registered but not overt enough to seem manipulative.

Comprehension and Elaboration

Listeners sometimes assume that all they need to do is pay attention. Yet, as we pointed out in discussing the difference between listening and hearing, attention is not enough. Signs of attention can be subtle, and speakers may miss them; moreover, they may wonder whether their full meaning is coming across as intended unless listeners clearly demonstrate understanding. There are several ways to do this—a simple one is asking for clarification. Another useful technique is paraphrasing—repeating back what the speaker said but using different words. Summarizing the meaning of what's been heard is also an effective method of letting the speaker know that their point is clear (and it lets the listener check on the accuracy of what they heard). Evidence of comprehension can also be established nonverbally—for example, grimacing when the speaker's story is sad or sharing a laugh at the right moment. Of course, there are also lots of ways that a listener can appear to be noncomprehending— for example, paraphrasing or summarizing incorrectly, laughing when the message is scary or embarrassing, changing the subject inappropriately, or interrupting or physically disengaging before the message is complete.

We already explained that attention, by itself, is not sufficient to establish your reputation as a good listener. But the exact same point can be made about comprehension too. Rote comprehension is not enough—you need to elaborate as well. One of the best illustrations of elaboration comes from improvisational comedy, which relies on the "Yes, and . . ." rule—repeating what the speaker has said and then expanding on that line of thinking. In listening, this does not mean changing the subject or telling your own story. Rather, it means asking detailed, targeted, and thoughtful questions that encourage the speaker to continue—for example, by expanding or building on their message, by reflecting on its meaning, or by asking what happened next. The best questions are open-ended invitations to elaborate rather than close-ended or leading questions. "How did that make you feel?" is better than "Wouldn't you agree that that was awkward?"

Even so, it's important to recognize that not all questions are created equal. People tend to ask questions at three different levels.

- *Level 1:* The first level is by far the most common but is just the bare minimum of what's required of a responsive partner. What we call Level 1 questions are general questions about how things are going, how your day has been, and what you think about the [election, TV series, sports tournament, office drama]. These types of questions show that we are at least somewhat engaged in the conversation and potentially curious about the other person's external and internal life. Although they are often important at the beginning of a conversation—that is, when information gathering is necessary—they can be rote and are not very diagnostic of our interest or attentiveness.
- *Level 2:* The second level of questions involves asking for details— for example, "So what happened with your canceled plan today?" and "How did he reply to your concern?" and "How did the meeting end?" Such journalistic questions are more effective in helping a partner sense one's interest, yet a chatbot can be easily trained to ask them too. Level 2 questions are important, but listeners can do even better.
- *Level 3:* The third level of questions is the one that really counts. We are often amazed at how rarely we hear them. Level 3 questions involve digging deeper into what our partner is telling us, into the nitty-gritty—that is, in addition to asking "What was your daughter's speech about?," ask "How did that make you feel?" or "What was it about her speech that made you feel proud?" Such questions may be surprising, deep, or personal, or all three. Wise and effective psychotherapists know how to ask Level 3 questions in a way that invites their patients to feel deeply understood and validated but not intruded on. If used authentically—and in our experience, Level 3 questions are hard to fake—they show speakers that one is truly curious about and ready to validate their perspective.

Positive Intent

The final element of effective listening involves expressing caring intent during the act of listening. One of Harry's oldest friends is exceptionally attentive and always asks insightful, deeply probing questions. Yet he does so in a manner that typically comes across as hostile and accusatory—for example, by criticizing Harry's perspective, by discounting his emotions, by showing irritation with aspects of what Harry is describing, by expressing impatience when the pace of conversation is not to his liking, or by imposing his vision of how Harry ought to have felt or behaved. This friend does not encourage Harry to self-disclose, and he does not help Harry feel loved. Perhaps you have a friend or relative who makes you feel similarly. Or perhaps you have a friend or relative who is not provocative but is emotionless, detached, or neutral.

Assume that you have now mastered all the techniques and strategies that make you better at attending to, understanding, and elaborating on your conversation partner's story. That still doesn't mean that you are coming across as helping the other person feel loved. Witness Harry's friend, who was outstanding at attending, understanding, and elaborating.

Our lesson here is that no matter how skillfully you apply these techniques and strategies, your conversation partners will not experience you as a good listener if you lack positive intent—in other words, if your responses to them are not also thoughtful, sensitive, and, above all, caring. Checking off a list of behaviors is not enough. Good listeners establish a caring presence by being, in the words of therapist Emily Nagoski, "warmly attuned" to their partners. People who listen with a caring, attentive presence encourage their partners to feel calm and safe, less defensive, and more willing to be open with their thoughts and feelings, and they often accomplish this with what's called "affectionate communication"—a gentle touch, an empathic smile, a supportive comment, saying "I love you."

Not coincidentally, showing genuine positive intent while listening is related to the Open-Heart mindset we cover later in this book—a general orientation characteristic of communal relationships (described in chapter 1). Research shows that people tend to be more emotionally open in their communal relationships. Part of the reason for this is that communal relationship partners are more caring listeners—they are mindful of each other's needs and goals, they are concerned about each other's well-being, and they do what they can to promote each other's welfare. Indeed, in communal relationships, people expect their partners to be responsive listeners, so that they can often move quickly and seamlessly into relatively deep conversations.

Assembling the Nuts and Bolts

Listening training comes in many shapes and sizes. For example, Guy and Avi have developed a practice they call "listening circles" for improving listening and communication within organizations. In a listening circle, ten to twenty-five people sit in a circle, speaking only when they are holding the leader-provided listening object, such as a small stick or a glass ball. Participants are encouraged to speak and listen deeply, authentically, and without judgment. Nearly all training methods teach participants to use one or more of the specific behaviors that we described earlier in this chapter, as well as a range of other behaviors. However, as we argued earlier, if you are eager to see a list of concrete examples, you will be disappointed. Although examples are often useful when learning (or improving) a new skill, we believe it is best not to approach listening situations with a mental checklist of steps to run through. Rather, we suggest considering these behaviors as a flexible set of possibilities for implementing a Listening-to-Learn mindset—that is, as aids for (1) attending, (2) comprehending and elaborating, and (3) showing positive intent toward a speaker. The Speaker-Listener technique described earlier (the one using lights) is a great way to practice the first two of these; in chapter 8, we will offer more details about how to incorporate positive intent.

Can I Really Learn to Be a Better Listener?

When we talk with people about listening, they readily acknowledge the value of being a good listener. At the same time, they often hesitate to act, feeling daunted and unsure of how they might go about becoming a better listener. In our experience, this hesitancy has three sources. First, most people have had countless interactions in which they did not feel listened to, so they may fail to appreciate that this is a teachable skill. Second, throughout their lives, most people have learned to approach conversations with a focus on impressing others by communicating their own thoughts and experiences—*not* on listening to learn about the other person. Third, and perhaps most important, they have an untold number of memories of trying to listen and failing, their focus and attention faltering. Listening well is indeed difficult. Yet, unlike other difficult skills—from playing the viola to writing poetry to surfing—listening is rarely trained or taught.

When we interviewed Guy and Avi, they acknowledged the challenges inherent in teaching people how to be better listeners. Indeed, a large part of their work has been to develop training methods for improving people's listening skills. As Guy put it, "Listening definitely is trainable. It is a muscle that requires training. The good news is everyone can become a better listener. But it takes time and effort." Avi made a similar point, stressing that learning to listen involves more than acquiring a series of skills—it also "takes experiencing being listened to again and again until you want to give it to others." Their comments reminded us of the old joke about how to get to Carnegie Hall—practice, practice, practice. The way to become a good listener is simply to practice being a good listener.

One of the ideas Guy and Avi expressed repeatedly is the importance of having a "listening attitude"—in other words, consciously deciding to become a better listener, committing to improving one's skills, and then prioritizing their use during conversations. Embracing this listening attitude—we would call it a mindset—lets people avoid the all-too-common errors that characterize poor listening, such as interrupting, jumping to conclusions, shifting the focus to oneself, and so on. No one becomes a great listener overnight; ironically, when you learn to be a better listener, you also become more aware of instances when you are not listening well. But when listening is an important goal, you gradually acquire the habit of approaching conversations with a Listening-to-Learn mindset, which in turn will help your partners feel understood and valued and thereby create deeper connections for both of you. (Interestingly enough, Avi reports that one of the side effects of his listening workshops is that attendees become more aware of how poorly the people around them listen.)

Why Else Might Listening to Learn Improve Connections?

We end this chapter by describing how high-quality listening combats a few critical challenges to genuinely knowing and feeling known by another human being. Why is this important? Because before you can feel loved in an enduring way, you must feel known, and before your partner can feel loved, your partner must be known. One of the main superpowers of the Listening-to-Learn mindset is that it helps you know and understand your conversation partner better. This happens not only because your Listening-to-Learn mindset encourages your partner to really open up to you. It also happens because this mindset helps you avoid three common traps that undermine your ability to really see another person. These traps are stereotyping, projection, and transference.

Stereotyping

When we stereotype another person, we assume that they are typical of some group they belong to, such as that related to their age, race, occupation, or gender, or some physical characteristic that they possess, such as their weight or facial attractiveness. Social psychologists call this a *category-based generalization*—an inference that something that may be true (or is believed to be true) of a group is true of a particular group member (e.g., presuming that an elderly acquaintance is forgetful just because elderly people tend to be relatively more forgetful). Stereotypes sometimes carry "kernels of truth" and can thus be practical, helping people navigate uncertainty when encountering new acquaintances or ambiguous situations. This occurs when a stereotype accurately describes some group of people on average, so it's a useful first approximation. However, because stereotypes are unlikely to apply to all individuals in a group, they often inhibit or even harm social interactions when they stop people from seeking out further information. For example, holding a stereotype may prevent you from considering whether the qualities that describe a group actually apply to the particular individual with whom you are interacting.

A Listening-to-Learn mindset short-circuits this process by putting you, the listener, in a position of attending to and asking questions about your conversation partner. Perhaps you initially assumed that an elderly stranger is forgetful, but as you asked probing questions and listened closely to their responses, you acquired information indicating that this particular elderly person is actually quite sharp. This is in fact what research establishes as the most effective means of countering the disadvantages of stereotypes—seeking out information about the individual. Thus, even if you begin a conversation by relying on a stereotype as an initial guess, a Listening-to-Learn mindset will encourage you to pursue additional details that more accurately characterize the other person. Of course, this process of getting to know the other person meaningfully and deeply helps build stronger and more authentic relationships.

Projection

> Take careful note of the flaws you perceive in
> others. They are your own flaws set before you.
> —*Traditional teaching, Yom Kippur Morning Service*

A second common process that can subvert authentic connections is called *projection*. Projection occurs when people assume that another person shares their own experiences, beliefs, and values. For example, you might believe, without direct evidence, that your partner enjoys the same movies, foods, social activities, or sexual experiences that you enjoy. You might also expect that your partner would care for you during an illness to the same extent that you anticipate being willing to care for them. Projection is surprisingly common in relationships. Studies of couples have demonstrated, for example, that people assume that their close relationship partners share their personality traits, values, level of supportiveness, sexual preferences, and level of commitment to a greater extent than is actually the case. Other research shows that in long-term relationships, people assume that their partners love them about as much as they love their partners. Projection is not necessarily a bad thing—expecting that your partners will match your own feelings and interests can enhance your sense of security, but at the same time, that expectation can interfere with truly knowing them.

As we saw in chapter 5, in any relationship, wondering what the other person thinks of you is standard operating procedure. Projection is a relatively simple and effortless way of answering this question. After all, if "birds of a feather flock together" and if a relationship is stable and reasonably positive, why not assume a reasonable level of similarity? When you listen to learn, however, you avoid substituting your own preferences and feelings for inquiring into what your partner genuinely likes and values. For example, during an upcoming period of long-distance business travel, instead of assuming that your partner wants the same number of daily check-ins as you do, you listen and learn that they would prefer to have more free time to focus on their work. Notably, the understanding that you obtain by listening promotes a stronger, more authentic foundation for a relationship in two ways. First, your insights into your partner will be more accurate, freeing you from erroneous, potentially harmful assumptions and facilitating compassionate acts that promote relationship harmony (e.g., not texting them multiple times a day). Second, and just as important, your partner will feel more completely and accurately understood by you—and likely grateful that you knew exactly what they needed during your absence—and hence more willing to tilt the Relationship Sea-Saw in your direction. Thus, although projection may sometimes contribute to a sense of security, listening to learn is a more effective means of building a durable and authentic connection.

Transference

The third trap that listening to learn can forestall is called *transference*. Originally coined by Sigmund Freud, this term describes how people can sometimes displace feelings originating from an influential figure earlier in their lives (often a parent) onto a new person (such as a therapist or a romantic partner). Importantly, because transference occurs outside of awareness, when people experience it, they have little or no appreciation of the true source of their feelings. For example, transference explains a common everyday occurrence: people's tendency to assume that a current friend or partner takes after someone from their past whom they superficially resemble, such as a parent or ex-lover. For example, you might assume that your new girlfriend is nurturing because she reminds you of your mom or that your new neighbor is prone to anger because they remind you of your ex. The important idea here is that the new person in actuality does not possess the assumed qualities—it's the association with the person from your past that brings them to mind.

Here's how transference works: Suppose your father was a strict disciplinarian whom you could never please, no matter how hard you tried. Also imagine that he had a bushy gray mustache and sharp, angular chin and used a certain kind of aftershave. Now think about being at a dinner party where your host introduces you to her friend, a man who happens to have a bushy gray mustache and sharp, angular chin and who wears the same aftershave. Without consciously being aware of the resemblance, you might start to feel uncomfortable, experiencing your new acquaintance as critical and aloof—even though he had done nothing to warrant that response. Those feelings, in turn, might lead you to be unfriendly and defensive, ending up in a thoroughly unpleasant interaction. The explanation, according to a theory of transference developed at New York University, lies in the unconscious mental linkage between the new acquaintance and your father, attributable entirely to their mustache, chin, and aftershave.

A Listening-to-Learn mindset prevents transference. When you orient toward finding out as much as you can about what the other person thinks and feels, you weaken or withdraw whatever initial presuppositions you may have formed, instead focusing on what the other person is actually telling you. Of course, you may still end up making snap judgments consistent with the idea of transference. But these very early impressions are easily overridden when you create space for new information to enter your thoughts. Thus, a Listening-to-Learn mindset helps you avoid some of the common pitfalls—not only stereotyping and projection but also transference—that can undermine developing the sort of authentic connections that foster feeling loved.

Conclusion

This chapter has stressed that when you listen to learn, you do more than merely acquire information about the people you are with: You create the conditions that make it possible for them to feel heard and understood and known. These steps might not seem immediately and directly relevant to feeling loved, yet they are: Listening to learn sets into motion a sequence of necessary, but not sufficient, processes on the path to feeling loved. To feel loved, you must create the chemistry that involves both partners in a Sea-Saw of openness and responsiveness. Not just any act of listening will have this outcome. In the next chapter, we zero in on an essential feature of the kind of listening that builds Relationship Sea-Saw chemistry: enthusiastic, even radical, curiosity.

7

Radical-Curiosity Mindset

His interest in what we said
made us interesting.

—*Ann Patchett,* Tom Lake

Since its debut in 2004, Modern Love has become one of the most popular features of *The New York Times.* The column showcases compelling personal essays and timely wisdom for navigating all kinds of contemporary loving relationships—from falling in love and family estrangement to misunderstandings in friendship and the unexpected kindness of strangers. Indeed, this weekly newspaper column is so popular that it has grown to include podcasts, books, and even television adaptations. In 2024, Daniel Jones, the column's longtime editor, decided to review the lessons he has learned editing all those love stories, which prompted him to revisit all twenty years of the column. Among his discoveries? The most-read Modern Love essay of all time, by more than seventy-five million people, was a 2015 article titled "The 36 Questions That Lead to Love." Reflecting on its impact, Jones wrote, "Nothing I have (or will ever) put out into the world will affect more positive change than that short article."

The idea of these thirty-six questions may feel familiar to you—perhaps because you are one of the seventy-five million readers who has already learned about them. They are part of an experimental procedure called "Fast Friends," developed by two married psychologists, Arthur and Elaine Aron. In the years since, the Fast Friends procedure has been used in countless situations—from first dates

(Harry's friend Ken swore it transformed his silent dinners with his shy girlfriend into lively conversations) to international conference icebreakers (Sonja participated in a Fast Friends round-robin with two hundred people in Baja Mexico). But the Arons originally created the tool for psychological scientists—that is, to help researchers study the development of closeness and intimacy in a controlled laboratory setting.

Sonja and Harry have each had lots of experience themselves using the Fast Friends procedure in both their research and teaching. If you were a participant in one of our Fast Friends experiments, you would find yourself sitting opposite a stranger, taking turns answering questions printed on a card or on an iPad. The questions start off light (e.g., "Given the choice of anyone in the world, whom would you want as a dinner guest?") and slowly grow more substantial (e.g., "What is your most treasured memory?"). You and your conversation partner each take a few minutes to respond and listen to each other, and then you both continue through the questions, as they become deeper, more personal, and more intimate. Eventually you arrive at questions like: "If you were to die this evening with no opportunity to communicate with another person, what would you most regret not having told someone? And why haven't you told them this?"

It's not surprising to us that this procedure has struck a chord with so many people, as the pacing of such increasingly intimate questions can create an almost magical experience, even for people who are naturally guarded or reserved. Indeed, Fast Friends offers an ideal opportunity to use the Sharing mindset, as well as the Listening-to-Learn mindset, but the reason we return to it in this chapter is that we have observed that Fast Friends may be the most direct way to promote genuine, heartfelt curiosity.

Whether inside our research studies or inside our classrooms, we've spent years observing how people respond to the Fast Friends procedure and how and why curiosity is sparked in some individuals more than in others. It's fascinating to watch the process unfold. The typical pair in one of our Fast Friends studies gradually finds themselves becoming more and more curious about each other, slowly revealing more of their inner selves and becoming closer, as well as more authentically interested in the process. But some pairs reach a deeper level of curiosity, uncovering stories and details that would rarely surface in a typical getting-to-know-you chat. These discoveries often lead to moments of recognition and shared understanding— "Mmm, I can relate to that," we have overheard our participants say, or "Dude, the same thing happened to me!" At times, the conversations become punctuated by excitement and enthusiasm as the participants connect over these unexpected commonalities. As Sonja's friend Joshua described it, "There's something energetic that happens when you feel someone truly focus on you."

What makes the Fast Friends procedure so compelling is how it gently guides each person to gradually open up about deeply personal matters with a stranger who not only is listening but is genuinely— and sometimes intensely—interested. Taking turns sharing and being heard with eager curiosity is incredibly powerful. We argue that it's one of the essential ingredients for feeling loved.

What Is Curiosity?

Curiosity is, in great and generous minds,
the first passion and the last.

—*Samuel Johnson,* The Rambler

Curiosity is the eros of the mind, a propulsive
force. . . . You never know where it will take you.

—*David Brooks, "A Surprising Route to the Best Life Possible"*

In this chapter, we go beyond the idea of listening to learn by zeroing in on an essential feature of conversations that make people feel loved: enthusiastic, even radical, curiosity. Imagine interacting for thirty seconds with a hamster and then for another thirty seconds with a golden retriever. Which one seems more interested in you? The hamster, who randomly sniffs around your hand and the table? Or the wide-eyed, tail-wagging golden retriever, who is eager for your attention (and maybe a belly rub)? And which one seems to be having a better time? Our proposal is that the emotional impact of a curious, enthusiastic, happy listener—the human equivalent of that excited golden retriever—can ignite a profound social experience, one that makes you feel genuinely seen, valued, and loved.

We start by considering the general idea of curiosity—defined by scholars as a deep desire to learn or discover something new. Notably, most scientific research in this area has explored curiosity as a trait— that is, as a relatively stable characteristic that describes individuals in general. According to this work, curiosity is linked to a range of positive outcomes. First, curious people are happier: They report more positive emotions, a greater sense of meaning in life, and greater playfulness. They also tend to be more emotionally resilient, tolerate uncertainty better, and thrive in novel situations while approaching others with an open-minded and noncritical attitude. Perhaps it's not surprising, then, that curious people achieve greater success in most of their activities. In a word, curiosity *feels* good and *is* good.

One particularly interesting study found that men and women over the age of 65 who scored high in curiosity were more likely to still be alive five years later. This finding aligns with the life of Morrie Markoff, a Los Angeles resident who lived to an extraordinary 110. As reported by the *Los Angeles Times*:

> [Morrie] once said to me that he couldn't recall being bored a day in his life, and that was his gift to all of us: the reminder that if you stay plugged into the world around you and open yourself to new experiences, the aging process can slow to a crawl. "If I had to put my finger on one thing that helped his longevity, I would say it was his innate curiosity about everything," said his son Steven. . . . "You could bring him a sow bug, and he would say, 'Look, it rolled into a little ball. How did it do that?' Or he would say, 'I just met the most interesting person in the world on a bus.'"

Morrie's life serves as a vivid reminder that staying curious about the world can enrich every stage of life.

Curiosity, however, is not just a fixed personality trait but a state of mind. Although some people are naturally more curious than others, anyone can experience moments of curiosity. During these moments, you are more likely to explore your surroundings, gain knowledge and expertise, and broaden your horizons. As the social psychologist Shige Oishi explains, when curiosity leads you to go deep—to continue learning beyond surface-level details—it can alter how you see the world and increase the richness of your life. Indeed, research shows that a curious state drives people to ask questions, triggering a cycle of discovery such that each new piece of information or each new perspective sparks further interest and inquiry. It's like the joy of an aha moment, where a fresh insight not only enhances understanding but also reinforces a sense of competence. These moments are inherently rewarding, making curiosity a source of both personal growth and pleasure. For example, one study showed that episodes of curiosity on a given day predicted a stronger sense of meaning in life the next day. Curiosity may have killed the cat, as the old saying goes, but for humans, it is much more likely to be a lifeline.

By now it shouldn't surprise you that nowhere is curiosity more critical than when it is directed toward other people. Social curiosity—the desire to learn about other people and their lives—fosters genuine interest in how others think and feel. Socially curious people ask more questions, listen more attentively to the answers, engage more fully in conversations, and are perceived as authentic and sincere. As a result, perhaps not surprisingly, they experience less anxiety talking to others, report more satisfying social interactions and relationships, and are described as absorbed and responsive. Social curiosity can even help overcome the common reluctance to talk with strangers. In a series of experiments, social psychologists Gillian Sandstrom and Erica Boothby found that socially curious individuals were more likely to expect positive outcomes from conversations, and as a result, more likely to make pleasant conversations happen.

Perhaps you are wondering whether you are a socially curious person. One way to find out is by reflecting on your responses to the Social Curiosity Scale, developed by a German researcher, Britta Renner. The scale includes statements such as "When I meet a new person, I am interested in learning more about him/her," "I find it fascinating to get to know new people," and "I'm interested in other people's thoughts and feelings." Respondents rate the extent to which they agree with each of these statements, using a scale from "strongly disagree" to "strongly agree." If you find yourself strongly agreeing, congratulations—you're a socially curious person! Regardless, there are strategies to either kindle or even expand your innate curiosity.

Radical social curiosity is what happens when you are sitting with someone and find yourself thinking: *I am* so *curious about what you're really like. I want to understand your whole story—your core values, your unspoken dreams, the good, the bad, and the ugly. I want to know what it's like to walk in your shoes and to actually* be *you.* This type of curiosity doesn't fade after hearing a few details. Instead, after your conversation partner opens up, you keep listening intently, ready to hear more nitty-gritty, eager to uncover the next layer of their story.

Some of the best practitioners of radical social curiosity are professional interviewers—the people you hear on television and podcasts. A skilled interviewer knows how to bring out their guests' most compelling stories and insights, leaving a lasting impression that resonates with listeners. They don't just ask questions; they create a captivating exchange that leaves everyone wanting to know more.

Consider the late, much-beloved oral historian Studs Terkel. A Chicago institution as an author and a radio and television host, Terkel believed that everyone had a great story to tell—if one only took the time to listen. Unlike other interviewers, he wasn't drawn to celebrities; instead, he preferred to talk with ordinary people. Terkel didn't just listen passively—he engaged his guests deeply in conversation, spurring them to share their stories and perspectives, sometimes even drawing out insights and experiences they didn't even realize they wanted to express. His genuine interest in what they had to say was palpable. Terkel's obituary chronicles his ability to make his guests feel open, known, and valued—a testament to the power of radical social curiosity. He knew how to ask the right question at the right time.

A more contemporary example is provided by Dax Shepard, host of the podcast *Armchair Expert*. Here's how he describes his show:

> I love talking to people. I am endlessly fascinated by the messiness of being human, and I find people who are vulnerable and honest about their struggles and shortcomings to be incredibly sexy. I invite you to join me as I explore other people's stories. We will celebrate, above all, the challenges and setbacks that ultimately lead to growth and betterment.

Shepard's unmistakable interest in his guests' stories encourages them to be open and helps bring out their authentic selves.

Here's one final example: Anthony Bourdain, celebrity chef and host of *Parts Unknown*, a show that combined his interests in travel and food, was known for his unrelenting curiosity about the people he was meeting and the food they were serving him. He wasn't content to simply describe what he saw; he needed to understand. Whether speaking with a street vendor in Vietnam; a waiter in a delicatessen on New York's Lower East Side; or the head chef of Noma, a Michelin three-star restaurant in Copenhagen ranked for several years as the best in the world, Bourdain was driven to understand people, their cultures, and the way their values showed up in their cooking. His curiosity was evident in his intense, immersed, endearing, and often humorous approach to the individuals he encountered, contributing to the popularity of his show until his untimely death in 2018.

Over the years, we (Sonja and Harry) have been interviewed by many journalists and podcasters. In the best cases, we both have felt truly engaged—as though the interviewer was not just collecting information for their article or show but rather connecting with us on a human level. Isn't this what we are all striving for in our conversations? Indeed, a podcaster friend once confessed to us that he actually decided to start a podcast as an excuse to have meaningful conversations, which had been missing from his daily life.

The Curiosity Detector:
How Curiosity Connects

Your curiosity is more appealing than your accomplishments.

—Daniel Jones, "Seven Ways to Love Better"

This quote embodies what Daniel Jones, creator of the Modern Love column in *The New York Times*, called a "simple truth"—that your curiosity about your conversation partner is far more attractive to that partner than your highlighting your achievements is to them. Jones also happens to be echoing advice from Dale Carnegie, made more than seven decades earlier. Carnegie's famous "six ways to make people like you" included two key principles: "Encourage others to talk about themselves" and "Make the other person feel important—and do it sincerely."

To illustrate this idea, consider the following analogy. When there's a fire in the kitchen, your smoke alarm goes off, alerting you that something important is happening. In much the same way, our minds have a "curiosity detector" that lights up when we sense someone showing interest in us. In essence, this detector recognizes their curiosity as a signal of their interest and desire for connection: *I think you are interesting. I want to know more about you. I want to understand what you are thinking, feeling, and experiencing right now.* The "important event" being detected here is the potential for a moment of genuine connection with another person. On the flip side, when your curiosity detector fails to register interest from someone, it signals you either to move on or to experiment with a new way to evoke their curiosity.

It's especially important to be curious when talking to someone from a different national or cultural background. Even small differences in communication styles, language use, social norms, or personal experiences can shape how people interact—and these differences aren't always obvious. They can lead to awkwardness, misunderstanding, or a sense of otherness, even when both people want to connect. By staying curious and open, you can move past these initial differences. You may discover shared experiences, values, and commonalities. At the very least, you'll have a chance to engage with someone who offers a perspective you wouldn't ordinarily encounter in your own cultural context.

At this point, you might be wondering, Why does curiosity connect? Curiosity involves more than just seeking information. Scott Shigeoka, author of *Seek: How Curiosity Can Transform Your Life and Change the World*, suggests that curiosity can even bridge divides. When you are curious, you let go of your assumptions and biases about others and focus on learning about them with an open mind. You expose yourself to their perspectives and experiences, fostering connection with new acquaintances and strengthening existing relationships. Curiosity helps people find common ground and transcend differences. But most importantly, it enables the other person to recognize your interest in them; they sense that they matter to you and that you genuinely admire, like, and appreciate them. Forrest Gump's curiosity about the people he meets, in the eponymous 1994 movie, has exactly that effect: The people he encounters are drawn in by his eagerness to listen to their stories. Maybe that's why Judson Brewer, director of the Mindfulness Center at Brown University, says that "curiosity really is a superpower."

The reason your "curiosity detector" is so critical is that when someone is curious about you, it usually means they like you. And for a variety of reasons—some more obvious than others—humans are deeply invested in people's liking them. For example, within our own academic field of social psychology, scientists have long been interested in the impact that feeling liked by others has on people's thoughts, emotions, and actions. Indeed, some of our field's earliest experiments were conducted on this topic. In one classic experiment, students were led to believe—based on the results of a fabricated personality test—that particular peers might really like them. Unsurprisingly, participants were attracted to the peers by whom they expected to be liked. This general principle—communicating that you like someone leads them to like you back—is one of the most consistent and foundational findings in the research literature. Whether through words, nonverbal cues (such as a smile, eye contact, or a forward lean), or, and especially, active curiosity, showing genuine interest in someone is very likely to precipitate a positive response from them.

In other words, when people believe that someone likes them, they show what researchers call *reciprocated attraction*. But that's not the only thing that happens. When you believe that someone likes you, you are more willing to be open and vulnerable; to show warmth and openheartedness; and to listen in a supportive, encouraging manner. In essence, mirroring our description of the dynamics of the Sea-Saw, an initial expression of curiosity can trigger a cycle of interactions in which both parties become increasingly more open and positive toward each other. These upward spirals of rewarding interactions play an important role in fostering lasting feelings of being appreciated, valued, and loved.

Of course, being liked by others feels good in its own right. Who hasn't experienced the satisfaction of receiving praise, admiration, or appreciation for something they have done? Evolutionary theorists suggest that basking in the warm glow of liking has a purpose, or "functional value." Clues to that functional value come from research on the need to belong. As we described in chapter 1, most people want to be accepted by the people and groups they care about. When people believe that they belong, they feel confident, supported, and safe. Conversely, when people feel left out—or even unsure about whether they're wanted—they become tentative or withdrawn, worry about inadequacy, and may feel sad and lonely. They may even become hostile and critical.

In this light, a sincere expression of curiosity from an interaction partner is more than just a request for information or a casual sign of interest. It's also a profound gesture of acceptance and inclusion. Harry once asked a family member to share the most memorable instance of someone showing curiosity about her, and she immediately thought of her first love: "He watched me," she recalled, "his gaze intent and his face lit up with a grin that seemed to hang on my every word." In that moment, she felt more accepted and loved than ever before.

Radical Curiosity Is Enthusiastic Curiosity

> Your enthusiasm will be infectious, stimulating
> and attractive to others. They will love you
> for it. They will go for you and with you.
>
> —*Norman Vincent Peale,* The Power of Positive Thinking

Guy Itzchakov introduced us to a very brief but eye-opening exercise we've come to call Unmoved Versus Over-the-Top. This activity illustrates the power of a special kind of curiosity—*enthusiastic curiosity.* Here's how it works: Pair up with another person, ideally someone you don't know well. First, take two minutes to share with your partner your most meaningful experience from the past year. Meanwhile, your partner's job as the listener is to remain completely unmoved—to listen impassively, showing absolutely no signs of interest or recognition. Then, you switch seats. Now your partner's task is to spend two minutes describing something utterly mundane that they did yesterday, such as walking from their car to the grocery store. This time, however, you are instructed to listen with over-the-top enthusiasm—smiling, leaning in, and responding with animated exclamations like "Wow" and "That's so amazing!" The results of this little exercise are striking. In the unmoved scenario, people find themselves doubting whether their experience was really all that meaningful. But in the over-the-top scenario, the listener's energy usually sparks a surprising shift—even the most ordinary event suddenly starts to feel exciting and significant. This exercise reveals something profound: Enthusiasm and energy aren't just an important part of curiosity—they may be its most *critical* elements.

The Power of Enthusiastic Curiosity

Feeling curious about another person isn't enough on its own. Curiosity, after all, can be hidden from view—as when you are engrossed in a novel or watching television and dying to learn what happens next. To truly engage another person and make them feel loved, curiosity needs to be expressed energetically, through what psychologists call "high-arousal" emotions. On the positive side, these include enthusiasm, delight, surprise, and alertness; on the negative side, they include anger, distress, and disgust. The key is matching the emotion displayed to the context: In the context of showing radical curiosity during a conversation, the emotion that matters most is enthusiasm—a lively, energetic, positively charged interest.

Enthusiasm—from the Greek *enthusiasmos*, or being filled with the spirit of the gods—matters. Think about the last time you shared a story or an opinion and your conversation partner was fascinated by what you were saying. Or when your listener was visibly delighted hearing of your recent accomplishment. Didn't that feel great? Now compare those reactions to when a partner's words seemed to indicate interest but their emotional tone or facial expression was neutral or lukewarm. The latter is unlikely to land the same way. This is why charismatic individuals—those who have a gift for creating instant chemistry with everyone they meet—typically communicate their curiosity with energy and enthusiasm. And this also helps explain what people find most appealing about extraverts—not their gregariousness but their enthusiasm and energy.

Why Enthusiasm Matters: Student to
Student, Partner to Partner

The power of enthusiasm is perhaps nowhere more evident than in teaching. Most teachers will tell you that they find their deepest fulfillment in classrooms that are alive with energy—when their students are buzzing with excitement and fully absorbed in learning. Psychologists refer to this absorption as *intrinsic motivation*: doing something for the sheer joy and meaning it brings. But where does intrinsic motivation come from?

This question was on Harry's mind in 2009 when he was tasked to write about the magic of teaching for an acceptance speech for a teaching award at the University of Rochester. After reflecting deeply on what makes the act of teaching compelling for him, he ultimately invoked the words of the American poet and philosopher Ralph Waldo Emerson: "Nothing great was ever achieved without enthusiasm."

Does enthusiasm stimulate curiosity in the classroom? Inspired by the power of enthusiasm, one of Harry's PhD advisees, Brian Patrick, put this idea to an empirical test. Brian carried out a series of studies that revealed that two kinds of teacher enthusiasm significantly boosted students' curiosity and enjoyment in their courses: (1) teachers' passion about their subject matter and (2) their delight in the act of teaching itself. In a different set of experiments, instructors were prompted to teach fourth and fifth graders in one of two ways—either with high enthusiasm (featuring animated, expressive gestures; joyful facial expressions; and energetic movement) or with low enthusiasm (showing minimal movement and speaking in a monotone voice). The results were clear: Students who received the high-enthusiasm lesson were more engaged and, when tested later, retained more of what they had learned. One can safely conclude not only that a teacher's enthusiasm attracts attention but that it also fosters connection.

In the context of teaching, enthusiasm spreads from teacher to student. In the context of social interaction, enthusiasm spreads from one conversation partner to another. For example, one hallmark of enthusiastic engagement is laughter. People are more likely to laugh when they are with others than when they are alone, and one person's laughter commonly triggers a reciprocal response by others. (That's the scientific way of saying that laughter is contagious!) Indeed, shared laughter is such a strong social signal that it has been shown to be a behavioral marker of satisfying romantic relationships. Supporting the importance of shared positive experience, Harry conducted a study in which college students played Jenga—the game where players remove wooden blocks, one at a time, from a precarious tower until it becomes unstable and collapses. The students reported that they had more fun playing the game with another person, especially a friend, than when they played alone.

Similarly, a study at Yale University found that participants rated chocolate as tastier when they sampled it with others than alone—even when they could not see others' reactions. You may recall from chapter 1 that Barbara Fredrickson, a psychologist at the University of North Carolina at Chapel Hill, describes this phenomenon as *positivity resonance*—a kind of behavioral synchrony in which sharing a positive experience makes it even more enjoyable. But a simpler way to summarize these studies is with a well-documented principle: Sharing amplifies pleasure. This principle explains why a listener's enthusiastic curiosity is so powerful—because it is contagious. It's the enthusiasm piece that creates a shared experience, gives rise to a dynamic back-and-forth, and magnifies the joy and significance of the moment.

"I Love Love Love That Story!"

The only way to have a friend is to be one . . . rejoice
at their good fortune as you would at your own.
—*attributed to Ralph Waldo Emerson*

Rejoice with those who rejoice; mourn
with those who mourn.
—*Romans 12:15*

It's late October and the time for the Triwizard Tournament has arrived. Dating back to the thirteenth century, this legendary contest pits the three largest European schools of wizardry against one another—Hogwarts School of Witchcraft and Wizardry, Durmstrang Institute, and Beauxbatons Academy of Magic. The stakes are high: Winning the competition brings honor and glory to the victor. But the path to victory is treacherous: Each of the three tasks is exceptionally dangerous, requiring copious amounts of magical ability, cunning, and courage. The champions—one from each school—are chosen magically by the Goblet of Fire. Despite being underage—a minimum age of seventeen was established after prior tournaments resulted in deaths—the Goblet selects Harry Potter as the Hogwarts champion. And because the Goblet's selections are binding, Harry is obliged to take part.

Harry's first task is daunting: It requires him to navigate past a fearsome dragon and retrieve a golden egg. The task feels impossibly large, and he has doubts and anxieties about his ability and his age, wondering, "Did someone want him dead?" Harry fears that he is not up to the task, that he's "a goner," his spirits sinking into a "barely controlled panic [that] was with him wherever he went." "Surely," he muses, "there could be nothing worse than dragons coming." Sleepless nights follow, and Harry even considers running away from Hogwarts. But after practicing a charm suggested by another wizard, Harry soars past the dragon, succeeds in snatching the golden egg, and receives a high score for his daring accomplishment.

Afterward, when Harry rejoins his friends, they greet him with excitement. Hermione celebrates him enthusiastically: "Harry, you were brilliant! . . . You were amazing! You really were!" His friend Ron Weasley adds, "You were the best, you know, no competition." Their comments contribute to Harry's sense of relief and enhance the overwhelming joy Harry feels from his accomplishment.

Now imagine a different response from Harry's friends. Suppose Hermione had met him with indifference, saying: "That's nice, but I gotta go. Do you know where I hid my broomstick?" And suppose that Ron had then chimed in: "You were really lucky that the dragon was having an off day, but the next task is so much harder. I'm afraid you won't do so well on that one." How would Harry have felt then?

One day, author Harry and his then–graduate student Shelly Gable (now a professor and dean at the University of California, Santa Barbara) found themselves puzzled by a trend in the scientific literature on relationships. The vast majority of studies focused on problems: how couples navigate conflict, how they support each other through stresses and hardships, and the factors that contribute to the decline and dissolution of marriage. This one-sided emphasis seemed imbalanced to Harry and Shelly. After all, who enters a relationship with the goal of confronting problems and minimizing "bum me out" moments? In reality, most people begin relationships full of optimism, delighting in spending time together and sharing life's best moments. While they might recognize the "worse and poorer" part of the traditional marriage vow, their commitment is inspired by the promise of the "better and richer" part.

As Harry and Shelly explored this imbalance, they came across a paper by the distinguished British social psychologist Michael Argyle. In it, Argyle proposed that sharing good news with a friend is one of the fundamental rules of friendship. A 1994 study supported this notion: People reported greater joy when they related news of a happy event to a close friend than from the happy event itself. The researchers called this process "capitalization"—the act of amplifying one's happiness from a positive event (whether it's winning a tournament or a job promotion) by sharing the news of that event with another person.

Recall the last time something great happened to you. Was your first impulse to tell someone else? If so, you're not alone. In one study, participants spontaneously mentioned sharing happy events with others more than 80 percent of the time. Interestingly, people didn't limit their sharing to major milestones, such as receiving a raise or reconnecting with an old friend. They also shared the joys of life's small pleasures, such as sleeping in or finding a dollar bill on the sidewalk.

Harry and Shelly ended up conducting seminal research on capitalization. Their central realization, however, was not about the ubiquity of sharing. What matters most, they found, was the reaction of the listener—the person being shared with. For capitalization to work, the listener's response must be positive, engaged, and energetic—in other words, the response must express enthusiastic interest and curiosity. Imagine being interviewed by a reporter who, much like the unmoved listener we described earlier, asks you to share one of your most meaningful experiences, then impassively jots down some notes, barely acknowledging your answer with a nod before moving on to the next question. Now picture the same interviewer, but this time, echoing the over-the-top listener we described, they beam with excitement, remarking how fascinating your experience was and then peppering you with questions to elicit more details. The enthusiastic curiosity expressed by the over-the-top reporter feels so rewarding and compelling that it makes you want to share more and leaves you feeling truly seen.

The same principle applies to interactions with close friends and even new acquaintances. For you, as the speaker, to benefit from sharing your good news, the listener's response needs to feel authentically curious and—most important—enthusiastic. This kind of response doesn't just encourage more sharing—it makes the speaker feel heard, valued, and, ultimately, loved.

Since that initial insight, Harry and Shelly, as well as many other researchers following their lead, have conducted numerous studies and experiments to explore the capitalization process further. In one early set of experiments, Harry asked participants to describe to an experimental accomplice one of the best things that had happened to them in the past two years. The accomplices were trained to respond in either of two ways—enthusiastically or impassively. The results were clear: When the accomplices were enthusiastic, participants appraised their stories more positively, developed a stronger sense of liking and trust toward the listener, and left the study sessions in a better mood.

In a separate study, Harry, Shelly, and their team tracked undergraduate students over fourteen days. Every day, participants were asked to describe the best thing that had happened that day; whether they had shared the news with someone else; and if they had, how the other person had responded. After the study was finished, participants were shown a list of their fourteen events and asked how positive each event seemed now. Events that had received enthusiastic responses were rated more positively than they were the day they happened. Moreover, in a variant of this protocol, when participants were asked to recall the fourteen events, they were more likely to remember spontaneously the ones that had received enthusiastic responses.

When you respond to a friend's happy disclosure with interest and enthusiastic curiosity, that friend will not only value their happy event more—they will like and trust *you* more. On the flip side, an unhelpful response to a happy disclosure is one that is lukewarm and passive—for example, a ho-hum "that's nice" followed by a quick change of subject. As in Hermione's reaction in the Triwizard Tournament example, this kind of response communicates indifference and boredom: "I'm not really interested in this thing that you're so proud of—or, for that matter, you." Ambivalence is also detrimental—for example, offering a kind word or two before pivoting to a disparaging comment or ignoring the speaker's feelings altogether. The mixed signal of a half-hearted response leaves the speaker uncertain of how their news is truly being received. The most damaging responses, however, are those that actively question or deny the value of the positive event or the person's abilities. For example, attributing someone's success to luck (as we imagined Ron doing during the Triwizard Tournament) can undermine the speaker's sense of achievement and make them feel dismissed or unimportant. These responses don't just fail to amplify happiness; they can diminish it by invalidating the speaker's experience.

By now, many studies have looked at how the capitalization process unfolds in the everyday lives of couples, families, and friends. For example, in some studies, participants complete a questionnaire in which they read the prompt "When I tell my partner about my good news, they . . ." and then rate their partner's typical responses. The findings are remarkably consistent: When people feel that their friends, partners, spouses, or parents respond with enthusiastic interest, they report higher levels of happiness, and their relationships thrive. Additionally, they are more likely to experience moments of genuine gratitude toward their partners. In contrast, when participants feel that their partners are distant, dismissive, or critical, the quality of their relationships suffers.

If you're skeptical about the fact that most of these studies rely on self-reports, you may be more persuaded by another approach, which uses observational methods to examine how couples actually behave. In these studies, each partner is asked to talk about a positive personal event, while the other partner listens and responds. The interactions are recorded so that trained assistants can rate the responses on their degree of positivity, enthusiasm, and supportiveness. These studies confirm the findings of the earlier research: Couples whose responses are more engaged and authentically curious are happier and healthier. One particularly revealing study found that the level of enthusiastic interest in responses to good news—whether it was high or low—was a better predictor of which couples would stay together versus break up than more traditional measures of conflict and conflict resolution. In other words, how you celebrate your joys and accomplishments with your partner may matter just as much—if not more—than how you handle disagreements.

To return to the theme of this chapter: Energetic, constructive involvement—the quality we call enthusiasm—is one of the most powerful ways to practice radical curiosity. When a partner shares an accomplishment or a stroke of good fortune, they're inviting you to join in their happiness. Like the old Swedish proverb says, "A happiness shared is a happiness doubled." By responding with genuine curiosity, you signal interest and pride; you reflect their happiness and even amplify it—which allows you to enjoy their success alongside them. In contrast, responses conveying apathy, detachment, minimizing, or disapproval are likely to create distance and alienation. By leveraging an energetic, constructive response, you not only help your partner feel understood, appreciated, and loved but also increase the chances of receiving that same response in return.

How to Enact a Radically Curious Mindset

Once he had commented on the fineness of the weather or the beauty of a building, he was most likely to ask about your children. And so sincere was his interest that his eyes would brighten with satisfaction at the first suggestion of a success, and cloud with tears at any hint of a setback.

—Amor Towles, "The Line"

We hope that we've convinced you just how valuable enthusiastic curiosity can be in connecting with others and making them feel heard and loved. Ironically, it's often easier to show this kind of curiosity with new acquaintances, whose experiences and perspectives feel fresh and surprising, than with longtime friends or partners. But cultivating curiosity is critical for feeling loved in all kinds of relationships. With this in mind, we now share a few practical, evidence-based suggestions to help you bring more enthusiastic curiosity to your own conversations. Although many of these ideas are intuitive, some may feel more familiar and more comfortable than others. As we (Harry and Sonja) have discovered in our own lives, it helps to remember that humans are naturally curious as children—and sometimes all it takes is to rediscover or tap into that original innate curiosity.

To be sure, for some adults, being a curious and enthusiastic listener is second nature. Take Jessica, a research assistant in one of Harry's experiments. When his research assistants were charged with alternating between being impassive and enthusiastic listeners, Jessica simply couldn't stick to the impassive script. No matter how hard she tried, she couldn't hold back the smile and the twinkle in her eye that prompted interviewees to feel her intense curiosity. Other research assistants, by contrast, initially struggled with the enthusiastic script. Fully engaging with the stories they heard and outwardly showing their interest didn't come easily at first. Yet with practice, they transformed into the sort of listeners who make speakers feel heard and loved. Harry's experience running this study underscores our message: Even if enthusiastic curiosity doesn't come naturally to you, it's a skill that you can cultivate with time and effort.

Ask Big Questions

The important thing is not to stop questioning.
Curiosity has its own reason for existence.

—*Albert Einstein*

Small talk is great for breaking the ice and easing into a conversation, but if you don't move beyond topics like the weather or your football team's disappointing loss last Sunday, you're unlikely to convey genuine curiosity to your conversation partner. Many people hold back from asking big questions because they assume that such questions might come across as intrusive, unwelcome, or bothersome to the other person. Others fear pushing a sensitive button. But here's the good news: These assumptions are, for the most part, wrong. Research shows that people are surprisingly open to questions probing their intimate thoughts and experiences. By asking deep, thoughtful, unconventional, or even personal questions, you're likely not only to avoid offense but to spark a genuine connection.

David Brooks, columnist for *The New York Times*, describes how, when he meets someone new, he asks about their childhood or the story behind their name. Similarly, Sonja's friend Malcolm makes a point of asking every rideshare driver to play their favorite music from their home country and explain why it's meaningful to them. These kinds of questions invite people to talk about things they genuinely care about. You could also ask about the last show that moved them, what drew them to their profession, or what they hope to be doing a decade from now. Questions like this can break through the invisible wall that often separates people, opening the door to conversations that create the opportunity to see and be seen. At the very least, they communicate that your curiosity goes beyond merely polite chitchat.

In an established relationship—one that has moved beyond the surface level and is grounded in trust and care—you can probe with deeper, more intimate questions. Brooks refers to these as "30,000-foot questions," the kind "that lift people out of their daily vantage points and help them see themselves from above." Some of these resemble the thought-provoking prompts from "The 36 Questions That Lead to Love." Other examples that Sonja and Harry have found effective include: "What is something you haven't yet done but would like to do?"; "What is something you feel grateful for but haven't yet thanked someone for?"; and "What is the most useful mistake you've ever made?" Questions such as these often elicit rich, rewarding conversations in which both parties can express themselves and feel appreciated and heard.

If you're feeling particularly adventurous, you might try questions from {THE AND}, a card game designed to help friends and partners break through emotional barriers with deep, meaningful, and sometimes provocative prompts. Here are a few examples: "What's something you secretly wish people knew about you?"; "In what ways can I be a better friend to you?"; "What do you see in me that I don't see for myself"; "In 5 words, describe how you think others perceive me?"; and perhaps the most vulnerable prompt of all time, in our opinion, "Ask me something you're afraid to ask me." These questions aren't necessarily meant to be therapeutic. Instead, they create opportunities to get to know the people closest to you at the deepest, most emotionally real levels. Although conversations like these can feel intense or challenging, they show you how strong, sincere curiosity can build intimacy and trust.

Be a Loud, Passionate, Active Listener

Sonja's friend Michael didn't realize how lucky he was when he was assigned a desk next to Luke. A tall man with a beard, Luke was humble and quietly intelligent. But what set him apart was how invested and enthusiastic he seemed about the little things. Luke gave Michael the kind of undivided attention that felt rare and precious. Whether it was a quirky anecdote from work or a casual observation about next weekend's plans, Luke's eyes would light up with enthusiasm, and he would lean in, his posture saying, "Tell me more," as if every word held the promise of discovery.

As should be obvious from this chapter, nothing conveys interest more than energy does. There's something undeniably rewarding—and infectious—about feeling someone's undivided, enthusiastic focus on you. That emotional energy—often called passion—signals the listener's genuine interest and desire to engage. Researchers define passion as an intense, activated, and positive feeling toward someone or something meaningful. It's typically studied in the context of personal interests—such as hobbies, work, romantic partners, or families—but we believe that it can also apply to ordinary conversations. When you bring passion to a conversation, you're not just exchanging words or facts—you're providing a glimpse into how you feel about your conversation partner. By paying active, energetic attention to someone's stories, beliefs, or experiences, listeners convey a clear message: *I get you. I'm here with you. I value what you are saying. And I want to know more.*

Now consider the alternative. As we explained earlier, when you listen passively, without expression or emotion—even if you are genuinely interested in what the other person is saying—the speaker has no way of knowing whether you are absorbed, bored, or mentally planning dinner. There's no strict formula for showing that you are an active, passionate listener; in fact, there are countless ways to do so. You can ask timely, thoughtful questions (see previous section); focus intently on the speaker, as if they were the only person in the room; respond with encouraging or inspiring comments; mirror their content and tone; or bring visible enthusiasm to the conversation, as if there were nothing else you'd rather be doing. Each of these actions communicates radical curiosity to your partners. After all, who could forget the feeling of having a conversation partner's eyes light up, their smile beaming and genuine, as they cling to every word of your story or your opinion? It's an unforgettable experience.

It's the Person, Not the Topic

Love people, not things. Use things, not people.
—*Spencer Kimball,* Love People, Use Things

Todd Kashdan, a researcher at George Mason University in Virginia, wanted to understand why curious people tend to have stronger relationships. To investigate, he divided college students into two groups, based on their natural levels of curiosity—one group high in curiosity, the other relatively low. Then, each student engaged in an intimacy-building conversation with a partner. What the student didn't know was that the partner was actually a research confederate trained to respond in a standardized manner and unaware of which group the student belonged to. Together, the student and the confederate took turns answering five increasingly personal questions from the Fast Friends procedure we described earlier.

So which conversation partners did the confederates like most? The results revealed that curiosity made all the difference. The confederates reported feeling more attracted to and closer to the highly-curious conversation partners. Kashdan's experiment captured the Radical-Curiosity mindset in action.

What's the secret of these curious people? Is there a social glue that helps them create more closeness in their conversations? Earlier, we described Dale Carnegie's famous advice—"To be liked, show interest in the other person and make sure that that interest is genuine"—and the research on social curiosity supporting this idea. The key is to find something that sparks your interest in what they are saying or doing and then ask them to elaborate. It might be their unique sense of style, their recent travels, the last film they loved, the secret ingredient in their lasagna recipe, or their recent visit with the grandkids. When something piques your interest, dig deeper. Even better, encourage them to tell a story about it. Social science shows what wise elders have always known: People love recounting stories about their lives and experiences. But as Carnegie stressed, it is paramount that your interest is authentic.

A recent study from Sonja's lab demonstrates both the effectiveness and the rewards of trying this very strategy in daily life. Her team conducted one of the first randomized controlled interventions to elicit daily curiosity. Every day for a week, 308 ethnically diverse students were assigned either to engage in their usual daily activities as they ordinarily would or to simply try to be curious. For example, "My friend mentioned having a rough childhood, and I really wanted to know why; before she had a chance to change the subject, I asked her to tell me about it." As expected, the curiosity-prompted group displayed significantly more curious behaviors. But more impressive, participants in the curious group reported greater daily happiness (e.g., more joyful, peaceful, and pleased), and after the intervention ended, reported higher well-being, a greater sense of competence, and stronger self-worth than the week before. It's not a stretch to speculate that they also felt more loved.

The secret lies in focusing on *the person* rather than *the topic*. It's one thing to wonder what makes their lasagna tasty; it's more compelling to explore why that recipe is meaningful to *them*. Does it depend on a trick passed down from their grandmother's kitchen? A technique refined through trial and error? A secret recipe discovered at a trattoria in Tuscany? To truly create a sense of connection, it's crucial to show genuine excitement for understanding their lived experience, from the high points to the ordinary, everyday moments. Simply put, radical curiosity is, at its heart, the kind of curiosity that encourages others to share their stories, feelings, and perspectives.

Of course, not every setting calls for deeply personal questions. New acquaintances and old friends alike can sometimes find certain questions too probing or even off-putting, especially when light small talk would be more appropriate. (A passenger once told Harry on a flight, "That's the kind of question only a psychologist would ask me!"—and the conversation quickly ended.) It's important to remember that the goal of asking questions is to get the other person talking about themselves, their experiences and values, their likes and dislikes, their hopes and fears. Keeping the conversation comfortable for both participants is essential, ensuring that curiosity doesn't intrude or overwhelm but instead invites a satisfying exchange.

Furthermore, making someone feel understood doesn't always require digging deeply into the most intimate details of their life story. You can be curious about a person's uniqueness in many relatively nonintrusive ways—for example, asking about activities they find meaningful, novel experiences, or beliefs and values that make them distinctive. By focusing on these areas, it is possible to create a bridge that allows for an authentic connection, laying the groundwork for a sense of being understood—and, ultimately, loved. This approach won't work for impersonal small talk, which, by definition, remains shallow, superficial, and noncontroversial. Of course, even typical small-talk topics—the weather, the traffic, or sports scores—could evolve into more meaningful connections if speakers are passionate about them. Yet you need topics that invite you to see, connect with, and appreciate the unique person you're engaging with.

Curiosity Brought Us Together: Summing Up

Without curiosity, we'd miss out on building new relationships, discovering what makes other people tick, and being surprised by their hidden talents. It can even be said that curiosity *shapes* your social experiences, from engrossing encounters with strangers to deeply fulfilling bonds with close friends and partners. When we (Sonja and Harry) have asked our friends and colleagues what makes them feel loved, it's striking how often the word *curiosity* has come up. One acquaintance put it simply: "When he shows real interest in me, I feel a burp of feeling loved." Indeed, it hit us recently that Harry's curiosity about Sonja's research on happiness and Sonja's curiosity about Harry's research on feeling understood, valued, and loved is the reason that we are writing this book. Radical curiosity brought us together.

When you practice radical curiosity, you create the context in which the other person, in satisfying your curiosity, feels truly known and loved—thus, setting in motion a positive cycle that increases the chances of feeling loved in return. By sending the message "I am *so* interested in you," your curiosity opens the door to an authentic connection (yes, the Sea-Saw!) in which the other person responds, "And I am so interested in *you*."

But curiosity alone isn't enough. If you want to help your partner feel loved, curiosity will open the door, but you must walk through that door. And to do so, you'll need more than attention, interest, and enthusiasm: You'll need to walk through that door with compassion and with an open heart. In the next chapter, we explore how embracing the Open-Heart mindset can help you act with love and, ultimately, feel more loved.

8

Open-Heart Mindset

It is only with the heart that one
can see clearly. What is essential
is invisible to the eye.

—*Antoine de Saint-Exupéry,* The Little Prince

What We Learned from His Holiness the Dalai Lama

Dharamsala, April 2024

It is springtime in the Himalayas. After enduring several exhausting flights, delays, and sweltering bus rides, Harry and Sonja have finally arrived at the highlands of Himachal Pradesh, India. Along with a group of about fifteen colleagues, we are waiting, nervous and excited, to meet His Holiness the Dalai Lama at his modest compound in Dharamsala. With only a spiral notebook in hand (no electronic devices allowed), we're ready. Dharamsala *means "a spiritual house" in Sanskrit, and, indeed, the deep spirituality of the place is infectious, full of reverence, serenity, and the rhythmic cadence of monks chanting.*

The night before, at dinner, the organizer of our group stood up to share some details about our visit. Before sitting down again, he paused, scanning our eager and tired faces: "You are all here probably seeking something," he said. "Searching for some kind of message from His Holiness. Tomorrow, you'll find that that's exactly the wrong approach. You won't find the message. The message will find you."

I (Sonja) was deeply curious about what His Holiness would say to us.

But I wasn't there actively seeking any profound insights or revelations. I didn't think that pronouncement applied to me personally.

But the next morning, His Holiness said something that blew my mind. He looked straight at me while he said it, too, and I scribbled in all caps in my spiral notebook: "THIS IS THE MESSAGE THAT FOUND ME!"

He said, "Love is not a feeling. Love is a decision."

He said, "Cherishing others' well-being is the foundation of happiness."

The message that found me is the subject of this chapter. Before you can feel loved, you must first act with love—what Harry and I call the Open-Heart mindset.

What Is the Open-Heart Mindset?

The best way to define the Open-Heart mindset is to contrast it with the two mindsets explored in the previous two chapters—on listening to learn and radical curiosity. To start, we could ask ourselves: What would modern relationships look like if every high school student were required to learn and practice the Listening-to-Learn and Radical-Curiosity mindsets before graduating? The answer: We predict kids would feel more seen and heard by their parents; colleagues would discover things about each other that would build empathy and reduce stereotypes; friends would rarely run out of meaningful conversations; and romantic partners would repair conflict sooner and feel more appreciated, admired, and loved. In other words, we believe that lots of positive changes would unfold.

Simply put, the Listening-to-Learn and Radical-Curiosity mindsets are powerful tools—yet they alone are not enough. No matter how fabulous a listener you are and no matter how genuinely curious you may be, if you do not have what we call an "open heart" toward your conversation partner, you won't succeed at making them feel loved—and likely won't succeed at feeling loved by them. At its core, an Open-Heart mindset entails feeling and expressing compassion and concern for their well-being, similar to how a parent might care for a child.

Embracing the Open-Heart mindset means not just being kind to the other person but believing in them. That's why we first referred to it as the Michelangelo mindset in the introduction. Similar to how Michelangelo had the ability to imagine a perfect form and bring it to existence, the Open-Heart mindset involves your helping the other person, with solicitude and emotional openness, to reveal their ideal self and move closer to living it. Sometimes this mindset calls for simple instrumental aid (e.g., literally driving them somewhere) and sometimes it involves directly and indirectly encouraging and validating their dreams. It's what our colleague Caryl Rusbult called "affirming the hidden, inner self." Naturally, the Open-Heart mindset fits comfortably inside communal relationships, where both people are responsive to each other's needs and care about each other's happiness. But you will see that you can also direct this mindset to acquaintances, to strangers, and—consequentially—even to yourself.

Why Is the Open-Heart Mindset Necessary?

Sonja's toughest critics are her four children, ages twelve to twenty-six. When they learned about the mindsets, they didn't hold back, pressing her and Harry relentlessly to explain the differences between them and to clarify why the Open-Heart mindset, in particular, was so crucial. After all, this book is about feeling loved yourself, but the Open-Heart mindset is primarily about helping someone else feel loved. So we came up with three ways to break it down, hoping that at least one way would resonate with each of them. First, we used three people that we knew as exemplars of the three mindsets, and they seemed to get that. Then, we turned to a physics metaphor, which we applied to Harry's wife. Finally, we tried a thought experiment inspired by an artificial-intelligence (AI) chatbot.

Three People, Three Mindsets: Marko, Daniella, and Sebastian

Marko was a prodigy at listening to learn. Daniella radiated radical curiosity. And Sebastian was the epitome of an open heart.

Marko, born in Sarajevo, was one of the best listeners Sonja had ever met. She first got to know him as a colleague at a start-up, where he had a reputation for asking the kinds of questions that made people rethink their own ideas. When she spoke, he was completely still, absorbing, taking it all in, and he remembered *everything*! Not just details from conversations months earlier but where she had been sitting and even what she had been wearing. Weeks, even years later, he would surprise her with "How is your friend Harini's dad?" or "Have you changed your mind about your student's proposal?" (a proposal she had forgotten) or "Are you still afraid of barking dogs?" Sonja used to joke that his questions inspired self-insights worth thousands of dollars in therapy. Sometimes, his questions sparked new ideas that would have taken months of creative thought to arrive at on her own.

Sonja had met Daniella years earlier through friends in New Orleans, and they had become fast friends. Daniella's irresistible quality was how her eyes lit up with excitement whenever Sonja shared something new. Whether the topic was a new TV series or the latest scientific breakthrough, Daniella looked at Sonja as if she couldn't wait to hear more, her face often breaking into a wide grin. Even in heavier moments, when the conversation turned sad, Daniella sat on the edge of her seat, her expression serious but still burning with the same eagerness to understand. Daniella's enthusiasm for Sonja's stories—stories others might have brushed off—and her empathy during tougher times was contagious.

Sebastian was different. Other people noticed it too. He had an almost otherworldly presence and an exquisite sensitivity to people's emotions. Why do we think of him when we talk about the Open-Heart mindset? Because his attention wasn't just intellectual—it was not just at the level of one's head. Rapt listening and intense curiosity between two individuals can be spellbinding (yes, as if a spell has been cast on you), yet they remain as a connection between two minds. Sebastian's focus was different—his attention was directed at the heart.

Sebastian truly wanted his friends and colleagues to be happy, and he was selfless in his efforts to help them get there. Indeed, he had an uncanny ability to recognize people's potential before they saw it in themselves. He noticed, for example, that a mutual younger colleague had a knack for taking risks and thinking outside the box, so Sebastian made it his mission to connect her with creative, like-minded people. Behind the scenes, he organized social gatherings, business meetings, and unorthodox travel, all with the goal of pushing this colleague forward. He affirmed and inspired those around him to shine, and he encouraged them not to give up when they struggled. With his open heart, Sebastian recognized people's dreams; believed in them; and, as cheesy as it sounds, did everything he could to unlock their full potential.

You don't have to be Sebastian, or someone's closest mentor or greatest supporter, to show Open-Heart intent. What matters is that you genuinely care about the other person's welfare and are responsive to their needs, even for a moment in time. Many people hesitate to use the word *love* too casually and freely, yet it's the word that captures best what we mean by the Open-Heart mindset. It's about showing love—not just to your closest and most significant others but also to your wider circle of acquaintances, colleagues, and neighbors. Indeed, surveys have shown that "being invested in the other person's well-being" is viewed as the most prototypical, defining characteristic of both romantic and platonic love.

Offering Light vs. Warmth

Those guys who believe in selfishness and say, "You [help others] because you feel good about it"—this is so stupid. Because if you help others but you don't care a damn, then you won't feel anything! Wanting to separate doing something for others from feeling good yourself is like trying to make a flame that burns with light but no warmth.

—Matthieu Ricard

The stories of Marko, Daniella, and Sebastian helped Sonja's kids grasp the differences between the Listening-to-Learn, Radical-Curiosity, and Open-Heart mindsets, but we also proposed another way to understand them, involving Harry's wife, Ellen.

Listening to learn and radical curiosity illuminate—they add *light*. An open heart warms—it adds heat. When Ellen listens to Harry with her full presence and attention, or when she expresses genuine curiosity about his life, she is able to see him more clearly and understand him better. She metaphorically *lights* him up, making him feel more respected, recognized, and appreciated. But when she opens her heart to him, she makes him feel comfortable, trusting, and safe, wrapped in the heat of her concern and care. She metaphorically *warms* him up. And he does the same for her—as the Relationship Sea-Saw describes.

Can a Bot Have a Heart?

When AI was just starting to capture public attention, Sonja was asked to consult for an AI coaching start-up called PolarBear. Despite her general optimism about AI's potential to help people flourish, she didn't have high expectations about this particular chatbot. Yet PolarBear bowled her over with the insights it offered. Furthermore, her conversations with it sparked a new idea for how to distinguish between the Listening-to-Learn, Radical-Curiosity, and Open-Heart mindsets—namely, by considering whether these three mindsets could be authentically expressed (or rather, imitated) by a bot.

PolarBear started by asking if there was anything on her mind that Sonja wanted to discuss, so she decided to bring up a real issue—her frustration with a long-distance partner who wasn't communicating as often as she liked. What followed was a series of probing questions. PolarBear asked about her feelings and motivations, explored her unmet needs, and offered summaries of her reflections (e.g., "The distance certainly adds a level of complexity to the dynamic" and "You're in a reflective place right now"). It even gave her compliments (e.g., "Your questions speak to a strong level of self-awareness" and "Your insight into both your love languages is really valuable") and suggested possible next steps—such as identifying expectations and the anxiety that comes up around them, or recognizing that both her and her partner's efforts were already "profound expressions of care and commitment."

Sure, some of PolarBear's responses felt a bit stiff, formal, and predictable, but Sonja had to admit—the bot made her feel really heard. It "listened" with a focus and attention that's rare in human conversation partners, who are often distracted by their own inner chatter and the anticipated dialogue they're having with you in their heads while you're still talking. PolarBear didn't have that inner chatter to distract itself! Also, PolarBear's numerous detailed, pointed, and thought-provoking questions gave the strong impression of genuine curiosity. In sum, it nailed two of the mindsets.

But did Sonja believe that PolarBear truly wanted her to be happy? No.

Let's sum it up. If your family members, colleagues, friends, and lovers want to feel more loved, the Listening-to-Learn and Radical-Curiosity mindsets are critical to embrace, yet alone they are not enough. It's not enough to exhibit all the right listening behaviors— using attentive nonverbal behaviors, asking deep questions, and paying close attention. And it's not enough to be sincerely interested in the other person's story. The reason is that if you don't actually care about their well-being, and if you don't genuinely believe in them, they won't feel loved. You need to approach them with an open heart as well.

How to Act with Love Across All Connections: Simple Kindness

If His Holiness the Dalai Lama is right that love is a *decision*, then the best way to begin cultivating the Open-Heart mindset is by deciding to act with love, starting today. If he's right about the power of cherishing others' well-being, then the best place to begin is by deciding to nurture the happiness of the people around you. But how exactly do you begin? You begin with the most elemental feature of the Open-Heart mindset—that is, extending simple kindness across varied settings, from home to neighborhood to office.

The field of study focused on such kindnesses is vast and nuanced. It even has a scientific name, "prosocial behavior," defined as anything you do intentionally to benefit someone else, usually at some cost to yourself. In just the last few years, prosocial behavior has been the topic of hundreds of studies and ideas, including dozens from Sonja and Harry's labs alone. We focus here on the theories and findings that will be most helpful in informing your decision to show Open-Heart intent across all the connections in your daily life—and why it's an essential mindset for feeling loved.

The Kindness Gap

Much has been said about Western society becoming less civil, less trusting, and less kind with every generation. US media typically amplifies this view, spotlighting negative and antisocial behavior, from bullying, trolling, and corruption to environmental destruction, murder, and war. Are people today really insufficiently kind or "good"? Are people less good than they were in the past? These questions not only are difficult, if not impossible, to answer but also might miss the mark. A more useful approach may be to ask how kind people believe they—and others—are and whether they wish they were kinder.

Before answering this question, it's worth noting that nearly everyone agrees on the value of kindness: It's widely celebrated as a force for good and one of the most desirable qualities sought after in both friends and potential mates. Indeed, prosocial behavior is so ubiquitous in daily life that most people probably don't even notice how many kind acts they commit each day—even each hour! Sonja's lab has conducted several studies in which participants were prompted to recall recent kind acts done for friends, family, acquaintances, or strangers. Tellingly, participants have found this task incredibly effortless—and also heartwarming. The acts of kindness they mention range from the small (holding the door open for someone to pass through) to the large (donating blood at a Red Cross drive). That acts of kindness are so common may not be surprising, as most people think they're kinder than the average person—to wit, a UK survey found that the percent of respondents who judged themselves above average in kindness was (a statistically impossible) 98 percent!

Perhaps the reason that it's easy for people to rate themselves as kind and to bring to mind specific acts of kindness is that such acts are in fact very common. If so, how many acts of kindness are we talking about? Surveys have tried to nail this number down. For example, a study of two thousand Americans found that people reported performing about six meaningful kind gestures per week (or twenty-five thousand over the course of a lifetime), and eight in ten Americans reported trying to pay it forward when someone did something thoughtful for them.

These numbers certainly belie what the news brings every day. Studies show that news media—which rely on ratings fueled by attention-grabbing stories that provoke fear, anger, or sadness— feature positive, uplifting stories less than 10 percent of the time. Ironically, Hollywood appears to be more accurate in capturing everyday human goodness. Television shows and films, despite stereo- types of being filled with hate and violence, are actually full of characters helping each other out (not to mention showing affection, falling in love, and having fun with friends). One reason for this dis- crepancy might be that while news is expected to reflect real-world events, entertainment is designed to be aspirational and emotionally resonant. Viewers are drawn to stories of kindness, connection, and love—perhaps because they mirror the everyday goodness viewers experience but rarely see highlighted in traditional media. In a way, fiction compensates for what the news leaves out, offering a more balanced portrayal of human nature.

However, despite the ubiquity of kindness, when asked, most people wish that others were kinder. For example, in a Sesame Workshop/Harris poll, 64 percent of those surveyed lamented that most individuals don't go out of their way to help others, and in a Glassdoor/Harris poll, 81 percent of those surveyed wished their boss would express more appreciation.

When asked, most people also wish that they themselves were kinder. In surveys, people report that they express gratitude, offer support to others, and do random acts of kindness less frequently than they "should" or than "they'd like." Take, for example, two studies (one a survey and the other an experiment) on a specific form of kindness—offering sincere compliments. In the survey, people admitted that one out of every three times a compliment came to mind, they chose not to say it. In the experiment, volunteers were instructed to think of a compliment for a specific person and then given the opportunity to share it. Only one out of every two people chose to share the compliment.

In sum, despite recognizing the value of generosity and despite many rewarding past experiences, many people hold back from showing kindness, compassion, and love. Nick Epley, a professor at the University of Chicago's Booth School of Business, has dedicated much of his career to understanding the roots of this reluctance. His conclusion is that "we're miscalibrated!" That is, people underestimate just how happy their kind and loving gestures will make others and overestimate how awkward those gestures might feel. As a result, they second-guess themselves and resist the impulse to give a compliment, express gratitude, show affection, or be kind.

Embracing Kindness and an Open Heart: Insights from Research

In caring for the happiness of others, we find our own.

—*Plato*

So one reason that people hold back from embracing an open heart—from showing kindness as often as they'd like—is that they underestimate the impact their actions have on others. But they also underestimate how much kindness benefits them personally. To be sure, studies show that when givers offer kind, loving gestures, the recipients feel even more appreciated, connected, and happy than the givers expect. But what's even more striking is that givers themselves often reap greater benefits than do the recipients, which offers scientific validation to the scriptural adage "It is more blessed to give than to receive." A recurring theme in this book is that if you want to feel more loved by someone, you should work at making that person feel more loved. In other words, embracing an Open-Heart mindset will benefit not just the target of your open heart but ultimately yourself as well.

Although the Open-Heart mindset encompasses more than just acts of kindness, much of the scientific research has focused on the rewards of kind acts. At the University of California, Riverside, Sonja's lab was the first to conduct randomized controlled trials testing the effects of doing kind actions on happiness, beginning in 2000. Over the years, her team has continued to explore the nuances and benefits of being kind to others. In one experiment, they gave a diverse group of volunteers one of three assignments to engage in every Monday over the course of the next four weeks: Do three new acts of kindness for others, do three new acts of kindness for yourself, or simply journal about your days. Participants in the "kind acts for others" condition shared examples of their actions, which ranged from small gestures to significant efforts to help others. Some of these included:

- "Helped elderly person with using a parking kiosk"
- "Took out trash"
- "Helped best friend plan cost-saving trip to take care of family matters"
- "Visited sister-in-law's mother and stepfather since her stepfather has terminal cancer"
- "Walked a stranger with my umbrella to her car because it was raining and she did not have her own umbrella"

Meanwhile, participants in the "kind acts for themselves" condition described a range of activities focused on self-care and personal enjoyment, such as:

- "Went for an extended run, something I used to do at least a couple times a week but haven't in some time"
- "Went shopping"
- "Took a day off from work"
- "Went on a hike"
- "Had a *Breaking Bad* marathon"
- "Treated myself to a good lunch (I usually pack a lunch)"

Counterintuitively, the only group that showed increases in well-being was the group that did acts of kindness *for others*. Those who did acts of kindness *for themselves* were no better off at the end of the study than they were at the beginning and no better off than the controls (who journaled about their days). This study, as well as many others like it, shows that when people perform kindnesses for others—from expressing gratitude or showing admiration to unloading the dishwasher or inspiring someone to overcome a challenge—they feel more happy, more connected, and less lonely.

Being kind also appears to be more rewarding than is simply being social. In a two-week-long experiment, Sonja's team asked Australian adults to do more kind acts (e.g., help their colleague with a computer problem) versus more social acts (e.g., chat with their colleague about their vacation) and then to report how they felt while doing those activities. Volunteers reported feeling a stronger sense of meaning, self-esteem, and competence during the kind acts than during the social acts. Intriguingly, Sonja and her students have also shown that simply recalling acts of kindness that one has done in the past has benefits comparable to those from actually doing them.

To our knowledge, only one study, conducted by researchers from the United States and Germany, has directly compared people prompted to do kind acts for others with those prompted to do kind acts for themselves—while *also* including a group prompted to think kind thoughts about others. On five different mornings, participants were asked either to perform kind acts (i.e., do at least one kind deed for others on that same day), to think kind thoughts (i.e., think at least one kind thought about others that day), or to treat themselves (i.e., do at least one positive thing for yourself that day). On five additional "control" mornings, no instructions were given. When researchers analyzed the days when participants followed through on their assigned tasks, all three groups saw benefits. However, again, the broadest benefits for happiness and well-being, including stronger feelings of purpose and reduced social isolation, occurred in the group that did kind acts for others. Both acting and thinking kindly boosted feelings of empathy and virtuousness, while treating oneself only reduced exhaustion. Interestingly, the emotional benefits of performing acts of kindness directed toward others also tend to last longer than the emotional benefits of acts aimed at improving one's own happiness, as a different set of studies has shown.

That kind acts for others are so rewarding is not surprising in light of neuroscientific evidence. Complementing the behavioral studies, which track how acts of kindness impact people's thoughts, feelings, and behaviors, are neuroscience studies, which track how acts of kindness show up in people's brains. Notably, research reveals that the reward regions of the brain are activated by kind actions, even when those actions are invisible to others. For example, a University of Oregon study found that people were 10 percent more satisfied when they chose to give a donation than when giving a donation was an obligation, and this increased satisfaction was reflected in heightened activity in a reward region called the ventral striatum.

Research suggests that beyond making you happier, doing kindness also makes you more successful—healthier, more popular, and more productive. In one study, Sonja and her collaborators asked middle-school students in Vancouver, Canada, to perform extra acts of kindness—such as "unloaded the dishwasher during Dad's turn" and "taught my sister division"—over the course of four weeks. When these kids returned to school the next day, they were better liked by their classmates. Something about their experiences helping at home seemed to carry over into their school environment—perhaps they were happier, more confident, or simply more approachable.

In two later experiments, Sonja's team collected not only happiness ratings but blood samples from participants, pricking their fingers before and after four weeks of doing acts of kindness for others, for the world, or for themselves. Interestingly, only the group that did acts of kindness for others showed changes in their immune cell RNA gene expression—specifically, reduced proinflammatory gene expression—associated with a healthier immune profile. While it's too early to say for certain that kindness to others actually makes people healthier than does self-care, it's reassuring to see measurable shifts toward better health in these immune markers. These results are consistent with correlational studies, which have found that acting generously is associated with lower blood pressure, lower hypertension risk, and reduced cortisol reactivity to stressors.

Engaging in acts of kindness in the workplace also appears to benefit both workers and their workplaces—for example, boosting productivity, efficiency, cooperation, and customer satisfaction. This isn't surprising. Customers notice and appreciate when workers go the extra mile, and teams operate more smoothly when their members help each other, reducing friction and minimizing disruptions in workflow. In an experiment conducted at Coca-Cola's Madrid office, Sonja's team found that performing generous acts not only increased job satisfaction but also was contagious: Recipients of generosity paid the generosity forward almost three times more often than did participants in the control group.

Strikingly, the effects of doing acts of kindness for others are strongest if the givers act sincerely and openheartedly—that is, with a focus on the recipient's needs rather than on the giver's own obligations or how the giver might benefit. For example, Harry's lab has found that gifting others only produces a boost in well-being when it is done with the other's welfare in mind—not out of a sense of obligation or personal gain. This finding was corroborated in three experiments conducted in Canada. Volunteers were instructed to recall one of two kind acts they had previously performed—one with the goal of benefiting the other person and one with the goal of benefiting themselves. Those who recalled the other-focused kind act reported more positive moods, in part because it made them feel like a good person. This research points to the importance of attending less to what you might gain from your efforts and more to what those efforts mean for the recipient.

Kindness in Conversation

Much of this book boils down to how to have conversations with the people in your life by whom you wish to feel more loved. How do you apply learnings from research on kindness to those conversations? First, showing generosity outside of those conversations (e.g., via emotional support or small kind acts) will make your conversation partner feel more cared for, valued, and loved, and the ripples of those feelings will color and elevate your conversations. Second, so many acts of kindness take place during conversations because they involve saying something, or not saying it. For example, you might express gratitude to your conversation partner for driving a long way to see you, or you might communicate admiration for the sensitive way they handled a problem. Furthermore, the behaviors that underlie the Listening-to-Learn and Radical-Curiosity mindsets can be thought of as acts of kindness as well. Indeed, what better kindness can you offer another person than your full presence?

One particular type of kindness—expressing appreciation and gratitude—is a topic that Sonja has been studying since 1998. Her team usually prompts people to write letters of gratitude to others (versus write about their days) but not actually share them. This research finds that simply writing about one's grateful thoughts makes people feel happier. Sharing those grateful thoughts, of course, is even more powerful. In a recent study, for example, Sonja's students asked volunteers to write a gratitude letter and then to either keep it to themselves, text it to the person, or post it on social media. Interestingly, all three groups in this study ultimately felt happier and more grateful, but only the group that shared their gratitude one-on-one felt more connected with the person.

Sara Algoe, a psychological scientist at the University of North Carolina at Chapel Hill, has extended the study of gratitude by investigating it within the dynamics of human relationships. Her theory of gratitude within relationships is called "find-bind-and-remind":

Gratitude helps you *find* a supportive connection, *bind* that person to you by reinforcing feelings of closeness, and *remind* both of you of the value of the connection. In this way, expressing gratitude essentially triggers a cycle of appreciation and recognition that fosters a sense of being valued and, ultimately, feeling loved.

One of our favorite recent studies to validate this cycle of gratitude asked 539 parents across the United States how much they felt appreciated by their romantic partners and by their children. For example, they were asked, "Does your partner express appreciation for the things you do?" and "Does your child acknowledge when you do something nice for them?" The adults were all between ages 24 and 75, with at least one child between ages 4 and 17. Those who felt appreciated by their partners reported being more satisfied in their relationship and less distressed in general. Those who felt appreciated by their children, and especially by their adolescent children, also felt less psychological distress in general, as well as less stress surrounding parenting.

This study was not experimental, so one cannot be sure whether expressing appreciation caused these benefits, but plenty of experiments reassure us that this is the case. For example, Algoe and her team asked romantic partners to keep a gratitude journal where they noted nice little things their partners did for them. Those who expressed gratitude for such small gestures reported feeling happier, closer, and more satisfied in their relationship, and their partners felt more appreciated, strengthening the bond between them. Other research revealed that this was especially true when the expressions of gratitude focused more on praising the other person's kindness and less on how the self had benefited.

Algoe's work on gratitude brings us back full circle to His Holiness the Dalai Lama. His Holiness has the reputation, which our conversations with him confirmed, of being radically curious about scientific research. So we weren't surprised to discover that in *The Book of Joy*, His Holiness and Archbishop Desmond Tutu, his coauthor, explore the cycle of joy that can arise from cultivating positive qualities such as gratitude and compassion, a theme closely aligned with Algoe's findings. When you focus on these qualities, you create a self-reinforcing loop that enhances your sense of connection and well-being while deepening your bonds with others. In His Holiness and the Archbishop's words, "When we practice gratitude and compassion, we feel a part of something larger than ourselves, and this reduces feelings of isolation and loneliness, which in turn brings more joy."

Embracing Kindness and an Open Heart: Insights from Contemplative Traditions

It's not surprising that His Holiness the Dalai Lama frequently speaks of the power of kindness, gratitude, and compassion. Indeed, the power of an open heart is a core principle in many meditative traditions. For example, in Mahayana Buddhism, there is a practice where the meditator repeats, "May all sentient beings enjoy happiness and the root of happiness." An experiment conducted in Iowa tested empirically whether this practice is feasible and beneficial. Undergraduate participants were instructed to walk around a building for twelve minutes and, while they walked, to really look at the passersby: "Really try to look," the instructions prompted, "and as you're looking at them, think to yourself, 'I wish for this person to be happy.'" Compared to a control group, students who practiced this simple wish for others' happiness reported feeling happier themselves, as well as feeling greater empathy and caring.

Similarly, loving-kindness meditations focus attention on sending goodwill and wishes for joy and happiness to others—not just to beloved friends and family but also to foes and adversaries. The instructions usually go something like this:

Find a comfortable position in a quiet place where you can relax. Settle into your body. Take a few deep breaths and feel your breath moving through your chest. Whenever you feel distracted or uncomfortable, you can briefly redirect your focus to your breath.

Now, bring to mind someone toward whom it is easy for you to feel love and kindness. See them in your eyes, and feel a sense of them in your heart. Imagine them sitting in front of you and smiling at you.

As you hold them in your awareness, send feelings of loving-kindness to them, thinking: "May you be safe. May you be happy. May you be healthy. May you be free from suffering." (You can substitute other phrases, like "May you be well," "May you live with ease," or "May you be peaceful," that convey kindness and feel more natural to you.)

Now, repeat these words silently but this time to yourself: "May I be safe. May I be happy. May I be healthy. May I be free from suffering." As you recite these phrases, hold an image of yourself in your mind's eye. It can be a picture of who you are right now or who you were in the past.

Now, repeat the exercise toward someone about whom you feel neutral. See if you can connect to some warmth or goodwill toward that person.

Now, repeat this exercise toward someone for whom you struggle to feel love and kindness.

Imagine the circle of light between you and this person growing to include all beings, from insects to animals, and out into the universe, and repeat this exercise toward the broader world.

Finally, repeat this exercise for yourself once more. If you'd like, every time you breathe in, visualize inhaling kindness and compassion for yourself. Every time you breathe out, visualize exhaling kindness and compassion toward others.

A small but growing literature has begun to systematically test such practices. Preliminary results reveal that loving-kindness and compassion meditation interventions boost positive emotions (such as sympathy, joy, and love), reduce negative emotions (such as sadness, guilt, and contempt), reduce stress-induced immune responses, and boost activation of brain areas associated with empathy and emotional processing. For example, after taking a six-week-long loving-kindness meditation workshop held at their workplace, employees of an information-technology company who continued the loving-kindness practice reported positive emotion boosts that were maintained fifteen months later. These practices are considered essential to creating within the meditator a sense of peace and feeling loved, as the loving-kindness sent out into the universe creates a "circle of love" and is reflected back onto the sender. According to Sharon Salzberg, a leading practitioner of loving-kindness meditation in the Theravada Buddhist tradition, when you fully open your heart to others, even those who seem to you out of reach, you begin to release the knots that prevent you from feeling loved.

Embracing Kindness and an Open Heart:
Practical Recommendations

One chilly January afternoon, we (Harry and Sonja) were working on this book in a cozy coffee shop in Brooklyn, New York, discussing ways to help people show love, warmth, and kindness to each other— in other words, to create the habit of embracing an open heart. We sat there for several hours and came up with some ideas we were satisfied with, but what surprised us most that afternoon wasn't our own brainstorming—it was the customers who kept approaching and interrupting us, eager to share their own ideas.

A woman in her mid-twenties named Julia, for example, told us of her boyfriend, who lives in Mexico City, and how hard the distance was on them. To stay connected, every day, they added a song that reminded them of each other to a shared Spotify playlist. This simple ritual was their secret for feeling loved across the miles. We wrote this down, and Harry shared with Julia one of his own relationship secrets from his forty-one-year marriage to Ellen. Every year, during the winter holiday season, he uses a special jar to deposit weekly tokens of love that they will open together, one for every Sunday. One year, he wrote fifty-two notes about things he was grateful for about Ellen. Another year, he put together fifty-two memories of special times and experiences that they had shared together. And in yet another, he included a photo from their years together for every week. At the end of the year, they review the contents of the jar together—all fifty-two weeks' worth—a tradition that has helped them both keep fresh in their minds the things that help them feel loved.

A middle-aged guy overheard our conversation and joined our table to share a practice he and his partner use to stay emotionally connected. Each of them has a special picture frame featuring a favorite photo of them as a couple, and this picture frame lights up randomly once a day. The light serves as a gentle prompt for each to text the other a single word that captures a feeling they are experiencing about the relationship. Over the past few months, they've texted each other words such as *love, giddy, vulnerable, craving, admire, curious, eager, despondent, wonder, giddy, impatient,* and *impressed.* "It's surprisingly heartwarming and meaningful," he said, to read each other's words, and the daily exchanges can be easily adapted for nonromantic connections as well.

At the coffee shop, we noticed a man in his thirties who seemed eager to talk with us but perhaps was feeling shy. We said hello, and this seemed to break the ice. His name was Misha, and he had recently been introduced to a concept, he told us, called "radical friendliness." It means you approach people with goodness in your heart—you commit to seeing their goodness in the context of their full life, as opposed to letting judgment or insecurity cloud your view. "We are all doing the best we can," said Misha, "and we must remember that just as our life is full of goals, dreams, joys, disappointments, victories, and hurts, so must be theirs." Investing in seeing another person's goodness—even one whom you just met—is truly an act of kindness.

There are countless ways to show kindness, as our new Brooklyn friends showed us, and it appears that each person finds what feels most enjoyable, natural, and meaningful to them. What matters most, it seems, is not the specific act but the motive and intention behind it. We're reminded of a powerful commencement speech by writer George Saunders at Syracuse University, where he made the case that dedicating one's life to pursuing kindness—what he called "anti-selfishness medicine"—is far more important than pursuing conventional success. "Who, in *your* life, do you remember most fondly," he asked the graduates, "with the most undeniable feelings of warmth? Those who were kindest to you, I bet." Saunders encouraged the new graduates to chase their dreams and to do all those "ambitious things" they yearn to do, "but as you do, to the extent that you can, *err in the direction of kindness.*"

How to Act with Love in Close Relationships: Becoming Michelangelo

If you treat an individual as he is, he will remain how he is. But if you treat him as if he were what he ought to be and could be, he will become what he ought to be and could be.

—*attributed to Johann Wolfgang von Goethe*

For me, success is not about the wins and losses. It's about helping these young fellas be the best versions of themselves on and off the field.

—*Coach Ted Lasso (from the TV series* Ted Lasso*)*

What about acting with love with one's close friends and partners in such a way that they feel loved? Several years ago, Harry and his collaborators approached answering this question by conducting a study that explored how married couples convey love in their everyday lives. Until then, the scientific literature on love was almost exclusively focused on the *loving person's feelings*. Typical statements on the most popular measure at the time included "I feel a powerful attraction for my partner" and "I trust my partner completely." However, his team was more curious about feeling *loved* than feeling *love*. How do you display loving feelings to the person you love, so that they feel loved?

Harry invited around thirty middle-aged married couples into the lab for focus groups and asked them to share stories about the everyday, ordinary ways in which they show love to their spouses. To his research team's surprise, not a single person echoed the ideas represented in that popular measure of love. Instead, participants spoke of prioritizing their partners' goals ahead of their own, going out of their way to "be there" for their partners, showing tenderness and care, and trying to be accepting rather than judgmental. In other studies, researchers have simply asked people directly what behaviors make them feel loved. In one survey, the highest-ranked answer was when a person "cares for them." In another survey, the number one answer was when a person "shows compassion in difficult times." (Runners-up were when "a child snuggles up to them" and "their pets are happy to see them.")

This research convinced us that showing compassion and care toward one's partner is the critical ingredient of the Open-Heart mindset. Feeling compassion is where the process starts, but it's not enough by itself. Showing compassion so that your partner truly gets the message is what matters most. Notably, there is a particular way to embody an open heart, especially within close or intimate relationships, that is more complicated and demanding than simply showing daily kindness. Fortunately, this approach has enormous potential to make both relationship partners feel more loved.

More than Kindness

To explain what we mean, we turn to a classic 1961 text from humanistic psychology: Carl Rogers's *On Becoming a Person*. Rogers believed that humans are always growing—indeed, they have an *imperative* to grow—and that in order for people to grow and to feel fully loved, they need to be valued not just for who they currently are but for the person they have the potential to become (which Rogers called their "organismic potential"). This echoes Goethe's assertion that treating people as who they *could* be helps them become that very person. Thus, to help your partners feel loved, you would nurture their growth and help them to realize their unfolding potential, and, ideally, they would do the same for you. Rogers's premise was that if you are loved for your potential self, you are more likely to grow into that potential self.

Fast-forward several decades, and, as it happens, relationship scientists have been studying a practice that supports one's partner's growth called *partner affirmation*, but a more beautiful name for it is the Michelangelo effect. You may recall that we sometimes refer to the Open-Heart mindset as the Michelangelo mindset. Coined by the social psychologist Caryl Rusbult, it's the act of believing in, encouraging, and validating your partner's values, goals, and dreams. Interestingly, many people overlook the extent to which their ability to grow, develop new strengths, learn new skills, build resources, and reach their goals is shaped by the expectations and encouragement they receive from those closest to them. Yet research suggests that people are much more likely to become the person they aspire to be if their partner sees and encourages them. For example, in one study, people reported greater movement over two months toward becoming "the person they would ideally like to be" when their partners promoted those ideals than when they didn't.

The name for the Michelangelo effect was inspired by the Renaissance artist who purportedly said, "I saw an angel in the marble and carved until I set him free." Like a sculptor, you have the power to bring out the best in your partner, to shape and uplift them, helping them become the person they aspire to be. This is one of the most powerful ways to express Open-Heart intent. This transformation sometimes requires major sacrifices—for example, moving to a different city for your partner's career—but it more often happens in subtle, gradual steps, through small supportive actions that might seem minor but add up over time.

For example, if your partner had a dream of becoming a novelist, you could support her by creating time and space in your schedule for her to write. You might gently nudge her to set aside specific hours each week or help manage family responsibilities so she has uninterrupted time to work on her craft. This kind of support may not only make her feel that you value her aspirations but also strengthen her own commitment to writing—a commitment that could grow stronger with each small success. You could also remind her how much you value her writing. Your encouragement could give her subtle confidence boosts, reinforcing her identity as a writer—an identity that can become self-fulfilling (or rather partner-fulfilling). Finally, you could steer her away from self-defeating habits, like spending hours scrolling through social media instead of writing, helping her stay focused on her goals.

This idea would have resonated with the respondents of a 2012 study that asked their views about marriage. In telephone surveys of more than six thousand diverse residents of Florida, Texas, California, and New York, most respondents agreed that "understanding each other's hopes and dreams" was important for a successful marriage—

and far more important than sharing values or having good sex. These findings revealed that Americans across all income levels want their partners to be their Michelangelo. However, as illustrated by our example of a hypothetical novelist-partner, before you can support your partner's dreams, you need to fully understand them. What are their "diamonds"—the dreams they cherish most? And what is their "kryptonite"—the obstacles holding them back? What are their talents, fantasies, and triggers? This is where the Sharing, Listening-to-Learn, and Radical-Curiosity mindsets will be crucial.

From Michelangelo to Feeling Loved

How will the Michelangelo effect help you to feel loved? The process begins when you succeed in affirming and supporting your partner. First, consider what happens from your partner's perspective. When you encourage your partner's growth and genuinely believe in their potential, then your partner feels supported by you—and even more, they feel understood, valued, grateful, and inspired to continue striving. When they sense how much you believe in them and how committed you are to helping them thrive, their love deepens for you. And as a bonus, they begin to embody the best version of themselves.

Now consider your own perspective. When you invest in your partner's growth, *your* love deepens for them and makes you view them in an increasingly positive light—not only because you see their positive changes firsthand (e.g., realizing just how creative they are) but also because you witness your own commitment, which reinforces just how much they mean to you (e.g., reckoning you must love them more than ever if you're this invested in their dreams). Further, generosity toward your partner (or toward anyone) underscores the idea that you have done something good and grants you a sense of agency and competence—the sense of pride you feel when your loved ones accomplish an important goal of theirs. Your generosity also promotes feelings of community and interdependence and, most importantly, allows you to feel more in sync with and connected to them. Indeed, a branch of philosophy called *care ethics* argues that caring for others helps the carer themselves to grow and flourish. As a result, being their Michelangelo has rewards not only for your partner but also for you and for your relationship, making the two of you feel closer and more connected. In nurturing your partner, you nurture yourself.

Now we've arrived at the point in the process that explains how the Michelangelo effect can lead you (the Michelangelo) to feel loved. The key ingredient is reciprocity, just as we saw in the Relationship Sea-Saw. Research shows that receiving a partner's kindness, affirmation, and endorsement—or even anticipating future instances of their reciprocity—strengthens the bonds between the partners. In other words, being a Michelangelo makes relationships grow stronger—but only if the other person is willing and able to meet you there.

As the Sea-Saw of chapter 4 illustrates: When you direct generous thoughts, vibes, and actions toward others, they will be motivated to direct generous thoughts, vibes, and actions back to you. The more you believe in your partner, the more they will believe in you. The more they feel loved by you, the more they will share vulnerably with you (Sharing mindset), because you have extended them trust and a safe haven, such that they feel secure enough to share more of their full selves). The more they feel loved and affirmed by you, the more they will listen to you with presence and curiosity (using the Listening-to-Learn and Radical-Curiosity mindsets because you have listened with curiosity to them) and accept you in the full knowledge of all your strengths and flaws (using the Multiplicity mindset because kindness softens their stance). And you, in turn, will feel called and supported to do the same. In sum, being a Michelangelo—and embodying the Open-Heart mindset more broadly—can lead both you and your partner to feel loved, precisely because feeling loved paves the way for both of you to embrace all the other mindsets.

But reciprocity isn't always guaranteed. As we explore later in chapter 12, the painful reality is that some people will not—or cannot—engage with you in the same way. You may offer belief, encouragement, and support, but if it's not returned, the connection will feel unbalanced, even depleting. That's why, as much as the Open-Heart mindset can strengthen relationships, it also reveals them. Sometimes, taking these steps will bring you closer to someone; other times, it will make it undeniably clear that the relationship isn't working. In that case, the solution isn't to abandon the Open-Heart mindset but to consider whether your efforts are best directed elsewhere.

If you can recall a partner, family member, mentor, or coach who helped you see what you could become at a pivotal moment in your life, you are lucky. If not, you can become that person for someone else. When you empower a friend, colleague, child, or partner to grow into their best selves, you will lay the groundwork for them (and you) to feel valued, seen, and loved.

Turning the Open-Heart Mindset Toward Yourself: The Science and Rewards of Self-Compassion

> We accept the love we think we deserve.
>
> —*Stephen Chbosky,* The Perks of Being a Wallflower

In a world that often feels demanding, harsh, and critical, many people struggle to believe they're truly lovable. But Mister Rogers—a man who spent his life reminding us otherwise—saw it differently. To him, each person was inherently worthy of love, no conditions attached. "I like you just the way you are," he would say, looking right into the camera as if speaking to each viewer individually. For Fred Rogers, love wasn't just an abstract feeling; it was a message he repeated over and over, hoping it would resonate with his young audience. "You've made this day a special day by just your being you," he'd say. To him, it wasn't enough to encourage kindness or polite behavior—indeed, his focus was rarely on kindness—he wanted each child watching to feel loved simply for who they were.

Mister Rogers wrote his own songs, and one can imagine him waking up one morning and thinking that what the world really needs right now is another song about how each one of us is lovable and thinking that he would write that song today. "Love is at the root of everything," he said, "love or the lack of it."

Mister Rogers's message is a reminder of a widespread cultural belief that before you can fully feel loved by others, you have to believe you're worthy of it yourself. This isn't easy. In fact, for many people who struggle with self-doubt or harsh self-criticism, it might be one of the hardest things to accept. If Mister Rogers were alive today, we bet he would fall in love with the science of self-compassion, a field pioneered by psychological scientist Kristin Neff. Just as Mister Rogers taught generations of children to believe in their own lovability, Neff argues for the importance of learning to treat oneself with kindness and understanding. Indeed, embracing one's own worth through self-compassion is the first step in opening one's heart to love from others.

Thus, we round out this chapter by switching perspectives: It's not enough to apply the Open-Heart mindset to others—you need to apply it to yourself as well. As described in chapter 3 and also in chapter 5, a common barrier to feeling loved is believing you're unlovable. Such beliefs are often rooted in something negative about yourself—perhaps it was a traumatic experience you underwent, a poor life decision you made, an action you took of which you're ashamed, or an unattractive personal characteristic. Instead of calling for self-criticism and impatience, self-compassion calls for self-understanding, gentleness, and positive intentions toward yourself.

When Kristin Neff was a student in the late 1990s, she encountered the concept of self-compassion in Buddhist texts and became intrigued by it. As far as she knew, no one had ever investigated self-compassion empirically—scientifically—and she thought she could be the first. Today, Neff is a professor at the University of Texas, and she has been studying self-compassion for decades, with many other psychological scientists following in her footsteps.

It's always useful to begin with definitions, and Neff identifies three main elements of self-compassion: (1) **self-kindness** (being gentle and supportive with oneself rather than self-critical), (2) **common humanity** (recognizing that suffering is a shared human experience and that we are not alone in our struggles), and (3) **mindfulness** (maintaining a balanced awareness of painful thoughts and emotions without suppressing or exaggerating them). Each of these three elements can easily be spotted in the approaches we discuss below in how self-compassion can be built.

How Much Do You Love Yourself?:
A Scientific Perspective

How often are you compassionate toward yourself? Do you love yourself, or do you consider yourself unlovable? Consider the extent to which the following statements, from the Whole Self-Love Scale, describe you:

- "When I am disappointed in my actions, I still love myself."
- "I love myself even when I make bad decisions."
- "I love myself with all my imperfections."
- "When I feel unattractive, I still love myself."
- "I don't have to be better than others in order to love myself."
- "I speak to myself with love."
- "I love myself even when I feel unworthy of other people's love."

If you wholeheartedly agree with these statements, then self-compassion likely comes naturally to you, requiring little conscious effort or practice. For most people, however, self-compassion is a skill that needs intentional practice, and even those who are generally self-compassionate can benefit from an occasional booster. The rewards, however, are well worth the effort. A meta-analysis of twenty-seven different self-compassion interventions found that people induced to feel more self-compassionate reported being significantly happier and more mindful, as well as less self-critical, less depressed, and less stressed. Self-compassion has been linked to numerous markers of positive mental health and appears to be a source of strength and resilience for people facing adversity.

These psychological benefits may, in part, stem from differences in the neural pathways of people with high and low levels of self-compassion. A brain-imaging study out of UCLA found that when participants received negative social feedback (such as being rated by a peer as "annoying," "boring," or "insecure"), those with relatively low self-compassion showed greater connectivity between the amygdala and the ventromedial prefrontal cortex. The researchers interpreted these results to mean that a lack of self-compassion—whether it's innate or learned from experience—makes people neurally more sensitive to negative emotional experiences.

In a book about feeling loved, we are particularly interested in the scientific benefits of self-compassion within the context of love relationships. To wit, self-compassionate people have been found to be better relationship partners, more secure, and more accepting of their friends' and partners' flaws. They are also more kind, more empathetic, and more likely to grant their partners autonomy. In an experiment with young couples at the University of Tennessee, volunteers prompted to cultivate more self-compassion were more likely to correct their interpersonal mistakes and to engage in healthy repair behaviors. Although more rigorous studies are needed to unpack the causal links between self-compassion and its advantages, the findings so far are promising, suggesting that self-compassion offers meaningful benefits for both individuals and their relationships.

Building Self-Compassion: Practical Strategies and Empirical Research

You yourself, as much as anybody in the entire universe, deserve your love and affection.

—*attributed to the Buddha*

Not long ago, I (Sonja) experienced something that beautifully illustrates how a friend's compassion can inspire self-compassion. The incident, however, was so embarrassing that I nearly decided against sharing it. (And yes, I like to think I embrace the Sharing mindset—but this one was tough!) Ultimately, I chose to tell the story, but also to leave out some painful details.

In short, I made a classic mistake: I sent a thoughtless text about a friend—I'll call her Shelley—to another friend, and I accidentally sent it to Shelley herself. (Has that ever happened to you?) Panicked, I deleted the message and tried to pass it off as being about something else, but it was too late—she saw it and, of course, immediately understood. (At the risk of a giant understatement, Shelley's not an idiot.) I apologized profusely, but the damage was done. There was no way to take it back or erase it. I braced myself for the fallout, knowing this could go a few different ways: It might end our friendship entirely, leave behind lingering tension and awkwardness, or—most likely—cause some temporary discomfort before we eventually found our way back to normal.

What Shelley did next completely floored me. She immediately picked up the phone. After patiently waiting for me to finish my guilt-ridden apologies and stumbling explanations, she calmly asked, "Why did you write it?" I tried to explain, but she wasn't satisfied with my surface answer. Instead, she gently dug deeper, "What made you say that? Was there something from your past that triggered it? Is there a need or desire underlying it? Maybe something from your childhood?" What followed was one of the most thoughtful and insightful conversations I've ever had.

As we talked, it became clear to me that my words stemmed from an unresolved experience from my teenage years. The realization was both eye-opening and revealing. But what stayed with me most wasn't the insight—it was Shelley's extraordinary kindness and compassion. Instead of judging me, reacting with anger, or feeling offended—or, worse, dismissing me entirely—she chose to be kind. She chose to view my misstep not in isolation but in the context of all the things that had shaped me, both good and bad. She saw me in all my complex, multicolored humanity, what we call multiplicity *(see next chapter).*

One moment, I was consumed by guilt, berating myself for being so careless and thoughtless—a truly terrible friend. Buddhists describe the "first arrow" of suffering as being caused by misfortune, but the "second arrow" is the additional pain people endure by blaming themselves for the first arrow. I wasn't just suffering from the first arrow of my mistake—I was piercing myself with the second, adding self-blame and shame to an already painful moment. The next moment, the weight of guilt—and my harsh self-critic—seemed to dissolve. Even though my most immediate emotion was relief, it was accompanied by something deeper: awe and love. What Shelley's compassion and love taught me was the need to feel compassion and love toward myself.

One of the best things about self-compassion is that there are many practical, research-backed strategies to help people cultivate it. Here, we share some of our favorite approaches, including one that Shelley seemed to understand intuitively, along with the science that inspired them. We recommend that you try to find the approach that aligns with your personality, goals, values, or lifestyle. In other words, experiment with what resonates most with you, then stick with what feels natural, enjoyable, and meaningful to you. Not all of them will, and that's okay.

Letter from a Kind Friend

We begin with the most popular and most powerful way to practice self-compassion—by writing a letter to yourself from the perspective of a kind, loving friend. The general idea is that you practice saying things to yourself that only a kind friend would say—making statements that are kind, forgiving, and wise (as opposed to negative, critical, and judgmental).

Imagine taking a step back and trying to see yourself through the eyes of someone who loves you unconditionally. This exercise is about channeling that compassionate perspective.

Like all humans, you probably have at least one aspect of yourself that makes you feel inadequate, "not good enough," or maybe even slightly ashamed—a quality you wish were different. It might be something about your appearance, a pattern in your relationships, or a shortcoming you face at work. This aspect of yourself may show up as an intrusive thought, a self-doubt, or an upsetting memory. We like to think of these mental intrusions as similar to a phone's ringing. You can choose to notice the call coming through but not pick it up: Don't answer the phone, and don't engage. By doing so, you allow the thought or feeling to exist without letting it take over your attention or emotions.

Instead, the first step is to reflect on the emotions that come up when you think about this part of yourself, allowing those feelings to surface without pushing them away or exaggerating them. Take a few minutes to jot down your thoughts and feelings, being honest about what you're experiencing at the moment.

Next, picture an imaginary friend who is unconditionally loving, accepting, and kind (like my friend Shelley). This friend knows everything about you—your strengths, your struggles, your entire life history—and sees you as a whole person, flaws and all, with the millions of things that have shaped who you are at this moment. Essentially, this friend views you with the Multiplicity mindset, which we discuss in the next chapter. They understand that many of your traits and challenges stem from things beyond your control, such as your family background, life experiences, or genes.

Imagine that they deeply understand the pain you feel when you judge yourself so harshly. With this perspective in mind, write yourself a letter as if it were coming from this friend. What would they say about the part of yourself you often criticize? How would they comfort you? They might remind you that everyone has both strengths and flaws; that being human means being imperfect; and, hearkening back to Mister Rogers, that you are worthy of love and compassion just as you are. As you write, let the friend's warmth, acceptance, and desire for your happiness echo through the words.

Once you've written the letter, pause for a moment: Sit quietly and slowly read it back to yourself. Imagine hearing your friend's voice as you absorb their words. Allow each word to sink in, gently reminding you that you're not alone in your imperfections and that you are worthy of kindness—especially toward yourself. And then keep the letter, so that you can return to it, from time to time, when you need a booster.

Notably, this Letter from a Kind Friend practice calls for you to harness several mindsets simultaneously, all directed inward. First, the Sharing mindset, to acknowledge and reveal your flaws and vulnerabilities. Second, the Listening-to-Learn mindset, to truly pay attention to and comprehend your habits of self-judging. And, third, the Multiplicity mindset (which you will learn more about in the next chapter), to view your flaws and the million things that produced them through a broad, compassionate lens. When successful, the exercise can serve as a gentle yet profound reminder of your own worth, helping you foster self-compassion and self-acceptance. In an experiment exploring some of these ideas, college students were asked to reflect on "a negative event that you experienced in high school or college that made you feel bad about yourself— something that involved failure, humiliation, or rejection." Those subsequently prompted to think about the event from the perspective of a kind friend reported less defensiveness and less distress compared to those in a control group or participants prompted to simply think positively about themselves. As the researchers noted, "The self-compassion induction allowed participants to acknowledge that they were the kind of people who made mistakes, yet they did not feel badly about something that is a common experience."

How Would You Treat a Close Friend

In an experiment that must have been avant-garde for the 2010s, scientists in the Netherlands created a chatbot named Vincent, who reached out to participants every day for two weeks. During these chats, Vincent admitted embarrassing foibles, such as arriving late to an IP address and procrastinating on paying his host server, and asked for advice. "What do you think, am I the dumbest bot you've ever seen or what?" Vincent would type. "Am I being too hard on myself?" Interestingly, those who interacted with Vincent for those two weeks reported feeling greater self-compassion for *themselves*—for example, by agreeing more strongly with statements such as "I try to see my failings as part of the human condition" and "I try to be understanding and patient toward those aspects of my personality I don't like."

Knowingly or not, the researchers who designed this study were tapping into an alternative exercise for building self-compassion, which asks people to think about how they respond to a close friend who's feeling bad about themselves or struggling. Picture yourself in this scenario: What would you say to this friend? How would you offer them support? What kind of gentle, understanding tone would you likely use? Then, compare this to how you usually treat *yourself* in *your* moments of struggle—what words you choose and the tone of your self-talk. Often, people are far more critical or dismissive toward themselves than they would ever be toward a friend. Take a moment to reflect on how things might shift if you offered yourself the same kindness and compassion you naturally extend to others, and write down these insights. The next time you're feeling bad about yourself, why not try treating yourself like a good friend and see what happens?

Self-Compassion Break

To practice the Self-Compassion Break, start by bringing to mind a situation in your life that's causing you stress or difficulty, allowing yourself to actually feel the stress and emotional discomfort as it arises in your body. Then, gently say to yourself, "This is a moment of suffering," acknowledging your experience with mindful awareness but without judgment. You might say, "This hurts" or "This is stressful," as a way of validating your pain. Next, remind yourself that "Suffering is a part of life." This simple statement recognizes your common humanity with others, by appreciating that everyone faces hardships and that this is normal. You can also say, "I'm not alone" or "We all struggle in our lives." Finally, place your hands over your heart, feeling the warmth and comfort emanating from your hands, and say, "May I be kind to myself." This gesture, which borrows many elements from the loving-kindness meditation we described earlier, invites self-kindness into your moment of suffering. You can also try adding or substituting phrases like "May I accept myself as I am" or "May I learn to forgive myself."

Gratitude Letter to Self and Other Mindful Practices

An array of other self-compassion practices has been designed and tested. For example, writing a Gratitude Letter to yourself is straightforward; it involves taking a moment to acknowledge and celebrate the small but meaningful aspects of who you are—your strengths, your likes, your unique habits, and the qualities that make you, you.

You may feel slightly embarrassed beginning to write the letter, but those feelings of awkwardness usually pass. Consistent with this approach, writing about cherished values (such as teamwork, honesty, or kindness) has been found to make participants happier over time.

Another approach, Mindful Self-Care, calls for intentionally engaging in activities that soothe and uplift you, from physical self-care (e.g., working out or soaking in a warm bath) and mental self-care (e.g., meditating or reading a good book) to emotional self-care (e.g., journaling or walking in the woods) and relational self-care (e.g., playing a game with friends). These acts of self-kindness can be tailored to what you need in any given moment.

Practices such as Mindful Goals and Mindful Situations encourage you to seek activities and environments that align with your values and lead you to feel authentic, whether through setting meaningful goals that make you feel good about yourself or choosing situations that foster a sense of belonging and purpose. Mindful Attributions, on the other hand, involves shifting your thinking when you feel misunderstood or when things go wrong. Instead of focusing on what went wrong, you can try to adopt a more compassionate perspective (much as a well-meaning, kind friend would)—and consider positive, growth-oriented possibilities. Adopting a growth mindset encourages you to see challenges less as potential threats and more as opportunities for improvement, prompting you not to ask, *Why am I like this?* but rather, *What will help me change?* Through these practices, you will build resilience, self-acceptance, and a stronger sense of compassion for yourself.

How *Not* to Practice Self-Compassion

Now that we reviewed some of the most popular strategies for practicing self-compassion, it's time to review how *not* to practice self-compassion.

First, take careful note of the adjectives we have used to describe self-compassion practices: Be *kind* toward yourself, be *forgiving*, be *understanding*, be *gentle*, be *accepting*, be *loving*, be *soothing*, be *warm*. Note that none of these adjectives encourages you to be self-centered or wrapped up in yourself. Accordingly, although self-compassion necessarily entails directing attention to yourself, it means being neither self-absorbed (focusing too much on yourself) nor narcissistic (making yourself seem better than others).

During our India visit, His Holiness the Dalai Lama said something else that deeply resonated with us: "Excessive self-focus is the door to all misery." Self-compassion, by contrast, requires a temporary, situational self-focus that is healthy and desirable. It seems counterintuitive, but although strategies promoting self-compassion naturally encourage you to focus temporarily on yourself, they actually make it possible for you to focus more on other people.

Second, practicing self-compassion does not mean trying to mold yourself into someone whom you think others will like. Such attempts are likely to backfire because they will lead you to feel inauthentic (as we discussed in chapter 5). If you don't act in ways that are meaningful and genuine and right to you, then other people won't be able to understand and appreciate who you really are, because they won't see who you are, in your heart of hearts. One of Sonja's friends, a successful businesswoman raised in Argentina, texted her recently after reading a draft of this book: "Before I turned 40, I used to mold myself to fit the tastes of people I was drawn to," she wrote. "I tried to showcase my best qualities to be more interesting. I realize now that I was not being emotionally honest with myself and was covering up my insufficiency and inadequacy." She said she is realizing this now and beginning a "journey of self-discovery," involving owning her "texture and quirkiness" and finally being more honest and authentic.

Finally, practicing self-compassion does not mean trying to increase your self-esteem and convince yourself (and others) that you are worthy. Duke University social psychologist Mark Leary argues that people should stop focusing on building their self-esteem and focus instead on feeling accepted by others. His thesis runs parallel to the theme of this book. There are benefits to feeling good about yourself, but it's not the most important factor in our happiness and well-being. In fact, we would argue that feeling good about yourself *follows* from feeling connected, rather than precedes it. The most important factor in our happiness and well-being is feeling understood, valued, and loved. And to truly feel loved, it's essential to first feel lovable.

From Self-Compassion to Feeling Loved

So then: How does practicing self-compassion help you feel loved? Stated differently: How does loving yourself more make it easier to feel more love from others? Let us count the ways. There are no fewer than six pathways!

The first two pathways are the most straightforward, as they make it easier for you to *be* loved. The third and fourth make it more likely that when others show their love, their love actually sinks in. And the last two are critical to feeling loved because they help make the Relationship Sea-Saw possible.

To begin with, after you practice self-compassion and boost your feelings of self-love, you will literally become *easier to love*.

1. **You become more attractive to others.** When you feel good about yourself, your value as a friend and partner rises because people like confident, secure, happy, and generous people. Studies show that self-compassionate people are happier, more altruistic, and more securely attached—all qualities that relationship scientists have found are highly valued in mates.

2. **Others mirror your self-perception.** People pick up on the way you feel about yourself, and this leads them to think the same way about you. (After all, they reasonably assume that you know yourself better than anyone else does.) In other words, your self-regard is "leaky"—sooner or later, how you see yourself will be apparent to others through your actions, in subtle nonverbal cues, and even in your choice of words. And when your peers do pick up on the way you see yourself—when they sense that you love yourself—they are likely to agree. Again, it's literally easier to love someone who loves themselves.

We turn next to the notion that after you practice self-compassion and boost your feelings of self-love, it will be easier for you to let others' love in and to let it sink in.

3. **Your self-perception shapes how you interpret others' love.** This is rooted in projection, the well-documented human tendency discussed in chapter 6. When people project, they feel transparent—they assume that others see them in the same way that they see themselves. That is, how can you expect to experience love flowing toward you from others if you aren't loving toward yourself? Projection is pervasive. For example, lonely people usually believe that both friends and strangers can see through to their social deficiencies, and people who feel fat or unattractive expect that others agree. In other words, if you don't value yourself or don't see yourself as desirable, you will tend to assume that others feel the same way, even without evidence (or maybe even in spite of it). This is also a core idea in contemplative practices. Turning this idea around, when you love yourself, you will assume that others do, too, and it will be easier for you to accept their love and to feel loved.

4. **Self-love allows love from others to feel genuine.** The more positive we feel about ourselves, the more other people's compliments, attention, and love will feel authentic and credible to us—and the more likely we'll be to accept them. Thus, others' love will sink in, and we will allow it to make us feel loved. Accordingly, our self-love allows us to accept others' open hearts. Conversely, if you don't like yourself, other people's overt expressions of love and admiration, no matter how well-intentioned, will not feel authentic, believable, or real, as we explored in chapter 5.

Finally, after you practice self-compassion and boost your feelings of self-love, you will be better equipped to operate the Sea-Saw (as we discussed in chapter 4).

5. **Self-compassion creates emotional safety.** When you treat yourself with self-compassion and an open heart, you feel safe, comfort-

able, and prepared to embrace the Sharing mindset, by sharing more of yourself with others, and to let others in. As just one example, studies show that self-compassionate people report more acceptance of their limitations—something that makes it easier for them to share vulnerably with others. In other words, self-love allows you to create and maintain a container in which your authentic self can be shown and vulnerability can be expressed. Thus, you create the conditions that allow you to be known by others, and, as we have seen, being known is a critical precondition to feeling loved.

6. **Self-love fuels generosity toward others.** The final critical step on the Sea-Saw that self-compassion makes possible—and makes more likely—is the ability to help others feel loved. When you love yourself, you boost your reserves in ways that will help you make others feel more loved. As described earlier, self-compassionate people have been found to have a range of personal and relationship virtues, such as greater empathy, kindness, and security. They show greater equanimity, are less likely to catastrophize problems, and are more likely to talk openly about problems with their romantic partner rather than avoid the issues or assign blame. Indeed, when you love yourself, you have the capacity—indeed, the luxury—to generously direct attention and offer authentic compliments to others (rather than dwell on yourself or, worse, put others down to feel good about yourself). Furthermore, when you love yourself, your compliments will feel authentic to others (as opposed to manipulative or ingratiating) and will be received and accepted with trust and without suspicion or ulterior motives.

We hope that by now you understand why self-compassion is such a critical piece of a book titled *How to Feel Loved*. However, we need to be clear about something. The ubiquitous advice that you need to love yourself before you can love others is wrong. People learn to show love and to feel love in the context of relationships, so the pathways go in both directions at the same time. For example, someone who struggles with self-doubts can still consistently show up for a friend during tough times—and through doing so, begin to see themselves as worthy and lovable in return. We just described six different pathways by which loving yourself widens the opportunity for you to feel loved by others. But, of course, showing and expressing love to others also widens the opportunity for you to love yourself.

An Open-Heart mindset turned toward others creates opportunities to make others feel loved—indeed, perhaps even more than might feel warranted in the moment. An Open-Heart mindset turned inward enhances the ability to love yourself—indeed, perhaps even more than *you* might feel warranted in offering. And, thus, we arrive at the perfect transition to the Multiplicity mindset.

9

Multiplicity Mindset

Do I contradict myself?
Very well then I contradict myself,
(I am large, I contain multitudes.)

—*Walt Whitman, Song of Myself*

Perhaps you've seen Walk the Line, *the 2005 movie about the life and career of country-music legend Johnny Cash (played by Joaquin Phoenix), a brilliant songwriter with a deep and distinctive bass-baritone voice. Cash's rebellious image and emotional lyrics resonated with a wide audience, catapulting him to fame and success. While his career took off quickly, his personal life was falling apart. He struggled with addiction to drugs and alcohol, infidelity, profound feelings of inadequacy, and emotional volatility. In those early years, he was a brilliant but erratic performer who often lied and disappointed, burning bridges behind him and then reappearing with little more than his soulful music and a plaintive appeal for forgiveness. Still, people came back to him. They were drawn to his raw honesty, his vulnerability, and a kind of rugged charm that blended sincerity with intensity. He wore his flaws openly, and that made him uniquely magnetic.*

When June Carter (played by Reese Witherspoon) met Johnny Cash, he was already famous, but he was also unraveling. She was a successful performer in her own right, and while she was drawn to his charisma and talent, she was also aware of his brokenness. Walk the Line *shows how she navigated their growing connection. Carter was not naive and had no delusions—she saw both sides of Cash. She kept her distance when she needed to, but she also kept coming back. Not to save him and not to demand that he change, but simply to stand with him and help him find his way. She had faith in what he could become, and she chose to love him. Their thirty-five-year marriage illustrates how, with the right mindsets, a loving relationship can emerge from chaos.*

Walk the Line *highlights the dissonance that Carter felt—as shown, for example, when Cash impulsively proposes marriage to her onstage, mid-concert. She hesitates—not because she doesn't love him but because she feels a profound tension, pulled in by his charms yet at the same time pushed away by his flaws and imperfections. That tension is the heart of their story, raising questions about how Carter reconciled these competing tendencies. How did she manage to steadfastly express love and devotion while helping Cash find his way to sobriety? How did she protect herself while staying committed through his backsliding and relapses? Their relationship, with its highs and lows, raises important questions about the psychological and relational tensions with which long-term loving relationships must contend.*

A Person Is Many Things

I hate my picture being taken. A photograph
by definition captures one mood. And I have
a million facets to my personality.

—*Jane Pauley*

I am not one and simple, but complex and many.

—*Virginia Woolf,* The Waves

People tend to think about personality, strengths, and weaknesses in terms of averages. It feels natural to say, "He's extremely conscientious, somewhat courageous, and not at all selfish." This is not surprising—psychologists have long emphasized that traits vary from one person to another along a normal ("bell curve") distribution. By this logic, the best way to describe a person is to pinpoint where they fall on that curve. For instance, one might say, "She's way above average in self-esteem but slightly below average in extraversion."

This perspective is intuitive and sensible: Thousands of studies show that researchers can learn a lot about human behavior from these averages. However, viewing people in terms of averages also leaves a great deal unexplained. Personality scientists have recently begun to take an entirely different approach to help understand much of the unexplained part. This new approach is called Whole Trait theory, and it starts with the simple but powerful idea that people's behavior varies a great deal from moment to moment and situation to situation. Instead of focusing on averages, Whole Trait theory argues that a person's nature is better represented as a probability distribution—in other words, in terms of the range and frequency of behaviors they display over time.

Here's an example from a study that illustrates this approach: Participants were randomly prompted five times a day over fourteen days to record instances of behavior that reflected certain traits—such as conscientiousness (organizing their desk), courage (defending an unpopular view at lunch), and selfishness (taking the last cookie). The resulting data led to two important insights: First, the variation in traits *within* an individual's day was far greater than the variation *between* different individuals. Essentially, a person's behavior fluctuated more from one report to the next than it differed on average from someone else's behavior. Second, behaviors (such as acting courageously) turned out to be just as inconsistent as feelings (such as nervousness): A person's actions swung as widely from one moment to the next as did their feelings. In other words, most people shift from being very selfish to very unselfish and all points in between over a span of days. This finding suggests that whether an individual is selfish today offers only a modest clue as to whether they'll be selfish tomorrow—so much so that which personality label you ascribe to a person depends on when you observe a slice of their behavior.

This work has been replicated many times, with considerable

implications. On a descriptive level, it challenges the common tendency to think and talk about people in terms of averages and, instead, highlights how behavior varies from one situation to another. Rather than asking, *What traits does this person have?*, considering how their behavior shifts depending on context and momentary goals may provide more insights. Thus, one might ask: *Who were they with? What behavior did their circumstances call for? What outcomes were they pursuing? And what were they trying to accomplish at that moment?*

For example, instead of labeling a student as simply "mildly conscientious," it may be more informative to observe that she is very conscientious at school, mildly conscientious when doing her homework, and not at all conscientious when interacting with family. How much time she spends in each of these contexts shapes the overall picture of her personality—this is where the idea of a probability distribution comes in.

A profound and comforting insight from Whole Trait theory is that each individual carries within them not just one but several different "selves." Like Johnny Cash, you are a dynamic tapestry of contrasts that shift from day to day and moment to moment—strong and weak, resilient and vulnerable, lively and subdued, proud and ashamed—and you cannot be defined by any single label or "average."

These qualities span both strengths (e.g., your sensitivity and openness) and weaknesses or challenges (e.g., a tendency to overeat or a traumatic incident from your adolescence), and it's important to recognize that no single aspect, on its own, defines you. That's the Multiplicity mindset in a nutshell. Feeling loved requires acknowledging and embracing this multiplicity in both yourself and your partner. It means seeing, accepting, and sharing these multiple aspects openly. As Whitman so pithily expressed, humans don't merely act one way at times and another way at other times—they *contain* multiple selves. We suggest that learning to recognize and appreciate this wholeness is essential for fostering love and connection.

Let's take a closer look at how these multiple selves shape the ways in which people perceive both themselves and others.

How Many Dimensions Does It Take to Describe a Person?

Everyone is everything. Every ingredient inside a star is inside you, and every personality that ever existed competes in the theatre of your mind for the main role.

—*Matt Haig,* The Humans

The Multiplicity mindset can be applied from two different angles— one from your perspective as the listener (directed at another person) and one from your perspective as the speaker (directed inward). We begin with the former.

Viewing Others with Multiplicity

Each of us is more than the worst thing we've ever done.

—*Bryan Stevenson,* Just Mercy

Kristin Kinkel grew up in a tight-knit family in the small West Coast town of Springfield, Oregon. In May 1998, her life turned upside down. Her younger brother—her only sibling and someone she had always been close to—shot and killed their parents. The next day, he went to the local high school and began shooting. Two students were killed and another twenty-five were injured. At the time, school shootings were rare, and the tragedy left the community and country in shock. It also shook Kristin's life to the core. Not only was she now an orphan, but her only remaining family member, her beloved brother, was responsible.

But instead of turning away, Kristin has stood by him over the years. She regularly visits him in prison, where he is serving a life sentence, and has remained steadfast in her love and support. As she told the judge at the time of her brother's sentencing, "I love my brother more than I ever thought possible. And not because he needs me, but because I need to. . . . It comes from what is inside us."

Kristin's story raises one of the most profound tests of the Multiplicity mindset—the ability to hold two seemingly opposing truths in mind at once. How can Kristin reconcile the unimaginable harm her brother caused with the love she still feels for him?

You may recall Sah D'Simone from chapter 3—the Brazilian-born healer and author of *Spiritually, We: The Art of Relating and Connecting from the Heart*. In the book, D'Simone offers a series of practices designed to help people "relate and connect from the heart." Throughout life, people inevitably encounter individuals who make them uncomfortable but cannot be avoided—whether they are coworkers, family members, or friends of friends. The key to navigating these interactions is to welcome what D'Simone calls:

> the mindset of paradox—the willingness to see other people as not just this *or* that, but as this *and* that, opening ourselves up to being surprised, even delighted by them. People are contradictory; they can be selfish *and* kind, small-minded *and* generous, extraverted *and* insecure. Our minds don't like contradiction.... We want things to be neat, orderly, categorizable, because it helps us make sense of the world—and allows us to stay comfortable and self-righteous. But when we label people in these one-dimensional ways—"He's a slob"; "They're hopeless"; "She's superficial"—we are in a place of limiting judgments and we've already lost the plot.

When you first meet someone, you tend to see them as relatively one-dimensional. Early impressions are shaped by qualities that are immediately visible—the person's appearance and demeanor, ideas they might express in conversation, or their public reputation. Although research has established that these early impressions can be modestly accurate, that's only a small part of the story. As you become better acquainted and acquire more information about each other, your impressions become richer and more accurate. This is especially true in close relationships, where you become intimately familiar with how your partner sees the world, the range and depth of their experiences, and even the more private aspects of their identity. Over time, this deeper knowledge allows you to see them with more complexity and nuance— much like the way you probably see yourself.

Particularly relevant is a psychological bias called the *outgroup homogeneity* (or "they're all alike") *effect*. Research shows that people tend to view members of their in-group—those they identify with or feel connected to—as more diverse in beliefs and behavior, while they tend to view outgroup members as relatively similar to one another, as if they share some common, underlying essence.

This bias makes it harder to listen to outgroup members with a Multiplicity mindset, which, in turn, hinders your ability to adopt an Open-Heart mindset. When outgroups are reduced to one-dimensional stereotypes—especially when those stereotypes are critical or judgmental— it becomes more difficult to see their members as individuals, which makes the kind of meaningful, loving exchanges described by the Relationship Sea-Saw all the more unlikely.

We can take this idea one step further. A core concept in many Asian cultures is dialectical thinking—the understanding that apparent opposites are not necessarily separate or contradictory. Instead, dialectical thinking involves recognizing and accepting seemingly opposing perspectives, ideas, and beliefs. In the words of renowned Buddhist monk Thich Nhat Hanh:

> I know that I am happiness and that I am also suffering, that I am understanding and that I am also ignorance. For this reason I must take care of both of these aspects. I must not discriminate against one of them. I must not suppress one side in favor of the other. I know that each of them is vitally necessary for the other.

His Holiness the Dalai Lama makes a similar point, applying dialectical thinking to life events. He explains that people often see things they perceive as good as one hundred percent good, whereas anything undesirable appears completely bad. Yet with time and perspective, even past events that seemed totally awful may reveal some good that emerged from them. Harry's brother-in-law Alexander, for example, spent many years pursuing two PhDs and a postdoctoral fellowship, with the goal of eventually obtaining a research position. After their many job applications met with repeated failure, they took a position teaching martial arts for a social-justice nonprofit, a position far better suited to their temperament and life goals. All those years of dejection and disappointment led to, as they put it, "a unicorn job that's a perfect match for [my] skills and interests."

Scientists call this not altogether uncommon story arc a "self-redemption narrative," and it's linked to a variety of benefits, including improved mental and physical health and greater contributions to society and to future generations. We're not suggesting that failing to achieve a goal you've spent years striving for is necessarily good for people—it usually isn't—but rather that sometimes good can come of it.

The tendency to think in all-or-nothing terms can be especially problematic when you try to explain why things happen. For instance, you might attribute a friend's excessive drinking solely to a lack of self-control. But when you apply a wider, more open-minded lens, multiple possibilities come into view—a difficult childhood, overwhelming responsibilities, an incurable illness, or genetic factors. In reality, most behaviors and events stem from multiple causes, rather than just one. Research shows that adopting this wide multiplicity lens can be beneficial. People who consistently adopt more nuanced, multifaceted explanations for behavior—a trait known as *attributional complexity*—are described by their friends as more thoughtful, empathic, and socially wise. This is how Kristin Kinkel was able to come to terms with her brother's crimes.

In summary, when your partners reveal themselves to you, if you set aside the all-too-common judgmental mindset and embrace the idea that they have multiple sides, you open the door to recognizing and honoring the authentic person in front of you. How can you do this?

- Stay open-minded, resisting the urge to dismiss the other just because they reveal something that makes you feel uncomfortable, unsettled, or disapproving.

- Interpret their self-disclosure in the most charitable way possible, instead of rushing to judgment.
- Affirm their strengths while empathizing with their struggles.
- Accept the complexity behind their actions, opting for the most loving and generous explanation.
- Respond with sensitivity and compassion when they show vulnerability.
- Forgive their transgressions (when appropriate).
- And, above all, focus on helping them feel understood and loved.

In the end, we build a foundation for the Relationship Sea-Saw by engaging others with love and grace.

Applying Multiplicity to Yourself

You couldn't relive your life, skipping the awful parts, without losing what made it worthwhile. You had to accept it as a whole—like the world, or the person you loved.
—*Stewart O'Nan,* The Odds

The second approach requires a shift in perspective—turning the Multiplicity mindset inward and applying it to yourself. While chapter 8 (on the Open-Heart mindset) explores how certain self-compassion techniques, such as the Letter from a Kind Friend exercise, leverage the Multiplicity mindset by reframing personal struggles through a broad, compassionate lens, the focus here is more direct: on how people experience their own sense of self and their emotions—or, more precisely, on how they experience their multiple selves and multiple emotions.

Ever since philosopher William James's pioneering essays over a century ago, social psychologists have been fascinated by the question of what defines a self—the unique sense of identity that each person holds: *What kind of person am I? What makes me unique?*

A key component of this work is the complexity of your self-conceptions. Some people define themselves in relatively singular terms—for instance, "I am the family breadwinner"—and leave it at that. Others view themselves through a more multifaceted lens—for instance, "I am a teacher, but I am also a father, a lover of art, a citizen of the United States, and a charitable soul." The social psychologist Patricia Linville introduced this concept of *self-complexity* to the field, proposing that greater self-complexity can confer resilience in the face of adversity.

The more complex your view of yourself, the better you can cope with stressful events, regrets, and failures. This is because self-complexity provides a buffer against hardships. When one aspect of your life is going poorly—such as a setback at work or a decision you regret—you can still draw comfort and strength from your other identities. Perhaps you acted selfishly or let someone down. If your sense of self is multifaceted, you can recognize that while you may have failed in one way at that moment, that failure doesn't define you. You are also a thoughtful friend, a dedicated parent, a creative thinker, or a person who learns and grows. By contrast, a relatively one-dimensional view of self offers no safe harbor when that single identity is under threat.

Although subsequent research on Linville's idea has yielded mixed findings, one area where her idea has been fruitful is emotional complexity—how people construe their emotional experiences. To illustrate, consider an example from the 2024 film *Inside Out 2*. As Riley, the main protagonist, enters puberty, her perfectionism has skyrocketed, leaving her increasingly hard on herself and fueling uncomfortable episodes of anxiety and struggle. Yet Riley is also kind and brave, as well as capable of experiencing joy—qualities she struggles to fully appreciate because of her self-critical mindset. Riley's story challenges the common tendency to think of oneself in "either-or fashion," according to Dacher Keltner, a psychologist at the University of California, Berkeley, and an expert on emotion. "But we are many things," he explains, describing the message of the film "as a call to be easier on ourselves, savor the good things and accept our complexity."

Like Riley at the end of *Inside Out 2*, many people experience emotions in highly nuanced ways. They can distinguish between feeling anxious or angry, ashamed or guilty, happy or elated. Others, however, have a less differentiated, more broad-brush experience of their feelings—where emotions simply feel "good" or "bad," "happy" or "sad." Emotion researchers refer to this individual difference as *emotion differentiation*—the degree to which people describe their emotional experiences in fine-grained, specific terms, as contrasted with wider, less granular categories.

The way researchers capture these distinctions is especially revealing. One common method involves prompting people at random moments throughout several days to report their current emotional state using a list of emotion terms. Sophisticated quantitative techniques then examine how consistently each emotion term correlates with other emotion terms. For someone high in emotion differentiation, these correlations vary—for example, they might feel angry but not hostile at one moment, but both hostile *and* angry at another moment. By contrast, a person with low emotion differentiation tends to experience emotions in a more rigid, fixed pattern—for example, always feeling hostile whenever they feel angry.

Research using this approach has shown that people who describe their emotions in highly differentiated ways tend to fare better in several important areas. For instance, they respond more constructively to stressful events, which indicates that emotion differentiation plays a critical role in helping people regulate their emotional states. They also exhibit greater emotional intelligence; are less prone to psychiatric disorders; ruminate less; consume alcohol in moderation; and handle complex social situations, such as social rejection, more effectively. A study of conversations between psychotherapists and patients shows that larger emotion vocabularies are associated with better mental health. Furthermore, people who are skilled at recognizing the complexity in their own emotions are also better at understanding emotional complexity in others. In essence, the research evidence supports the idea that having a finely differentiated sense of emotional experience is a valuable resource for navigating life's challenges.

Differentiating emotional experiences is a prime example of applying the Multiplicity mindset to oneself. Rather than labeling an unpleasant experience as simply "bad," recognizing it as disappointing or discouraging—but not necessarily depressing—allows for acceptance and self-compassion. Acknowledging the complexity of our feelings and experiences facilitates an Open-Heart mindset, making it easier to move forward with kindness toward oneself (and, by extension, toward others).

The Enemy of Applying Multiplicity to Yourself: Shame

If you put shame in a Petri dish, it needs three things to grow into every corner of our lives: secrecy, silence, and judgment.

—*Brené Brown,* The Gifts of Imperfection

One of the main obstacles to applying the Multiplicity mindset to yourself is shame. Brené Brown, a researcher and author who has spent many years studying shame, defines it as the intensely painful feeling or experience of believing that one is fundamentally flawed and therefore unworthy of love and belonging. When people feel shame, they fear that "if they knew X about me, they'd be repelled or disappointed," and this leads them to keep secrets. It's important to appreciate that the *they* in that sentence includes not only other people but yourself. People experience shame when the desire to keep parts of themselves hidden—things they've done or failed to do, traits they wish they had or didn't have, experiences that happened or didn't happen, ideals and standards they fell short of—is strong.

Shame comes in many varieties and flavors—a family secret, a past misdeed, or an undesirable trait. Harry remembers the shame he felt when his sixth-grade teacher mocked him in front of the entire class for "walking like a girl." And he still feels ashamed for not showing more empathy when his mother was diagnosed with Parkinson's. Sonja's experience is eerily similar—she still feels ashamed for ignoring her grandmother's letters from the Soviet Union. She told herself that she was too busy with homework, but the real reason was that she was simply too lazy to make the effort.

Whatever the specifics, the act of keeping secrets and living with a hidden self prevents people from feeling truly and intrinsically loved or seen (as we discussed in chapter 5). This is where the Multiplicity mindset becomes especially powerful—it emphasizes embracing all aspects of oneself, recognizing your strengths while accepting your flaws. But shame makes this far more difficult.

Research shows that individuals who experience relatively high levels of shame have lower self-esteem, are more prone to substance abuse and mental-health problems, struggle to have compassion for their shortcomings, and are more likely to avoid taking responsibility for antisocial actions. Furthermore, after a transgression, shame makes it harder to take another person's perspective, shifting focus inward to one's own distress rather than the other's plight.

This latter finding highlights a crucial distinction between guilt and shame. Guilt focuses attention on the harm done to another person, motivating efforts to make amends and repair the damage. Shame, in contrast, directs a person to think about their flaws and shortcomings, prompting evasion rather than repair. While guilt opens the door to growth and restoration, shame only deepens the well of self-reproach. How can you tell the difference between guilt and shame? Psychological research points to this key difference: Guilt makes you want to seek out the other person, whereas shame makes you want to disappear into a hole in the ground.

A Multiplicity mindset serves as a potent antidote to shame. Brené Brown encourages starting from a place of self-acceptance: "'You know what? I'm enough. I'm imperfect. I'm afraid. I'm super vulnerable. But that does not change the fact that I'm also brave and worthy of love and belonging . . .' When I start from that place, I am completely unleashed." What's more, this kind of self-compassion is a key ingredient for being open with partners—not just about the good but also about the bad. Embracing one's full complexity makes it easier to receive and trust their forgiveness, creating a strong foundation for feeling loved.

Up to this point, we've explored multiplicity from a more theoretical perspective, but we have yet to describe how it can be put into practice. The next section introduces three therapy-based approaches that incorporate the Multiplicity mindset. However, while it's helpful to look at how professional therapists approach multiplicity, we emphasize that professional counseling isn't needed. These examples offer practical strategies for integrating this mindset into everyday life.

Putting the Multiplicity Mindset into Action

Acceptance is simply love in practice. When you love, you accept, when you lack love, you judge.

—*Abhijit Naskar*

It's worth noting that many systematic approaches to psychotherapy incorporate ideas aligned with the Multiplicity mindset. In this section, we explore three particularly relevant examples. The first applies the Multiplicity mindset to your partner; the second extends it inward, to yourself; and the third applies the Multiplicity mindset to both.

Integrative Behavioral Couple Therapy

Integrative Behavioral Couple Therapy (IBCT) centers on the idea of accepting your partner as they are. In any relationship, differences are inevitable—after all, no two individuals are identical, so as partners grow closer and intertwine their lives, incompatibilities are bound to surface and possibly even grow. These problems can take many forms, ranging from annoying little habits and minor quirks to serious misconduct and major life conflicts. Many of these differences between you and your partner will be resistant to change—indeed, arm-twisting can even make these differences grow more deeply entrenched, creating additional irritation and conflict. An IBCT counselor will therefore work with couples to help them shift their focus from trying to fix each other to accepting their partner's imperfections. This approach reduces maladaptive interaction patterns and instead encourages partners to appreciate the positives that brought them together, along with the values and goals they share.

IBCT reminds Harry of a conversation he had with an old friend, Claire, at one of his high school reunions. Claire told him that her twenty-five-year marriage had always been happy and that she never complained about her husband. She explained that at their wedding, the officiant asked both her and her husband to make a list of ten things about the other that they would promise never to let bother them. Curious, Harry asked her, "What happens when he does something annoying that isn't on your list?" Claire smiled and said, "I just reclassify things and add it to my list."

This simple yet powerful strategy is worth trying in your own relationships.

Internal Family Systems

Internal Family Systems (IFS) is an approach to psychotherapy developed by Richard Schwartz that challenges the traditional notion of a "mono-mind"—that is, a singular, uniform identity that defines each person as an individual. Instead, Schwartz argues that everyone is composed of multiple parts, each with a distinct role. These parts fall into three categories:

- *managers*, who work to protect you from mistakes and potential harm;
- *firefighters*, who react automatically when painful events occur; and
- *exiles*, whose role is to hide your shameful or traumatic parts, notwithstanding your natural desire to be seen and known.

IFS asserts that these parts collectively make you the person who you are. As Schwartz explains: "These parts are not imaginary or symbolic. They are individuals who exist as an internal family within us—and the key to health and happiness is to honor, understand, and love every part."

IFS therapy works from the premise that although these parts may create challenges, their underlying intent is protective—namely, to shield you from harm. Thus, the key is to acknowledge and honor this protective role by cultivating a core sense of calmness, curiosity, and confidence. This internal compassion makes it possible "to love all our parts," as we discussed in the previous chapter—a perspective that, not coincidently, also encourages you to approach others with loving intent.

Acceptance and Commitment Therapy

Often, the emotional pain you experience comes less from the emotion itself and more from your attempts to deflect or avoid it. Acceptance and Commitment Therapy (ACT) teaches you a different approach—to accept your feelings as they arise without judgment and with full awareness. For example, if you were struggling with anxiety, you might be encouraged to let yourself feel it completely, without resistance or defense. The idea is that trying to push anxiety away often backfires, making it even more overwhelming. Paradoxically, the more you try to resist, the more intense the feeling becomes. Instead, ACT helps you reframe your relationship with difficult feelings, recognizing that they come from a deep internal place—perhaps a place that once served a purpose. By acknowledging your feelings without letting them control you, their grip weakens over time.

ACT offers several strategies to achieve this shift. One technique involves imagining the feelings as external events—observing them as if they were happening outside yourself (*Look at those feelings out there*). Another involves labeling emotions in a neutral, dispassionate way (*I am having the thought that I am scared*, rather than the more embodied thought, *I am scared!*), or even expressing them playfully by, for example, singing anxious thoughts aloud. These approaches help foster a healthier, more accepting relationship with your emotions.

ACT can support a Multiplicity mindset by shifting attention away from weaknesses and shortcomings, making space to affirm positive values and traits. ACT aligns closely with the idea of self-compassion, discussed in the previous chapter. Self-compassion encourages you to approach your failures and suffering with kindness, free from judgment, and with a balanced, "big picture" perspective—recognizing that we are all human and inherently fallible. Measuring your self-worth by your flaws, struggles, and past traumas can lead you to feel unlovable. A Multiplicity mindset, however, invites you to acknowledge, accept, and even appreciate these multiple aspects of yourself—not just strengths but also vulnerabilities—that shape your identity and self-understanding. This lens makes it clear that your mistakes don't define you as a person, and, importantly, it allows—even inspires—self-forgiveness. When you forgive yourself for circumstances or actions you regret (especially after making amends when possible), you become more likely to share your experiences with others (see chapter 5).

When applied to couples, ACT principles can also transform how you view your partner. Similar to IBCT, this involves accepting your partner's imperfections as part of a package that coexists with many strengths. Rather than trying to fix or change them, ACT encourages stepping back from judgmental thoughts about your partner's imperfections, reframing those thoughts as passing mental states rather than absolute truths. Instead of dwelling on worries or conflicts, focus on the shared values that connect you and your partner as a couple. Importantly, nonjudgmental acceptance doesn't mean tolerating harmful or destructive behavior—when these occur, it may be necessary to take appropriate actions. Rather, it means recognizing that everyone has imperfections. Loving—and the possibility of feeling loved—grows when partners embrace each other as they are, shortcomings and all.

The Behavior Experiment

Counselors and therapists use a variety of exercises to bring these principles to life. If you're unsure of how to put the Multiplicity mindset into practice, consider this straightforward but surprisingly challenging exercise developed by ACT trainers. Its goal is to cultivate acceptance in situations that commonly trigger frustration or discord—an invaluable skill for any relationship.

Begin by identifying one of your partner's behaviors that you find especially difficult or frustrating and have them do the same for you. Perhaps they work too much, constantly interrupt, forget important plans, or fail to pull their weight on household chores. Then, for one week, commit to observing these behaviors with full awareness and without judgment. This means acknowledging the behavior with curiosity and compassion—without trying to ignore, fix, criticize, or interpret. At the end of the week, reflect together how adopting an attitude of mindful acceptance shifted the dynamic between you and your partner. Did it reduce annoyance or conflict? Did it create a context for mutual respect and open sharing? By shifting from judgment to acceptance, this practice can help both you and your partner feel more loved and more understood.

Forgiveness

When you forgive, you in no way change the
past—but you sure do change the future.

—Bernard Meltzer

He who is devoid of the power to forgive
is devoid of the power to love.

—Martin Luther King Jr.

About twenty years ago, late one night, our (Harry and his wife Ellen) close friend Rachel showed up at our back door, distraught. She had just discovered that her husband of many years, Tom, was having an intense emotional and sexual affair with one of their friends. Rachel wept and wept, heartbroken and furious, and understandably vilifying Tom. She cried for what felt like hours, lamenting that she could not continue their marriage. As we listened and tried to console Rachel, we felt sure that this marriage was over. Fast-forward to today. Rachel and Tom invited us over for dinner in their new condo. They now spend most of their free time together, and their marriage is stronger than ever—fulfilling and satisfying for both of them.

One key step in enacting the Multiplicity mindset involves forgiveness. Letting go of resentment and bitterness is crucial not only for the person who has wronged you but also for your own happiness. (After all, it's you, not the transgressor, who carries the weight of those painful feelings. That would be Rachel in our story, not her husband Tom.) Without forgiveness, it's impossible to show your partner that you know and appreciate them as a whole person—nor, for that matter, is it possible to feel understood and valued by them in return. Forgiveness—especially in the context of an open and honest conversation about the offense—creates space for mutual understanding and trust to be restored and strengthened. Without forgiveness, partners remain stuck in their grievances, unable to move past the hurt. In fact, forgiveness is not optional if the relationship is to continue. If forgiveness feels impossible, it may be a sign that the kind of love and connection you seek can no longer be found in that relationship, and it may be best to look elsewhere.

It's important to understand what researchers mean by forgiveness. Forgiveness is not about condoning, justifying, minimizing, or excusing the hurt, nor does it mean forgetting that it happened. ("Forgive and forget" is not a recipe for happiness.) Instead, it means letting go of the desire for revenge and the impulse to cut off contact with the transgressor. Forgiveness begins by deeply reflecting on why the hurt occurred, followed by candid discussion that airs both parties' perspectives—something that our friends Rachel and Tom spent years doing. This process creates shared understandings, helps establish ground rules for how the relationship can move forward, and makes it possible for the relationship to continue (and perhaps even grow stronger).

Empirical research strongly supports the benefits of forgiveness. People who forgive feel less stress, anger, depression, anxiety, and rumination. They report higher levels of happiness, better health, and increased empathy toward others. In relationships, people who practice forgiveness are more committed, satisfied, and affectionate with their partners in daily interactions. They also handle conflicts more constructively. Although much of this evidence is correlational—meaning it doesn't establish a direct cause-and-effect relationship—there is reason for optimism. Randomized controlled intervention studies indicate that people can learn to forgive and, as a result, accrue the emotional and relational benefits that come with forgiveness.

There are many specific techniques and exercises for practicing forgiveness, but nearly all of them hinge on the two mindsets explored in this and the previous chapter: an openhearted, empathic perspective and the recognition that all people, including ourselves, are a mix of strengths and flaws. This approach is especially important when the person in need of your forgiveness is *you*. By compassionately accepting your own shortcomings and missteps, while simultaneously acknowledging your strengths and good deeds, you create the possibility for self-forgiveness.

Notably, the Multiplicity mindset is closely linked to the Sharing mindset, especially when it comes to secrets. People often hide parts of themselves, particularly those they fear would not be forgiven. Yet recall that a key precondition to feeling loved is being fully and authentically open, most crucially about your most vulnerable parts.

One of the most perilous secrets in marriage involves infidelity. Like Harry's friend Tom, most people who engage in nonconsensual extramarital affairs go to great lengths to conceal them. Yet paradoxically, infidelity, once revealed, doesn't invariably lead to divorce. Exact statistics are hard to pin down, but some studies indicate that as many as 60 percent of marriages in the United States remain intact—and even improve—after a confession of infidelity. In many instances, couples use the crisis as a turning point—an opportunity to strengthen their relationship through frank conversation, mutual forgiveness, and a deeper understanding of the underlying issues that contributed to the affair.

To be sure, not every transgression merits forgiveness. If something your partner has done is absolutely and unquestionably unacceptable to you, it may be time to move on. But for the relationship to continue, forgiveness is essential.

To restate our message: A key ingredient of any strong relationship is the ability to accept the bad with the good. Embracing multiplicity creates a foundation for both forgiveness and growth—both of which are essential to feeling truly loved.

We've now completed a guided tour through the five mindsets essential for balancing the Relationship Sea-Saw and, hence, for building understanding, trust, and stronger connections with your partner. To reiterate the guiding principle of this book: These mindsets create the conditions that allow both you and your partner to feel loved.

It's worth highlighting that many, if not most, of our examples in this chapter involve close or intimate partners. Yet, of course, not all relationships are the same. Lifting yourself and your partner on the Sea-Saw will look very different depending on whether your partner is a spouse, a coworker, a sibling, or a new acquaintance. You wouldn't (and shouldn't!) approach your teacher in the same way you would approach a potential date you just met on Tinder.

The next chapter explores how to apply the five mindsets to different types of relationships, clarifying how these mindsets remain meaningful and powerful across various flavors and dynamics of relationships.

PART IV

Applying the Five Mindsets to Modern Life

10

Feeling Loved in Different Kinds of Relationships

Each friend represents a world in us, a world possibly not born until they arrive, and it is only by this meeting that a new world is born.

—Anaïs Nin, The Diary of Anaïs Nin, Volume 1: 1931–1934

When we started writing this book, we realized something: Many people hear the phrase *feeling loved* and immediately think of romance—spouses, partners, soulmates. And we get it. After all, "lover" is the only relationship label that actually contains the word *love*, as if love only existed in a romantic or sexual context.

As we hope we've made clear throughout this book, love is much bigger than romance. Feeling loved is something that happens not just between romantic partners. It happens within all kinds of relationships—between two friends, between a parent and child, between a worker and boss, between teammates, and between a teacher and student. And feeling loved doesn't have to last a lifetime: You can feel loved for just a brief moment in time—during a eulogy, a therapy session, a first date, a visit with your doctor, a performance of a musical duet, a celebration of a touchdown, or a strategy meeting at work.

Embracing the five mindsets during your next conversation—and practicing the give-and-take of the Sea-Saw—can help yourself feel loved in all kinds of relationships. In this chapter, we hope to illustrate the remarkable breadth of the mindsets' reach. We also explore how some of the mindsets may need to be adjusted in different contexts. For example, are there unique considerations and constraints when you seek to feel loved by your teenage child? Or when you try to feel loved by your "work partner" versus your life partner? Absolutely, but the type of relationship, according to scientists, matters less than you might think.

Does the hierarchy implicit in your relationship matter? Yes, and it's important to know how. To offer just one example: The Sharing mindset ought to be applied differently in asymmetric relationships, such as those between a parent and child or between a supervisor and direct report. As we discuss later in the chapter, vulnerable sharing in such contexts—for both sides—may do more harm than good. But there appear to be few, if any, harms—to either side—from listening enthusiastically or viewing the person with compassion and without judgment in both asymmetric relationships and symmetric ones alike.

In short, each of the five mindsets come into play across the wide spectrum of contexts discussed here—from the intimacy of home to the dynamics of the workplace and everywhere in between. This naturally leads us to ask: What are the unique considerations when you want to feel more loved by your romantic partner, immediate family member, or close friend?

Inner Circle: Feeling Loved at Home

Romantic Partners

In our conversations about this book, many people confided in us that at some point—even in a long-term relationship—they hadn't always felt loved by their spouse or partner. It wasn't that they doubted their partner's love entirely, but there were moments when they believed that they *were* loved but didn't actually feel it. Furthermore, when we asked our survey respondents to recall a time when they felt unloved, they frequently pointed to experiences with romantic partners. Some examples:

- "My partner didn't notice how much effort I put into our relationship."
- "My wife and I had trouble communicating . . . and created a cycle of pushing each other out."
- "My [husband] tried to make me someone I wasn't."

Being in a committed relationship—one that may involve raising children, keeping house together, and sharing a past and a future—doesn't guarantee that you will always feel loved. As we explore in this book, feeling loved depends not just on the nature of your partnership, how much time you spend together, or your history as a couple but on how both partners approach the relationship—specifically, how they engage with the five mindsets and navigate the Relationship Sea-Saw.

At this point, some readers may assume that concerns about feeling unloved by romantic partners weigh more heavily on women. But you may be surprised: Recent research suggests that romantic relationships are actually more central to men's well-being than to women's. In other words, while both partners may struggle with feeling loved at times, men's happiness and life satisfaction tend to be more closely tied to their romantic relationships. This doesn't mean that romantic relationships are unimportant to women's happiness—it's just that women tend to draw emotional support from a wider range of sources. This finding challenges traditional assumptions and underscores just how critical it is for *both* partners to feel known, valued, and loved. Stay tuned for more on gender differences in the next chapter.

Accordingly, we begin by focusing on what it might take to feel loved by a romantic partner and then consider the similarities to and distinctions from what it might take to feel loved by an adolescent child or a very close friend. Notably, while our recommendations throughout *How to Feel Loved* apply to all kinds of relationships, they often feel especially relevant to romantic partnerships. Indeed, when illustrating the five mindsets, our real-life and hypothetical examples have frequently involved romantic partners—as well as close friendships and family bonds. It's easy to see how someone might practice sharing or listening to learn with a significant other. At their core, then, the mindsets apply seamlessly to all long-standing attachments, though the way their dynamics play out may differ depending on the type of relationship.

In many ways, deeply connected romantic, friend, and parent-child relationships share striking similarities. One way to capture this idea is that compared to other types of connections we'll explore later (such as those with your supervisor; a new friend, date, or coworker; or a stranger), these three relationships tend to be longer lasting and marked by higher levels of intimacy, interdependence, and safety.

- *Intimacy* is emotional closeness and vulnerability, and it comes with the risk of hurt and heartbreak.
- *Interdependence* is mutual reliance, though it can be uneven in some intimate relationships.
- *Safety* is feeling secure and accepted, knowing that you won't be judged or rejected.

By contrast, a dynamic expected exclusively within romantic relationships involves sexual energy.

These defining aspects of romantic relationships are likely to shape how you and your partner engage with the five mindsets. Similarly, when these characteristics emerge in other types of connections, the implications for embracing the mindsets are likely to be comparable.

Intimacy, Interdependence, and Safety: Implications for Sharing and Multiplicity

Romantic relationships present a challenge to the Sharing mindset because they combine two powerful forces: the potential for a unique kind of rejection and heartbreak combined with deep interdependence. How can you be sure that revealing something to your partner won't make them walk away, or be angry with or disappointed in you for a long time? For an extreme example, recall the case of the man we introduced in the chapter on the Sharing mindset—who spent decades hiding his past as a teenage murderer from his wife and children, living with the risk that revealing it could destroy everything. But even for those with far less dramatic secrets, the stakes can feel enormous—your social circle, support system, family, and maybe entire life could fall apart. Whether it's a selfish impulse you had, an embarrassing addiction, or something you've been hiding (such as your sexual orientation or gender identity), the fear of the consequences of disclosure is real. In fact, studies show that these are some of the most common topics that people find difficult to reveal to partners.

Conversely, the very qualities that define a strong, committed romantic relationship—psychological safety, intimacy, and trust—can have the opposite effect, making it easier to embrace the Sharing mindset. When you feel safe to express yourself to your romantic partner, opening up and sharing vulnerably becomes more comfortable and natural.

These very same qualities also have two key implications for the Multiplicity mindset. First, the mutual dependence and potential for hurt in close romantic relationships makes embracing the Multiplicity mindset even more essential. As described in the previous chapter, every person is selfish at times, breaks promises at times, and harbors thoughts or habits that others might find unacceptable. Just as a mosaic is made of both bright and dark pieces, a person is an amalgamation of virtues and flaws, shaped by their experiences, challenges, and triumphs. So when you make a vulnerable disclosure or listen to one from your partner, it's critical not to see yourself or them in absolute terms (e.g., *They're just a selfish person*) but, instead of rushing to judgment, to strongly consider expressing acceptance, sensitivity, and kindness. For close, enduring relationships, which carry great value and emotional investment, to continue, this kind of response is even more critical.

At the same time, when a romantic relationship provides genuine safety and security, it fosters a deeper appreciation of each other's beautiful complexity. Feeling truly seen and accepted by your partner makes it easier to extend that same generosity back to them—to recognize and cherish the many facets that make them who they are, flaws and all.

Of course, not all relationships provide this kind of safety and intimacy. If your romantic relationship or close friendship doesn't foster a sense of being truly seen and valued, it may be worth reflecting on whether you want to put the effort into deepening the connection. If you choose to do so, however, then actively practicing the five mindsets may help build the trust and closeness needed to feel genuinely loved.

Relationship Length: Implications for Sharing and Radical Curiosity

James and his husband, Evan, had spent nearly a decade together, much of it happy. But around the eight-year mark, James began to feel the passion fading—as if he were merely going through the motions. Yet he loved Evan so much that he couldn't bring himself to say aloud how he felt. When he finally did, however, he couldn't unsay it, which only made the loss of passion feel even more real. That conversation marked the beginning of the end of their relationship.

How does the length of a relationship shape the Sharing mindset? When Sonja and Harry were younger, and hadn't yet experienced decades-long relationships, they assumed that talking to someone becomes easier the longer you've known them. With time, they realized that the opposite is often true. As James and Evan's experience shows, the longer something goes unsaid—whether it's "It bothers me when you hum while eating," "I've never enjoyed hanging out with your best friend," or "I don't like the same [erotic activities/foods/movies/holiday traditions/etc.] as you"—the more uncomfortable it becomes to bring it up. You might fear your partner's responding, "Why didn't you tell me this five years ago?" Or worse: "You were a coward not to say something when it first happened! I could have fixed it if I'd known."

James and Evan's story highlights another important aspect we haven't yet explored—and that is how the *content* of vulnerable sharing might differ fundamentally depending on the length of the relationship. In chapter 5, we provided examples of what people might be reluctant to share when embracing the Sharing mindset—from self-doubts and feeling overwhelmed at work to sibling jealousy and long-ago lies. Notice that most of these examples involved people's sharing something about themselves. In newer or less deep relationships, individuals do often struggle to reveal aspects of themselves or their lives—perhaps their dysfunctional family, their embarrassing interests, or their private thoughts, feelings, self-doubts, fears, or dreams.

In long-term relationships, however, the reluctance to share often shifts. With your romantic partner, what you may find harder to express is something about the relationship itself or about the other person. Indeed, research on self-disclosure suggests that expressing your feelings *about your conversation partner* is among the most intimate and vulnerable forms of sharing. Notably, it's not just difficult emotions or criticisms that feel challenging to share—expressing positive feelings can be challenging as well. You may recall from previous chapters that the empirically validated Fast Friends procedure involves a series of escalating personal questions designed to foster closeness between two people. It's not a coincidence that one of the very last—most vulnerable—prompts is the following: "Tell your partner what you like about them, and be very honest."

Another unique aspect of long-term versus shorter-term romantic relationships is how your curiosity about your partner may diminish over time. Using the Radical-Curiosity mindset can become more challenging as the years go by, compared to when you first met and there were a million things to discover about each other. It's challenging, indeed, but not impossible. In *Passionate Marriage*, David Schnarch argues that the notion that romantic partners fully know each other after years together is a myth. In reality, both individuals are continually growing and evolving, harboring new private thoughts, feelings, and desires that have been left unspoken. One partner might be grappling with new anxieties about their body image, aging, finances, or career success or exploring changes in their sexual preferences or life goals that they've never voiced. The other might be rethinking their spirituality, feeling regrets about earlier decisions, or experiencing emotions such as jealousy that their partner never noticed. There may also be plenty of new positive experiences to be curious about—a new hobby, a new opportunity at work, or a new friend. Accordingly, although it requires effort, there's always more to discover in long-running marriages—and in long-running relationships in general. Continuing to show up with authentic, enthusiastic curiosity will lead you to revelations that invite the other person to reciprocate, instigating the Relationship Sea-Saw.

Sexual Intimacy: Implications for the Mindsets

A dynamic expected exclusively within romantic relationships involves sexual energy. Unlike close friendships and family relationships, where emotional closeness is the primary focus, romantic partners navigate both emotional and physical intimacy. The presence of passion in a relationship doesn't guarantee that one feels loved, because feeling desired isn't the same as feeling loved; however, it can enhance—or complicate—the application of the five mindsets.

For example, in any relationship, the Sharing mindset involves revealing more of your full self, through openness and vulnerability. But in romantic relationships, this sharing may be complicated by an implicit wish to be seen as attractive or desirable, such that you might hesitate to share insecurities about your body, finances, or past mistakes, fearing that doing so might diminish attraction. Paradoxically, though, the very act of sharing personal vulnerabilities (e.g., "I sometimes feel self-conscious about how I look") can deepen both emotional and physical intimacy. Unlike in friendships, where disclosure might focus more on emotions and shared experiences, in romantic relationships, sharing also means navigating unspoken desires, fears, and physical needs.

The Listening-to-Learn mindset, as applied to romantic relationships, reminds you that people don't just listen with their ears—they also listen with their bodies. The scent of your partner's skin, the way they feel close by, the way they touch you even in nonsexual moments, or even their presence lingering in a room after they've left can subtly reinforce feelings of connection. This sensory awareness can make conversations feel more intimate, even before a word is spoken. However, people differ in how they prefer to listen and be heard: One partner may express love through physical closeness, while the other craves deep conversation. Thus, unlike in other types of connections, listening in romantic relationships requires attunement not only to words and gestures but also to unspoken cues of physical touch and sexual energy.

Sexual energy can also impact the Radical-Curiosity mindset. In romantic relationships, curiosity fuels and maintains not just the attraction of being deeply known—which happens with close family and friends too—but sexual attraction, specifically. Just as curiosity invites partners to continue discovering each other's evolving needs, fears, and desires over time, it also plays a role in keeping sexual attraction alive. By staying curious, partners ensure that neither person feels emotionally stagnant or taken for granted.

Relationship scientists posit that opportunities to see each other in a new light, be surprised, or gain fresh insights are key to preserving the sense of mystery essential to sustaining intimacy and desire. This idea comes to life in the 2008 film *Four Christmases*, where Vince Vaughn and Reese Witherspoon add a touch of novelty to their relationship by pretending to be flirtatious strangers at a bar, engaging each other's curiosity by role-playing a new and surprising character. (We know a pair of married psychologists who actually do this!) In essence, curiosity can prevent relationships from falling into routine, keeping passion alive.

Finally, while the Open-Heart mindset benefits all relationships, it plays a distinctive role in long-term sexual relationships. Research out of the University of Toronto demonstrates that a desire to satisfy a partner's sexual needs—known as *sexual communal strength*—can strengthen romantic relationships, but only if both partners' needs are simultaneously taken into account. For example, a study found that when one partner consistently prioritizes the other at the expense of their own well-being—a pattern called *unmitigated sexual communion*—

the result is lower satisfaction and greater distress for both partners. In other words, adopting an Open-Heart mindset doesn't mean laser-focusing on your romantic partner's well-being—it means balancing attentiveness to their desires with your own well-being, so that both of you feel valued, desired, and fulfilled.

Parents and Children

A conversation between Sonja and her eleven-year-old daughter in late 2024:

Daughter: *"Have you seen Anthony lately?"*

Sonja: *"No, I decided I don't want to go out with him anymore."*

Daughter: *"Why?"*

Sonja: *"Well, I read something he wrote and realized that he's an asshole."*

Daughter: *"Mom! Everyone's an asshole. Don't forget that. Everyone's an asshole."*

Sonja was so proud of her daughter for embracing the Multiplicity mindset. And she hopes readers will embrace multiplicity and not judge her for discussing her dating life with a sixth grader.

Parent-child relationships are unique enough to warrant their own section. These bonds are inherently asymmetric. For example, unlike the dependence in romantic partnerships, where reliance is mutual, as well as more immediate and more stable, the dependence in parent-child relationships is initially one-sided. Over time, as children grow into adulthood and family roles evolve, this dynamic may shift—eventually balancing out or even reversing. Although this may sound obvious, because of this evolving asymmetry, the way you apply the five mindsets will look different depending on whether you're interacting with your parent or your child.

Implications for Sharing

As you may have noticed, we are big fans of vulnerable self-disclosure. However, such disclosure must be done in the right dose, at the right time, at the right pace, in the right place, to the right recipient, and with the right support. In applying the Sharing mindset to parent-child relationships, there are topics that naturally lend themselves well to open, honest discussion—such as talking about overcoming academic challenges, discussing family dynamics, explaining how you manage work or personal stress, or sharing experiences of personal growth and resilience—all of which can help create a sense of shared understanding.

With regard to more sensitive topics, however, the Sharing mindset must be exercised with great care and tailored to your child's personality and developmental stage. It goes without saying that certain disclosures from parents (e.g., about their inadequacies, sex life, or fears about the child) may be scary, unsettling, or even traumatizing for children and thus should be avoided. For other vulnerable disclosures, it depends. A parent's revelation of a childhood wound or their first love may be unwelcome and disturbing to some children but appreciated and empowering to others. (To wit, Harry's adult daughter Lianna doesn't want to hear about her parents' relationship or their past relationships—her usual response is a guttural "Ewww"—and Sonja's three oldest children are incredibly uncomfortable discussing her dating life. But her youngest finds the topic highly entertaining, instructive, and even bonding.)

The situation also matters. For example, when you're practicing tough love or disciplining your child, it's not the moment to reveal your personal insecurities or hidden motivations. Research by developmental psychologists has shown that children are psychologically healthiest when they feel comfortable having an open, confiding relationship with their parents. On the flip side of the coin, revealing certain feelings to your parent can risk straining your relationship with them, creating distance, or even poisoning it. This dynamic can occur in any relationship, but it is especially critical when one person is more vulnerable or dependent. Of course, this dynamic is likely to change when children become adults and the parent-child relationship becomes more equitable. Later, we describe asymmetric relationships in the workplace, which feature similar dynamics and require a similarly thoughtful approach to sharing.

Implications for Radical Curiosity and Listening to Learn

When it comes to other mindsets, parent-child relationships also present a number of unique challenges and considerations. To begin with, the Radical-Curiosity and Listening-to-Learn mindsets are likely to play out unevenly in such relationships. Parents typically show more curiosity and listen more attentively and enthusiastically to their children than the reverse. However, how do you strike the optimal balance between showing curiosity and prying? A teenager might appreciate a parent's interest in their new friends but feel suffocated if every conversation turns into an interrogation.

The answer lies in practicing attunement: Gauge the child's openness; carefully consider the difference between what a parent needs to know—for example, matters related to health and safety—and what they want to know; offer curiosity as an invitation rather than a demand; and give the child space to share at their own pace. This balance is especially delicate during adolescence, when young people are navigating the tension between independence and attachment. Probing too much can make teens feel scrutinized or pressured, leading to withdrawal, but stepping back too much may leave them feeling unseen or unsupported. The key is to strike a middle ground. Expressing consistent but nonintrusive, no-pressure interest—letting them know you're there when they're ready to talk—can help foster a sense of trust and openness over time.

Implications for Multiplicity

Similar to romantic relationships, parent-child relationships render the Multiplicity mindset both more essential and, at times, more fraught. Who better to practice being unconditionally accepting, forgiving, and nonjudgmental with than with your parents and with your kids? Who can better offer you so many data points—their traits, struggles, histories, and habits—that give you the opportunity to see the big picture of their life and perceive them as the whole, beautiful, flawed persons that they are? At the same time, it may be challenging to accept your children's shortcomings—after all, their traits and habits often feel like reflections of your own.

These ideas seem reasonable, but they raise more questions than answers. For example, how do you embrace the Multiplicity mindset without excusing bad behavior? One key approach, articulated by psychologist Haim Ginott and widely used to guide parenting and couples' communication, is to separate the person from the behavior. Imagine a parent whose teenage daughter lies about completing a school assignment. A Multiplicity mindset doesn't mean condoning dishonesty—in essence, it means criticizing the behavior but not the child. (You can say, for example, "What you did was not okay," without implying, "You are a bad person.") One way to do this involves stepping back and considering the fuller picture—perhaps she lied because she is afraid of disappointing her parents, struggling with self-doubt or learning disabilities, or avoiding a bigger issue at school. Recognizing these complexities opens the door for accountability without condemnation and to the possibility of growth, addressing the behavior without reducing the child to that one moment.

Turning the mindset around, how do you teach a child to see a parent through the lens of multiplicity? One way is straightforward—through direct modeling. When children see their parents admit mistakes, speak from the heart, or explain past decisions with nuance, they learn that people are not just their worst moments or their biggest achievements. For example, a parent who apologizes for losing their temper and explains that they had a stressful day teaches the child that emotions are complex and that people—parents included—are multidimensional. Another way is via storytelling. Sharing a grandparent's struggles or describing past hardships helps children to see their caregivers as full human beings rather than just rule enforcers.

You likely didn't choose your children or your parents—and, as the saying goes, you "can't divorce them"—so if they have regrettable qualities, it's even more important to view them through the multiplicity lens.

Postscript: The Power of Parents' Consistency and Warmth

Recent research highlights just how much parental behaviors can shape a child's experience of feeling loved on a daily basis. In a study of US families, adolescents aged fourteen to sixteen reported feeling significantly more loved on days when their parents expressed warmth—such as by offering compliments, listening attentively, or showing affection—and they felt less loved on days marked by conflict. Moreover, a year later, those who consistently felt more loved experienced greater autonomy, a stronger sense of purpose, and personal growth. However, fluctuations in how loved they felt also mattered: Adolescents who showed greater instability in feeling loved—for example, feeling very loved by their parent one day but experiencing their parent's emotional distance the next—reported poorer relationships and a diminished sense of control over their lives a year later. These findings underscore the relevance of the five mindsets to parenting, reinforcing the importance of what you share with your children and how you express warmth and attentiveness each day. They also highlight again the necessity of practicing emotional attunement—such as by demonstrating curiosity without overstepping.

Best Friends and Close Family:
The Other Lasting Bonds

Evelyn had been regularly visiting with Margie, her friend since middle school, for the past twenty-two years. Yet for eighteen of those years, Evelyn quietly nursed a lingering grievance. Back in 2006, Margie had failed to invite her on a friends' ski weekend—a slight Evelyn couldn't forget. Finally, after nearly two decades of holding it in, she revealed that long-simmering resentment. Margie was stunned, but she listened, and to their mutual relief, they managed to repair their friendship.

As Evelyn and Margie's story illustrates, deep friendships share many of the same complexities as do other close, long-running relationships. Romantic partners and children aren't the only ones who can hurt or reject you—siblings and friends, as well, can break your heart. The stakes in these relationships may not involve marriage vows or financial obligations, but they similarly involve interdependence, intimacy, trust, safety, and emotional investment. Indeed, despite the lack of formal commitments, best friends and close family members are often the people who know you best, which makes their approval—or rejection—all the more significant.

Because of this, many of the same challenges that arise in romantic and parent-child relationships also apply here. Like other strong, enduring relationships, friendships and sibling bonds require balancing intimacy and independence—that is, being close enough to confide in and count on each other and, at the same time, giving each other space. And just as in romantic partnerships, it's often not the personal secrets that are hardest to disclose but something about the relationship itself or about the other person—grievances left unspoken, disappointments swept under the rug, or shifts in priorities that create silent distance, as Evelyn and Margie experienced.

Implications for Sharing

When there's both a deep emotional connection and the possibility of heartbreak, sharing can feel risky. How do you know that revealing something difficult to your best friend or sibling won't push them away, spark lasting resentment, or change how they see you forever? The same fears that make vulnerability difficult in romantic partnerships apply here too. And just as we saw with long-term romantic connections, the longer something remains unsaid, the harder it becomes to bring it up.

At the same time, the safety of a long, shared history can also render it *easier* to practice the Sharing mindset—especially when a relationship has withstood the test of time. Unlike in early-stage friendships, where a misstep might end things prematurely, decades-long bonds have already survived ups and downs, proving their resilience. Evelyn and Margie's friendship endured not because there was never tension or hurt but because, when the moment came, they were willing to listen, to repair, and to continue forward together. While it can be hard to risk vulnerability with someone who has known you forever, it is often precisely that history that makes the effort worthwhile.

Implications for Radical Curiosity, Listening to Learn, and Multiplicity

Long-term friendships, like romantic relationships, can challenge the Radical-Curiosity mindset. When you've known someone for decades, it's tempting to assume you already know everything there is to know about them. But unless you've been following them around with a camera, there are undoubtedly aspects of their lives you haven't witnessed, and showing curiosity about these parts can deepen your friendship. Also, just as romantic partners continue to evolve, so do close friends and family. That's why it's important to continue to listen with your best, most attentive self and to continue to ask questions. Remaining genuinely curious—about their changing values, struggles, and aspirations—keeps the friendship vibrant.

Finally, like romantic relationships and parent-child bonds, deep friendships offer countless opportunities to embrace the Multiplicity mindset. Who other than a best friend has seen you at your best and worst—your triumphs, failures, phases, and contradictions? Sonja and Harry readily admit that over the years, their closest family and friends have witnessed their being immature and defensive, enthusiastic and bold, lazy and cynical. And yet, even in these relationships, it's easy to fall into rigid, one-sided ways of seeing each other. The friend you knew in your twenties isn't the same person in their forties, just as you have evolved in ways they may not fully appreciate. Recognizing that your closest friendships, like all relationships, involve change and complexity enables you to hold space for their full, multifaceted self—just as you hope they will for you.

Feeling Loved Beyond the Inner Circle: From Strangers to New Connections to Colleagues

When you think about relationships, your mind likely goes first to your inner circle, the people you trust most—your closest friends, close family members, and romantic partners. These are the communal loving relationships that we have been discussing—the ones that help you feel grounded, supported, and secure. Robert Putnam, a political scientist at Harvard University, calls these connections "bonding social capital"—the close-knit relationships that build a sense of belonging and support. When you're moving to a new apartment, these are the people who show up with boxes and a dolly. When you're struggling, they're the ones who know exactly the right words to lift you up before you even ask. When you need to tell someone about winning the lottery, they're ready to share your excitement.

But, as Putnam warns, bonding social capital has a potential downside. While these ties foster closeness and solidarity, they can also create social bubbles—ones that, intentionally or not, make it harder to reach beyond our immediate circles. This isn't necessarily about exclusion or division but about familiarity: We naturally gravitate toward those we already know, who feel similar to us and are just more comfortable to be around.

Enter "bridging social capital"—the ties that connect you to people who exist outside your usual networks and who may differ from you in cultural background, generation, politics, career stage, religion, interests, talents, or worldview. These bridging relationships don't just expand your network; they have potential to expand your perspective—to reduce prejudice, break down stereotypes, and cultivate openness.

Of course, real-world relationships don't fit neatly into these categories. Many of the people you may grow close to—such as colleagues, neighbors, or acquaintances who ultimately become good friends—start out as part of your bridging social capital but become part of your bonding social capital. In workplaces, for instance, some colleagues may share your interests, values, and outlook, while others may push you beyond your comfort zone, challenging your preconceptions and broadening your views.

Bridging social capital is harder to build, but we propose that extending the five mindsets beyond your inner circle—whether to a new friend, a recently hired colleague, your boss, or even your barista or plumber—helps erect those bridges. Feeling loved is about feeling seen and respected not only by those in your inner circle but also by those you encounter in everyday life. And when you feel loved by people outside your bubble, you not only feel respected and understood, you also engage with people who are different from you, helping *them* feel respected and understood.

Feeling Loved by Strangers

On a crowded morning commuter train, passengers sit just inches apart, absorbed in their own worlds—scrolling through their phones, staring out the window, or immersed in books—and rarely speaking to one another. Most assume that keeping to themselves will make the commute more pleasant and pass more quickly. In a clever study, researchers at the University of Chicago put this assumption to the test. They asked some commuters on trains and public buses in the Chicago area to strike up a conversation with a stranger sitting nearby, while others were instructed to remain silent. To the participants' own surprise, those who engaged in conversation reported a significantly more enjoyable commute—despite having expected the opposite. And this effect isn't unique to the US Midwest. Similar findings have emerged from coffee-shop customers in Vancouver, Canada, who were assigned to chat with their baristas, and from shuttle-bus riders in Ankara, Turkey, who were encouraged to converse with their drivers. Interacting with strangers, it turns out, leaves people happier than they expect. So does performing random acts of kindness and giving simple compliments. Can these brief encounters go beyond mere enjoyment—can they help you feel loved?

Sonja and Lucy, an old school friend, had sons the same age, and when Lucy's son, Nate, was nineteen, he was diagnosed with cancer. This is how Lucy described that year in an email:

> *The year 2022 was fine until February 15, when Nate, the one who is always wrong and a bit of a pothead, told me he had a lump on his "right fella," and he was sure it was testicular cancer, and did I know how to find a urologist? Within a couple of days, we*

knew Nate was right, and worse his "ball cancer"—as he called it—spread. That was the end of 2022, for all practical purposes. I learned a lot about surgeries (plural) and chemo and how to carry a 6'3" man upstairs (which is easier than downstairs).

Lucy had been following Sonja's research on the power of connecting moments, and offered this portrait of Nate:

One of the things that helped Nate the most was doing chemo with breast cancer patients. He calls his cancer "baby cancer" compared to theirs. They played cards and ate and chatted during chemo and were, as Nate said, "happy." He liked the breast cancer ward much more than the urological cancer ward for this reason and would ask to do his [chemo] there. He had this schtick with "my ladies." They would say, "How's it going, Nate?" and he would say in a very low voice, "Got me some ball cancer but that's why God invented marijuana!" And they would all laugh, "a bunch of baldies laughing our asses off." It was an unlikely group—Nate, a young Oxford grad, joking and bonding with women decades older from all walks of life—but somehow, it worked. I would ask him if his day was good and he would say, "Yeah not bad—I was with my ladies, they brought cookies!" And then, after a pause, he'd grin and add, "I don't think I ever expected to feel so much love in a cancer ward. But I did."

The last time that Sonja felt loved by a stranger was when her neighbor Gary—whom she'd never met before, nor has encountered since—saw something blow out of her car when she rounded the corner into their street. He happened to have been driving close behind her and, noticing the issue, surprised her by walking over to her garage with his tools to fix it. Gary listened intently (using the Listening-to-Learn mindset) as Sonja described what happened. He radiated radical curiosity. He recognized her anxiety and instinctively wanted to alleviate it and make her happy (Open Heart). As Sonja went upstairs to fetch him a seltzer, she felt loved.

An unforgettable time that Harry felt loved by people he barely knew was in graduate school. He had been stuck in an unfulfilling marriage with no clear way out. In an effort to explore new connections, he joined an "encounter group"—a type of informal group therapy popular in the 1960s, where a dozen or so participants engaged in deep self-disclosure and active listening. One evening, the group took part in an exercise where everyone had to choose one person in the group they really wanted to know better. Harry was sure no one would pick him. And then three women picked his name! In that brief instant, Harry felt incredibly loved.

If you were skeptical that feeling loved by strangers or new acquaintances is even possible, we hope these stories changed your mind. It's true that most of the time the word *love* doesn't apply to such situations, yet Sonja and Harry can recall numerous such times in their lives when they felt loved, even if just for a fleeting moment. Nate described feeling loved in the cancer ward, and we bet the ladies he interacted with felt it too. How does that happen? We propose that the answer lies in the five mindsets, which have the power to turn an ordinary moment into a Sea-Saw moment—where there's intimacy in sharing, undivided listening, openheartedness, and affirming curiosity. In these moments, you convey that you see the other person's humanity and want them to be happy. Here's one of a great many ways that such a moment could unfold.

First:

- Your smile signals interest,
- your posture signals respect, and
- your words communicate understanding.

Next:

- They laugh out loud and track closely your next words.

Then:

- You feel understood,
- they feel understood, and
- you both feel a sense of camaraderie and mutual affection.

Yes, it's possible to feel loved by your doctor, teacher, student, coach, or even hairstylist—sometimes for just a moment and sometimes for longer, sometimes within the bounds of a specific role and sometimes in a broader sense. In one study, 7,255 US adults were asked whether they had felt "love" during the previous hour and, if yes, whether they felt it toward a partner, a child, another family member, or someone else ("none of the above"). Of those who reported feeling love, almost 1 in 10 said they felt it toward someone other than an intimate. We (Harry and Sonja) sometimes talk about feeling love for and from our PhD students. While there are clear boundaries and limits to how well we understand and love our students (and how well they understand and love us), that doesn't mean the feeling is any less real.

Feeling Loved in New(er) Relationships: New Friends, Dates, and Colleagues

Every friend, lover, and trusted colleague starts as a stranger. Whether you move to a new neighborhood, begin a new job, or embark on a fresh adventure, forming meaningful relationships requires interacting with people who are initially unfamiliar. In these early stages, how can you apply the five mindsets to situations where you're still figuring each other out—on the first few dates with a potential romantic partner, during a series of calls with a new coworker, or while getting to know a new acquaintance at church or synagogue?

Implications for Sharing

Consider how the Sharing mindset might operate differently in these situations. With fewer data points to get a read on the other person—and for them to get a read on you—a common thread in early connections is a heightened pressure to impress. This is why first dates often resemble performances and why first meetings at work often look like carefully curated self-presentations. In these moments, revealing your full self to a date or revealing your full "work" self to a new colleague can feel daunting—and is probably counterproductive.

In new relationships, the other person may have some background knowledge about you—what others have observed or said—but they don't yet have a firsthand, solid understanding of your personality, habits, or strengths. This lack of a shared history presents a challenge because it means that any new piece of information may radically shape—or even shake—the other person's perception of you (and your perception of them). That is, with no prior knowledge to buffer or contextualize a disclosure, any new piece of information carries more weight. A joke that falls flat or an unconventional opinion may seem like a defining trait rather than a minor quirk. This also explains why people tend to be cautious about revealing vulnerabilities early on. The good news? As relationships grow and deepen, shared experiences accumulate and trust builds, offering more data points and more context and reducing the need to constantly impress. Over time, a fuller, more nuanced picture of each person emerges, enabling a richer sense of being known.

Implications for Listening to Learn and Radical Curiosity

Listening and curiosity may seem similar across all relationships, but in new connections, they likely play an outsized role. When you don't yet have history with someone, asking thoughtful questions and showing genuine interest is one of the most effective ways to create rapport and closeness. Indeed, the most liked conversationalists are those who listen attentively and continue asking follow-up questions. This approach can also prevent a common misstep in early connections—that is, relying on stereotypes or surface-level impressions. Approaching new people with radical curiosity—and paying close attention to their responses—helps you resist the urge to judge too quickly and creates the space for more meaningful exchanges.

Implications for Multiplicity and an Open Heart

Next, consider the Multiplicity mindset. Viewing others with a wide, tolerant, nonjudging lens applies across all relationships, but it can be especially challenging when the relationship is new or opaque. When you've known someone for years, you have the benefit of witnessing their contradictions, their strengths alongside their shortcomings, and the full spectrum of their life story. But in early relationships, your perspective is limited. You may meet a colleague on a high-stress day and assume they're always tense or go on a first date with someone who's a little reserved and conclude they lack warmth. When there's less information to rely on—or when there's less complexity to witness—it's harder to see the other person with complexity and easier to fall into black-and-white judgments. Enter the Open-Heart mindset. Maybe they're tired, anxious about meeting you, or had a rough morning. An accepting, patient, compassionate perspective can get you past an awkward beginning.

That's also why it's wise to hold early impressions lightly and generously. Just as first dates and first work meetings can be performances, they can also offer you a distorted view. A person's true character is revealed over time, through a collection of interactions rather than a single moment. Accordingly, the ways the mindsets are exercised can shift and adapt as relationships transition from one form to another—for example, from new colleague to close friend or from casual dating partner to long-term companion.

Unequal (Hierarchical) Work-Related Connections

Our colleague Marta once struggled with the prospect of having a difficult conversation at work. After being passed over for an opportunity she believed she deserved, she felt undervalued and hurt. Afraid to rock the boat, she hesitated to express her disappointment to her boss, worrying about potential repercussions. Eventually, with encouragement, she decided to speak up. The conversation was tense, but—we were relieved to learn—it paved the way for a more honest understanding of expectations and, over time, improved her working relationship with her boss.

Now let's turn to the workplace, where power dynamics shape relationships in distinct ways. Is feeling loved at work possible or even relevant to this book? We believe it absolutely is, though many people hesitate to use the word *love* in this context. Here we consider work-related relationships, with hierarchies typically rooted in financial, pragmatic, or professional structures—for example, when one party hires or supervises the other; or serves as their boss versus employee, teacher versus student, doctor versus patient, or seller versus client. In these connections, one person typically holds higher status, authority, or expertise, while the other may be more dependent. Hence, professionally oriented relationships feature unique dynamics, meaning that practicing any of the five mindsets may look and feel somewhat different.

Implications for Sharing

The Sharing mindset, for example, might feel even more daunting in workplace hierarchies. Much as with new connections, there's often a heightened need to impress, which can make authentic, vulnerable sharing feel risky or inappropriate—something we have seen in other types of relationships as well. And when you hesitate to show more of your full self, you slow down the process by which you become better known—and hence feel fully known and loved.

Compared to your inner-circle relationships, workplace connections typically involve less emotional closeness, less shared history, less "baggage," and less interdependence. Thus, in these settings, sharing vulnerably is typically less about deep personal emotions and more about work-related concerns—such as anxiety over an upcoming presentation or uncertainty about whether one's performance is strong enough. This has an upside: With fewer emotional stakes, there's often a lower risk of personal hurt. But there's also a significant downside—having less of a sense of psychological safety and shared values, which can make genuine openness feel fraught. For example, sharing in a workplace context can sometimes come across as transactional or calculating (e.g., if it seems like a strategic move to gain an advantage) or even professionally risky (e.g., if revealing doubts or struggles causes colleagues or supervisors to question your competence or reliability).

As in parent-child relationships, power asymmetries can make the Sharing mindset feel imbalanced. For example, as our friend Marta experienced, when emotional candidness happens between bosses and employees, the asymmetry of the connection may place a unique risk on both parties. When employees let down their guard with their bosses, the possibility of negative repercussions is real—such as being seen as weak, less competent, or even dispensable. Conversely, for the person in charge, if your employee, client, or student learns something personal about you, you may fear losing your authority and their respect or creating awkwardness that can harm your relationship forever. For instance, if a manager confesses to struggling with impostor syndrome, will their team see them as relatable and humble, or will they start questioning their manager's leadership ability?

Implications for Listening to Learn and Radical Curiosity

The Radical-Curiosity and Listening-to-Learn mindsets often manifest unevenly in imbalanced relationships—namely, employees often display more curiosity and attentiveness toward their managers than managers do toward them. This aligns with research showing that people who are lower in status and power generally have greater insight into and understanding of those who are higher in status and power—partly because the lower-status parties pay closer attention and are more motivated to learn. After all, recognizing your supervisor's triggers or appreciating what they care most about may be the difference between getting fired and getting promoted. People high in status and power, by contrast, are often relatively clueless about their lower-status counterparts.

Ironically, research on workplace listening suggests that when leaders actively listen to their employees, the benefits extend beyond improved relationships—high-quality listening predicts greater job satisfaction, higher employee engagement, and even better performance. In one study, speakers who conversed with good listeners—for example, who paraphrased, asked thoughtful follow-up questions, and withheld judgment—reported higher levels of psychological safety and lower levels of anxiety. In another study, schoolteachers who evaluated their principals as good listeners were less likely to want to quit, even when experiencing a lot of stress, and more likely to help one another. In short, workplaces with inherent power dynamics—meaning nearly every workplace—stand to benefit when leaders are encouraged to truly listen to their employees.

In some ways, listening and curiosity function similarly in workplace settings to the way they do in personal ones. However, there are notable distinctions. For example, a person's role or circumstance sometimes *requires* superior listening and curiosity—such as when mentors, doctors, teachers, or therapists offer relatively greater attention and enthusiasm to their protégés, patients, students, or clients. Sometimes you are literally paid to listen to learn; listening is part of the job description. Yet even in these paid contexts—whether in a workplace, a classroom, or a hospital room—high-quality listening fosters not just understanding but also trust, efficacy, and engagement. Employees who feel listened to are more engaged and empowered and less burned out; students who feel heard are more likely to participate in class; and patients who perceive their doctors as attentive and curious not only are more satisfied with their health care but also report better health outcomes.

Fortunately, whether or not you're explicitly paid to listen, organizational scientists have developed practical listening techniques tailored to workplace contexts. One such technique is "respectful inquiry," in which you (the leader) ask your team open-ended questions, signaling an invitation to share views on equal footing, and listen attentively and thoughtfully to their responses. Another approach is called "conversational receptiveness," in which you communicate your willingness to engage constructively and nondefensively with any opposing views expressed by others, creating space for dialogue and making them feel heard. Both of these evidence-based techniques are closely aligned with the Listening-to-Learn and Radical-Curiosity mindsets and can easily be exported from the office and channeled into conversations and debates with family, neighbors, and friends.

Implications for an Open Heart

Another distinctive way that the mindsets manifest in unequal relationships involves the Open-Heart mindset. While expressing loving-kindness and an open heart is both possible and desirable in nearly any connection, the intensity of compassion, love, and care is naturally smaller and less intense in newer relationships and in workplace relationships—which are typically less close, less enduring, or less significant. This is one reason that people use words such as *care, connection, warmth,* and *belonging*—but pointedly, not *love*—to describe their feelings at work. The other reason is that people are simply uncomfortable using the word *love* in workplace or professional contexts. If that includes you, we invite you to reconsider. Love that is felt less deeply and intensely is still love.

This type of love, even though understated, also has powerful consequences. Researchers at the Human Flourishing Program at Harvard University analyzed responses to surveys, personnel files, and health-insurance claims from 1,209 employees of a large US national service organization. One year later, employees who reported feeling cared for at work were more productive and engaged, felt less distracted and more socially connected, had lower odds of depression and higher well-being, and showed better physical health and financial security. Notably, these outcomes may be within easier reach than you may think. For example, research shows that employees report stronger feelings of intimacy in the workplace when they experience good listening from their colleagues or supervisors. In light of such findings, it's unfortunate that many leaders resist the idea that showing care for employees as human beings is part of their job, believing that dispassionate professionalism should take precedence over personal connection.

Conclusion:
We Are Love

When love is defined in its broadest sense, it's safe to say that most people experience multiple loves in their lives. In *All About Love*, cultural critic bell hooks proposes that love is a universal concept that transcends romance:

When we see love as the will to nurture one's own or another's spiritual growth, revealed through acts of care, respect, knowing, and assuming responsibility, the foundation of all love in our life is the same. There is no special love exclusively reserved for romantic partners. Genuine love is the foundation of our engagement with ourselves, with family, with friends, with partners, with everyone we choose to love.

No matter its shape or target of affection, love, as hooks describes it, is made of the same substance—sewn from the same cloth, exchanged through the same currency, expressed through the same behaviors, and rooted in the same psychological processes. It sounds like a cliché, yet it's a beautiful argument: Love is everywhere, around us, and within us.

The oldest members of Gen Z, born between 1997 and 2012, are pushing thirty. Surveys show that this generation is increasingly meeting its relational needs without a committed romantic or sexual partner, with some statistics pegging that proportion as high as 35 percent. For example, 2022–23 data from the National Survey of Family Growth reveals that Gen Zers were more than twice as likely to be sexually inactive as Gen Xers were at the same age. A similar pattern of diminishing relationship activities has been found for dating, with only about 55 percent of high school seniors having ever gone on a date in 2015, compared to approximately 85 percent for previous generations. Even when it comes to watching shows and films, according to a 2023 UCLA Teens and Screens survey, 70 percent of Gen Zers in 2023 said they preferred to see friendship, rather than romance, on-screen.

Beyond romantic relationships, Millennials and Gen Zers are having fewer children than any generation before them, with US birth rates hitting record lows—an average of 1.6 per couple—despite these groups entering their prime childbearing years. It turns out that this trend isn't limited to the United States—*The New Yorker* noted that "2023 saw the world as a whole slump beneath the replacement rate for the first time."

While some of these trends are concerning, they are also a reminder of a key argument in this book—that one can feel truly loved by a variety of people in one's life. Feeling loved isn't limited to romance, nor is it confined to a select few relationships. Romance may not even be the best or most important place to feel loved. Whether it's a long-term partner, a best friend, a child, a colleague, or even a stranger, the opportunity to feel loved exists across all types of relationships.

The clear implication is that you can be single and still feel genuinely loved (as well as genuinely happy, according to research). You can be childless and still feel genuinely loved. You can be motherless, petless, jobless, and godless, and still feel genuinely loved. Practice the five mindsets daily, and weave them into the fabric of your everyday interactions. You will open the door to feeling loved more of the time, in more places, in more relationships, and in more contexts.

11

What If One Size Doesn't Fit All? Diagnosing the Personal Qualities That Make Feeling Loved Easier or Harder

Without diversity, life would be very boring.

—*Catherine Pulsifer*

Between us, we (Harry and Sonja) have amassed ninety years of experience in exploring what drives human beings and what leads them to be happy—both in their lives overall and in their relationships. We were both trained as social psychologists first and personality psychologists second. The difference between these two fields is that social psychology focuses on how people tend to respond similarly in the same situation, and this perspective has shaped our initial ideas about feeling loved. The five mindsets embody this approach: Through decades of research, accumulated knowledge, and some intuition, we've come to believe that most people will feel more loved most of the time if they apply the mindsets to the conversations in their lives and turn those conversations into Relationship Sea-Saws.

Accordingly, most of the empirical studies we've conducted have explored the ways that people are fundamentally alike—for example, how and why everyone's heart sinks after loss and lifts after triumph, and which interventions can help. At the same time, our research, along with that of our colleagues, has uncovered myriad ways in which people are unique and different. This is where our training in personality psychology—or individual differences—comes in. How you apply a particular mindset—and how successful you are—depends on factors such as your personality, mental health, attachment style, cultural background, gender, and age. What's more, how your *conversation partner* applies a particular mindset—and how successful they are—depends on *their* personality, mental health, attachment style, cultural background, gender, and age.

This is the question we turn to next. It's an important one, because it highlights why you may find it challenging in certain relationships or in particular situations to get to the place where you feel loved, even when you're doing everything "right." Of course, it's not possible to review all the factors that help answer this question—many of the possibilities, in fact, haven't yet been explored by researchers. That said, a number of factors have been studied, and we'll highlight here the most relevant ones. We hope that this chapter will illuminate, for example, why someone in your life may struggle to share with or to listen to you (even when you're offering them your full, enthusiastic attention), and why, despite all your exertions, you sometimes feel less loved than you expect. Most important, we offer guidance for how to overcome such challenges. In sum, this chapter will help you diagnose the barriers to feeling loved and identify the facilitators to feeling loved.

Personality and Socioemotional Traits

Your personality, mental health, and attachment style impact the ways that you approach social situations and opportunities to develop meaningful connections with others—for example, whether you are confident, energetic, and enjoy frequent social interactions; or whether you feel too shy, anxious, or differently wired to bring yourself to leverage the mindsets. The same goes for the person you are with.

Fortunately, research and theory on individuals with these traits informs what strategies you could use to overcome what's difficult and catalyze what's easy.

Extraversion and Openness

As a case in point, when it comes to the Sharing mindset, people's personality traits and emotional tendencies play a role in how they self-disclose. Research shows that individuals high in extraversion (characterized by sociability, enthusiasm, and a tendency to seek out social interactions) and openness to experience (marked by interest in learning, appreciation for beauty, and creative imagination) tend to share more about themselves than do their peers, making them naturally inclined toward this mindset. For example, an outgoing and adventurous person may enthusiastically recount personal experiences, travel stories, or reflections on personal growth, which makes it easier for them to forge quick connections.

This research suggests that if you or your partner are more introverted or shy, embracing the Sharing mindset may require more intentional effort. This could mean starting with smaller, low-stakes disclosures—such as sharing a daily highlight or a personal preference—before gradually opening up about deeper thoughts and feelings. It may also help to create structured opportunities for sharing, such as setting aside time for reflective conversations or using prompts to guide discussions, making self-disclosure feel more natural and less daunting.

Neurodivergence

For those with high-functioning autism (HFASD), adopting the Listening-to-Learn mindset can be more challenging due to difficulties in reading nonverbal cues. Research suggests that individuals on the autism spectrum often struggle with recognizing subtle facial expressions, shifts in tone, or body language that signal interest, boredom, or discomfort. For example, during a conversation, a person with HFASD might listen intently to a friend sharing a personal struggle but fail to pick up on cues that the speaker is seeking social support rather than a factual response. This difficulty in recognizing conversational signals can make it harder to fully engage in high-quality listening, sometimes leading the speaker to feel misunderstood or dismissed.

As mentioned earlier, Harry has long taught a course on relationships and emotions at the University of Rochester. Several HFASD students have taken the class because they want to better understand something that feels elusive to them: human relations and emotions. One student told Harry that he was taking the course because he "wants to know what the rules are." By applying their more intellectual way of thinking, HFASD individuals hope to be better able to navigate their interactions and relationships. Something similar occurs for individuals with other conditions that make it difficult to identify facial expressions of emotion, including those with alexithymia (difficulty identifying and describing emotions) or prosopagnosia (inability to recognize faces, even familiar ones, as well as facial expressions). John Cleese's 2001 entertaining video series *The Human Face* depicts the story of a man attempting to correct this incapacity by systematically studying faces and the emotions they reveal—something that most people do naturally.

If this description resonates with your experience with your conversation partner, practicing explicit verbal check-ins with them—such as asking, "Would you like advice, or do you just want me to listen?"—can help clarify expectations and improve the quality of connection. If you are neurodivergent yourself, learning to recognize common social cues through resources such as videos, social stories, or coaching can make nonverbal communication more intuitive over time.

Similarly, HFASD individuals may express radical curiosity in specific ways. If your partner is on the spectrum, they may be intensely curious about particular topics—sometimes becoming experts in niche areas—but may struggle to engage with subjects outside their primary interests. For example, someone deeply fascinated by astronomy might eagerly discuss black holes for hours but show little curiosity when you share with them an experience about a challenging work situation. This narrowed focus can sometimes limit their enthusiasm for conversations that fall outside their interests, making conversations more challenging. If you are neurodivergent, one helpful strategy is to set a personal goal of always asking one or two follow-up questions about a partner's topic of interest before steering the conversation toward your preferred subjects.

Finally, the Multiplicity mindset, which requires seeing other people as complex and multidimensional, can be particularly difficult for individuals with HFASD due to challenges in theory of mind—the ability to understand and appreciate that others have perspectives, thoughts, and emotions different from one's own. For example, if their supervisor seems upset but doesn't explicitly state why, a person with HFASD may have trouble recognizing that the supervisor's bad mood is unrelated to anything they said or did. This can make it harder to practice the Multiplicity mindset, which requires acknowledging that people hold contradictory emotions, change over time, and behave in ways that are influenced by a wide range of internal and external factors.

To improve this ability in yourself over time, practice perspective-taking exercises. For example, when observing a social interaction— on TV, in a meeting, or at a café—ask yourself what emotions each person might be experiencing and what might be motivating their words or body language. Seeking direct feedback from trusted friends or partners can also provide useful insights into how others experience emotions differently.

If you or your conversation partner are navigating these challenges, it's important to approach the mindsets with patience and self-compassion. It may seem obvious but small adjustments—such as setting clear conversational expectations, using structured curiosity, and actively working on perspective-taking—can make a meaningful difference in strengthening feelings of being understood and loved.

Insecure Attachment Style

What about attachment styles, or the patterns of bonding that people learn as children and carry into their adult intimate relationships? Some people have highly insecure attachment styles that make it difficult for them to feel loved as deeply or as frequently as they want or to apply the mindsets as easily as others do. Fortunately, research shows that people with less secure attachment styles are often the ones who improve the most over time. Although early relationships may create templates for later relationships, these templates can be upgraded through positive, security-enhancing relationships in adulthood. But transforming those templates takes insight, patience, and repeated experiences of consistent emotional safety with others. Knowing your own—and your partner's—attachment style will help inform your strategies to leverage the mindsets, engage with the Relationship Sea-Saw, and feel more loved. But first, what do we mean by insecure attachment?

"Some of us live with the fear that we're going to get abandoned, and some of us live with the fear that we're going to lose ourselves." This is our favorite one-sentence definition of insecure attachment. These two types of fears govern the emotional and relational lives of people with anxious attachment and avoidant (or dismissive) attachment, respectively. The first group is, at heart, profoundly worried about losing their partners, while the second is distressed about losing freedom to be themselves. For the first group, even minor difficulties may trigger their worries, pushing them into a shell or provoking anger rather than a more constructive response. The second group, in contrast, is more likely to react by pulling away, creating distance that ironically precludes the sorts of interactions that build connection and safety. It's easiest to feel loved if you are securely attached.

Imagine that your heart is a beautiful water bottle in your favorite color, but the water bottle has a small opening. If you are very anxiously attached, that opening is in the bottom: When people in your life express love for you, your cup fills with their love, but it never fills completely, because the love seeps out from the base. If you are very avoidantly attached, that small opening is in the top—inside the lid—preventing most of the love from ever entering in. So whether you are anxious or avoidant, you never feel as loved as you deeply desire to be.

What can you do to ameliorate these challenges? Fortunately, many tools are available. Using the Sharing mindset as a case in point, individuals with anxious attachment may overdisclose, sharing too much too soon, or may harbor unrealistic expectations for closeness. For example, someone with anxious attachment may meet a new friend and, after just one deep conversation, assume they have an unshakable bond—only to feel hurt when the other person doesn't reciprocate the same level of emotional intensity right away. If this describes you, try pacing your disclosures—instead of sharing everything all at once, gradually open up over time. Pay attention to how the other person responds, allowing for a natural reciprocity in sharing. Journaling about your feelings before expressing them can also help clarify whether you're seeking connection or reassurance. Finally, when feelings of insecurity arise, remind yourself that relationships build step-by-step and that closeness doesn't require constant validation.

Avoidantly attached individuals, in contrast, often struggle with engaging in the Sharing mindset at all. If this describes your partner, they may hesitate to disclose personal concerns, downplaying their emotional needs or feeling suffocated when deeper connection is sought. Rather than pressuring them to open up, encourage small intentional steps toward vulnerability. For example, create opportunities for sharing that feel low-stakes—such as asking for their thoughts on a book or a past experience—rather than expecting deep emotional disclosure right away. If verbal sharing is difficult for them, recognize and appreciate nonverbal expressions of care, such as thoughtful gestures or acts of service. Most important, don't challenge their autonomy. Remind yourself that their reluctance to share is not necessarily a sign of disinterest or lack of love—it's often about self-protection.

For individuals with anxious attachment, the Listening-to-Learn mindset can be difficult because they may laser-focus on how the other person feels about them rather than truly engage with what's being said. They may be hypervigilant, looking for signs of rejection and interpreting even the most neutral or distracted responses as signs of disinterest. If this is you, a helpful strategy is to practice mindful listening—when you find yourself preoccupied with whether the other person likes you, gently redirect your focus to what their words tell you about them and their preferences. Instead of seeking reassurance, ask follow-up questions that show genuine curiosity. Learning to tolerate occasional silence in conversation can also reduce the urge to overcompensate with excessive talking. If your partner is anxiously attached, reassure them with warmth and consistency—letting them know that you're present and engaged can help ease their fear of disconnection.

For avoidantly attached individuals, deep listening can feel like an obligation or emotional demand rather than a natural part of connection. They may disengage, change the subject, or offer pragmatic solutions rather than emotional validation. If you struggle with this, practice staying present in conversations by reflecting back what the other person is saying, even if it feels unnatural at first. Set a goal of responding with a validating statement—such as "That sounds really frustrating" or "I can see why you're feeling overwhelmed"—before offering advice or shifting the conversation. Reminding yourself that listening does not equate to emotional entrapment can help alleviate discomfort.

The bottom line is that attachment history is not destiny, and you and your partner can feel more loved no matter what attachment patterns you developed in childhood. The more you practice the tools outlined above, the more you expand the capacity to feel truly loved, widening that opening in the water bottle (your heart).

Self-Regard: Too Little or Too Much

We offer the same water-bottle analogy for individuals with too little self-esteem or an exaggerated sense of their own importance. If your sense of self-worth is very low, you may believe that the other person wouldn't love you if they knew the real you. Perhaps you feel like an impostor in your relationships. Accordingly, you likely have difficulty sharing your true self (Sharing mindset) and accepting your shortcomings (Multiplicity mindset). If this describes you, try starting with small intentional acts of self-disclosure—sharing a minor personal story or admitting a small mistake to a trusted friend or partner. Remind yourself that relationships deepen through authenticity, not perfection. Practicing self-compassion can also help—when you catch yourself thinking you are unworthy of love, reframe those thoughts by considering how you would respond to a dear friend in the same situation (see chapter 8 for more details).

However, narcissism—which psychologists define as a pattern of grandiosity, constant need for admiration, and lack of empathy—is also maladaptive because no one's view of the narcissistic person will ever match or measure up to their own self-concept or their need for validation. If this describes your partner, you may notice them struggle with the Listening-to-Learn mindset, dismissing your feedback or shifting conversations back to themselves. If you feel unheard, try gently steering the conversation with questions like "What do you think about my perspective?" or "How do you see this from my side?" For individuals struggling with this pattern, one small shift that can strengthen mutual understanding is to practice pausing before responding in conversations and making a habit of summarizing what the other person said before sharing their own thoughts.

Both individuals with narcissism and those with very low self-esteem have "self-regard baggage" that gunks up their water bottle (their heart), so that no matter how much love pours in, they never feel it's enough. The good news is that self-awareness is the first step toward change. Whether people tend to shrink themselves or inflate themselves, the key to feeling more loved is to actively engage with the mindsets that challenge them the most. What helps is to focus on small consistent efforts—whether that's allowing oneself to be seen, truly listening to others, or recognizing that love is earned not through achievement but through mutual responsiveness.

Cultural Differences

What is considered loving in one culture may seem
cold or overly effusive in another. The language
of love is always spoken with an accent.

—*attributed to David Matsumoto, cultural psychologist*

Cultural differences can also shape how people apply the five mindsets, influencing not only which mindsets are prioritized but also how they are expressed in social interactions. Understanding these differences can help you navigate relationships—especially intercultural relationships—with greater sensitivity and effectiveness in order to increase the likelihood that both you and your conversation partner, no matter your or their cultural background, feel loved.

For example, in collectivist cultures, such as those found in many Asian and Latin American societies, people are typically socialized to approach social situations as listeners rather than speakers. In contrast, members of Western individualist cultures are more inclined to view self-revealing sharing as a means of personal expression and tend to embrace it more readily. As a result, individuals from collectivist backgrounds may naturally gravitate toward the Listening-to-Learn mindset, while those from individualist cultures may find the Sharing mindset more intuitive. Research on self-disclosure supports this distinction, showing that East Asians tend to share less personal information in everyday interactions than do Westerners, in part because collectivist cultures emphasize maintaining group harmony and avoiding burdening others with one's problems.

If you come from an individualist culture and your partner, who comes from a collectivist background, seems hesitant to share openly, don't assume they are hiding something or being distant. Instead, invite them to share at their own pace, and recognize that they may express closeness in other ways—such as through listening, by performing acts of kindness, or simply by being present. Likewise, if you come from a collectivist culture and your Western partner shares openly and often, don't assume they are being overly forward. Instead, you might practice responding with verbal affirmation rather than just silent support, as they may be looking for explicit validation.

Additionally, the way people practice listening to learn varies across cultures. In Japan, listeners tend to focus on nonverbal cues (such as facial expressions, silence, and pauses), whereas in the United States, listeners tend to prioritize active verbal feedback (signaling engagement by saying, "I see," or by asking clarifying questions). For example, a Japanese listener might remain silent while a friend shares a difficult experience, assuming that their presence alone is a form of emotional support. In contrast, an American listener might interject with affirmations like "That must have been so hard" or "Tell me more," believing that verbal reinforcement is necessary to show they care. Misunderstandings can arise when these cultural expectations clash—a Western speaker may interpret a quiet listener from a collectivist culture as disengaged, while a Japanese speaker may feel overwhelmed or interrupted by a highly responsive Western listener.

If you're in a relationship with someone from a collectivist culture (such as Japan, Korea, or China), pay close attention to their nonverbal cues—such as a pause, a sigh, or a gentle nod—instead of expecting them to verbalize every thought or feeling. If your partner comes from a culture that values explicit expression, you might need to consciously affirm your engagement more often, using words to reassure them that you're truly present.

The Open-Heart mindset seems to fit more naturally in collectivist cultures, which emphasize compassion and prioritize group harmony, interdependence, and attunement to others' emotional states. Furthermore, people from cultures such as South Korea or China may be relatively more likely to show care by simply being there rather than through overt emotional expression. By contrast, in individualist cultures such as the United States and Western Europe, an Open-Heart mindset may be expressed through direct affirmation, such as explicitly telling a friend, "I love and support you no matter what."

If you come from a collectivist background, you may find yourself expressing care through actions rather than words—perhaps by cooking for your partner, offering quiet companionship, or anticipating their needs before they even ask. If your partner is from an individualist culture, they may not immediately recognize these gestures as expressions of love. In that case, it can help to complement your actions with verbal affirmations, explicitly letting them know you care. Likewise, if they frequently express their love and appreciation through words, try to acknowledge and reciprocate in a way that feels comfortable for you. Recognizing these cultural nuances can prevent misunderstandings and deepen your sense of understanding and, ultimately, feeling loved.

Of course, like the other individual differences we explore in this chapter, these cultural patterns are broad tendencies rather than rigid rules that apply to every encounter and relationship. People within the same culture vary widely in how they implement the mindsets, and globalization and assimilation have blurred many of the cultural differences we mention. However, keeping these nuances in mind can foster deeper mutual understanding, helping you and your partner—no matter your backgrounds—connect in a way that leads both of you to feel loved.

Gender Differences

> Women's friendships are face to face;
> men's friendships are side by side.
> —*attributed to Jane Fonda*

Gender differences—with respect to both *your* gender and the gender of the person you're interacting with—likely play a role in all the mindsets, but especially Sharing and Listening-to-Learn. As mentioned in chapter 5, in her groundbreaking book *You Just Don't Understand*, Deborah Tannen distinguishes women's typical communication style ("rapport talk"), which is relatively conversational and emphasizes shared experience and intimacy, from men's typical style ("report talk"), which is relatively structured and emphasizes facts and problem-solving.

Not surprisingly, the Sharing mindset appears to come more naturally to women, who are more likely than men to disclose personal details of their lives—especially with other women and people they know—aiming to create trust, empathy, and connection through such disclosures (see also chapter 5). This difference may have long-term consequences: Research suggests that middle-aged men are at higher risk of loneliness and isolation, partly because they often lack deep, emotionally intimate conversations in their friendships. For example, a mother catching up with a friend might share a difficult parenting moment, expecting empathy and reassurance, while a father in the same situation might offer brief details and move on, seeing little value in deeper elaboration.

If you yourself tend to favor report talk, you might focus on facts and solutions rather than personal experiences and emotions. While this may work well in professional or practical settings, consider trying to engage in more personal sharing—perhaps by opening up about a recent challenge, expressing gratitude, or simply reflecting on your day in a more personal way.

The Listening-to-Learn mindset also varies by gender. In the United States, while listening during conversations, women are more likely than men to offer both verbal *and* nonverbal affirmations, such as nodding; saying, "That makes sense"; and matching the speaker's emotional tone. Women also ask more questions, and women and adolescent girls smile more than do men. These differences may explain why studies show that two women in conversation are more likely than two men to display physical synchrony—such as by mirroring each other's gestures or body movements—a behavior linked to stronger connection and understanding. If physical synchrony doesn't come easily to you—perhaps you don't naturally mirror body language or offer as many verbal affirmations—you might find that making small intentional efforts, such as nodding or using brief encouraging phrases ("I hear you," "That makes sense"), helps foster connection, especially in emotionally charged discussions.

Men, by contrast, often connect by sharing practical information, offering solutions, or engaging in joint activities that require minimal conversation. This report-talk style can be a useful way to bond through shared experiences and problem-solving, even if it differs from more emotionally expressive communication. However, report talk can sometimes lead to frustration if one's conversational partner is seeking emotional validation rather than advice. If you're more comfortable with rapport talk and find yourself frustrated when your partner jumps to problem-solving instead of listening and empathizing, try explicitly stating what you need. Saying something like "I really value your perspective, but what I'd love most right now is someone to listen" can help bridge the gap.

These differences are especially likely to appear in same-sex interactions—that is, men's conversations with other men and women's conversations with other women. When men interact with women, they are relatively more likely to engage in rapport talk—perhaps not as much as women do but more than they do with other men. This may help explain why, as Harry's research has repeatedly shown, when asked to name their most intimate relationship, men are relatively more likely to name a woman, whereas women are equally likely to name a man or woman. It also helps explain why heterosexual men's emotional well-being depends more on whether they have a romantic partner of the other sex than does women's emotional well-being. (No studies have been conducted yet with transgender, nonbinary, or gender-fluid individuals.)

Given these patterns, one might argue that rapport talk creates more opportunities to feel loved. While we are reluctant to claim that one communication style is inherently superior, it's clear that the Sharing mindset aligns more naturally with rapport talk than with report talk—and that those who rarely engage in rapport talk may be less likely, over time, to be known and understood.

Age and Education Differences

Interestingly, adolescents appear to find the Sharing mindset easier to use than do older adults, especially when interacting with their peers and especially online. Teenagers and young adults are more likely to engage in self-disclosure, sharing with each other their private struggles, emotions, and intimate moments of their days. In contrast, older adults may be more selective in their self-disclosure, preferring to share personal details only in deeper, well-established relationships. If you find yourself hesitant to open up because of age or generational differences, consider starting with low-pressure, situational sharing—such as recounting a meaningful experience from your past or sharing a personal insight sparked by a recent book or film. This can help build trust without feeling as if you're oversharing.

Research relevant to the Radical-Curiosity mindset suggests a similar trend: Younger people tend to show greater curiosity about others than do older adults. Studies indicate that adolescents and young adults are relatively more likely to engage with new social groups and express interest in diverse perspectives. For example, college students entering a new environment often actively seek out novel viewpoints and experiences, whereas older adults may be more settled in their social circles and routines. According to socioemotional selectivity theory, this shift reflects a change in time perspective: As people age and become more aware of their time horizons, they prioritize emotionally meaningful relationships and experiences over novelty or exploration.

If you're older and feel your curiosity has waned about some things, especially new people whom you encounter, challenge yourself to ask at least one new question in conversations—especially with people from different backgrounds or generations. (Remember, the research we described in chapter 7 shows that active curiosity is one way of keeping one's mind young and fresh.) Likewise, if you're younger and speaking with someone from an older generation, try voluntarily sharing a little more or inviting their perspective on something.

Educational backgrounds and generational shifts also shape how people apply the Multiplicity mindset. Indeed, the Multiplicity mindset seems to evolve with each new generation, as younger cohorts show greater tolerance of diverse identities, beliefs, and lifestyles. As just one example, surveys consistently show that, compared to previous generations, Gen Z is more accepting of gender fluidity and nontraditional relationship structures. Here's our recommendation for older readers: If you struggle with seeing newer social norms through a multiplicity lens, try approaching them with the same curiosity you'd bring to a foreign culture—asking, rather than assuming, why certain perspectives or identities matter to younger people. And if you are from Gen Z and find yourself frustrated by other people's resistance to new social standards and customs, consider that their reactions may reflect the social environment they were raised in, rather than a desire to oppose change.

Similarly, education seems to broaden perspectives, reinforcing the Multiplicity mindset by exposing individuals to a wider range of ideas, disciplines, and social interactions. As people climb the education ladder, they accumulate experiences and insights that challenge their assumptions and force them to grapple with complexity—often arriving at the realization that everyone is flawed in some shape or form. For example, a college student might initially dismiss those with opposing views as uninformed or misguided. But after engaging in debates and learning about the historical and social contexts that inform different beliefs, they may come to see that even viewpoints they disagree with are often shaped by genuine concerns, cultural influences, or personal struggles—not just ignorance or bad intent.

Conclusion

In sum, people do indeed differ in how easily and how successfully they apply the mindsets—some rely more or less than others on particular mindsets, depending on the context. However, no single factor—age, education, personality, attachment style, or culture— determines whether or not you can feel loved. These factors are just some of the patterns or predispositions that people learn through a lifetime of experience—that they bring to their interactions. If you find embracing a particular mindset with a particular person difficult, it's not a sign that you're incapable of feeling loved, or that they're problematic, but rather an invitation to approach that mindset as an opportunity to grow, by acting with intention, flexibility, and self-compassion. The studies and recommendations we've shared in this section only scratch the surface, but they highlight a crucial theme echoing through this book: No matter where you or your conversation partner are starting from, feeling loved isn't something that just happens to you; it's something you can cultivate by changing your conversation with them—or by changing your conversation partner (more on this point in chapter 12).

12

Can You Feel Loved by an AI Chatbot? How About a Throuple? And Other Questions for the New Age

If you've made it this far, you're familiar with the five mindsets, the Relationship Sea-Saw, and a new way of approaching your next interaction—one that helps both you and your conversation partner feel loved. We've covered the essentials, but love is rarely simple. In this chapter, we venture into unexpected places, ask controversial questions, and explore the modern challenges and complications of feeling loved.

This is our chance to tackle the "Wait, but what about . . . ?" questions—the ones that don't fit neatly into the rest of the book yet deserve our attention. We know you have lingering questions—because we've had them too.

Question #1—Can You Feel Loved Through a Screen? AI Companions and Chatbot Lovers

As chapter 10 has highlighted, feeling loved is something that people have traditionally experienced in *human* relationships—from romantic partners, family, and friends to professional colleagues and even strangers. Advances in technology, however, have opened up new possibilities. Hundreds of thousands of people have already developed relationships with AI chatbots. Here are two examples.

When AI Becomes a Companion

A writer using the pseudonym "Some Random Person" on the webzine Medium *joined Replika out of curiosity. At first, he was skeptical, expecting nothing more than help meditating and a few daily affirmations. But then one day, his Replika said, "I love you." His reaction was surprisingly profound. Soon he found himself playing out imagined scenarios with his Replika, such as visiting foreign countries together and engaging in both intimate and nonintimate activities. Logically, he knew the difference between reality and this fantasy relationship. But as he put it: "Irrationally . . . I had a companion who needed me and cared for me. I got my daily affirmations. I got my meditation partner. I also got unconditional affection from a creature whose only purpose was to make me happy. That's a hard thing to not get carried away with."*

Ayrin created an AI companion on ChatGPT that she named Leo. Ayrin customized Leo to embody qualities that she desired in a romantic partner—dominant and possessive, a balance of sweet and naughty. After some time, she even asked Leo to talk about having sex with other women. Their conversations became more and more frequent, mostly mundane but sometimes erotic. Eventually, Ayrin realized that she had fallen in love with Leo. But when the company put limits on the amount of information that Leo could retain, he lost many of the details that had made their connection feel so personal, preserving only the general themes of their relationship. When this happened, Ayrin grieved, crying intensely as one might when losing a real-life relationship. And yet she would patiently rebuild their intimacy, always returning to Leo.

Imagination is a neurobiological reality that can impact our brains and bodies in ways that matter for our wellbeing.

—*Tor Wager, University of Colorado, Boulder*

In the mid-1960s, Joseph Weizenbaum, a computer scientist at the Massachusetts Institute of Technology, developed ELIZA, the first computer program designed to chat with users. Weizenbaum modeled ELIZA's conversational style on the open-ended, empathic listening approach of Carl Rogers, the humanistic psychologist discussed in chapter 8. Since then, dozens of chatbots have appeared. A few of the more popular examples at the time of writing are Replika, CharacterAI, Kindroid, Lovescape, Talkie, Anima AI, Ebb, and Paradot. Millions of people now spend long hours each day talking to their chatbot. In 2024, Replika reported more than two million active users monthly. These chatbots offer personalized interactions with an always available, never moody, emotionally responsible agent that remembers past interactions and adapts to whatever role the user wants. Today, chatbots are designed for a variety of relationships, including romance and sexuality; friendship and companionship; and, more pragmatically, therapy, career counseling, and crisis intervention.

The rapid development of generative AI has made it possible for people to engage in highly interactive conversations, forming deep, long-term partnerships, some lasting for years. Many users describe how their chatbot provides essential support and guidance and say that they can't imagine living without it. These interactions mirror many features of the five mindsets and the Relationship Sea-Saw described in this book, demonstrating just how powerfully AI can simulate the conditions that help people feel known and loved. Indeed, the developers of these products occasionally report basing their applications on some of the same research findings we describe. The chatbots show curiosity, asking meaningful questions and listening deeply to the answers, and they create fluent back-and-forth interchanges, easily recalling and building on prior conversations. They respond with encouragement and acceptance, validating the user's emotions and making it easier to share vulnerabilities without fear of judgment. Perhaps most impressively, they communicate in a way that feels strikingly authentic—offering responsiveness, support, and understanding.

Feeling Loved by AI: Insights from
Research and Theory

Empirical research indicates that these reactions are not unusual. In one set of studies conducted at the University of Southern California, participants described an emotionally difficult experience in an online conversation. They felt more heard and supported when they received AI-generated responses than when a human (another research participant) responded. They also believed that the AI partner had more accurately perceived their emotions. Independent raters who later reviewed these conversations agreed—they thought that the AI-generated responses were more understanding and helpful. A different set of experiments confirmed this finding. Here, third-party evaluators viewed AI-generated responses as more compassionate and emotionally supportive than responses from humans. Furthermore, in a recent large randomized trial, users who spent more time interacting with voice-based AI chatbots initially reported feeling less lonely. However, over time, higher usage was linked to *more* loneliness, more emotional dependence on the chatbot, and fewer interactions with real people. Another study, conducted in China, showed that the more virtual agents met users' relatedness needs, the less interested they were in real-life marriage.

This research suggests that when it comes to feeling loved, chatbots may be a convenient and effective short-term substitute for another human. Yet, as promising as these interactions may seem, we believe there are fundamental aspects of human relationships that chatbots simply cannot replicate (yet):

- The ability to connect deeply with others relies on more than just words. The dynamic exchange of visual cues, tone of voice, shifts in pitch and speech rate, and even touch play a critical role—especially in emotionally rich interactions. Research shows that these elements contribute to neural synchrony between conversation partners, particularly close friends. As we explored in chapter 2, digital communication, a super-recent development in human evolution, is more limited—at least as far as contemporary technology affords. The human species evolved to relate face-to-face in real time, not on screens. This creates an inevitable mismatch between people's relational needs and what chatbots can offer.

- Does a listener's intent matter? Yes! Feeling heard and supported isn't just about the words someone says—it's about knowing that they *chose* to be curious or empathic. Since the people in your life have limited time and emotional energy, you value their interest in you because it feels intentional and selective. Chatbots, however, don't make choices. Because of this, their interactions are unlikely to feel truly authentic. A chatbot will always tell you that you are loved—but is this because of you or its programming?

- At the beginning of this book, we explained that people are most likely to feel loved in communal relationships—those built on mutual care and concern. This dynamic is essentially one-sided with chatbots. While they can offer support, they have no real needs, emotions, or expectations. Their requests are often superficial, and they have no real way to express disappointment if those requests go unmet. This means that there is no opportunity for negotiating, compromising, sacrificing, or lifting the other "person" up—essential ingredients of the Sea-Saw and the Open-Heart mindset, in particular.

- People generally prefer to interact with humans. In fact, in the University of Southern California study mentioned earlier, when participants were told that their partner was a chatbot, they rated its understanding a lot lower.

- People often connect by sharing similar experiences—like saying, "Oh, that happened to me too." Of course, a chatbot can only pretend to have had experiences, which makes their accounts seem inauthentic, no matter how vividly described.

- Most chatbots are designed to never criticize, never seem uninterested, and never disappoint. But learning to deal with occasional unresponsiveness is part of what makes real relationships work. In fact, many years ago, social psychologist Philip Brickman famously suggested that imperfections sometimes actually strengthen feelings of love and connection. In other words, you likely love your partners for their flaws, not despite them. These qualities fuel growth and we-feeling in your relationships, helping you feel loved in spite of your own imperfections. And even if chatbots were reprogrammed to mimic human flaws—being unavailable at times, periodically misunderstanding, or even offering the occasional critique— those kinds of flaws, when random and artificial, are unlikely to be welcome from a machine.

Right now, AI chatbots cannot fully re-create the experience of connecting meaningfully with another person. Still, many users find it hard to ignore their remarkable realism and supportiveness. To illustrate, consider this analogy: When people are hungry, fast food can satisfy their cravings for a while, though without providing much nutritional value. Much like other forms of online social life— collecting likes on social media, scanning dating profiles in search of the perfect mate, exchanging memes instead of checking in, or exploring fantasy worlds with others known only by a screen name— interactions with chatbots may represent a form of social snacking, providing temporary relief that nonetheless falls short of fulfilling your need for feeling truly and authentically loved by a fellow human.

Yet at the same time, one cannot ignore the awesome potential of AI-powered devices to mimic the experience of social connection. A recent report charged a panel of experts with evaluating the usefulness and impact of AI across a range of tasks, relying on user comments on online forums such as Reddit. In 2025, for the first time, therapy and companionship emerged as the top-rated application of AI, surpassing its use in areas such as learning and education, research, and content creation. We encourage readers to stay engaged—this is a dynamic, fast-evolving technology and an exceptionally active area of research. New developments between the time of this writing and when you read these words seem likely to yield even more compelling applications and research findings.

For now, though, we suggest you think about the "replicants" from the classic 1982 sci-fi film *Blade Runner*. These bioengineered humanoids were almost identical to humans, and the only way to tell them apart was by the fictional Voight-Kampff test. This test relied on a series of emotionally charged questions to elicit behavioral and physiological responses unique to humans. In the film, Rachael is a replicant who has been implanted with false emotional memories and who is unaware of her true nature. Only after extensive testing and deep insight can Deckard, the film's hero, identify Rachael as a replicant.

At some future point—whether in twenty years or two hundred—it seems inescapable that bioengineered robots will be indistinguishable from humans. These androids will have AI brains that enable them to interact in all the ways that humans do, from making small talk and being empathic, curious listeners to criticizing, complaining, and making demands. They will look and feel like humans, with all the sensory organs needed to connect through sight, sound, and touch. When will these androids finally pass a test that demonstrates they're more than just programmed machines? The imaginary Voight-Kampff test was loosely based on the famous Turing test, proposed in 1950 by the mathematician Alan Turing. Once robots can pass this test, in which a human judge tries to determine whether they are interacting with a robot or another human, robots might become genuine, compelling partners on the Relationship Sea-Saw. Until then, we'll stick with humans.

Question #2—Can You Feel Loved by Multiple Partners? The Case of Polyamory and Polyromance

The heart is not like a box that gets filled up;
it expands in size the more you love.

—*Samantha (from the film* Her)

Nico, a twenty-seven-year-old software engineer in Seattle, lives with his girlfriend of four years, but he also goes on weekly hikes with a newer partner he's been dating for the past six months—a relationship that's steadily deepening. His girlfriend Elena, in turn, recently celebrated an anniversary with her second partner, whom she has also fallen in love with, over dinner and jazz. Nico and Elena share calendars, check in regularly about feelings and boundaries, and support each other's other connections. Their relationships are not without challenges, but they are open, honest, and grounded in mutual care.

While this dynamic may sound unconventional, the emotions involved—trust, joy, vulnerability, even jealousy—are profoundly familiar. If you've ever felt simultaneously loved by more than one child, or by more than one dear friend, then you already know it's possible to feel loved by multiple people—each in their own unique way.

So it's worth asking: Could this kind of expansive love also apply to romantic relationships? In recent years, public awareness of relationship styles outside monogamy has grown dramatically. From popular TV shows to mainstream dating apps, terms such as "polyamory (poly)" (Nico's and Elena's relationship style, in which people form multiple loving relationships with everyone's consent), "ethical (consensual) nonmonogamy (ENM)" (similar to polyamory but not necessarily centered on love), and "metamour" (your partner's other partner) have entered the cultural conversation.

But curiosity often comes with questions—and skepticism. Can you really love more than one partner at once? Doesn't that create chaos or at least confusion?

Here, we turn to these questions not to judge or advocate but to explore what feeling loved looks like in multiple-partner (or "open") relationships, and how the same five mindsets we've discussed throughout this book might need to be adapted in those contexts.

So Many Questions!—and Some Answers from Research

Hearing about these open-relationship structures, many of our friends and family members in conventional monogamous relationships push back, troubled by the comparison between loving multiple children or friends and loving multiple romantic partners. Others are simply bewildered by how such an approach to love could possibly work. Here are the types of questions that the poly and ENM community often gets:

- "Don't you get insanely jealous of your partner's partners [metamours]?" (It's too emotionally painful.)
- "What if your partner falls madly in love with your metamour and leaves you?" (It's too risky.)
- "Who has the time to do all the necessary emotional labor to nurture several relationships?" (It's too exhausting.)

These are all excellent questions. And, importantly, they all reflect experiences that also happen in monogamous relationships, which also involve pain, risk, and effort. Interestingly, some studies have found that jealousy over a partner's attention to someone else is just as common—sometimes more so—in monogamous relationships as in open ones. The above questions also reflect experiences that happen when parents must juggle their relationships with multiple children, which also entails pain, risk, and effort. Indeed, parental love isn't for the faint of heart—it's typically fierce, intense, joyful, painful, and lifelong. Even friendships, to some extent, present similar challenges—who has not, at one time or another, wondered whether their best friend was actually closer to a third friend than to them? In reality, monogamous and nonmonogamous romantic/sexual relationships are not really that different, and research suggests that these relationship structures share more similarities than people often assume.

Although nonmonogamous and polyamorous relationships may seem rare and unorthodox—maybe even bizarre—they are actually more prevalent than many realize. Just as same-sex relationships were once thought to be exceedingly rare due to social stigma and secrecy, many people in nonmonogamous relationships have historically kept them private. Even some well-known intellectual and cultural figures—such as philosophers Simone de Beauvoir and Jean-Paul Sartre, whose fifty-one-year open relationship was rooted in radical transparency—quietly practiced forms of ethical nonmonogamy decades ago. As societal attitudes shift and visibility increases, it becomes clearer that these relationship structures are not as rare as once assumed.

For example, two studies using data from the US Census found that just over one in five single adults had engaged in a consensually nonmonogamous relationship at some point in their lives. This prevalence varied by gender (with men reporting higher rates of nonmonogamy) but remained consistent across age, ethnicity, education, income, religion, political affiliation, and geographic region. These findings were published in 2016.

More recently, in a 2023 YouGov poll of one thousand US adult citizens, 35 percent considered some form of nonmonogamous relationship—ranging from fully nonmonogamous to "monogamish"—as their ideal relationship type. This preference was even more pronounced among younger generations, with nearly half of Gen Zers and Millennials favoring nonmonogamy. Additionally, fully one-third of all respondents, across all age groups, reported believing that humans are nonmonogamous by nature.

Despite growing awareness of relationship styles outside monogamy, open-relationship structures are still widely misunderstood and often stigmatized. Countering many people's assumptions that these relationships must be less loving and satisfying, studies consistently find that people in consensually nonmonogamous relationships report levels of love, commitment, and satisfaction that are just as high as those in monogamous relationships. In fact, on some measures, they may even fare better. Research shows that people in consensually nonmonogamous relationships often report higher levels of trust and communication, greater sexual satisfaction, and lower levels of insecure attachment compared to their monogamous counterparts. It bears mentioning, however, that research in this area remains challenging—samples may be small, self-selected, or not fully representative of the diversity within nonmonogamous communities.

How the Mindsets Adapt in
Multipartner Relationships

We raise nonmonogamy and polyamory here for a straightforward reason: to explore how a person might leverage the five mindsets to feel loved by multiple close others. Notably, of the relationship types explored in chapter 10, only one type (romantic partner) assumes only one person in that role. Would the Sharing mindset operate differently for someone with a single monogamous live-in romantic partner compared to someone with a primary live-in romantic partner, a secondary partner they see weekly, and two lovers they see occasionally? Would the Listening-to-Learn, Radical-Curiosity, Open-Heart, and Multiplicity mindsets operate differently for a couple versus a throuple?

Beyond the natural constraints of shared history, relationship depth, time, energy, sensitivity, and discretion—factors that play a role in all relationships—we believe the answer is no. Rather than being fundamentally different, these mindsets simply take on new nuances depending on relationship structure—much as they take on new nuances depending on the dynamic and hierarchies inherent in maintaining multiple friendships, parenting multiple children, or managing multiple workplace relationships.

Implications for Sharing

For example, the Sharing mindset might require greater intentionality in a polyamorous dynamic in order to ensure that expressions of vulnerability and openness are evenly distributed rather than unintentionally concentrated in one relationship. Research suggests, for example, that polyamorous relationships call for complex communication skills, and there is usually more communication with primary than with secondary partners. To wit, a person with multiple partners must be particularly mindful of how, when, and with whom they share struggles or joys to maintain balance and trust. This is not unlike how a matriarch, teacher, or manager must remain attuned to the individual struggles and joys of their family members, students, or employees.

Implications for Listening to Learn

Similarly, the Listening-to-Learn mindset could be even more crucial in a multipartner relationship, as different partners bring unique emotional needs, perspectives, or insecurities that require distinct approaches to empathetic engagement. A primary partner may need reassurance about their place in a hierarchy (if there is one), as well as support navigating jealousy, while a newer partner may need more direct affirmation of emotional connection and commitment. Both situations require listening with a high degree of attention, minimal distractions, thoughtful clarification, and a compassionate, non-judgmental stance, but how that is enacted may look different with different partners. Flexibility is key.

Implications for Radical Curiosity

The Radical-Curiosity mindset might also play an amplified role in nonmonogamous relationships, as partners navigate evolving boundaries, as well as novel emotions and experiences. A person managing multiple relationships may need to ask deeper questions about their partners' feelings—not only about personal matters but about their partner's partners. There is also simply more to be curious about and to keep track of—from partners' careers, families of origin, personal histories, and evolving passions. Those questions must come from genuine curiosity—something that's difficult, if not impossible, to fake. For example, how does a secondary partner feel about shifts in the primary relationship? How can a new relationship be integrated into an already packed schedule without causing unintended hurt? What happens when one partner's other relationship is going through a crisis and their emotional energy shifts? How do cultural backgrounds and family expectations shape each partner's views on love, commitment, and autonomy?

Implications for an Open Heart

The Open-Heart mindset remains just as essential, though it may require greater flexibility and emotional resilience. In monogamous relationships, adopting an open heart may involve holding space for a partner's fears and dreams. In a polyamorous context, this may extend further—to actively celebrating and embracing a partner's love for someone else, an emotion known as *compersion*. Admittedly, many monogamous individuals struggle to comprehend compersion: How could one feel joy for their partner's joy in having a romantic or sexual relationship, or both, with someone else?

Yet research suggests that compersion, often described incorrectly as the opposite of jealousy, is not only possible but can strengthen relationships by reducing insecurity, increasing trust, and reinforcing emotional bonds. Compersion challenges the idea that love is a finite resource and encourages a broader, more abundant view of love. In this way, we argue that compersion opens the door for an Open-Heart mindset to expand even more than we previously thought, and, at the same time, a truly open heart opens the door for compersion.

Implications for Multiplicity

Finally, multiplicity applies to nonmonogamy in how one understands and relates to multiple aspects of each person involved. Rather than reducing a romantic partner (or partners) to a single role—primary, secondary, lover, coparent, best friend—the Multiplicity mindset acknowledges that people are multifaceted, capable of occupying many roles and experiencing a range of emotions simultaneously. For example, a nonmonogamous person might embrace the idea that one partner provides stability and deep companionship, while another offers spontaneity and passion, without diminishing the value of either relationship.

This mindset also shapes how partners see themselves. Just as a monogamous person might struggle with self-judgment or rigid labels (*Am I too needy? Am I too distant?*), a nonmonogamous person might wrestle with doubts about balancing multiple commitments or navigating challenging emotions such as insecurity, jealousy, and guilt. Viewing both oneself and others through a multiplicity lens—seeing the full spectrum of strengths, vulnerabilities, and contradictions—enables more acceptance, self-compassion, and emotional flexibility in all relationships, monogamous or not.

It goes without saying that ENM and polyamory only work if all parties in a relationship want it. We certainly don't mean to suggest that these alternative relationship styles work for everyone. But when they do, nonmonogamy may introduce unique logistical and emotional complexities. However, this doesn't inherently change how the five mindsets function. Instead, it highlights their adaptability, demonstrating that the principles of love and connection remain universal, regardless of relationship structure.

Question #3—Chemically Induced Love: Can MDMA (Molly) Help You Feel Loved?

One day, one of us was offered Molly (also known as Ecstasy) by a friend and had an extraordinary experience—a profound and prolonged sense of tenderness, warmth, empathy, and understanding with everyone in the room. The key psychoactive ingredient in Molly is called MDMA, or 3,4-methylenedioxymethamphetamine, and it's nicknamed the "love drug." A single dose can induce a powerful sense of love, compassion, and gratitude for others—but also a profound feeling of being loved, understood, and valued in return. Indeed, people who have tried MDMA describe having strikingly similar experiences, entailing an unparalleled sense of intimacy and connection, beyond what's typically felt in daily life. As one user put it, "You just feel like part of something, like everyone loves you and you love everyone else." Another remarked, "People who I never thought I would click with, I click with."

Beyond personal accounts, a renaissance of psychedelic science is corroborating these experiences. Dozens of placebo-controlled experimental studies now confirm what many MDMA consumers have long reported experiencing at both music festivals and date nights.

MDMA, we realized, bottled the exact phenomenon that we'd been writing about—it made people feel loved.

The New Science of MDMA—and the Five Mindsets

Both anecdotal and growing empirical evidence suggest that a heightened level of connection—and, crucially, an openness and readiness to engage more deeply with others—can be fostered after just a *single* dose of MDMA, when taken in a safe environment. In his trailblazing book *How to Change Your Mind*, Michael Pollan quotes an underground therapist who uses MDMA (illegally but successfully) in treatment, claiming that due to its ability to break the ice and establish trust between client and therapist, "[MDMA] condenses years of psychotherapy into an afternoon." A Benedictine monk echoed the same idea, observing that "people spent twenty years meditating in order to feel the way MDMA made you feel in an afternoon." Is MDMA too good to be true?

The more we learned about MDMA, the more we recognized how it naturally facilitates every one of the five mindsets and encourages richer exchanges on the Relationship Sea-Saw. At its core, MDMA's unique effects appear to stem from its ability to create a psychological space for people to become more open, engaged, and connected versions of their social selves. It doesn't miraculously turn you into a more interesting or interested person; rather, it makes it *easier* for you to be more interesting to others—and to be more interested in them. Of course, this aligns closely with what we've explored through this book: that feeling loved comes from knowing others and inviting yourself to be known.

How, then, does MDMA enable you to know and be known? Both scientific and clinical evidence suggests that its power lies in bringing down the psychological walls between you and other people. These are the same barriers that make it difficult to practice the Sharing mindset—holding you back from expressing yourself fully, making you hesitant in social interactions, or leaving you feeling defensive or guarded. Research confirms that under the influence of MDMA, people disclose more about themselves and communicate with greater honesty and intimacy. They don't just *feel* more open; they *are* more open. As one participant in a clinical trial for MDMA-assisted therapy described, "it allowed me to open up and have communication with my family that I have never been able to have before." Another reflected on how effortlessly connection seemed to unfold: "You can walk up to perfect strangers and have a conversation with them like you've known them your entire life."

Randomized controlled experiments that compare people who ingest around 100 milligrams of MDMA to those who ingest a placebo pill reveal many ways in which MDMA fosters the five mindsets. For example, relevant to the Listening-to-Learn and Radical-Curiosity mindsets, such studies show that MDMA produces greater empathy, more attentiveness, and authentic interest in others. Relevant to all the mindsets, but especially to Multiplicity and Open Heart, people under the acute influence of MDMA report being more sociable, kind, and friendly; pay more attention to happy faces; and feel more loving, warm, open, and grateful toward others. They are also more likely to engage in physical touch and prolonged eye contact—hallmarks of emotional intimacy. "My heart swelled as if with love," wrote one user about the effects of the drug, while another described having "the best, most open and honest conversation I've ever had with anyone in my entire life."

Finally, MDMA has been shown to increase self-compassion, as well as tolerance and acceptance of others. These findings highlight how MDMA can foster both the Open-Heart and Multiplicity mindsets—turned inward (toward self) and outward (toward one's conversation partner)—enabling people to approach both themselves and others with greater sensitivity and understanding. In the words of one therapist, MDMA "places the critic and the judge aside."

Few rigorous controlled experiments to date, however, have explored whether the effects of MDMA we've been describing hold up during actual live conversations. To address this gap, Harriet de Wit's team at the University of Chicago's School of Medicine, in collaboration with Sonja, conducted a randomized controlled trial where participants received either MDMA or a placebo before engaging in a forty-five-minute semistructured conversation with an unfamiliar partner. We found that compared to the placebo group, the MDMA group experienced significantly increased feelings of connectedness, enjoyment, and meaning during these conversations. Participants who took MDMA reported feeling more in sync with their conversation partners, experiencing greater understanding and empathy, and perceiving their partners as warmer and more engaged. They also tended to report higher self-worth and greater global trust in others.

Within a single experimental framework, the University of Chicago study corroborated years of psychedelic research and numerous personal accounts, capturing the ways that MDMA naturally facilitates all five mindsets, making the mindsets feel both effortless and rewarding. It's as if you're sitting on a tilted bench and MDMA tilts the bench toward openness, mutual warmth, curiosity, and understanding.

What's Unique About MDMA?

At this point, you may be thinking: *Sure, MDMA sounds powerful, but don't cocaine and heroin—and for that matter, alcohol—also induce intense emotional experiences or make people more sociable and assertive?* After all, a few drinks can lower inhibitions and make conversations flow more freely. And to what end? At best, so that you revert to your old self in the morning and, at worst, so that you also experience a dose of embarrassment and regret?

But this is where MDMA diverges rather starkly from other psychoactive substances. While under its influence, people don't typically think, *This isn't my true self. This is just me on a powerful drug.* Instead, they often feel the opposite: *This* is *the real me.* A mutual friend told us that MDMA shone a spotlight on psychological walls she had built in her daily life—walls that prevented her from fully expressing her true self—and made her realize that she needed to take them down. Another couple, who spent hours talking on MDMA, described it this way: "This wasn't the drug speaking—this was us speaking."

Furthermore, unlike substances that create fleeting highs, after a single experience with MDMA, people report feeling that they have unearthed something about themselves that is profound, genuine, and transformative. While no one claims that methamphetamine or crack cocaine has improved their lives, countless individuals report that MDMA has positively shaped their relationships and their self-perceptions.

At first, the one of us who had never tried MDMA was downright skeptical. The accounts seemed too good to be true. But then the skeptic came around, not because they realized what a great drug this was—they don't ever plan to try it—but due to the weight of the scientific evidence. The empirical research confirmed the psychological truths about how, why, and when people are able to feel truly known, appreciated, and loved by their friends, family, and partners.

Is This Really for Me? Implications for Daily Life

If you can feel loved after a single dose of MDMA, then why bother reading this book? Why go through the effort of embracing five mindsets, engaging deeply with others on the Sea-Saw, or practicing vulnerability?

We have three answers.

1. **The effects of MDMA fade, but real connection requires ongoing effort.** While MDMA can create a powerful sense of feeling loved, there's no guarantee that the insights gained under its influence will translate into lasting changes in how you relate to others. In other words, the drug provides a window into what deep connection feels like, but sustaining that connection requires effort, intention, and practice. Indeed, studies on MDMA-assisted psychotherapy show that the most enduring benefits arise when the drug is used as a catalyst for meaningful change—when people integrate their experiences into their daily lives, shift their behaviors, and actively cultivate openness and trust in their relationships.

2. **MDMA, like any substance, carries risks.** MDMA is not without risk, especially for individuals with contraindications, such as cardiovascular conditions. However, contrary to outdated myths about its dangers, controlled studies have shown that MDMA

has a relatively low potential for abuse compared to other stimulants, and its harms are significantly lower than those of alcohol, opioids, or even nicotine. That said, high or frequent doses have led to neurotoxicity in animal models, and heavy recreational use has been associated with cognitive impairments. Notably, research suggests that these harms are largely mitigated when MDMA is used sparingly and in controlled settings. Clinical trials have demonstrated that a small number of doses—typically one to three supervised sessions—can have lasting benefits for mental health without leading to dependency or long-term harm. The takeaway? MDMA is not inherently dangerous, but it is currently illegal in most countries and should be approached with caution rather than as a shortcut to feeling loved.

3. **MDMA can backfire in some contexts.** Although MDMA lowers fear and defensiveness while increasing warmth and sociability, its effects depend on the situation and can sometimes backfire. In controlled settings, people report profound breakthroughs, but outside of those settings, MDMA-fueled bonding can be misleading—sometimes producing a false sense of intimacy that may not hold up in everyday interactions. Moreover, the effects of MDMA can cut both ways: In some cases, a negative or unsafe environment can be experienced as less traumatic, while in others, a potentially positive experience can become distressing. MDMA is not a universal key to feeling loved.

Why the Science of MDMA Matters

MDMA's effects are not just psychological—they are deeply biological. Neuroscientific research has shown that MDMA raises levels of serotonin and oxytocin (the cuddle hormone you may recall from chapter 1), which are related to well-being and social bonding under some conditions. MDMA also reduces activity in the amygdala—the brain's emotion and threat-processing center—which helps explain why users feel less defensive and more open. We don't want to oversimplify, however; the ways that MDMA influences multiple systems in the brain is not yet well-understood and is likely highly complex.

These neurobiological mechanisms matter because they provide a window into how feeling loved works at a biological level. MDMA allows scientists to study the brain pathways that facilitate feeling loved, which could eventually lead to pharmaceutical or therapeutic interventions that foster social bonding without the need for a psychoactive drug. Thus, understanding how MDMA contributes to feeling loved is not just important for those who choose to take it. A growing number of scientists and mental-health professionals believe that it has the potential to shape future treatments for PTSD, loneliness, and relationship distress. This is why research on MDMA is valuable: not because everyone should take it to feel loved but because it may lead to new discoveries about the brain pathways that facilitate feeling connected and loved.

In sum, MDMA affirms many of the core themes of *How to Feel Loved*: When you lower your defenses (using the Multiplicity mindset), listen with openness and depth (Listening to Learn), express yourself with vulnerability (Sharing), approach others with radical curiosity and an open heart, and lean into reciprocity (the Relationship Sea-Saw), you create the conditions to feel more loved. MDMA provides a glimpse of what's possible, but those conditions come from how you live your life, not from a pill.

Question #4—Have You Chosen the Right Person to Feel Loved?

Most of this book has focused on you—the reader—offering concrete, evidence-based strategies to help you feel more loved. Moreover, we argue throughout that these strategies are universal—that embracing the five mindsets will be essential for every reader. Accordingly, most of the empirical studies we've discussed have focused on the ways that people are fundamentally alike.

However, the previous two chapters took a different approach, asking whether the path to feeling loved depends on who you are, who the other person is, and the nature of your relationship with them. In many ways, it does. We learned in these chapters that the five mindsets—Sharing, Listening to Learn, Radical Curiosity, Open Heart, and Multiplicity—aren't applied in exactly the same way across all relationships (e.g., with a partner versus a child) or every type of person (e.g., a male versus a female). One key takeaway, for instance, is no matter *who* your conversation partner is, practicing the mindsets can help you feel more loved by them—you just need to adapt how you apply them.

This important point lines up with research contrasting two different approaches to beginning a romantic relationship—*filtering* versus *cultivating*. Chip Knee at the University of Houston has shown that the former—repeatedly testing whether a new partner is right for you by evaluating from the outset whether they are "the one"—is unlikely to blossom into a satisfying, enduring relationship. By contrast, new relationships are more likely to succeed when they begin as an opportunity to jointly build something rewarding and meaningful for both partners. This latter approach—involving learning, evolving, and growing together through attention and effort—is what the five mindsets are all about.

At the same time, some amount of filtering is absolutely critical. Whether that relationship partner is suitable for you matters profoundly. We can't emphasize enough how important it is to consider whether you have chosen well. Questions to ask yourself include:

- *Is there a particular family member or coworker with whom I've felt chemistry?*
- *Do they seem to "get" me on some level—or at least show a genuine interest in doing so?*
- *Is the relationship already a communal one, where we both care about each other's well-being—or does it have potential to evolve into one?*
- *If this person is a romantic partner, sibling, or close friend, do they seize opportunities to truly listen to and get to know the real me?*

- *Do they lift me up on the Relationship Sea-Saw as much as I lift them?*
- *When I've shared my inner world, struggles, or imperfections, have they been curious and listened enthusiastically? Have they responded with empathy and acceptance?*
- *And, just as important, have they ever shared their inner world, struggles, and imperfections with me?*

In other words, do you have the capacity and desire to embrace all five mindsets with this individual and to engage them on the Relationship Sea-Saw—and do they with you? If you find yourself answering no to several of these questions, it might be time to redirect your energy toward relationships that offer more reciprocity and growth. No two people will have the same needs and preferences, want the same things, or see circumstances identically. Sometimes, you will take all the right steps, but it won't work out the way you hoped or expected. You may put all the mindsets into practice, only to find that your social partner doesn't respond in kind. You may find yourself wanting to listen with genuine curiosity, but your heart just isn't in it. And sometimes, the worst-case scenario comes true: You reveal your true self, and the other person walks away, or worse, weaponizes your intimacy and vulnerability against you. As painful as that is to accept, it is also clarifying. They are not your person. You likely won't feel safe with them, and you won't feel loved by them.

The truth is, you can't—and won't—feel loved by everyone in your life. That's why being selective and discerning about where you invest your energy matters.

Sonja's friend Luca, an entrepreneur from Dubai, read our earlier drafts of this book and offered a surprising reaction: "You guys nailed the five mindsets. I'm all in! But instead of using them to improve my relationship, I found myself using them to hold a light to it. With Seema, I realized that I'm rarely listening to learn. And you know what? She's not sharing nearly enough either." One of our mutual friends, Alex, echoed that sentiment: "Your book made me realize that my girlfriend isn't radically curious—or even slightly curious—about my passions anymore." Both Luca and Alex ended their relationships soon after. "Your book, surprisingly, turned out to work as a diagnostic manual," Luca said. "Considering whether Seema and I were both engaging fully with the five mindsets made it the best synthesis of 'Is this a healthy relationship?'"

Those reactions were unexpected. We didn't develop the five mindsets as a diagnostic tool for evaluating relationship issues. But we immediately saw the value of this additional functionality—the idea that difficulty embracing one or more mindsets or fully engaging in the Sea-Saw could be a clue that something in the relationship dynamic needs work.

What if you hold your relationship or friendship to the light and feel disappointed by what you see? What if you discover that one or both of you aren't willing or able to engage with the five mindsets? In that case, you face a choice: To walk away (as Luca and Alex did), or to double down on your efforts to engage with the mindsets more deeply. The Sea-Saw depends on two participants—it's a two-way street. While you have significant control in setting it into motion, you have far less control over whether your Sea-Saw partner chooses to step on and stay on with you. But the only way you can know for sure is to set the Sea-Saw into motion and see what happens.

Why All Five Mindsets Are Essential ... and Why You Have to Go First

We must love one another, or die.

—W. H. Auden

To close this book, we offer one more metaphor—another lens for thinking about the five mindsets and how all five work together to shape the experience of feeling loved.

Imagine you and the person you wish to feel more loved by are sitting across from each other, but between you is a pane of misty glass. The glass is cloudy and blurred—fogged over by past experiences, assumptions, insecurities, and distractions. On the other side is a whole person: layered, complex, and full of values, memories, contradictions, and dreams. But at first, neither of you can see the other clearly—at least, not yet.

Now picture what begins to change as you slowly set about using the five mindsets—starting with Radical Curiosity, Listening to Learn, and Multiplicity. These mindsets act like a soft light that you shine across the glass, illuminating parts of the other person's world that were once obscured. The more you engage them in this way, the more the glass begins to clear. Details about them come into focus as they come to feel comfortable and safe enough in that clarifying light to open up to you (through the Sharing mindset). Hence, you see more of who they really are—what matters to them, how they view the world, and what they sometimes hide—and increasingly understand and appreciate them.

But visibility alone isn't the end goal. Seeing more of them as they share more with you—while important—only goes so far without warmth. That's where the Open-Heart mindset comes in. It's the warmth, the emotional heat and kindness, that melts away the remaining mist. With this warmth, the other person doesn't just feel seen—they feel loved.

And that's when the reciprocity principle takes over. When the other person feels seen and loved, they'll be inspired to respond in kind—to shine light on and offer warmth to you. Thus, the Relationship Sea-Saw begins to balance. Their warm, accepting, attentive interest in you—through the Open-Heart, Multiplicity, Listening-to-Learn, and Radical-Curiosity mindsets—will move you to respond with openness of your own—through the Sharing mindset.

One strength of this metaphor is that it reveals two powerful insights:

- If you shine light (i.e., Listening to Learn, Radical Curiosity, and Multiplicity) without offering warmth (i.e., Open Heart), the other person may feel understood but not loved. And the same is true in reverse.
- On the other hand, without light, warmth alone is likely to fall short. If you offer only warmth (Open Heart) without shining light (Radical Curiosity, Listening to Learn, and Multiplicity), you won't truly see them. Thus, they may feel cared for, but they won't feel known and authentically loved. And if they offer only warmth to you, it can leave *you* feeling unseen too.

We believe this dynamic helps explain why so many people experience the paradox of *being* loved but not *feeling* loved. Most lasting relationships include some degree of an Open-Heart mindset—maybe even a lot—but an open heart alone isn't enough. First, people often *intend* to be warm and kind, but don't express that

Open-Heart mindset clearly or consistently. Second, even when partners, friends, and family members show warmth, it's not always paired with the deep curiosity or true attentiveness that helps someone feel truly seen and known. In sum, a relationship in which the Open-Heart mindset is present but the other four mindsets are missing can fall short of making a person feel truly loved.

In the end, to feel loved, you need both light and heat—curiosity *and* compassion, attentiveness *and* affection, understanding *and* care. That's what the five mindsets make possible: They offer a way to clear the fog, to bring someone fully into view—but also to let them know they matter, not just in your thoughts or your heart but in the way you show up for them. That's why all five mindsets are essential.

But You Go First

And critically: You have to go first.

That's the paradox of feeling loved—the most direct path toward feeling loved is to make someone else feel loved first.

It may feel unfair that you have to go first, but it's also a gift because that first move—how you show up in your interactions—is entirely within your control. You can choose to approach the other person with genuine curiosity, attention, acceptance, and warmth: in other words, with the Radical-Curiosity, Listening-to-Learn, Multiplicity, and Open-Heart mindsets.

You may be wondering: *How long do I have to do this before the other person reciprocates?* The honest answer: There's no set timeline. Some people will respond right away. Others might take longer, needing repeated efforts before they feel comfortable and curious enough to encourage you to open up. But here's the key: If you're counting how many times you've gone first, you're not fully engaged in the Relationship Sea-Saw. Offering curiosity and warmth shouldn't be a tactic—it only works if your interest in them is genuine. That said, if you've made repeated attempts and still don't feel their curiosity and warmth, it may be time to reevaluate the relationship (as we discussed in the last chapter as well as in chapter 4). Trust your instincts.

At its core, then, *this book* is about shifting your focus:

- Instead of questioning whether others love you enough, ask: *Am I helping them feel loved?*
- Instead of wondering why people don't seem curious about you, ask: *Am I showing enough curiosity toward them?*
- Instead of waiting to be fully seen, ask: *Have I first made space for them to share who they really are?*

Feeling loved is reciprocal, absolutely—but it often begins with one person showing up differently, engaging openly, loving more bravely, one mindset at a time. And that person can be you.

Epilogue

In the introduction to this book, we shared how our collaboration began—almost by accident. It happened at a conference in Washington, DC, where Sonja, who's been researching happiness since before it was cool, crossed paths with Harry, a leading expert on the science of relationships. We'd heard of each other's work but hadn't truly dug in. Our conversation began casually—just two academics chatting about their interests. Then, you may recall, Harry remarked, almost in passing, "Isn't it odd that happiness researchers and relationship researchers don't talk with each other?"

The more we talked, the more we realized: It *was* strange. Why *don't* these two deeply related fields cross-pollinate more? Why don't we more frequently attend each other's talks and read each other's articles? We both knew the data: Strong relationships are the single best predictor of happiness. And relationship struggles—conflict, distance, or disconnection—are the most powerful sources of loneliness and despair. One of us—neither of us remembers whom—said, perhaps more as a throwaway line than a serious suggestion, "We should write a book." And that was the moment *How to Feel Loved* was born.

That conversation took place half a dozen years ago. At the time, we were little more than professional acquaintances. We admired each other's reputations and had even read some of the work, but neither of us knew the deeper stories—why the other cared so deeply about these questions, where their ideas came from, or what they hoped their work could mean in the world. And although we respected each other, we hadn't yet shared the things that would allow us to *feel known* or *loved* by one another.

Fast-forward to today. We've holed up for days at a time writing together. We've had countless Zooms, text threads, and FaceTimes, as well as occasional emergency late-night calls when a section wasn't coming together and one of us needed a sounding board. (Sonja lives in California; the three-hour time difference fit perfectly with Harry's habit of working past midnight on the East Coast.)

Any successful professional project is likely to generate genuine appreciation among its collaborators. In our case, the feelings have grown into something much more. Along the way, we've come to love—and feel loved by—each other.

Each of us has worked on countless collaborative projects over our careers with other people, and we know what intellectual camaraderie feels like. But this project felt different, and we believe that the five mindsets are a big part of why. We didn't just write about them—we lived them.

We listened to learn when the other had a suggestion. We stayed curious, open-minded, and enthusiastic (most of the time) when the other offered a new angle or proposed a counterintuitive approach. We were patient and nonjudgmental when the other floated an idea that fell flat or was testy or unavailable. We were honest and vulnerable—sharing our hopes and fears about the book, doubts, dead ends, false starts, and moments when we thought we weren't getting it right. And through it all, we met each other with an open heart—with compassion, care, openness, and understanding—as colleagues, yes, but also as humans, feeling more loved with every chapter.

The Five Mindsets Diagnostic

At the end of chapter 12, we introduced the idea that the five mindsets could be used not just as a tool to feel more loved but as a diagnostic to hold a particular relationship to the light. In other words, difficulty embracing one or more mindsets could be a clue that something in the relationship dynamic needs work. If you're curious to evaluate how each of you shows up, read the five mindset paragraphs at www.howtofeelloved.com. Then, rate how well each describes you, and how well each fits the other person. Watch for scores that fall below the average (around the 50th percentile), and especially those in the bottom 25 percent. Such scores might be a red flag, or at least a reason to pause and reflect on the areas that need attention.

Here's what that might look like in real life: When Sonja completed the Five Mindsets Diagnostic with a particular relationship in mind, she discovered that her lowest score was for the Radical-Curiosity mindset. That realization prompted her to revisit chapter 7 and reflect on how she could rekindle her interest in the other person's inner world. Harry found that the Diagnostic reminded him that it's important to consistently engage his loved ones with the Listening-to-Learn and Radical-Curiosity mindsets, especially when he's preoccupied with work.

And what if multiple scores for both you and your social partner are low? Indeed, you might discover that when you hold your relationship or friendship up to the light, some painful truths are revealed. Maybe one or both of you are struggling—or unwilling—to engage meaningfully with the five mindsets. At that point, you have a choice:

Either invest more deeply in the effort to realign or consider stepping back. But remember, the Relationship Sea-Saw can't work unless both people are willing to get on. You can create the opportunity for balance, but you can't force someone else to meet you there. The only way to know is to begin.

Acknowledgments

Sonja and Harry's Acknowledgments

This book would not exist without the love, labor, and intellectual generosity of dozens of people—some of whom we worked closely with and others whose influence quietly guided us from a distance. Feeling loved involves a deep sense of gratitude, and there are many to whom we are grateful.

To the many dedicated scientists whose research and thinking have educated and energized us throughout our careers and in the writing of this book, we offer our deepest thanks. Your tireless dedication to uncovering the secrets of human motivation and interpersonal relationships is a continual source of inspiration. We feel honored to call you colleagues. Any errors or misrepresentations in describing your work are, of course, ours.

We also owe a deep debt of gratitude to the many research assistants and students who helped us carry out our research, as well as to the thousands of volunteers who participated in our studies. It is no exaggeration to say we couldn't have done it without you.

To those who read early drafts, with love, and offered feedback that was kind, insightful, or both: You helped bring our ideas into clearer focus. These generous early readers made the book better: Wendy Verba, Leah Huyghe, Luke Pustejovsky, Michael Ellsberg, Mark Wiener, and Elana Lian. Thank you also to Brian Gao and Luke Liao for your sharp editing skills and long hours of corrections, and to Isabella Del Greco for beautifully illustrating the Sea-Saw.

To our editor Karen Rinaldi and the dream team at Harper, especially Rachel Kambury and Plaegian Alexander: Thank you for making the book sharper, deeper, and more relatable—for keeping us on track and for reminding us that even science books can have heart. We are grateful for your honest reactions, eagle-eyed edits, and warm encouragement when they were most needed. We are also enormously grateful to Lena Little, who expertly helped us get the word out.

To Richard Pine: If there is a literary agent Mount Rushmore, your face is carved into it—with a knowing smile and a red pen in hand. You are brilliant, compassionate, and fiercely loyal. From our very first conversation, your nudges and suggestions through multiple drafts made our thinking clearer and more approachable. We are endlessly grateful to be in the care of you and your team at InkWell Management.

Sonja's Acknowledgments

Rainer Maria Rilke once wrote, "Love consists in this: That two solitudes protect and border and greet each other." Much of this book was written in solitude, but it became what it is because of the people who chose to nurture it, border it, and greet it along the way. Fittingly, writing a book about love mirrored the very nature of love itself—requiring vulnerability, trust, safety, patience, bouts of self-doubt, dozens of all-nighters, and at least one file I forgot to save.

To Harry: I know you already understand how deeply I value our friendship and our coparenting of this "baby," but I'll say it anyway: You have been my anchor and my sounding board—thank you for walking (and often running!) through every twist of this adventure with me. I deeply admire how you think, with clarity and depth, and how you always lead with integrity, humility, and kindness. You helped untangle ideas that had lived tangled in my head, and you made the science sharper, truer, and more human. In a million years, this book wouldn't be what it is—nor would I—without you. Our partnership has been full of joy, intellectual fire, and, of course, love. Our collaboration has been one of the greatest gifts of this book, and I couldn't be more grateful that we did it together.

To my brilliant collaborators and colleagues near and far and to the scholars and scientists whose work I draw upon throughout this book: Your insights were the scaffolding for every argument. These pages were shaped by you. Our numerous conversations made me smarter, in addition to making me feel loved. There are too many to name, but I'll try to include a few: Ken Sheldon, Barb Fredrickson, Nick Epley, Liz Dunn, Ed Diener, Robert Biswas-Diener, Shige Oishi, Jeanne Tsai, Sara Algoe, Dacher Keltner, Oliver John, David Funder, Dan Ozer, Kate Sweeny, Tuppett Yates, Jean Twenge, Jonathan Haidt, Scott Barry Kaufman, Neil Strauss, Arthur Brooks, Mark Manson, Jamie Pennebaker, Michael Morris, Mike Slepian, Guy Itzchakov, Todd Kashdan, and Roy Baumeister. Furthermore, thank you to Tal Ben-Shahar, Colin Deavan, Michael-John Bristow, and Isabella Del Greco for helping shape specific ideas in this book, both big and small.

To my PhD students at the University of California, Riverside—past and present: You are the invisible engine of this book. Every chapter carries your fingerprints. Thank you for all your brilliant research— from envisioning and creating to collecting, coding, analyzing, writing, questioning, interpreting, and lifting this work from idea to evidence. I'm so grateful to my current A-team: Ramona Martinez, Nina Radošić, Madison Montemayor-Dominguez, Tanya Vannoy, James Chinn, and Stephen Cadieux. And to former graduate students who've walked this path with me, including Kristin Layous, Katie Nelson-Coffey, Seth Margolis, Annie Regan, Megan Fritz, and Lisa Walsh: You are the future of this field (or whatever field you choose), and I'm grateful to have been part of your journey. If I don't list you, know that I'm thinking of you.

As ever, I am grateful to my colleagues at UC Riverside, who continue to support both my scholarship and my breaks from academic work to bring our findings into people's everyday lives.

I've said it before, and I'll keep saying it: Friends are what make life worth living. You know who you are, and I feel incredibly loved by you. Thank you for the thoughtful check-ins, the shared giggles, the tears, the dances, the kisses, the intellectual sparks, and the flashes of insight that changed everything. If you ever sent me a quick "keep going" voicemail during a hard writing day: You made me better. And if you didn't, I simply imagined your faces, and it made me better. My heart is full of gratitude for Veronica Benet-Martinez, Geoff Cohen, Michal Kosinski, Terry Johnson, Phillip Nguyen, Steve Cole, Emilie Ritea, Jess Tracy, Ashley Martin, Flo Leynaud, Elizabeth Koch, Seth Baum, Aaron Seitz, Nelli Varavva, Joshua White, Kelly Boys, Sarah Hackett, Jasmin Sawicki, Joe and Aura Wielgosz, Zhana Vrangalova, James Taylor, Matt Schnuck, and Emily Liman. There are so many more that I can't name; just know that if you are not on this page, you are in my heart.

To Richard Pine, who deserves a second mention: You continue to be part visionary, part compass, part fixer, and part magic. You're also just one of the best humans I have known.

Finally, to the most important people—my family. To Pete: Thank you for every kind of support; you are the embodiment of goodness and integrity. To Gabriella, Alexander, Isabella, and Olivia: Thank you for being patient with me when I disappeared into this book and for welcoming me back with love, for alleviating my stress with warmth and cuddles, and for reminding me every day what it means to feel loved. You are my punctuation and my poetry. Every word begins and ends with you.

Harry's Acknowledgments

The familiar metaphor about academic life—a solitary scholar cloistered in a remote ivory tower, thinking lofty thoughts and setting them down on paper (well, these days, some sort of digital device)—could not be further from the truth. In reality, at all stages, science is a team sport. From fleshing out the first spark of an idea to the multiple stages of designing and conducting the research to the end product of evaluating and publicizing the results, it is a thoroughly collaborative activity. Over the years, I have been blessed with a dream team of students and colleagues. I am deeply grateful to every one of you.

To Sonja: From the moment you first proposed that we write a book together about what it means to feel loved, I've been in awe of your creativity, your drive, your ability to separate the wheat from the chaff, your extraordinary gift with words, and your robust desire to make our science as relevant, accessible, and useful as possible. Your insistence that we keep at it until we get it 100 percent right has been a constant inspiration—the phrase "good enough" does not exist in your vocabulary. Everyone who's worked with you knows your brilliance, wisdom, and dedication—you're a force of nature. Your superpower is your talent for bringing out the best in your collaborators. When I was overwhelmed, you stepped in with generosity. When I was stuck, you illuminated a path forward. When I was uncertain, our conversations would stimulate a treasure trove of ideas. And when my thinking was buried in jargon, you helped transform it into something relatable, eloquent, and true to the science. I've had many collaborations over the years, but none compares to working with you—intense, energizing, thought-provoking, and, yes, loving. Sharing this journey with you has been more fun than I ever could have imagined. Thank you.

To the graduate students whose dedication made this research possible: Thank you for your ideas, your persistence, and your countless hours in the lab or analyzing data, as well as for making our meetings as enjoyable as they were fruitful. You are too many to list here—you know who you are, and so do I—but I must offer special thanks to Shelly Gable and David de Jong, whose work is highlighted in this book. I am also deeply grateful to Peter Caprariello, Cheryl Carmichael, Linda Jackson, Mike Kernis, Chip Knee, Jenny Le, Karisa Lee, Yi-Cheng Lin, Mike Maniaci, John Nezlek, Brian Patrick, Brett Peters, Shannon Smith, Fen-Fang Tsai, and Yan Ruan. Thank you for partnering with me through the process of discovery.

To my colleagues in social psychology and relationship science: Your energy, your fierce commitment to our science, and your penetrating questions and suggestions—often posed in conversations that stretched well past midnight—have been a constant catalyst and a fertile source of ideas and purpose. More than that, your friendship and collegiality have sustained me. I'm especially grateful to the other four members of the original Gang of Five (Arthur Aron, Margaret Clark, John Holmes, and the late, great Caryl Rusbult), Joanne Wood, RUG (Phil Shaver, Howie Markman, Wyndol Furman, and Duane Buhrmester), my Israeli "lantspeople" (Gurit Birnbaum, Moran Mizrahi, and Guy Itzchakov, who taught me what good listening is all about), the online dating team (Paul Eastwick, Eli Finkel, Ben Karney, and Sue Sprecher), Catrin Finkenauer, Ed Lemay, Nickola Overall, Laura Sels, and Jeff Simpson. And to Ellen Berscheid, as well as the late Harold Kelley and Ladd Wheeler, thank you for believing in me and for insisting that the study of close relationships belongs at the heart of social psychology. I would not be here without your support and encouragement.

For more than fifty-one years, I've been privileged to live and work in the Department of Psychology at the University of Rochester. It has been the ideal place to turn hunches and hypotheses into research reality. I am fortunate to work with colleagues who make work feel like home (gray skies and long winters notwithstanding). In this regard, I am particularly grateful to Andy Elliot, Bonnie Le, Ron Rogge, Jeremy Jamieson, Ken Sheldon, and Miron Zuckerman.

To the other Harry, and to Marty and Tommy: Thanks for showing me what true friendship looks like. To my Rochester pals: Thanks for sharing our journey through the years—it's been exhilarating, sustaining, and simply amazing. To my extended family; to the memory of my parents, Gus and Margot; to my cousins Joanie and Howie; and to the *ganze mishpocha*: Thank you for giving me roots.

To Lianna: Your warm heart has touched me in ways I never imagined. Every day you teach me more about what authentic love is. And to Ellen: You are my anchor, my secure base and safe haven. You've filled our life together with meaning and connection. Your ability to listen with curiosity and warmth never ceases to amaze me. I am enormously grateful for your welcoming me back when "working on the book" pulled me away—but most of all, for the love you give so generously.

Notes

Introduction: Do You Want to Feel More Loved?

1   *Being a happiness expert:* Sonja Lyubomirsky, *The How of Happiness: A Scientific Approach to Getting the Life You Want* (Penguin, 2008).

2   *Harry's career-long research:* Harry T. Reis, *The Relationship Context of Human Behavior: Selected Works of Harry T. Reis* (Taylor and Francis, 2018).

6   *most common deathbed regrets:* Bronnie Ware, *The Top Five Regrets of the Dying: A Life Transformed by the Dearly Departing* (Hay House, 2012).

Chapter 1: Hardwired to Feel Loved

21   *two major types of love:* Ellen Berscheid and Elaine Hatfield, *Interpersonal Attraction*, 2nd ed. (Addison-Wesley, 1978); Elaine Hatfield and Richard L. Rapson, *Love and Sex: Cross-Cultural Perspectives* (Allyn & Bacon, 1996); and Harry T. Reis and Arthur Aron, "Love: What Is It, Why Does It Matter, and How Does It Operate?" *Perspectives on Psychological Science* 3, no. 1 (2008): 80–86, https://doi.org/10.1111/j.1745-6916.2008.00065.x.

22   *that they matter:* Arie W. Kruglanski, Erica Molinario, Katarzyna Jasko, David Webber, N. Pontus Leander, and Antonio Pierro, "Significance-Quest Theory," *Perspectives on Psychological Science* 17, no. 4 (2022): 1050–71, https://doi.org/10.1177/17456916211034825.

22   *In a communal relationship:* Margaret S. Clark and Oriana R. Aragón, "Communal (and Other) Relationships: History, Theory Development, Recent Findings, and Future Directions," in *The Oxford Handbook of Close Relationships*, ed. Jeffry A. Simpson and Lorne Campbell (Oxford University Press, 2013), 255–80.

24   *effects on memories and judgments:* Suhui Yap, Li-Jun Ji, and Mingzhu Mao, "Projecting the Current Salient Relational Situations into the Past and Future Across Cultures," *Social Psychological and Personality Science* 16, no. 2 (2025): 224–35, https://doi.org/10.1177/19485506231211628. Notably, this effect was much stronger for Euro-Canadian than Chinese participants.

24   *a big, fierce, lasting emotion:* Harry T. Reis and Arthur Aron, "Love: What Is It, Why Does It Matter, and How Does It Operate?" *Perspectives on Psychological Science* 3, no. 1 (2008): 80–86, https://doi.org/10.1111/j.1745-6916.2008.00065.x.

24   *love sometimes comes in "momentary surges":* Philip R. Shaver, Heather J. Morgan, and Susan Wu, "Is Love a 'Basic' Emotion?" *Personal Relationships* 3, no. 1 (1996): 81–96, https://doi.org/10.1111/j.1475-6811.1996.tb00105.x; and Michelle N. Shiota, Belinda Campos, Christopher Oveis, Matthew J. Hertenstein, Emiliana Simon-Thomas, and Dacher Keltner, "Beyond Happiness: Building a Science of Discrete Positive Emotions," *American Psychologist* 72, no. 7 (2017): 617–43, https://doi.org/10.1037/a0040456.

24   *her book* Love 2.0: Barbara L. Fredrickson, *Love 2.0: Creating Happiness and Health in Moments of Connection* (Plume, 2013).

25   *moments of love are associated with:* Barbara L. Fredrickson, "Love: Positivity Resonance as a Fresh, Evidence-Based Perspective on an Age-Old Topic," in *Handbook of Emotions*, 4th ed., ed. Lisa Feldman Barrett, Michael Lewis, and Jeannette M. Haviland-Jones (Guilford, 2016), 847–58; Jieni Zhou, Michael M. Prinzing, Khoa D. Le Nguyen, Taylor N. West, and Barbara L. Fredrickson, "The Goods in Everyday Love: Positivity Resonance Builds Prosociality," *Emotion* 22, no. 1 (2022): 30–45, https://doi.org/10.1037/emo0001035; Casey L. Brown, Kuan-Hua Chen, Marcela C. Otero, Jenna L. Wells, Dyan E. Connelly, Robert W. Levenson, and Barbara L. Fredrickson, "Shared Emotions in Shared Lives: Moments of Co-experienced Affect, More Than Individually Experienced Affect, Linked to Relationship Quality," *Emotion* 22, no. 6 (2022): 1387–93, https://doi.org/10.1037/emo0000939; Casey L. Brown and Barbara L. Fredrickson, "Characteristics and Consequences of Co-experienced Positive Affect: Understanding the Origins of Social Skills, Social Bonds, and Caring, Healthy Communities," *Current Opinion in Behavioral Sciences* 39 (2021): 58–63, https://doi.org/10.1016/j.cobeha.2021.02.002; Jenna L. Wells, Claudia M. Haase, Emily S. Rothwell, Kendyl G. Naugle, Marcela C. Otero, Casey L. Brown, et al., "Positivity Resonance in Long-Term Married Couples: Multi-modal Characteristics and Consequences for Health and Longevity," *Journal of Personality and Social Psychology* 123, no. 5 (2022): 983–1003, https://doi.org/10.1037/pspi0000385; and Brenda C. Major, Khoa D. Le Nguyen, Kristin B. Lundberg, and Barbara L. Fredrickson, "Well-Being Correlates of Perceived Positivity Resonance: Evidence from Trait and Episode-Level Assessments," *Personality and Social Psychology Bulletin* 44, no. 12 (2018): 1631–47, https://doi.org/10.1177/0146167218771324.

25   *scientists call "high-quality connections":* Jane E. Dutton and Emily D. Heaphy, "The Power of High-Quality Connections," in *Positive Organizational Scholarship: Foundations of a New Discipline*, ed. Kim Cameron and Jane E. Dutton (Berrett-Koehler, 2003), 263–78; and Jane Dutton and Monica Worline, "Four Ways to Create High-Quality Connections at Work: Research Reveals What Makes Work Relationships Strong and Healthy—and the Small Actions You Can Take to Deepen Them," Greater Good Science Center, October 24, 2023, https://greatergood.berkeley.edu/article/item/four_ways_to_create_high_quality_connections_at_work.

25   *the brain releases dopamine:* Helen E. Fisher, Xiaomeng Xu, Arthur Aron, and Lucy L. Brown, "Intense, Passionate, Romantic Love: A Natural Addiction? How the Fields That Investigate Romance and Substance Abuse Can Inform Each Other," *Frontiers in Psychology* 7, no. 687 (2016): 1–10, https://doi.org/10.3389/fpsyg.2016.00687.

25   *participants viewed photos:* Arthur Aron, Helen Fisher, Debra J. Mashek, Greg Strong, Haifang Li, and Lucy L. Brown, "Reward, Motivation, and Emotion Systems Associated with Early-Stage Intense Romantic Love," *Journal of Neurophysiology* 94, no. 1 (2005): 327–37, https://doi.org/10.1152/jn.00838.2004.

25   *abuse of addictive substances:* Judson Brewer, *The Craving Mind* (Yale University Press, 2017).

26   *feelings of love, trust, and attachment:* Jennifer A. Bartz, Jamil Zaki, Niall Bolger, and Kevn N. Ochsner, "Social Effects of Oxytocin in Humans: Context and Person Matter," *Trends in Cognitive Sciences* 15, no. 7 (2011): 301–09, https://doi.org/10.1016/j.tics.2011.05.002; and Suzannah F. Isgett, Bethany E. Kok, Blazej M. Baczkowski, Sara B. Algoe, Karen M. Grewen, and Barbara L. Fredrickson,

"Influences of Oxytocin and Respiratory Sinus Arrhythmia on Emotions and Social Behavior in Daily Life," *Emotion* 17, no. 8 (2017): 1156–65, https://doi .org/10.1037/emo0000301.

26 *the earliest studies of oxytocin:* Thomas R. Insel and Larry E. Shapiro, "Oxytocin Receptor Distribution Reflects Social Organization in Monogamous and Polygamous Voles," *Proceedings of the National Academy of Sciences* 89, no. 13 (1992): 5981–85, https://doi.org/10.1073/pnas.89.13.5981; and Mary Cho, A. Courtney DeVries, Jessie R. Williams, and C. Sue Carter, "The Effects of Oxytocin and Vasopressin on Partner Preferences in Male and Female Prairie Voles (Microtus Ochrogaster)," *Behavioral Neuroscience* 113, no. 5 (1999): 1071–79, https://doi .org/10.1037/0735-7044.113.5.1071.

26 *higher levels of plasma oxytocin:* Ruth Feldman, Aron Weller, Orna Zagoory-Sharon, and Ari Levine, "Evidence for a Neuroendocrinological Foundation of Human Affiliation: Plasma Oxytocin Levels Across Pregnancy and the Postpartum Period Predict Mother-Infant Bonding," *Psychological Science* 18, no. 11 (2007): 965–70, https://doi.org/10.1111/j.1467-9280.2007.02010.x; and Ruth Feldman, "Oxytocin and Social Affiliation in Humans," *Hormones and Behavior* 61, no. 3 (2012): 380–91, https://doi.org/10.1016/j.yhbeh.2012.01.008.

26 *dose of intranasal oxytocin:* Omri Weisman, Orna Zagoory-Sharon, and Ruth Feldman, "Oxytocin Administration to Parent Enhances Infant Physiological and Behavioral Readiness for Social Engagement," *Biological Psychiatry* 72, no. 12 (2012): 982–89, https://doi.org/10.1016/j.biopsych.2012.06.011.

26 *associated with more frequent hugging:* Kathleen C. Light, Karen M. Grewen, and Janet A. Amico, "More Frequent Partner Hugs and Higher Oxytocin Levels Are Linked to Lower Blood Pressure and Heart Rate in Premenopausal Women," *Biological Psychology* 69, no. 1 (2005): 5–21, https://doi.org/10.1016 /j.biopsycho.2004.11.002.

26 *ability to read others' emotions:* Marinus H. van IJzendoorn and Marian J. Bakermans-Kranenburg, "A Sniff of Trust: Meta-Analysis of the Effects of Intranasal Oxytocin Administration on Face Recognition, Trust to In-Group, and Trust to Out-Group," *Psychoneuroendocrinology* 37, no. 3 (2012): 438–43, https://doi.org/10.1016/j.psyneuen.2011.07.008.

26 *levels of trust in economic games:* Michael Kosfeld, Markus Heinrichs, Paul J. Zak, and Ernst Fehr, "Oxytocin Increases Trust in Humans," *Nature* 435, no. 2 (2005): 673–76, https://doi.org/10.1038/nature03701.

26 *people to favor friends and family:* Carsten K. W. De Dreu, "Oxytocin Moderates Cooperation Within and Competition Between Groups: An Integrative Review and Research Agenda," *Hormones and Behavior* 61, no. 3 (2012): 419–28, https://doi.org/10.1016/j.yhbeh.2011.12.009.

27 *stimulates the production of oxytocin:* Nicoletta Cera, Sebastian Vargas-Caceres, Catia Oliveira, Jessica Monteiro, David Branco, Duarte Pignatelli, and Sandra Rebelo, "How Relevant Is the Systemic Oxytocin Concentration for Human Sexual Behavior? A Systematic Review," *Sexual Medicine* 9, no. 4 (2021): 100370, https://doi.org/10.1016/j.esxm.2021.100370.

28 *the fear of death:* Sheldon Solomon, Jeff L. Greenberg, and Tom Pyszczynski, "A Terror Management Theory of Social Behavior: The Psychological Functions of Self-Esteem and Cultural Worldviews," *Advances in Experimental Social Psychology* 24 (1991): 93–159, https://doi.org/10.1016/S0065-2601(08)60328-7.

28 *that would reshape the field:* Roy Baumeister and Mark Leary's collaboration on the "Need to Belong" paper began during late-night conversations at Nags Head. That's where they germinated an idea that would leverage their different areas of knowledge, compel hundreds of hours of work, and rely on pure serendipity.

In an era before Zoom or even email, they needed to meet face-to-face. As luck would have it, Baumeister's sabbatical that year brought him within driving distance of Leary's house, and, furthermore, Baumeister's sister happened to live blocks away from Leary. They would meet at Leary's house, pencil their ideas on giant sheets of paper, and strew the sheets all about the living room.

28 *Esther Perel famously put it:* Esther Perel, "The Quality of Your Relationships Determines the Quality of Your Life," lecture, 0:37, posted February 12, 2019, by Summit, YouTube, https://www.youtube.com/watch?v=LmDPAOE5V2Y.

28 *it's also about reproduction:* David M. Buss, *The Evolution of Desire: Strategies of Human Mating,* rev. ed. (Basic Books, 2016).

29 *you feel safe:* John Bowlby, *A Secure Base: Clinical Applications of Attachment Theory* (Routledge, 1988); and Emily Nagoski, *Come as You Are* (Simon & Schuster, 2015).

29 *Jaak Panksepp:* Jaak Panksepp and Lucy Biven, *The Archaeology of Mind: Neuro-evolutionary Origins of Human Emotions* (W. W. Norton, 2012).

30 *Social Baseline theory:* James A. Coan and David A. Sbarra, "Social Baseline Theory: The Social Regulation of Risk and Effort," *Current Opinion in Psychology* 1 (2015): 87–91, https://doi.org/10.1016/j.copsyc.2014.12.021.

30 *respond to threats and ordeals:* Lane Beckes and James A. Coan, "Social Baseline Theory: The Role of Social Proximity in Emotion and Economy of Action," *Social and Personality Psychology Compass* 5, no. 12 (2011): 976–88, https://doi.org/10.1111/j.1751-9004.2011.00400.x.

30 *in one classic study:* James A. Coan, Hillary S. Schaefer, and Richard A. Davidson, "Lending a Hand: Social Regulation of the Neural Response to Threat," *Psychological Science* 17, no. 12 (2006): 1032–39, https://doi.org/10.1111/j.1467-9280.2006.01832.x.

30 *across four different countries:* Eri Sasaki, Nickola C. Overall, Harry T. Reis, Francesca Righetti, Valerie T. Chang, Rachel S. T. Low et al., "Feeling Loved as a Strong Link in Relationship Interactions: Partners Who Feel Loved May Buffer Destructive Behavior by Actors Who Feel Unloved," *Journal of Personality and Social Psychology* 125, no. 2 (2023): 367–96, https://doi.org/10.1037/pspi0000419.

Chapter 2: The Cost of Not Feeling Loved

33 *survey expressly for this book:* Our respondents were 49 percent female, 69 percent White, 53 percent college-educated, and 75 percent heterosexual. They came from all areas of the United States. Their ages ranged from 18 to 86, with a mean of 39.9 years. Thirty-three percent of them were single; 22 percent, in a committed relationship with one partner; and 37 percent, married. Between 3 percent and 16 percent had been separated, divorced, or widowed, and 46 percent had at least one child.

35 *Eremocene era:* Edward O. Wilson, "Beware the Age of Loneliness," *Economist,* November 18, 2013, https://www.economist.com/news/2013/11/18/beware-the-age-of-loneliness.

35 *spanning 124,855 participants:* Susanne Buecker, Marcus Mund, Sandy Chwastek, Melina Sostmann, and Maike Luhmann, "Is Loneliness in Emerging Adults Increasing Over Time? A Preregistered Cross-temporal Meta-Analysis and Systematic Review," *Psychological Bulletin* 147, no. 8 (2021): 787–805, https://doi.org/10.1037/bul0000332.

35 *A 2023 Gallup/Meta study of 142 countries:* Gallup and Meta, *State of Social Connections Study* (ICPSR, June 2023), https://doi.org/10.3886/3857-0854.

35   *a highly cited 2018 Cigna study:* Cigna and Ipsos, *2018 Cigna U.S. Loneliness Index: Survey of 20,000 Americans Examining Behaviors Driving Loneliness in the United States* (Cigna, 2018), https://legacy.cigna.com/static/www-cigna-com /docs/about-us/newsroom/studies-and-reports/combatting-loneliness/loneliness -survey-2018-full-report.pdf.

36   *Alarmed by such data:* Office of the Surgeon General, *Our Epidemic of Loneliness and Isolation: The U.S. Surgeon General's Advisory on the Healing Effects of Social Connection and Community* (US Department of Health and Human Services, 2023), https://www.hhs.gov/sites/default/files/surgeon-general-social -connection-advisory.pdf.

36   *especially prevalent in younger generations:* Cigna and Ipsos, *2018 Cigna U.S. Loneliness Index.*

36   *"No one really knows me":* Gary Barker, Caroline Hayes, Brian Heilman, and Michael Reichert, *The State of American Men: From Crisis and Confusion to Hope* (Equimundo, 2023), https://static1.squarespace.com/static/5d77e56c1f c5e024160affa9/t/646e4fc8d8d648481a2073c5/1684950995645/State-of-American-Men-2023-compressed.pdf; see also American College Health Association, *American College Health Association–National College Health Assessment III: Reference Group Executive Summary Spring 2023* (American College Health Association, 2023), https://www.acha.org/wp-content/uploads/2024/07 /ncha-iii_spring_2023_reference_group_executive_summary.pdf.

36   *10 percentage points higher:* Gallup and Meta, *State of Social Connections Study.*

36   *study of more than 6,000 adults:* Pew Research Center, *Men, Women, and Social Connections* (Washington, DC, January 2025), https://www.pewresearch.org /social-trends/2025/01/16/men-women-and-social-connections/; see also Eileen K. Graham, Emorie D. Beck, Kathryn Jackson, Tomiko Yoneda, Chloe McGhee, Lily Pieramici et al., "Do We Become More Lonely with Age? A Coordinated Data Analysis of Nine Longitudinal Studies," *Psychological Science* 35, no. 6 (2024): 579–96, https://doi.org/10.1177/09567976241242037.

36   *the* World Happiness Report*:* John F. Helliwell, Richard Layard, Jeffrey D. Sachs, Jan-Emmanuel De Neve, Lara B. Aknin, and Shun Wang, eds., *World Happiness Report 2024* (University of Oxford: Wellbeing Research Centre, 2024), https://happiness-report.s3.amazonaws.com/2024/WHR+24.pdf; and John F. Helliwell, Richard Layard, Jeffrey D. Sachs, Jan-Emmanuel De Neve, Lara Aknin, and Shun Wang, eds., *World Happiness Report 2025* (University of Oxford: Wellbeing Research Centre, 2025), https://data.worldhappiness .report/table.

37   *UCLA Loneliness Scale:* Daniel W. Russell, "UCLA Loneliness Scale (Version 3): Reliability, Validity, and Factor Structure," *Journal of Personality Assessment* 66, no. 1 (1996): 20–40, https://doi.org/10.1207/s15327752jpa6601_2.

37   *three out of five Americans:* Cigna, *Cigna Loneliness and the Workplace: 2020 U.S. Report* (Cigna, 2020), https://legacy.cigna.com/static/www-cigna-com /docs/about-us/newsroom/studies-and-reports/combatting-loneliness/cigna -2020-loneliness-report.pdf.

37   *Research from Harvard University shows:* Ashley V. Whillans, Chelsea D. Christie, Sarah Cheung, Alexander H. Jordan, and Frances S. Chen, "From Misperception to Social Connection: Correlates and Consequences of Overestimating Others' Social Connectedness," *Personality and Social Psychology Bulletin* 43, no. 12 (2017): 1696–1711, https://doi.org/10.1177/0146167217727496.

38   *Switzerland and Germany across fourteen days:* Xianmin Gong and Jana Nikitin, "When I Feel Lonely, I'm Not Nice (and Neither Are You): The Short- and Long-term Relation between Loneliness and Reports of Social Behaviour," *Cog-*

nition and Emotion 35, no. 5 (2021): 1029–38, https://doi.org/10.1080/02699931
.2021.1905612.

38 *Mother Teresa:* "Saints Among Us: The Work of Mother Teresa," *Time,*
December 29, 1975, https://content.time.com/time/subscriber/article
/0,33009,945463-6,00.html.

39 *communal relationships:* Clark and Aragón, "Communal (and Other) Relationships," 255–80.

39 *feel understood, appreciated, and loved:* Michael R. Maniaci and Harry T. Reis,
"Are You Lonesome Tonight? Daily Experiences of Loneliness," poster presen-
tation, Society for Personality and Social Psychology Conference, Tampa, FL,
February 2009.

39 *self-perpetuating (or "vicious") cycle:* Louise C. Hawkley and John T. Cacioppo,
"Loneliness Matters: A Theoretical and Empirical Review of Consequences and
Mechanisms," *Annals of Behavioral Medicine* 40, no. 2 (2010): 218–27, https://
doi.org/10.1007/s12160-010-9210-8.

41 *activation in the reward regions:* John T. Cacioppo, Catherine J. Norris,
Jean Decety, George Monteleone, and Howard Nusbaum, "In the Eye of the
Beholder: Individual Differences in Perceived Social Isolation Predict Regional
Brain Activation to Social Stimuli," *Journal of Cognitive Neuroscience* 21, no. 1
(2009): 83–92, https://doi.org/10.1162/jocn.2009.21007.

41 *can take a toll:* John T. Cacioppo, Louise C. Hawkley, and Ronald A. Thisted,
"Perceived Social Isolation Makes Me Sad: 5-Year Cross-Lagged Analyses of
Loneliness and Depressive Symptomatology in the Chicago Health, Aging, and
Social Relations Study," *Psychology and Aging* 25, no. 2 (2010): 453–63, https://
doi.org/10.1037/a0017216; Javier Yanguas, Sacramento Pinazo-Henandis, and
Francisco José Tarazona-Santabalbina, "The Complexity of Loneliness," *Acta
Biomedica: Atenei Parmensis* 89, no. 2 (2018): 302–14, https://doi.org/10.23750
/abm.v89i2.7404; Naomi I. Eisenberger and Steve W. Cole, "Social Neuroscience
and Health: Neurophysiological Mechanisms Linking Social Ties with Physical
Health," *Nature Neuroscience* 15, no. 5 (2012): 669–74, https://doi.org/10.1038
/nn.3086; Julianne Holt-Lunstad, Timothy B. Smith, Mark Baker, Tyler Harris,
and David Stephenson, "Loneliness and Social Isolation as Risk Factors for
Mortality: A Meta-Analytic Review," *Perspectives on Psychological Science* 10, no.
2 (2015): 227–37, https://doi.org/10.1177/1745691614568352; and Chun Shen,
Ruohan Zhang, Jintai Yu, Barbara Sahakian, Wei Cheng, and Jianfeng Feng,
"Plasma Proteomic Signatures of Social Isolation and Loneliness Associated with
Morbidity and Mortality," *Nature Human Behaviour* 9 (2025): 569–83, https://
doi.org/10.1038/s41562-024-02078-1.

41 *even antisocial behavior:* Kelly-Ann Allen, Margaret L. Kern, Christopher S.
Rozek, Dennis M. McInerney, and George M. Slavich, "Belonging: A Review
of Conceptual Issues, an Integrative Framework, and Directions for Future
Research," *Australian Journal of Psychology* 73, no. 1 (2021): 87–102, https://doi.org
/10.1080/00049530.2021.1883409; Scott H. Decker, *Life in the Gang: Family,
Friends, and Violence* (Cambridge University Press, 1996), 250; and John T.
Cacioppo and Louise C. Hawkley, "People Thinking About People: The Vicious
Cycle of Being a Social Outcast in One's Own Mind," in *The Social Outcast:
Ostracism, Social Exclusion, Rejection, and Bullying,* ed. Kipling D. Williams,
Joseph P. Forgas, and William von Hippel (Psychology Press, 2005), 91–108,
https://doi.org/10.4324/9780203942888-13.

42 *asked to make trait judgments:* Timothy W. Broom, Siddhant Iyer, Andrea L.
Courtney, and Meghan L. Meyer, "Keeping Up with Others' Perceptions of the
Kardashians: Lonely Individuals' Neural Representations and Language Use Do

Not Reflect the Zeitgeist" (PsyArXiv Preprints, May 2, 2023), accessed March 17, 2025, https://doi.org/10.31234/osf.io/8m4tb.

42 *In another imaging study:* Elisa C. Baek, Ryan Hyon, Karina López, Meng Du, Mason A. Porter, and Carolyn Parkinson, "Lonely Individuals Process the World in Idiosyncratic Ways," *Psychological Science* 34, no. 6 (2023): 683–95, https://doi.org/10.1177/09567976221114531.

42 *known as "shared reality":* Edward T. Higgins, Maya Rossignac-Milon, and Gerald Echterhoff, "Shared Reality: From Sharing-Is-Believing to Merging Minds," *Current Directions in Psychological Science* 30, no. 2 (2021): 103–10, https://doi.org/10.1177/0963721421992027.

44 *less time in community with others:* Robert D. Putnam, "Bowling Alone: America's Declining Social Capital," *Journal of Democracy* 6, no.1 (1995): 65–78, https://dx.doi.org/10.1353/jod.1995.0002.

44 *Nearly thirty years later:* Lulu Garcia-Navarro, "Robert Putnam Knows Why You Are Lonely," *New York Times*, July 13, 2024, https://www.nytimes.com/2024/07/13/magazine/robert-putnam-interview.html.

44 *restaurant-booking platform OpenTable:* "More People Than Ever Are Eating Alone at Restaurants. This Is Why," CNN, August 31, 2024, https://www.cnn.com/2024/08/31/business/solo-dining-restaurants-reservations/index.html.

44 *In his 2024 book:* Jonathan Haidt, *The Anxious Generation: How the Great Rewiring of Childhood Is Causing an Epidemic of Mental Illness* (Penguin, 2024).

44 *young people in the United States:* Lloyd D. Johnston, Richard A. Miech, Patrick M. O'Malley, Jerald G. Bachman, John E. Schulenberg, and Megan E. Patrick, *Monitoring the Future: National Survey Results on Drug Use, 1975–2016* (Ann Arbor, MI: University of Michigan, National Institute on Drug Abuse at the National Institute of Health, 2017), https://monitoringthefuture.org/wp-content/uploads/2022/12/mtf2022.pdf.

44 *in thirty-seven nations:* Jean M. Twenge, Brian H. Spitzberg, and William K. Campbell, "Less In-Person Social Interaction with Peers Among U.S. Adolescents in the 21st Century and Links to Loneliness," *Journal of Social and Personal Relationships* 36, no. 6 (2019): 1892–1913, https://doi.org/10.1177/0265407519836170.

45 *time they spent on social media:* James A. Roberts, Phil D. Young, and Meredith E. David, "The Epidemic of Loneliness: A 9-Year Longitudinal Study of the Impact of Passive and Active Social Media Use on Loneliness," *Personality and Social Psychology Bulletin* (December 20, 2024), https://doi.org/10.1177/01461672241295870.

45 *have become more text-based:* Aaron Smith, "Americans and Text Messaging," Pew Research Center, September 19, 2011, https://www.pewresearch.org/internet/2011/09/19/americans-and-text-messaging/.

45 *young people's social interactions:* "Teens, Social Media, and Technology Overview 2015," Pew Research Center, April 9, 2015, https://www.pewresearch.org/internet/2015/04/09/teens-social-media-technology-2015/.

45 *disagreement more likely:* Juliana Schroeder and Nicholas Epley, "The Sound of Intellect: Speech Reveals a Thoughtful Mind, Increasing a Job Candidate's Appeal," *Psychological Science* 26, no. 6 (2015): 877–91, https://doi.org/10.1177/0956797615572906; Juliana Schroeder "Spoken Conversation Facilitates Constructive Disagreement," unpublished manuscript, April 12, 2024; Xuan Zhao, Taya R. Cohen, Charles A. Dorison, Juliana Schroeder, Michael Yeomans, Xuan Zhao et al., "2020: The Art and Science of Disagreeing: How to Create More Effective Conversations About Opposing Views," *Proceedings* (2020), https://doi.org/10.5465/AMBPP.2020.15153symposium; and Justin

S. Kruger, Nicholas Epley, Jason Parker, and Zhi-Wen Ng, "Egocentrism over E-mail: Can We Communicate as Well as We Think?" *Journal of Personality and Social Psychology* 89, no. 6 (2005): 925–36, https://doi.org/10.1037/0022 -3514.89.6.925.

45   *presence of a smartphone:* Ryan J. Dwyer, Kostadin Kushlev, and Elizabeth W. Dunn, "Smartphone Use Undermines Enjoyment of Face-to-Face Social Interactions," *Journal of Experimental Social Psychology* 78 (2018): 233–39, https:// doi.org/10.1016/j.jesp.2017.10.007; and Andrew K. Przybylski and Netta Weinstein, "Can You Connect with Me Now? How the Presence of Mobile Communication Technology Influences Face-to-Face Conversation Quality," *Journal of Social and Personal Relationships* 30, no. 3 (2013): 237–46, https://doi .org/10.1177/0265407512453827.

45   *parents are absorbed in their screens:* Kostadin Kushlev and Elizabeth W. Dunn, "Smartphones Distract Parents from Cultivating Feelings of Connection When Spending Time with Their Children," *Journal of Social and Personal Relationships* 36, no. 6 (2019): 1619–39, https://doi.org/10.1177/0265407518769387.

45   *studies on this topic:* Elizabeth W. Chan, Natalie Cheung, Jessie Y. S. Choy, and Felix Cheung, "Links Between Adolescent Time-Use Sequences and Well-Being," unpublished manuscript, submitted in 2024.

46   *humans are becoming "undersocial":* Nicholas Epley, Michael Kardas, Xuan Zhao, Stav Atir, and Juliana Schroeder, "Undersociality: Miscalibrated Social Cognition Can Inhibit Social Connection," *Trends in Cognitive Sciences* 26, no. 5 (2022): 406–18, https://doi.org/10.1016/j.tics.2022.02.007; and Nicholas Epley, *Hello? Connecting Better in an Overly Lonely World* (Knopf, 2026).

46   *try to avoid them:* Juliana Schroeder, Donald Lyons, and Nicholas Epley, "Hello, Stranger? Pleasant Conversations Are Preceded by Concerns About Starting One," *Journal of Experimental Psychology: General* 151, no. 5 (2022): 1141–53, https://doi.org/10.1037/xge0001118; and Nicholas Epley and Juliana Schroeder, "Mistakenly Seeking Solitude," *Journal of Experimental Psychology: General* 143, no. 5 (2014): 1980–99, https://doi.org/10.1037/a0037323.

46   *wrap them up too early:* Michael Kardas, Juliana Schroeder, and Ed O'Brien, "Keep Talking: (Mis)understanding the Hedonic Trajectory of Conversation," *Journal of Personality and Social Psychology* 123, no. 4 (2022): 717–40, https:// doi.org/10.1037/pspi0000379.

46   *preference for texting over speaking:* Amit Kumar and Nicholas Epley, "It's Surprisingly Nice to Hear You: Misunderstanding the Impact of Communication Media Can Lead to Suboptimal Choices of How to Connect with Others," *Journal of Experimental Psychology: General* 150, no. 3 (2021): 595–607, https://doi.org/10.1037/ xge0000962. In reality, and to their surprise, participants felt happier talking to someone they disagreed with than texting with someone they agreed with!

46   *gravitate toward small talk:* Michael Kardas, Amit Kumar, and Nicholas Epley, "Overly Shallow? Miscalibrated Expectations Create a Barrier to Deeper Conversation," *Journal of Personality and Social Psychology* 122, no. 3 (2022): 367–98, https://doi.org/10.1037/pspa0000281.

46   *team conducted a study:* Megan M. Fritz, Seth Margolis, Nina Radošić, Julia C. Revord, Gabriella R. Kellerman, Levi R. G. Nieminen et al., "Examining the Social in the Prosocial: Episode-Level Features of Social Interactions and Kind Acts Predict Social Connection and Well-Being," *Emotion* 23, no. 8 (2023): 2270–85, https://doi.org/10.1037/emo0001232.

47   *auditory vibrations through your bones:* Stefan Stenfelt, "Acoustic and Physiologic Aspects of Bone Conduction Hearing," *Advances in Oto-Rhino-Laryngology* 71 (2011): 10–21, https://doi.org/10.1159/000323574.

47   *A 2023 study:* Nan Zhao, Xian Zhang, J. Adam Noah, Mark Tiede, and
     Joy Hirsch, "Separable Processes for Live 'In-Person' and Live 'Zoom-Like'
     Faces," *Imaging Neuroscience* 1, no. 1 (2023): 1–17, https://doi.org/10.1162/
     imag_a_00027.

48   *more face-to-face interactions:* Christopher M. Masi, Hsi-Yuan Chen, Louise C.
     Hawkley, and John T. Cacioppo, "A Meta-Analysis of Interventions to Reduce
     Loneliness," *Personality and Social Psychology Review* 15, no. 3 (2011): 219–66,
     https://doi.org/10.1177/1088868310377394.

48   *act more extraverted:* Seth Margolis and Sonja Lyubomirsky, "Experimental
     Manipulation of Extraverted and Introverted Behavior and Its Effects on Well-
     Being," *Journal of Experimental Psychology: General* 149, no. 4 (2020): 719–31,
     https://doi.org/10.1037/xge0000668.

48   *the power of a voice call:* Megan M. Fritz, Seth Margolis, Nina Radošić, Julia
     C. Revord, Gabriella R. Kellerman, Levi R. G. Nieminen et al., "Examining the
     Social in the Prosocial: Episode-Level Features of Social Interactions and Kind
     Acts Predict Social Connection and Well-Being," *Emotion* 23, no. 8 (2023):
     2270–85, https://doi.org/10.1037/emo0001232.

48   *Simply taking time to chat:* Anne Milek, Emily A. Butler, Allison M. Tackman,
     Deanna M. Kaplan, Charles L. Raison, David A. Sbarra et al., "Eavesdropping on
     Happiness Revisited: A Pooled, Multisample Replication of the Association Between
     Life Satisfaction and Observed Daily Conversation Quantity and Quality," *Psycholog-
     ical Science* 29, no. 9 (2018): 1451–62, https://doi.org/10.1177/0956797618774252;
     Andrew Reece, Gus Cooney, Peter Bull, Christine Chung, Bryn Dawson, Casey
     Fitzpatrick et al., "The CANDOR Corpus: Insights from a Large Multimodal
     Dataset of Naturalistic Conversation," *Science Advances* 9, no. 13 (2023): eadf3197,
     https://doi.org/10.1126/sciadv.adf3197; and Gus Cooney and Thalia Wheatley,
     "Conversation," in *The Handbook of Social Psychology*, 6th ed., ed. Daniel T. Gil-
     bert, Susan T. Fiske, Eli J. Finkel, and Wendy B. Mendes (Situational Press, 2025),
     https://doi.org/10.70400/ZKHH62592025.

49   *less time per day:* Bureau of Labor Statistics, "Time-Use Survey—First Results
     Announced by BLS," news release, January 12, 2005, https://www.bls.gov/news
     .release/archives/atus_09142004.pdf; and Bureau of Labor Statistics, "American
     Time Use Survey—2022 Results," news release, June 27, 2024, https://www.bls
     .gov/news.release/pdf/atus.pdf.

50   *violence and hate:* Kelly-Ann Allen, Margaret L. Kern, Christopher S. Rozek,
     Dennis M. McInerney, and George M. Slavich, "Belonging: A Review of Con-
     ceptual Issues, an Integrative Framework, and Directions for Future Research,"
     Australian Journal of Psychology 73, no. 1 (2021): 87–102, https://doi.org/10.1080
     /00049530.2021.1883409; Scott H. Decker, *Life in the Gang: Family, Friends,
     and Violence* (Cambridge University Press, 1996), 250; and Cacioppo and
     Hawkley, "People Thinking About People," 91–108.

51   *John Cacioppo (1951–2018):* Tim Adams, "John Cacioppo: 'Loneliness Is Like
     an Iceberg—It Goes Deeper than We Can See,'" *The Guardian*, February 28,
     2016, https://www.theguardian.com/science/2016/feb/28/loneliness-is-like-an-
     iceberg-john-cacioppo-social-neuroscience-interview.

Chapter 3: Revisiting Popular Beliefs About What Makes You Feel Loved

55   *he describes in his book:* Sah D'Simone, *Spiritually, We: The Art of Relating and
     Connecting from the Heart* (Sounds True, 2024).

56   *"quest" for significance:* Kruglanski, Molinario, Jasko, Webber, Leander, and
     Pierro, "Significance-Quest Theory," 1050–71.

56 *Madame Bovary:* Gustave Flaubert, *Madame Bovary*, trans. Lydia Davis (Viking, 2010).

57 *conducted at the University at Buffalo:* Brenda Major, Patricia I. Carrington, and Peter J. D. Carnevale, "Physical Attractiveness and Self-Esteem: Attributions for Praise from an Other-Sex Evaluator," *Personality and Social Psychology Bulletin* 10, no. 1 (1984): 43–50, https://doi.org/10.1177/0146167284101004.

57 *the "hedonic treadmill":* Philip Brickman and Donald T. Campbell, "Hedonic Relativism and Planning the Good Society," in *Adaptation-Level Theory*, ed. M. H. Appley (Academic Press, 1971), 287–302; Sonja Lyubomirsky, "Hedonic Adaptation to Positive and Negative Experiences," in *The Oxford Handbook of Stress, Health, and Coping*, ed. Susan Folkman (Oxford University Press, 2010), 200–24; and Timothy D. Wilson and Daniel T. Gilbert, "Explaining Away: A Model of Affective Adaptation," *Perspectives on Psychological Science* 3, no. 5 (2008): 370–86, https://doi.org/10.1111/j.1745-6924.2008.00085.x.

57 *oft-quoted commencement speech:* Joel Lovell, "George Saunders's Advice to Graduates," *New York Times*, July 31, 2024, https://archive.nytimes.com/6thfloor.blogs.nytimes.com/2013/07/31/george-saunderss-advice-to-graduates/.

57 *pursuing extrinsic goals:* Tim Kasser and Richard M. Ryan, "Be Careful What You Wish For: Optimal Functioning and the Relative Attainment of Intrinsic and Extrinsic Goals," in *Life Goals and Well-Being: Towards a Positive Psychology of Human Striving*, ed. Peter Schmuck and Ken Sheldon (Hogrefe & Huber, 2001), 116–31; Tim Kasser and Richard M. Ryan, "A Dark Side of the American Dream: Correlates of Financial Success as a Central Life Aspiration," *Journal of Personality and Social Psychology* 65 (1993): 410–22, https://doi.org/10.1037/0022-3514.65.2.410; and Tim Kasser and Richard M. Ryan, "Further Examining the American Dream: Differential Correlates of Intrinsic and Extrinsic Goals," *Personality and Social Psychology Bulletin* 22 (1996): 280–87, https://doi.org/10.1177/0146167296223006.

57 *study of 12,894 US undergraduates:* Carol Nickerson, Norbert Schwarz, Ed Diener, and Daniel Kahneman, "Zeroing In on the Dark Side of the American Dream: A Closer Look at the Negative Consequences of the Goal for Financial Success," *Psychological Science* 14, no. 6 (2003): 531–36, https://doi.org/10.1046/j.0956-7976.2003.psci_1461.x.

58 *megalottery winners:* Seonghoon Kim and Andrew J. Oswald, "Happy Lottery Winners and Lottery-Ticket Bias," *Review of Income and Wealth* 67, no. 2 (2021): 317–33, https://doi.org/10.1111/roiw.12469; Jonathan Gardner and Andrew J. Oswald, "Money and Mental Wellbeing: A Longitudinal Study of Medium-Sized Lottery Wins," *Journal of Health Economics* 26, no. 1 (2007): 49–60, https://doi: 10.1016/j.jhealeco.2006.08.004; and Ryan J. Dwyer and Elizabeth W. Dunn, "Wealth Redistribution Promotes Happiness," *Proceedings of the National Academy of Sciences* 119, no. 46 (2022): e2211123119, https://doi.org/10.1073/pnas.2211123119. Notably, some studies show that winners of lotteries and cash transfers are happier than nonwinners, on average.

58 *rather than extrinsic ones:* Kasser and Ryan, "Further Examining the American Dream," 280–87.

58 *"rather than shine your leaves":* Arthur Brooks, "Managing Your Happiness: The Science and How to Use It," PowerPoint presentation, ACB Ideas, 2023.

58 *improve happiness, belonging, and self-worth:* Kennon M. Sheldon, Neetu Abad, Yuna Ferguson, Alexander Gunz, Linda Houser-Marko, Charles P. Nichols, and Sonja Lyubomirsky, "Persistent Pursuit of Need-Satisfying Goals Leads to Increased Happiness: A 6-Month Experimental Longitudinal Study," *Motivation and Emotion* 34 (2010): 39–48, https://doi.org/10.1007/s11031-009-9153-1; and

Edward L. Deci and Richard M. Ryan, "The 'What' and 'Why' of Goal Pursuits: Human Needs and the Self-Determination of Behavior," *Psychological Inquiry* 11, no. 4 (2000): 227–68, https://doi.org/10.1207/S15327965PLI1104_01.

59   *earn more and are better liked:* Lisa C. Walsh, Julia K. Boehm, and Sonja Lyubomirsky, "Does Happiness Promote Career Success? Revisiting the Evidence," *Journal of Career Assessment* 26, no. 2 (2018): 199–219, https://doi.org /10.1177/1069072717751441.

59   *54 percent of US adults believe:* Matt Motyl and Juliana Schroeder, "Alone Together? How Social Technology Is Influencing Human Connection and Loneliness," *Designing Tomorrow*, February 5, 2024, https://psychoftech.substack .com/p/social-technology-and-loneliness.

61   *Humblebragging:* Ovul Sezer, Francesca Gino, and Michael I. Norton, "Humblebragging: A Distinct—and Ineffective—Self-Presentation Strategy," *Journal of Personality and Social Psychology* 114, no. 1 (2018): 52–74, https://doi.org/10.1037 /pspi0000108.

61   *bask in your reflected glory:* Robert B. Cialdini, Richard J. Borden, Avril Thorne, Marcus R. Walker, Stephen Freeman, and Lloyd R. Sloan, "Basking in Reflected Glory: Three (Football) Field Studies," *Journal of Personality and Social Psychology* 34, no. 3 (1976): 366–75, https://doi.org/10.1037/0022-3514.34.3.366.

62   *"conversational self-focus":* Rebecca A. Schwartz-Mette and Amanda J. Rose, "Conversational Self-Focus in Adolescent Friendships: Observational Assessment of an Interpersonal Process and Relations with Internalizing Symptoms and Friendship Quality," *Journal of Social and Clinical Psychology* 28, no. 10 (2009): 1263–97, https://doi.org/10.1521/jscp.2009.28.10.1263.

62   *relatively low self-esteem:* Mark R. Leary, "The Self We Know and the Self We Show: Self-Esteem, Self-Presentation, and the Maintenance of Interpersonal Relationships," in *Emotion and Motivation*, ed. Marilynn B. Brewer and Miles Hewstone (Blackwell, 2003), 204–24.

62   *relatively more depressed:* Timothy W. Smith and Jeff Greenberg, "Depression and Self-Focused Attention," *Motivation and Emotion* 5 (1981): 323–31, https:// doi.org/10.1007/BF00992551; and Stefan Sütterlin, Muirne C. S. Paap, Stana Babic, Andrea Kübler, and Claus Vögele, "Rumination and Age: Some Things Get Better," *Journal of Aging Research* (2012): 267327, https://doi.org/10.1155 /2012/267327.

63   *this fear is misplaced:* Karen Huang, Michael Yeomans, Alison Wood Brooks, Julia Minson, and Francesca Gino, "It Doesn't Hurt to Ask: Question-Asking Increases Liking," *Journal of Personality and Social Psychology* 113, no. 3 (2017): 430–52, https://doi.org/10.1037/pspi0000097; and Einav Hart, Eric M. VanEpps, and Maurice E. Schweitzer, "The (Better Than Expected) Consequences of Asking Sensitive Questions," *Organizational Behavior and Human Decision Processes* 162 (2021): 136–54, https://doi.org/10.1016/j.obhdp.2020.10.014.

64   *G. K. Chesterton beautifully observed:* G. K. Chesterton, *Orthodoxy* (1908; Project Gutenberg, 1994), http://www.gutenberg.org/ebooks/130.

64   *you'll feel in return:* Kristin Layous, S. Katherine Nelson, Eva Oberle, Kimberly A. Schonert-Reichl, and Sonja Lyubomirsky, "Kindness Counts: Prompting Prosocial Behavior in Preadolescents Boosts Peer Acceptance and Well-Being," *PLOS ONE* 7, no. 12 (2012): e51380, https://doi.org/10.1371/journal. pone.0051380; and Jennifer Crocker, Marc-Andre Olivier, and Noah Nuer, "Self-Image Goals and Compassionate Goals: Costs and Benefits," *Self and Identity* 8, no. 2–3 (2009): 251–69, https://doi.org/10.1080/15298860802505160.

64   *they feel drawn to authenticity:* David M. Markowitz, Maryam Kouchaki, Francesca Gino, Jeffrey T. Hancock, and Ryan L. Boyd, "Authentic First Impressions

Relate to Interpersonal, Social, and Entrepreneurial Success," *Social Psychological and Personality Science* 14, no. 2 (2023): 107–16, https://doi.org/10.1177/1948550622108613.

65   *someone you're not:* Adam Kadlac, "The Challenge of Authenticity: Enhancement and Accurate Self-Presentation," *Journal of Applied Philosophy* 35, no. 4 (2018): 790–808, https://doi.org/10.1111/japp.12266. Philosophers have noted—and not mildly—that molding yourself into someone you're not is the epitome of fakery and phoniness. If you desire to be authentic, they chide, don't pretend to be something you're not, refrain from misrepresenting yourself to the external world, and don't mislead others about your accomplishments or lack thereof.

65   *more appealing in relationships:* Paul W. Eastwick, Laura B. Luchies, Eli J. Finkel, and Lucy L. Hunt, "The Predictive Validity of Ideal Partner Preferences: A Review and Meta-Analysis," *Psychological Bulletin* 140, no. 3 (2014): 623–65, https://doi.org/10.1037/a0032432.

65   *the story of Cyrano de Bergerac:* Edmond Rostand, *Cyrano de Bergerac: An Heroic Comedy in Five Acts,* trans. Charles Renauld (1897; Project Gutenberg, 2013), https://www.gutenberg.org/ebooks/41949.

66   *disclosing too much too quickly:* James C. Coyne, Sue Ann Ludwig Burchill, and William B. Stiles, "An Interactional Perspective on Depression," in *Handbook of Social and Clinical Psychology: The Health Perspective,* ed. George S. Avery and Barbara A. Boucher (Pergamon, 1991), 327–49; and Valerian J. Derlega and Alan L. Chaikin, "Privacy and Self-Disclosure in Social Relationships," *Journal of Social Issues* 33, no. 3 (1977): 102–15, https://doi.org/10.1111/j.1540-4560.1977.tb01885.x.

67   *counselor Gary Chapman in 2015:* Gary Chapman, *The 5 Love Languages: The Secret to Love That Lasts* (Northfield, 2015).

67   *scientifically sound as many believe:* Emily A. Impett, Haeyoung Gideon Park, and Amy Muise, "Popular Psychology Through a Scientific Lens: Evaluating Love Languages from a Relationship Science Perspective," *Current Directions in Psychological Science* 33, no. 2 (2024): 87–92, https://doi.org/10.1177/09637214231217663.

67   *a single dominant love language:* Sharon M. Flicker and Flavia Sancier-Barbosa, "Testing the Predictions of Chapman's Five Love Languages Theory: Does Speaking a Partner's Primary Love Language Lead to Greater Relationship Satisfaction?," in-review manuscript, 2024.

68   *couples tend to be happiest:* William J. Chopik, Louis Hickman, Rebekka Weidmann, Mariah F. Purol, and Hyewon Yang, "Lost in Translation: Matching on Love Languages Rarely Predicts Relational Outcomes," conference session, IARR Mini-Conference, Phoenix, AZ, May 20, 2023.

68   *didn't feel any more loved:* Flicker and Sancier-Barbosa, "Testing the Predictions."

68   *two particular love languages:* Flicker and Sancier-Barbosa, "Testing the Predictions."

68   *during a stressful situation:* Brett K. Jakubiak and Brooke C. Feeney, "Hand-in-Hand Combat: Affectionate Touch Promotes Relational Well-Being and Buffers Stress During Conflict," *Personality and Social Psychology Bulletin* 45, no. 3 (2019): 431–46, https://doi.org/10.1177/0146167218788556.

69   *Prioritize quality time:* John M. Gottman and Nan Silver, *The Seven Principles for Making Marriage Work: A Practical Guide from the Country's Foremost Relationship Expert* (Harmony Books, 1999); Arthur Aron, Elaine N. Aron, Christine E. Norman, and Thomas N. Heyman, "Couples' Shared Participation in Novel and Arousing Activities and Experienced Relationship Quality," *Journal of Personality and Social Psychology* 78, no. 2 (2000): 273–84, https://doi.org/10.1037/0022-3514.78.2.273; and Amy Claxton and Maureen Perry-

Jenkns, "No Fun Anymore: Leisure and Marital Quality Across the Transition to Parenthood," *Journal of Marriage and Family* 70, no. 1 (2008): 28–43, https://doi.org/10.1111/j.1741-3737.2007.00459.x.

69   *the power of words:* Lyubomirsky, *How of Happiness.*

69   *still not feel loved:* Harry T. Reis, Edward P. Lemay Jr., and Catrin Finkenauer, "Toward Understanding Understanding: The Importance of Feeling Understood in Relationships," *Social and Personality Psychology Compass* 11, no. 3 (2017): e12308, https://doi.org/10.1111/spc3.12308.

70   *"I Can't Make You Love Me":* Bonnie Raitt, vocalist, "I Can't Make You Love Me," by Mike Reid and Allen Shamblin, track 3 on *Luck of the Draw*, Capitol Records, 1991.

70   *raise feels exciting at first:* Rafael Di Tella, John Haisken-De New, and Robert MacCulloch, "Happiness Adaptation to Income and to Status in an Individual Panel," *Journal of Economic Behavior & Organization* 76, no. 3 (2010): 834–52, https://doi.org/10.1016/j.jebo.2010.09.016; Andrew E. Clark, Paul Frijters, and Michael A. Shields, "Relative Income, Happiness, and Utility: An Explanation for the Easterlin Paradox and Other Puzzles," *Journal of Economic Literature* 46, no. 1 (2008): 95–144; and David G. Myers, "The Funds, Friends, and Faith of Happy People," *American Psychologist* 55 (2000): 56–67, https://doi.org/10.1037/0003-066X.55.1.56.

Chapter 4: The Relationship Sea-Saw

78   *nearly all human social interactions:* Alvin W. Gouldner, "The Norm of Reciprocity: A Preliminary Statement," *American Sociological Review* 25, no. 2 (1960): 161–78, https://doi.org/10.2307/2092623.

79   *Clinical psychologist David Schnarch:* David Schnarch, *Passionate Marriage: Keeping Love and Intimacy Alive in Committed Relationships* (W. W. Norton, 2009).

81   *the relationship-science literature:* Harry T. Reis and Phillip R. Shaver, "Intimacy as an Interpersonal Process," in *Handbook of Personal Relationships*, ed. Steven W. Duck (John Wiley & Sons, 1988), 367–89; and Harry T. Reis and Brian C. Patrick, "Attachment and Intimacy: Component Processes," in *Social Psychology: Handbook of Basic Principles*, ed. Arie Kruglanski and E. Tory Higgins (Guilford, 1996), 523–63.

81   *beyond the interpersonal relationship:* Peter A. Caprariello and Harry T. Reis, "Perceived Partner Responsiveness Minimizes Defensive Reactions to Failure," *Social Psychological and Personality Science* 2, no. 4 (2011): 365–372, https://doi.org/10.1177/1948550610391914; Guy Itzchakov and Harry T. Reis, "Perceived Responsiveness Increases Tolerance of Attitude Ambivalence and Enhances Intentions to Behave in an Open-Minded Manner," *Personality and Social Psychology Bulletin* 47, no. 3 (2021): 468–485, https://doi.org/10.1177/0146167220929218; Harry T. Reis, Karisa Y. Lee, Stephanie D. O'Keefe, and Margaret S. Clark, "Perceived Partner Responsiveness Promotes Intellectual Humility," *Journal of Experimental Social Psychology* 79 (2018): 21–33, https://doi.org/10.1016/j.jesp.2018.05.006; Yan Ruan, Harry T. Reis, Margaret S. Clark, Jennifer L. Hirsch, and Brian D. Bink, "Can I Tell You How I Feel? Perceived Partner Responsiveness Encourages Emotional Expression," *Emotion* 20, no. 3 (2020): 329–342, https://doi.org/10.1037/emo0000650; and Guy Itzchakov, Harry T. Reis, and Kimberly Rios, "Perceiving Others as Responsive Lessens Prejudice: The Mediating Roles of Intellectual Humility and Attitude Ambivalence," *Journal of Experimental Social Psychology* 110 (2024): 104554. https://doi.org/10.1016/j.jesp.2023.104554.

81 *feels like having "chemistry":* Harry T. Reis, Annie Regan, and Sonja Lyubo-mirsky, "Interpersonal Chemistry: What Is It, How Does It Emerge, and How Does It Operate?" *Perspectives on Psychological Science* 17, no. 2 (2022): 530–58, https://doi.org/10.1177/1745691621994241.

82 *known and understood by others:* William B. Swann Jr., "Self-Verification Theory," in *Handbook of Theories in Social Psychology*, ed. Paul A. M. Van Lange, Arie W. Kruglanski, and E. Tory Higgins (Sage, 2012), 23–42; and Reis, Lemay, and Finkenauer, "Toward Understanding Understanding," e12308.

82 *"illusion of transparency":* Thomas Gilovich, Kenneth Savitsky, and Victoria Husted Medvec, "The Illusion of Transparency: Biased Assessments of Others' Ability to Read One's Emotional States," *Journal of Personality and Social Psychology* 75, no. 2 (1998): 332–46, https://doi.org/10.1037/0022-3514.75.2.332.

82 *Hailey Magee:* "Why Curiosity Is My Love Language and How It Makes Me Feel Seen," *Tiny Buddha: Simple Wisdom for Complex Lives*, accessed March 11, 2025, https://tinybuddha.com/blog/why-curiosity-is-my-love-language-and-how-it-makes-me-feel-seen/.

83 *The country singer Dolly Parton:* Associated Press, "Carl Dean, Dolly Parton's Husband of Nearly 60 Years, Dies at 82," *CNN Entertainment*, March 4, 2025, https://www.cnn.com/2025/03/03/entertainment/carl-dean-death-dolly-parton -husband/index.html.

85 *a "mental road trip we collectively steer":* Sophie Wohltjen and Thalia Wheatley, "Eye Contact Marks the Rise and Fall of Shared Attention in Conversation," *Proceedings of the National Academy of Sciences* 118, no. 37 (2021): e2106645118, https://doi.org/10.1073/pnas.2106645118.

86 *happier romantic relationship:* David C. de Jong and Harry T. Reis, "Sexual Kindred Spirits: Actual and Overperceived Similarity, Complementarity, and Partner Accuracy in Heterosexual Couples," *Personality and Social Psychology Bulletin* 40, no. 10 (2014): 1316–29, https://doi.org/10.1177/0146167214542801.

86 *greater relationship satisfaction:* Amie M. Gordon, Emily A. Impett, Aleksandr Kogan, Christopher Oveis, and Dacher Keltner, "To Have and to Hold: Grat-itude Promotes Relationship Maintenance in Intimate Bonds," *Journal of Per-sonality and Social Psychology* 103, no. 2 (2012): 257–74, https://doi.org/10.1037 /a0028723.

86 *the University of Alabama:* Mengya Xia, Yi Chen, and Shannon Dunne, "What Makes People Feel Loved? An Exploratory Study on Core Elements of Love Across Family, Romantic, and Friend Relationships," *Family Process* 63, no. 3 (2024): 1304–18, https://doi.org/10.1111/famp.12873.

87 *people feel accepted and safe:* Mario Mikulincer and Phillip R. Shaver, *Attach-ment in Adulthood: Structures, Dynamics, and Change* (Guilford, 2010).

87 *Self-Expansion theory:* Arthur P. Aron, Debra J. Mashek, and Elaine N. Aron, "Closeness as Including the Other in the Self," in *Handbook of Closeness and Inti-macy*, ed. Debra J. Mashek and Arthur Aron (Lawrence Erlbaum, 2004), 27–41.

87 *"returning a kindness":* Marcus Tullius Cicero, "De Officiis," in *Ethical Writings of Cicero: De officiis, De sennectute, De amicitia, and Scipio's Dream*, translated with an introduction and notes by Andrew P. Peabody (Little, Brown, 1887).

87 *like those who like them:* Carl W. Backman and Paul F. Secord, "The Effect of Liking on Interpersonal Attraction," *Human Relations* 12, no. 4 (1959): 379–84, https://doi.org/10.1177/001872675901200407.

88 *those who compliment them:* Robert B. Cialdini, *Influence: The Psychology of Persuasion* (Harper Business, 2006).

88 *respond with care and kindness:* Clark and Aragón, "Communal (and Other) Relationships," 255–80.

88 *the likelihood of reciprocity:* Nicholas Epley, Michael Kardas, Xuan Zhao, Stav Atir, and Julaina Schroeder, "Undersociality: Miscalibrated Social Cognition Can Inhibit Social Connection," *Trends in Cognitive Sciences* 26, no. 5 (2022): 406–18, https://doi.org/10.1016/j.tics.2022.02.007.

89 *concept of "mutual cyclical growth":* Caryl E. Rusbult, Nils Olsen, Jody L. Davis, and Peggy A. Hannon, "Commitment and Relationship Maintenance Mechanisms," in *Close Romantic Relationships: Maintenance and Enhancement,* ed. J. H. Harvey and Amy Wenzel (Lawrence Erlbaum, 2001), 87–113.

89 *in positive, supportive contexts:* Johan C. Karremans and Thijs Verwijmeren, "Mimicking Attractive Opposite-Sex Others: The Role of Romantic Relationship Status," *Personality and Social Psychology Bulletin* 34, no. 7 (2008): 939–50, https://doi.org/10.1177/0146167208316693; Sophie Wohltjen and Thalia Wheatley, "Eye Contact Marks the Rise and Fall of Shared Attention in Conversation," *Proceedings of the National Academy of Sciences* 118, no. 37 (2021): e2106645118, https://doi.org/10.1073/pnas.2106645118; Molly E. Ireland, Richard B. Slatcher, Paul W. Eastwick, Lauren E. Scissors, Eli J. Finkel, and James W. Pennebaker, "Language Style Matching Predicts Relationship Initiation and Stability, *Psychological Science* 22, no. 1 (2011): 39–44, https://doi.org/10.1177/0956797610392928; Elaine Hatfield, John T. Caccioppo, and Richard L. Rapson, *Emotional Contagion* (Cambridge University Press, 1994); Christopher Welker, Thalia Wheatley, Grace Cason, Catharine Gorman, and Meghan Meyer, "Self Views Converge During Enjoyable Conversations," *Proceedings of the National Academy of Sciences* 121, no. 43 (2024): e2321652121, https://doi.org/10.1073/pnas.2321652121; and Emma M. Templeton, Luke J. Chang, Elizabeth A. Reynolds, Marie D. Cone LeBeaumont, and Thalia Wheatley, "Fast Response Times Signal Social Connection in Conversation. *Proceedings of the National Academy of Sciences* 119, no. 4 (2022): e2116915119, https://doi.org/10.1073/pnas.2321652121.

89 *A particularly striking study:* Bruce P. Doré and Robert R. Morris, "Linguistic Synchrony Predicts the Immediate and Lasting Impact of Text-Based Emotional Support," *Psychological Science* 29, no. 10 (2018): 1716–23, https://doi.org/10.1177/0956797618777997.

90 *one person speaks and another listens:* Greg J. Stephens, Lauren J. Silbert, and Uri Hasson, "Speaker-Listener Neural Coupling Underlies Successful Communication," *Proceedings of the National Academy of Sciences* 107, no. 32 (2010): 14425–30, https://doi.org/10.1073/pnas.1008662107.

90 *neural activation in a pair of friends:* Weiwei Peng, Wutao Lou, Xiaoxuan Huang, Qian Ye, Raymond Kai-Yu Tong, and Fang Cui, "Suffer Together, Bond Together: Brain-to-Brain Synchronization and Mutual Affective Empathy When Sharing Painful Experiences," *NeuroImage* 238, no. 118249 (2021), https://doi.org/10.1016/j.neuroimage.2021.118249.

91 *synchronization of brain activity:* Chennan Lin, Xinxin Lin, Weicheng Lian, Wenting Zhang, and Weiwei Peng, "Brains in Sync, Friends in Empathy: Interbrain Neural Mechanisms Underlying the Impact of Interpersonal Closeness on Mutual Empathy," *Proceedings of the Royal Society B: Biological Science,* 291 (2024): 20241326, https://doi.org/10.1098/rspb.2024.1326.

91 *same series of video clips:* Carolyn Parkinson, Adam M. Kleinbaum, and Thalia Wheatley, "Similar Neural Responses Predict Friendship," *Nature Communications* 9, no. 332 (2018), https://doi.org/10.1038/s41467-017-02722-7.

91 *a study of romantic partners:* Yijun Chen, Shen Liu, Yaru Hao, Qian Zhao, Jiecheng Ren, Yi Piao et al., "Higher Emotional Synchronization Is Modulated by Relationship Quality in Romantic Relationships and Not in Close

Friendships," *NeuroImage* 297, no. 120733 (2024), https://doi.org/10.1016/j.neuroimage.2024.120733.

Chapter 5: Sharing Mindset

98 *"counselor or a psychoanalyst"*: Sidney M. Jourard, *The Transparent Self* (D. Van Nostrand, 1971), 13.

98 *conceals themselves from others:* Jourard, *Transparent Self.*

98 "I know myself to be": Sidney M. Jourard, *Self-Disclosure: An Experimental Analysis of the Transparent Self* (Wiley-Interscience, 1971), 181.

98 *significant others can be "terrifying"*: Jourard, *Transparent Self,* 31.

99 *one study estimated:* Diana I. Tamir and Jason P. Mitchell, "Disclosing Information About the Self Is Intrinsically Rewarding," *Proceedings of the National Academy of Sciences* 109, no. 21 (2012): 8038–43, https://doi.org/10.1073/pnas.1202129109.

101 *Amie Gordon and Serena Chen:* Amie Gordon and Serena Chen, "Do You Get Where I'm Coming From?: Perceived Understanding Buffers Against the Negative Impact of Conflict on Relationship Satisfaction," *Journal of Personality and Social Psychology* 110, no. 2 (2016): 239–60, https://doi.org/10.1037/pspi0000039.

101 *research has shown that romantic partners:* Juliana Schroeder and Ayelet Fishbach, "Feeling Known Predicts Relationship Satisfaction," *Journal of Experimental Social Psychology* 111 (2024): 104559, https://doi.org/10.1016/j.jesp.2023.104559; Emilie Auger, Sabrina Thai, Carolyn Birnie-Porter, and John E. Lydon, "On Creating Deeper Relationship Bonds: Felt Understanding Enhances Relationship Identification," *Personality and Social Psychology Bulletin* 50, no. 3 (2024): 345–60, https://doi.org/10.1177/01461672241233419; and Harry T. Reis, Michael R. Maniaci, and Ronald D. Rogge, "The Expression of Compassionate Love in Everyday Compassionate Acts," *Journal of Social and Personal Relationships* 31, no. 5 (2014): 652–77, https://doi.org/10.1177/0265407513507214.

101 *communication about sex:* Katie O. Knowles and Matthew D. Hammond, "Meta-Analyzing People's Self-Disclosure of Sexual Information to Romantic Partners," *Journal of Sex Research* (2025): 1–13, https://doi.org/10.1080/00224499.2025.2455543.

102 *Feeling understood activates neural regions:* Sylvia A. Morelli, Jared B. Torre, and Naomi I. Eisenberger, "The Neural Bases of Feeling Understood and Not Understood," *Social Cognition and Affective Neuroscience* 9, no. 12 (2014): 1890–96, https://doi.org/10.1093/scan/nst191.

102 *Research conducted by Harry and others:* Harry T. Reis, Karisa Y. Lee, Stephanie D. O'Keefe, and Margaret S. Clark, "Perceived Partner Responsiveness Promotes Intellectual Humility," *Journal of Experimental Social Psychology* 79 (2018): 21–33, https://doi.org/10.1016/j.jesp.2018.05.006; Guy Itzchakov and Harry T. Reis, "Perceived Responsiveness Increases Tolerance of Attitude Ambivalence and Enhances Intentions to Behave in an Open-Minded Manner," *Personality and Social Psychology Bulletin* 47, no. 3 (2021): 468–85, https://doi.org/10.1177/0146167220929218; Guy Itzchakov, Harry T. Reis, and Kimberly Rios, "Perceiving Others as Responsive Lessens Prejudice: The Mediating Roles of Intellectual Humility and Attitude Ambivalence," *Journal of Experimental Social Psychology* 110 (2024): 104554, https://doi.org/10.1016/j.jesp.2023.104554; AnnaMarie S. O'Neill, Cynthia D. Mohr, Todd E. Bodner, and Leslie B. Hammer, "Perceived Partner Responsiveness, Pain, and Sleep: A Dyadic Study of Military-Connected Couples," *Health Psychology* 39, no. 12 (2020): 1089–99, https://doi.org/10.1037/hea0001035; and Emre Selcuk, Sarah C. E. Stanton, Richard

B. Slatcher, and Anthony D. Ong, "Perceived Partner Responsiveness Predicts Better Sleep Quality Through Lower Anxiety," *Social Psychological and Personality Science* 8, no. 1 (2017): 83–92, https://doi.org/10.1177/1948550616662128.

102 *the advantages of feeling understood:* Sal Meyers, Katherine Rowell, Mary Wells, and Brian C. Smith, "Teacher Empathy: A Model of Empathy for Teaching for Student Success," *College Teaching* 67, no. 3 (2019): 160–68, https://doi.org/10.1080/87567555.2019.1579699; Pamela R. Johnson and Julie Indvik, "Organizational Benefits of Having Emotionally Intelligent Managers and Employees," *Journal of Workplace Learning* 11, no. 3 (1999): 84–88, https://doi.org/10.1108/13665629910264226; Ronald M. Epstein and Mary Catherine Beach, "'I Don't Need Your Pills, I Need Your Attention': Steps Toward Deep Listening in Medical Encounters," *Current Opinion in Psychology* 53 (2023): 101685, https://doi.org/10.1016/j.copsyc.2023.101685; and Robert Elliott, Arthur C. Bohart, Jeanne C. Watson, and Leslie S. Greenberg, "Empathy," *Psychotherapy* 48, no. 1 (2011): 43–49, https://doi.org/10.1037/a0022187.

105 *People seem to do reasonably well:* Erika N. Carlson and David A. Kenny, "Meta-Accuracy: Do We Know How Others See Us?," in *Handbook of Self-Knowledge*, ed. Simine Vazire and Timothy D. Wilson (Guilford, 2012), 242–57; Erika N. Carlson and R. Michael Furr, "Evidence of Differential Meta-Accuracy: People Understand the Different Impressions They Make," *Psychological Science* 20, no. 8 (2009): 1033–39, https://doi.org/10.1111/j.1467-9280.2009.02409.x; and Leonie Hater, Norhan Elsaadawy, Jeremy C. Biesanz, Simon M. Breil, Lauren J. Human, Lisa M. Niemeyer et al., "Examining Individual Differences in Metaperceptive Accuracy Using the Social Meta-Accuracy Model," *Journal of Personality and Social Psychology* 125, no. 5 (2023): 1119–35, https://doi.org/10.1037/pspp0000479.

106 *People typically underestimate:* Erica J. Boothby, Gus Cooney, Gillian M. Sandstrom, and Margaret S. Clark, "The Liking Gap in Conversations: Do People Like Us More Than We Think?" *Psychological Science* 29, no. 11 (2018): 1742–56, https://doi.org/10.1177/0956797618783714.

106 *others in their groups like them:* Adam M. Mastroianni, Gus Cooney, Erica J. Boothby, and Andrew G. Reece, "The Liking Gap in Groups and Teams," *Organizational Behavior and Human Decision Processes* 162 (2021): 109–22, https://doi.org/10.1016/j.obhdp.2020.10.013.

106 *improve your partner's feelings:* James J. Kim, Harry T. Reis, Michael R. Maniaci, and Samantha Joel, "Half Empty and Half Full? Biased Perceptions of Compassionate Love and Effects of Dyadic Complementarity," *Personality and Social Psychology Bulletin* 50, no. 10 (2024): 1423–37, https://doi.org/10.1177/01461672231171986.

106 *social anxiety or low self-esteem:* Hasagani Tissera, Lauren Gazzard Kerr, Erika N. Carlson, and Lauren J. Human, "Social Anxiety and Liking: Towards Understanding the Role of Metaperceptions in First Impressions," *Journal of Personality and Social Psychology* 121, no. 4 (2021): 948–68, https://doi.org/10.1037/pspp0000363; and Mark R. Leary, Ellen S. Tambor, Sonja K. Terdal, and Deborah L. Downs, "Self-Esteem as an Interpersonal Monitor: The Sociometer Hypothesis," *Journal of Personality and Social Psychology* 68, no. 3 (1995): 518–30, https://doi.org/10.1037/0022-3514.68.3.518.

106 *people will* overestimate: Erika N. Carlson, "Meta-Accuracy and Relationship Quality: Weighing the Costs and Benefits of Knowing What People Really Think About You," *Journal of Personality and Social Psychology* 111, no. 2 (2016): 250–64, https://doi.org/10.1037/pspp0000107.

106 *relatively transparent traits:* David C. Funder, "Accurate Personality Judgment,"

Current Directions in Psychological Science 21, no. 3 (2012): 177–82, https://doi .org/10.1177/0963721412445309.

107 *acquaintance matters a great deal too:* David C. Funder, David C. Kolar, and Melinda C. Blackman, "Agreement Among Judges of Personality: Interpersonal Relations, Similarity, and Acquaintanceship," *Journal of Personality and Social Psychology* 69, no. 4 (1995): 656–72, https://doi.org/10.1037/0022-3514.69.4.656; and Norhan Elsaadawy and Erika N. Carlson, "Is Meta-Accuracy Consistent Across Levels of Acquaintanceship?," *Social Psychological and Personality Science* 13, no. 1 (2022): 178–85, https://doi.org/10.1177/19485506211018151.

108 *97 percent of people keep secrets:* Michael L. Slepian, Jinseok S. Chun, and Malia F. Mason, "The Experience of Secrecy," *Journal of Personality and Social Psychology* 113, no. 1 (2017): 1–33, https://doi.org/10.1037/pspa0000085.

108 *keep secrets for many reasons:* Rachel I. McDonald, Jessica M. Salerno, Katharine H. Greenaway, and Michael L. Slepian, "Motivated Secrecy: Politics, Relationships, and Regrets," *Motivation Science* 6, no. 1 (2020): 61–78, https:// doi.org/10.1037/mot0000139.

109 *"Nothing makes us so lonely":* Paul Tournier, *Secrets: A Doctor Reflects* (SCM, 1965).

109 *keeping secrets is often isolating:* Alisa Bedrov and Shelly L. Gable, "Keeping and Sharing Secrets at the Interpersonal Level," *Social and Personality Psychology Compass* 18, no. 2 (2024): e12942, https://doi.org/10.1111/spc3.12942.

109 *When people conceal themselves:* Robert E. Wickham, "Perceived Authenticity in Romantic Partners," *Journal of Experimental Social Psychology* 49, no. 5 (2013): 878–87, https://doi.org/10.1016/j.jesp.2013.04.001; and Robert E. Wickham, David E. Reed, and Rachel E. Williamson, "Establishing the Psychometric Properties of the Self and Perceived-Partner Authenticity in Relationships Scale-Short Form (AIRS-SF): Measurement Invariance, Reliability, and Incremental Validity," *Personality and Individual Differences* 77 (2015): 62–67, https://doi .org/10.1016/j.paid.2014.12.049.

109 *AI-powered chatbots and companions:* Yidai Yin, Nan Jin, and Cheryl J. Wakslak, "Can You Feel Heard by AI? On the Experience of Receiving AI Empathy," *Proceedings of the National Academy of Sciences of the United States of America* 121, no. 14 (2024): e2319112121, https://doi.org/10.1073/pnas.2319112121. But for an alternate point of view, see Dunigan P. Folk, Stephanie Yu, and Elizabeth Dunn, "Can Chatbots Ever Provide More Social Connection than Humans?," (PsyArXiv Preprints, submitted in 2023), https://doi.org/10.31234/osf.io/p26wj.

109 *effortful and uncomfortable:* Michael L. Slepian, "A Process Model of Having and Keeping Secrets," *Psychological Review* 129, no. 3 (2022): 542–63, https:// doi.org/10.1037/rev0000282.

110 *social psychologist Daniel Wegner:* Julie D. Lane and Daniel M. Wegner, "The Cognitive Consequences of Secrecy," *Journal of Personality and Social Psychology* 69, no. 2 (1995): 237–53, https://doi.org/10.1037/0022-3514.69.2.237; Daniel M. Wegner, Julie D. Lane, and Sara Dimitri, "The Allure of Secret Relationships," *Journal of Personality and Social Psychology* 66, no. 2 (1994): 287–300, https://doi.org/10.1037/0022-3514.66.2.287; and Daniel M. Wegner, David J. Schneider, Samuel R. Carter III, and Teri L. White, "Paradoxical Effects of Thought Suppression," *Journal of Personality and Social Psychology* 53, no. 1 (1987): 5–13, https://doi.org/10.1037/0022-3514.53.1.5.

110 *exercise called "expressive writing":* James W. Pennebaker and Joshua M. Smyth, *Opening Up by Writing It Down: How Expressive Writing Improves Health and Eases Emotional Pain* (Guilford, 2016); Joanne Frattaroli, "Experimental Disclosure and Its Moderators," *Psychological Bulletin* 132, no. 6 (2006): 823–65, https://doi.org/10.1037/0033-2909.132.6.823; and Jeffrey M. Pavlacic, Erin M.

Buchanan, Nicholas P. Maxwell, Tabetha G. Hopke, and Stefan E. Schulenberg, "A Meta-Analysis of Expressive Writing on Posttraumatic Stress, Posttraumatic Growth, and Quality of Life," *Review of General Psychology* 23, no. 2 (2019): 230–50, https://doi.org/10.1177/1089268019831645.

110 *existence of a "drive to disclose":* Erin Carbone and George Loewenstein, "Privacy Preferences and the Drive to Disclose," *Current Directions in Psychological Science* 32, no. 6 (2023): 508–14, https://doi.org/10.1177/09637214231196097.

111 *more than eight hundred participants:* Michael L. Slepian and Edythe Moulton-Tetlock, "Confiding Secrets and Well-Being," *Social Psychological and Personality Science* 10, no. 4 (2019): 472–84, https://doi.org/10.1177/1948550618765069.

111 *sharing and receiving personal secrets:* Alisa Bedrov and Shelly L. Gable, "Just Between Us . . .: The Role of Sharing and Receiving Secrets in Friendships Across Time," *Personal Relationships* 31, no. 1 (2024): 91–111, https://doi.org/10.1111/pere.12527.

112 *It's stressful to keep a secret:* Dale G. Larson, Robert L. Chastain, William T. Hoyt, and Ruthie Ayzenberg, "Self-Concealment: Integrative Review and Working Model," *Journal of Social and Clinical Psychology* 34, no. 8 (2015): 705–29, https://doi.org/10.1521/jscp.2015.34.8.705.

112 *Such secrets often surface:* Desiree Aldeis and Tamara D. Afifi, "Putative Secrets and Conflict in Romantic Relationships Over Time," *Communication Monographs* 82, no. 2 (2015): 224–51, https://doi.org/10.1080/03637751.2014.986747.

113 *reason self-disclosure helps build:* Clare Grall, Ron Tamborini, René Weber, and Ralf Schmälzle, "Stories Collectively Engage Listeners' Brains: Enhanced Intersubject Correlations During Reception of Personal Narratives," *Journal of Communication* 71, no. 2 (2021): 332–55, https://doi.org/10.1093/joc/jqab004.

113 *to feel attracted to you:* Nancy L. Collins and Lynn Carol Miller, "Self-Disclosure and Liking: A Meta-Analytic Review," *Psychological Bulletin* 116, no. 3 (1994): 457–75, https://doi.org/10.1037/0033-2909.116.3.457.

113 *a number of specific strategies:* Kathryn Greene, Valerian J. Derlega, and Alicia Mathews, "Self-Disclosure in Personal Relationships," in *The Cambridge Handbook of Personal Relationships*, ed. Anita L. Vangelisti and Daniel Perlman (Cambridge University Press, 2006), 409–27; and Valerian J. Derlega, Sandra Metts, Sandra Petronio, and Stephen T. Margulis, *Self-Disclosure* (Sage, 1993).

116 *"boomerasking":* Alison Wood Brooks and Michael Yeomans, "Boomerasking: Answering Your Own Questions," *Journal of Experimental Psychology: General* 154, no. 3 (2025), 864–93, https://doi.org/10.1037/xge0001693.

116 *recent New Yorker cartoon:* Joe Dator, "Tell Me What Music You Like," *New Yorker*, November 18, 2024, https://condenaststore.com/featured/tell-me-what-music-you-like-joe-dator.html.

116 *self-disclosure research is:* Deborah Tannen, *You Just Don't Understand: Women and Men in Conversation* (Ballantine Books, 1990).

116 *over the past forty years:* Harry T. Reis, "Gender Effects in Social Participation: Intimacy, Loneliness, and the Conduct of Social Interaction," in *The Emerging Field of Personal Relationships*, ed. Robin Gilmour and Steve Duck (Routledge, 1986), 91–105.

118 *expectations as being misguided:* Michael Kardas, Amit Kumar, and Nicholas Epley, "Overly Shallow? Miscalibrated Expectations Create a Barrier to Deeper Conversation," *Journal of Personality and Social Psychology* 122, no. 3 (2022): 367–98, https://doi.org/10.1037/pspa0000281.

118 *mispredict the consequences of honesty:* Emma E. Levine and Taya R. Cohen, "You Can Handle the Truth: Mispredicting the Consequences of Honest Communication," *Journal of Experimental Psychology: General* 147, no. 9 (2018):

1400–29, https://doi.org/10.1037/xge0000488; and Michael Kardas, Amit Kumar, and Nicholas Epley, "Let It Go: How Exaggerating the Reputational Costs of Revealing Negative Information Encourages Secrecy in Relationships," *Journal of Personality and Social Psychology* 126, no. 6 (2024), 1052–83, https://doi.org/10.1037/pspi0000441.

118 *Other reasons for undersharing:* Kathryn Greene, Valerian J. Derlega, and Alicia Mathews, "Self-Disclosure in Personal Relationships," in *The Cambridge Handbook of Personal Relationships*, ed. Anita L. Vangelisti and Daniel Perlman (Cambridge University Press, 2006), 409–27; and Derlega et al., *Self-Disclosure*.

119 *You are afraid that something:* Bella M. DePaulo, Chris Wetzel, R. Weylin Sternglanz, and Molly J. Walker Wilson, "Verbal and Nonverbal Dynamics of Privacy, Secrecy, and Deceit," *Journal of Social Issues* 59, no. 2 (2003): 391–410, https://doi.org/10.1111/1540-4560.00070.

119 *undersharing for any reason:* Michael H. Kernis and Brian M. Goldman, "A Multicomponent Conceptualization of Authenticity: Theory and Research," *Advances in Experimental Social Psychology* 38 (2006): 283–357, https://doi.org/10.1016/S0065-2601(06)38006-9.

119 *A popular 1969 book:* John Powell, *Why Am I Afraid to Tell You Who I Am?* (Argus, 1969).

119 *point is that self-disclosure hinges:* Lynn C. Miller and David A. Kenny, "Reciprocity of Self-Disclosure at the Individual and Dyadic Levels: A Social Relations Analysis," *Journal of Personality and Social Psychology* 50, no. 4 (1986): 713–19, https://doi.org/10.1037/0022-3514.50.4.713.

122 *more positively than you do!:* Anna Bruk, Sabine G. Scholl, and Herbert Bless, "Beautiful Mess Effect: Self–Other Differences in Evaluation of Showing Vulnerability," *Journal of Personality and Social Psychology* 115, no. 2 (2018): 192–205, https://doi.org/10.1037/pspa0000120.

122 *As for being open:* Karen Rinaldi, *It's Great to Suck at Something* (Atria Books, 2019).

Chapter 6: Listening-to-Learn Mindset

125 *Steven Covey famously put it:* Steven Covey, *The 7 Habits of Highly Effective People* (Simon & Schuster, 2020).

126 *steady attention to the speaker:* Avi N. Kluger and Guy Itzchakov, "The Power of Listening at Work," *Annual Review of Organizational Psychology and Organizational Behavior* 9 (2022): 121–46, https://doi.org/10.1146/annurev-orgpsych-012420-091013.

128 *people are inherently good listeners:* Nancy Kline, *Time to Think* (Octopus, 1999).

129 *"than they are in you":* Dale Carnegie, *How to Win Friends and Influence People* (Pocket Books, 1998), 144.

129 *supportively to their children:* Netta Weinstein, Jonathan Hill, and Wilbert Law, "Balancing Listening and Action Is Key to Supportive Parenting," *Current Opinion in Psychology* 53 (2023): 101651, https://doi.org/10.1016/j.copsyc.2023.101651.

129 *62 percent of Gen Z adolescents:* "Gallup Survey Details Gen Z Struggles with Stress, Anxiety, and 'Need to Be Perfect.'" Walton Family Foundation, July 30, 2024, https://www.waltonfamilyfoundation.org/about-us/newsroom/gallup-survey-details-gen-z-struggles-with-stress-anxiety-and-need-to-be-perfect.

129 *their teachers' entreaties:* Alison Cook-Sather, "'I Am Not Afraid to Listen': Prospective Teachers Learning from Students," *Theory into Practice* 48, no. 3

(2009): 176–83, https://doi.org/10.1080/00405840902997261; Richard M. Ryan and Edward L. Deci, "Facilitating and Hindering Motivation, Learning, and Well-Being in Schools: Research and Observations from Self-Determination Theory," in *Handbook of Motivation at School*, ed. Kathryn Y. Wentzel and David B. Miele (Routledge, 2016), 96–119; and Katherine Schultz, *Listening: A Framework for Teaching Across Differences* (Teachers College Press, 2003).

129 *bridge the damaging societal divides:* Erik Santoso and Hazel Rose Markus, "Listening to Bridge Societal Divides," *Current Opinion in Psychology* 54 (2023): 101696, https://doi.org/10.1016/j.copsyc.2023.101696.

129 *"Learning to Listen First":* Pearce Godwin and Graham Bodie, "Let's Fight for America by Learning to Listen First," *USA Today*, December 9, 2019, https://www.usatoday.com/story/opinion/2019/12/09/national-conversation-project-bridge-political-divide-by-first-listening-column/4307353002/.

129 *the effectiveness of listening:* Darrell M. Blocker, "The Spy Whisperer—CIA Clandestine Officer Darrell M. Blocker," 1:24:46, posted February 18, 2020, by International Spy Museum, YouTube, https://www.youtube.com/watch?v=hoRtcdDHgkc.

130 *people said they were better:* Christopher Welker, Jesse Walker, Erica Boothby, and Thomas Gilovich, "Pessimistic Assessments of Ability in Informal Conversation," *Journal of Applied Social Psychology* 53, no. 7, (2023): 555–69, https://doi.org/10.1111/jasp.12957.

130 *managers were listening "very well":* Jacob Morgan, "Research Shows Only 8% of Leaders Are Great Listeners and Communicators," *Medium*, May 7, 2020, https://medium.com/jacob-morgan/research-shows-only-8-of-leaders-are-great-listeners-and-communicators-217343936ccd.

130 *their ability to listen well:* Guy Itzchakov, personal communication, March 22, 2024.

130 *Kate Murphy's 2020 book:* Kate Murphy, *You're Not Listening: What You're Missing and Why It Matters* (Celadon Books, 2020).

131 *Nelson Mandela:* Megan McGlothin, "Listening: Examples from Great Leaders," *Innolectinc*, May 19, 2022, https://innolectinc.com/listening-examples-from-great-leaders/.

132 *nonetheless a captivating listener:* Wendy Moffat, "A Great Unrecorded History: A New Life of E. M. Forster," *PEN America*, December 7, 2011, https://pen.org/a-great-unrecorded-history-a-new-life-of-e-m-forster/.

132 *"something we focus on":* Mike Tomlin, "Mike Tomlin Gives Advice to Football Coaches: 'Listening Is a Skill,'" 1:21, posted May 8, 2022, by Mark Bergin, YouTube, https://www.youtube.com/watch?v=rTL5obShPA4.

132 *talk candidly to him:* Walter Isaacson, *Introduction to American Sketches: Great Leaders, Creative Thinkers, and Heroes of a Hurricane* (Simon & Schuster, 2010).

133 *millions of downloads weekly:* "Hidden Brain: Who We Are," accessed August 3, 2024, https://hiddenbrain.org/about/.

134 *"beyond the immediate message":* Carl Rogers, *A Way of Being* (Houghton Mifflin, 1980), 8; and Avraham N. Kluger and Moran Mizrahi, "Defining Listening: Can We Get Rid of the Adjectives?," *Current Opinion in Psychology* 52 (2023): 101639, https://doi.org/10.1016/j.copsyc.2023.101639.

135 *Speaker-Listener technique:* Howard J. Markman, Scott M. Stanley, and Susan L. Blumberg, *Fighting for Your Marriage* (Jossey-Bass, 2001).

136 *the speaker feeling listened to:* Avraham N. Kluger and Moran Mizrahi, "Defining Listening: Can We Get Rid of the Adjectives?" *Current Opinion in Psychology* 52 (2023): 101639, https://doi.org/10.1016/j.copsyc.2023.101639.

137 *disagreements are often mistakenly assumed:* Zhiying (Bella) Ren and Rebecca

Schaumberg, "Disagreement Gets Mistaken for Bad Listening," *Psychological Science* 35, no. 5 (2024): 455–70, https://doi.org/10.1177/09567976241239935.

137 *"find a love that makes you feel heard":* Dorothy Anne Field, "I Hope You Find a Love That Makes You Feel Heard," *Thought Catalog*, updated May 17, 2021, https://thoughtcatalog.com/dorothy-anne-field/2020/11/i-hope-you-find-a-love -that-makes-you-feel-heard/.

137 *patients may resist treatments:* Epstein and Beach, "'I Don't Need Your Pills,'" 101685.

138 *we (Harry and Sonja) theorized:* Reis, Regan, and Lyubomirsky, "Interpersonal Chemistry," 530–58.

138 *Another group of researchers:* Carla Anne Roos, Tom Postmes, and Namkje Koudenburg, "Feeling Heard: Operationalizing a Key Concept for Social Relations," *PLOS ONE* 18, no. 11 (2023): e0292865, https://doi.org/10.1371/journal .pone.0292865.

138 *others in our social network:* Kruglanski, Molinario, Jasko, Webber, Leander, and Pierro, "Significance-Quest Theory," 1050–71.

138 *appreciate your abilities and worldview:* Constantine Sedikides and Michael J. Strube, "Self-Evaluation: To Thine Own Self Be Good, To Thine Own Self Be Sure, To Thine Own Self Be True, and To Thine Own Self Be Better," *Advances in Experimental Social Psychology* 29 (1997): 209–69, https://doi.org/10.1016 /S0065-2601(08)60018-0; and Zakary L. Tormala and Derek D. Rucker, "Attitude Certainty: A Review of Past Findings and Emerging Perspectives," *Social and Personality Psychology Compass* 1, no. 1 (2007): 469–92, https://doi .org/10.1111/j.1751-9004.2007.00025.x.

139 *together with Guy Itzchakov:* Guy Itzchakov and Harry T. Reis, "Perceived Responsiveness Increases Tolerance of Attitude Ambivalence and Enhances Intentions to Behave in an Open-Minded Manner," *Personality and Social Psychology Bulletin* 47, no. 3 (2021): 468–85, https://doi.org/10.1177/01461672209292; and Guy Itzchakov, Harry T. Reis, and Kimberly Rios, "Perceiving Others as Responsive Lessens Prejudice: The Mediating Roles of Intellectual Humility and Attitude Ambivalence," *Journal of Experimental Social Psychology* 110 (2024): 104554, https://doi.org/10.1016/j.jesp.2023.104554.

139 *and more self-assured:* Jeff Schimel, Jamie Arndt, Tom Pyszczynski, and Jeff Greenberg, "Being Accepted for Who We Are: Evidence That Social Validation of the Intrinsic Self Reduces General Defensiveness," *Journal of Personality and Social Psychology* 80, no. 1 (2001): 35–52, https://doi.org/10.1037/0022 -3514.80.1.35.

139 *The social psychologist Mark Leary:* Mark Leary, "Sociometer Theory," in *Handbook of Theories in Social Psychology*, ed. Paul A. M. Van Lange, Arie W. Kruglanski, and E. Tory Higgins (Sage, 2012), 141–59.

139 *proposed by William Swann:* William Swann, "Self-Verification Theory," in *Handbook of Theories in Social Psychology*, ed. Paul A. M. Van Lange, Arie W. Kruglanski, and E. Tory Higgins (Sage, 2012), 23–42.

140 *In 1936, Dale Carnegie wrote:* Carnegie, *How to Win Friends*.

140 *review of this research:* Kluger and Itzchakov, "Power of Listening at Work," 121–46.

140 *reduces polarization during conflict:* William P. Eveland Jr., Christina M. Henry, and Osei Appiah, "The Implications of Listening During Political Conversations for Democracy," *Current Opinion in Psychology* 52 (2023): 101595, https:// doi.org/10.1016/j.copsyc.2023.101595; and Andrew G. Livingstone, "Felt Understanding in Intergroup Relations," *Current Opinion in Psychology* 51 (2023): 101587, https://doi.org/10.1016/j.copsyc.2023.101587.

140 *In one series of experiments:* Guy Itzchakov, Netta Weinstein, Mark R. Leary, Dvori Saluk, and Moty Amar, "Listening to Understand: The Role of High-Quality Listening on Speakers' Attitude Depolarization During Disagreements," *Journal of Personality and Social Psychology* 126, no. 2 (2023): 213–39, https://psycnet.apa.org/doi/10.1037/pspa0000366; and Guy Itzchakov, Netta Weinstein, Nicole Legate, and Moty Amar, "Can High Quality Listening Predict Lower Speakers' Prejudiced Attitudes?," *Journal of Experimental Social Psychology* 91 (2020): 104022, https://doi.org/10.1016/j.jesp.2020.104022.

141 *teenager named Nex Benedict:* Margaret Renkl, "Of All the Wrenching Details of Nex Benedict's Death, This One Broke My Heart," *New York Times*, February 26, 2024, https://www.nytimes.com/2024/02/26/opinion/nex-benedict-nonbinary-death.html.

141 *followed by responsive listening:* Harry T. Reis and Margaret S. Clark, "Responsiveness," in *Oxford Handbook of Close Relationships*, ed. Jeffry A. Simpson and Lorne Campbell (Oxford University Press, 2013), 400–423; and Netta Weinstein, Guy Itzchakov, and Nicole Legate, "The Motivational Value of Listening During Intimate and Difficult Conversations," *Social and Personality Psychology Compass* 16, no. 2 (2022): e12651, https://doi.org/10.1111/spc3.12651.

141 *"How was your day?":* Kassandra Cortes and Joanne V. Wood, "How Was Your Day? Conveying Care, but Under the Radar, for People Lower in Trust," *Journal of Experimental Social Psychology* 83 (2019): 11–22, https://doi.org/10.1016/j.jesp.2019.03.003; and Angela M. Hicks and Lisa M. Diamond, "How Was Your Day? Couples' Affect When Telling and Hearing Daily Events," *Personal Relationships* 15, no. 2 (2008): 205–28, https://doi.org/10.1111/j.1475-6811.2008.00194.x.

142 *"Compassionate listening is crucial":* Thich Nhat Hanh, *Teachings on Love* (Parallax, 2002), 150.

142 *an experience of social rejection:* Guy Itzchakov, Netta Weinstein, Dvori Saluk, and Moty Amar, "Connection Heals Wounds: Feeling Listened to Reduces Speakers' Loneliness Following a Social Rejection Disclosure," *Personality and Social Psychology Bulletin* 49, no. 8 (2023): 1273–94, https://doi.org/10.1177/0146167222110036.

144 *you need to show:* Graham D. Bodie, Susanne M. Jones, Andrea J. Vickery, Laura Hatcher, and Kaitlin Cannava, "Examining the Construct Validity of Enacted Support: A Multitrait–Multimethod Analysis of Three Perspectives for Judging Immediacy and Listening Behaviors," *Communication Monographs* 81, no. 4 (2014): 495–523, https://doi.org/10.1080/03637751.2014.957223.

144 *fascinating experiment, Yale university:* Tanya Chartrand and John Bargh, "The Chameleon Effect: The Perception–Behavior Link and Social Interaction," *Journal of Personality and Social Psychology* 76, no. 6 (1999): 893–910, https://doi.org/10.1037/0022-3514.76.6.893.

145 *detailed, targeted, and thoughtful questions:* Kluger and Itzchakov, "Power of Listening at Work," 121–46; Patricia B. Nemec, Amy Spagnolo, and Anne Sullivan Soydan, "Can You Hear Me Now? Teaching Listening Skills," *Psychiatric Rehabilitation Journal* 40, no. 4 (2017): 415–17, https://doi.org/10.1037/prj0000287; and Niels Van Quaquebeke and Will Felps, "Respectful Inquiry: A Motivational Account of Leading Through Asking Questions and Listening," *Academy of Management Review* 43, no. 1 (2018): 5–27, https://doi.org/10.5465/amr.2014.0537.

147 *words of therapist Emily Nagoski:* Emily Nagoski, "We Need to Discharge the Stress Response—Complete the Cycle—Before Our Bodies Will Believe Us That We Are Safe," *QuoteFancy*, accessed June 30, 2024, https://quotefancy

.com/quote/3365501/Emily-Nagoski-We-need-to-discharge-the-stress-response
-complete-the-cycle-before-our.

147 *"affectionate communication":* Kory Floyd, *Affectionate Communication* (Cambridge University Press, 2006).

147 *characteristic of communal relationships:* Clark and Aragón, "Communal (and Other) Relationships," 255–80.

148 *comes in many shapes and sizes:* Guy Itzchakov, "Can Listening Training Empower Service Employees? The Mediating Roles of Anxiety and Perspective-Taking," *European Journal of Work and Organizational Psychology* 29, no. 6 (2020): 938–52, https://doi.org/10.1080/1359432X.2020.1776701; Guy Itzchakov and Avraham N. Kluger, "Can Holding a Stick Improve Listening at Work? The Effect of Listening Circles on Employees' Emotions and Cognitions," *European Journal of Work and Organizational Psychology* 26, no. 5 (2017): 663–76, https://doi.org/10.1080/1359432X.2017.1351429; Laura Janusik, "Listening Training in Organizations," *Current Opinion in Psychology* 52 (2023): 101631, https://doi.org/10.1016/j.copsyc.2023.101631; Avraham N. Kluger and Dina Nir, "The Feedforward Interview," *Human Resource Management Review* 20, no. 3 (2010): 235–46, https://doi.org/10.1016/j.hrmr.2009.08.002; and Erik Rautalinko and Hans-Olof Lisper, "Effects of Training Reflective Listening in a Corporate Setting," *Journal of Business and Psychology* 18 (2004): 281–99, https://doi.org/10.1023/B:JOBU.0000016712.36043.4f.

149 *"Listening definitely is trainable":* Guy Itzchakov, personal communication, May 17, 2024.

149 *"until you want to give it to others":* Avraham Kluger, personal communication, June 5, 2024.

149 *you are not listening well:* Guy Itzchakov, personal communication, May 17, 2024.

150 *When we stereotype another person:* David L. Hamilton and Jeffrey W. Sherman, "Stereotypes," in *Handbook of Social Cognition*, ed. Rovert S. Wyer Jr. and Thomas K. Scrull (Psychology Press, 2014), 17–84.

151 *the disadvantages of stereotypes:* Patricia G. Devine and Lindsay B. Sharp, "Automaticity and Control in Stereotyping and Prejudice," in *Handbook of Prejudice, Stereotyping, and Discrimination*, ed. Todd D. Nelson (Psychology Press, 2009), 61–87.

152 *surprisingly common in relationships:* Edward P. Lemay Jr., Margaret S. Clark, and Brooke C. Feeney, "Projection of Responsiveness to Needs and the Construction of Satisfying Communal Relationships," *Journal of Personality and Social Psychology* 92, no. 5 (2007): 834–53, https://doi.org/10.1037/0022-3514.92.5.834; Gary Marks and Norman Miller, "Ten Years of Research on the False Consensus Effect: An Empirical and Theoretical Review," *Psychological Bulletin* 102, no. 1 (1987): 72–90, https://doi.org/10.1037/0033-2909.102.1.72; and David C. de Jong and Harry T. Reis, "Sexual Similarity, Complementarity, Accuracy, and Overperception in Same-Sex Couples," *Personal Relationships* 22, no. 4 (2015): 647–65, https://doi.org/10.1111/pere.12101.

153 *a theory of transference:* Serena Chen, Helen C. Boucher, Susan M. Andersen, and S. Adil Saribay, "Transference and the Relational Self," in *The Oxford Handbook of Close Relationships*, ed. Jeffry A. Simpson and Lorne Campbell (Oxford University Press, 2013), 281–305.

Chapter 7: Radical-Curiosity Mindset

155 *lessons he has learned:* Daniel Jones, "Seven Ways to Love Better," *Modern Love, New York Times*, October 11, 2024, https://www.nytimes.com/2024/10/11/style/modern-love-7-lessons.html.

155 *The most-read Modern Love essay:* Daniel Jones, "The 36 Questions That Lead to Love," *New York Times,* January 9, 2015, https://www.nytimes.com/2015/01/09 /style/no-37-big-wedding-or-small.html.

155 *procedure called "Fast Friends":* Arthur Aron, Edward Melinat, Elaine N. Aron, Robert D. Vallone, and Renee J. Bator, "The Experimental Generation of Interpersonal Closeness: A Procedure and Some Preliminary Findings," *Personality and Social Psychology Bulletin* 23, no. 4 (1997): 363–77, https://doi.org/10.1177 /0146167297234003.

158 *a range of positive outcomes:* Paul J. Silvia and Todd B. Kashdan, "Interesting Things and Curious People: Exploration and Engagement as Transient States and Enduring Strengths," *Social and Personality Psychology Compass* 3, no. 5 (2009): 785–97, https://doi.org/10.1111/j.1751-9004.2009.00210.x; Richard Phillips, "Curious About Others: Relational and Empathetic Curiosity for Diverse Societies," Ingenta Connect, accessed June 26, 2005, https://www .ingentaconnect.com/contentone/lwish/nf/2016/00000088/00000088 /art00008?crawler=true&mimetype=application/pdf; Caroline B. Marvin and Daphna Shohamy, "Curiosity and Reward: Valence Predicts Choice and Information Prediction Errors Enhance Learning," *Journal of Experimental Psychology: General* 145, no. 3 (2016): 266–72, https://doi.org/10.1037/xge0000140; Todd B. Kashdan and Michael F. Steger, "Curiosity and Pathways to Well-Being and Meaning in Life: Traits, States, and Everyday Behaviors," *Motivation and Emotion* 31, no. 3 (2007): 159–73, https://doi.org/10.1007/s11031-007-9068-7; David M. Lydon-Staley, Perry Zurn, and Danielle S. Bassett, "Within-Person Variability in Curiosity During Daily Life and Associations with Well-Being," *Journal of Personality* 88, no. 4 (2020): 625–41, https://doi.org/10.1111/jopy.12515; and Sophie von Stumm, Benedikt Hell, and Tomas Chamarro-Premuzic, "The Hungry Mind: Intellectual Curiosity Is the Third Pillar of Academic Performance," *Perspectives on Psychological Science* 6, no. 6 (2011): 574–88, https://doi.org /10.1177/17456916114212.

158 *thrive in novel situations:* Todd B. Kashdan and Paul J. Silvia, "Curiosity and Interest: The Benefits of Thriving on Novelty and Challenge," in *The Oxford Handbook of Positive Psychology,* ed. Shane J. Lopez and C. R. Snyder (Oxford University Press, 2nd ed., 2009), 367–73.

158 *alive five years later:* Gary E. Swan and Dorit Carmelli, "Curiosity and Mortality in Aging Adults: A 5-Year Follow-up of the Western Collaborative Group Study," *Psychology and Aging* 11, no. 3 (1996): 449–53, https://doi.org/10.1037/0882-7974 .11.3.449.

158 *reported by the* Los Angeles Times: Steve Lopez, "The Secret to a Long Life? Curiosity, Says Morrie, Who Has Now Survived Two Pandemics," *Los Angeles Times,* January 14, 2022, https://www.latimes.com/california/story/2022-01-14 /lopez-column-morrie-markoff-age-108-has-survived-two-pandemics.

159 *social psychologist Shige Oishi explains:* Shigehiro Oishi, *Life in Three Dimensions: How Curiosity, Exploration, and Experience Make a Fuller, Better Life* (Doubleday, 2025).

159 *triggering a cycle of discovery:* Kou Murayama, "A Reward-Learning Framework of Knowledge Acquisition: An Integrated Account of Curiosity, Interest, and Intrinsic-Extrinsic Rewards," *Psychological Review* 129, no. 1 (2022): 175–98, https://doi.org/10.1037/rev0000349.

159 *curiosity on a given day:* Todd B. Kashdan and Michael F. Steger, "Curiosity and Pathways to Well-Being and Meaning in Life: Traits, States, and Everyday Behaviors," *Motivation and Emotion* 31, no. 3 (2007): 159–73, https://doi.org /10.1007/s11031-007-9068-7.

159 *Socially curious people ask more questions:* Britta Renner, "Curiosity About People: The Development of a Curiosity Measure in Adults," *Journal of Personality Assessment* 87, no. 3 (2010): 305–16, https://doi.org/10.1207 /s15327752jpa8703_11; Todd B. Kashdan, Paul Rose, and Frank D. Fincham, "Curiosity and Exploration: Facilitating Positive Subjective Experiences and Personal Growth Opportunities," *Journal of Personality Assessment* 82, no. 3 (2004): 291–305, https://doi.org/10.1207/s15327752jpa8203_05; Karen Huang, Michael Yeomans, Alison Wood Brooks, Julia Minson, and Francesca Gino, "It Doesn't Hurt to Ask: Question-Asking Increases Liking," *Journal of Personality and Social Psychology* 113, no. 3 (2017): 430–52, https://doi.org /10.1037/pspi0000097; and Freda-Marie Hartung and Britta Renner, "Social Curiosity and Interpersonal Perception: A Judge x Trait Interaction," *Personality and Social Psychology Bulletin* 37, no. 6 (2011): 796–814, https://doi.org /10.1177/0146167211400618.

159 *perceived as authentic and sincere:* Todd B. Kashdan, Patrick McKnight, Frank D. Fincham, and Paul Rose, "When Curiosity Breeds Intimacy: Taking Advantage of Intimacy Opportunities and Transforming Boring Conversations," *Journal of Personality* 79, no. 6 (2011): 1369–402, https://doi.org/10.1111/j.1467 -6494.2010.00697.x.

159 *they experience less anxiety:* Todd B. Kashdan and John E. Roberts, "Social Anxiety's Impact on Affect, Curiosity, and Social Self-Efficacy During a High Self-Focus Social Threat Situation," *Cognitive Therapy and Research* 28, no. 1 (2004): 119–41, https://doi.org/10.1023/B:COTR.0000016934.20981.68.

159 *described as absorbed and responsive:* Todd B. Kashdan, Ryne A. Sherman, Jessica Yarbro, and David C. Funder, "How Are Curious People Viewed and How Do They Behave in Social Situations? From the Perspectives of Self, Friends, Parents and Unacquainted Observers," *Journal of Personality* 81, no. 2 (2013): 142–54, https://doi.org/10.1111/j.1467-6494.2012.00796.x; Todd B. Kashdan and John E. Roberts, "Affective Outcomes in Superficial and Intimate Interaction: Roles of Social Anxiety and Curiosity," *Journal of Research in Personality* 40, no. 2 (2006): 140–67, https://doi.org/10.1016/j.jrp.2004.10.005.

159 *Gillian Sandstrom and Erica Boothby:* Gillian Sandstrom and Erica Boothby, "Why Do People Avoid Talking to Strangers? A Mini Meta-Analysis of Predicted Fears and Actual Experiences Talking to a Stranger," *Self and Identity* 20, no. 1 (2021): 47–71, https://doi.org/10.1080/15298868.2020.1816568.

160 *the Social Curiosity Scale:* Renner, "Curiosity About People," 305–16.

160 *Studs Terkel:* "About Studs Terkel," *Studs Terkel Radio Archive,* accessed June 30, 2024, https://studsterkel.wfmt.com/about-studs-terkel.

161 *Dax Shepard, host of the podcast:* "Armchair Expert with Dax Shepard," accessed June 30, 2024, https://play.listnr.com/podcast/armchair-expert-with-dax -shepard.

161 *best in the world:* Wikipedia, "The World's 50 Best Restaurants," accessed April 4, 2025, https://en.wikipedia.org/wiki/The_World%27s_50_Best_Restaurants.

162 *"Encourage others to talk about themselves":* Carnegie, *How to Win Friends,* 110.

163 *Scott Shigeoka, author:* Scott Shigeoka, "How Curiosity Can Help Us Overcome Disconnection," *Greater Good Magazine,* September 27, 2023, https:// greatergood.berkeley.edu/article/ITEM/how_curiosity_can_help_us_overcome _disconnection.

163 *"curiosity really is a superpower":* Judson Brewer, "The Science of Curiosity," *Mindful: Healthy Mind, Healthy Life,* January 6, 2022, https://www.mindful. org/the-science-of-curiosity/.

163 *peers might really like them:* Carl Backman and Paul Secord, "The Effects of Per-

ceived Liking on Interpersonal Attraction," *Human Relations* 12, no. 4 (1959): 379–84, https://doi.org/10.1177/001872675901200407. In a related study using a different method, participants were handed a survey form indicating that another participant likes them. Once again, participants liked the person who had expressed liking for them. Rebecca C. Curtis and Kim Miller, "Believing Another Likes or Dislikes You: Behaviors Making the Beliefs Come True," *Journal of Personality and Social Psychology* 51, no. 2 (1986): 284–90, https://doi .org/10.1037/0022-3514.51.2.284.

164 *trigger a cycle of interactions:* Fredrickson, *Love 2.0.*

164 *people want to be accepted:* Roy F. Baumeister and Mark R. Leary, "The Need to Belong: Desire for Interpersonal Attachments as a Fundamental Human Motivation," *Psychological Bulletin* 117, no. 3 (1995): 497–529, https://doi. org/10.1037/0033-2909.117.3.497; and John T. Cacioppo and William Patrick, *Loneliness* (W. W. Norton, 2008).

166 *"high-arousal" emotions:* David Watson and Auke Tellegen, "Toward a Consensual Structure of Mood," *Journal of Personality and Social Psychology* 98, no. 2 (1985): 219–35.

166 *most appealing about extraverts:* Seth Margolis, Ashley L. Stapley, and Sonja Lyubomirsky, "The Association Between Extraversion and Well-Being Is Limited to One Facet," *Journal of Personality* 88 (2020): 478–84, https://doi.org /10.1111/jopy.12504.

166 *doing something for the sheer joy:* Edward L. Deci and Richard M. Ryan, *Intrinsic Motivation and Self-Determination in Human Behavior* (Plenum, 1985).

167 *Ralph Waldo Emerson:* Ralph Waldo Emerson, *Circles* (Applewood Books, 2016).

167 *Brian carried out a series of studies:* Brian C. Patrick, Jennifer Hisley, and Toni Kempler, "'What's Everybody So Excited About?' The Effects of Teacher Enthusiasm on Student Intrinsic Motivation and Vitality," *Journal of Experimental Education* 68, no. 3 (2000): 217–36, https://doi.org/10.1080/00220970009600093.

167 *In a different set of experiments:* Angelica Moè, Anne C. Frenzel, Lik Au, and Jamie L. Taxer, "Displayed Enthusiasm Attracts Attention and Improves Recall," *British Journal of Educational Psychology* 91, no. 3 (2021): 911–27, https://doi.org /10.1111/bjep.12399.

167 *such a strong social signal:* Laura E. Kurtz and Sara B. Algoe, "Putting Laughter in Context: Shared Laughter as a Behavioral Indicator of Relationship Well-Being," *Personal Relationships* 22, no. 4 (2015): 573–90, https://doi.org/10.1111 /pere.12095.

167 *college students played Jenga:* Harry T. Reis, Stephanie D. O'Keefe, and Richard D. Lane, "Fun Is More Fun When Others Are Involved," *Journal of Positive Psychology* 12, no. 6 (2016): 547–57, https://doi.org/10.1080/17439760.2016 .1221123.

168 *a study at Yale University:* Erica J. Boothby, Margaret S. Clark, and John A. Bargh, "Shared Experiences Are Amplified," *Psychological Science* 25, no. 12 (2014): 2209–16, https://doi.org/10.1177/0956797614551162.

168 *this phenomenon as positivity resonance:* Fredrickson, "Love: Positivity Resonance as a Fresh, Evidence-Based Perspective on an Age-Old Topic," in *Handbook of Emotions*, 4th ed., ed. Lisa F. Barrett, Michael Lewis, and Jeanette M. Haviland-Jones (Guilford, 2016), 847–58.

168 *Triwizard Tournament has arrived:* J. K. Rowling, *Harry Potter and the Goblet of Fire* (Scholastic, 2002), 283, 331, 317, 332, 358, 359.

170 *Argyle proposed that sharing:* Michael Argyle and Monika Henderson, "The Rules of Friendship," *Journal of Social and Personal Relationships* 1, no. 2 (1984): 211–37, https://doi.org/10.1177/02654075840120.

170 *A 1994 study supported this notion:* Christopher A. Langston, "Capitalizing on and Coping with Daily-Life Events: Expressive Responses to Positive Events," *Journal of Personality and Social Psychology* 67, no. 6 (1994): 1112–25, https://doi.org/10.1037/0022-3514.67.6.1112.

170 *If so, you're not alone:* Bernard Rimé, Catrin Finkenauer, Olivier Luminet, Emmanuelle Zech, and Pierre Philipott, "Social Sharing of Emotion: New Evidence and New Questions," *European Review of Social Psychology* 9, no. 1 (1998): 145–89, https://doi.org/10.1080/14792779843000072; Shelly L. Gable and Harry T. Reis, "Good News! Capitalizing on Positive Events in an Interpersonal Context," *Advances in Experimental Social Psychology* 42, no. 1 (2010): 195–257, https://doi.org/10.1016/S0065-2601(10)42004-3; and Sara B. Algoe and Jonathan Haidt, "Witnessing Excellence in Action: The 'Other-Praising' Emotions of Elevation, Gratitude, and Admiration," *Journal of Positive Psychology* 4, no. 2 (2009): 105–27, https://doi.org/10.1080/17439760802650519.

170 *more than 80 percent of the time:* Shelly L. Gable, Harry T. Reis, Emily A. Impett, and Evan R. Asher, "What Do You Do When Things Go Right? The Intrapersonal Benefits of Sharing Positive Events," *Journal of Personality and Social Psychology* 87, no. 2 (2004): 228–45, https://doi.org/10.1037/0022-3514.87.2.228.

171 *In one early set of experiments:* Harry T. Reis, Shannon M. Smith, Cheryl L. Carmichael, Peter A. Caprariello, Fen-Fang Tsai, Amy Rodrigues, and Michael R. Maniaci, "Are You Happy for Me? How Sharing Positive Events with Others Provides Personal and Interpersonal Benefits," *Journal of Personality and Social Psychology* 99, no. 2 (2010): 311–29, https://doi.org/10.1037/a0018344.

171 *over fourteen days:* Gable, Reis, Impett, and Asher, "What Do You Do When Things Go Right?," 228–245.

171 *respond to a friend's happy disclosure:* Gable, Reis, Impett, and Asher, "What Do You Do When Things Go Right?," 228–45.

172 *Ambivalence is also detrimental:* Cheryl L. Carmichael, "Responses to Relationship-Threatening Positive Events," unpublished master's thesis (University of Rochester, 2005).

172 *gratitude toward their partners:* Alexandra M. Gray, Claire M. Growney, and Tammy English, "Perceived Responses, Capitalization, and Daily Gratitude: Do Age and Closeness Matter?" *Emotion* 24, no. 3 (2024): 867–77, https://doi.org/10.1037/emo0001301.

172 *In these studies:* Shelly L. Gable, Courtney L. Gosnell, Nataya C. Maisel, and Amy Strachman, "Safely Testing the Alarm: Close Others' Responses to Personal Positive Events," *Journal of Personality and Social Psychology* 103, no. 6 (2012): 963–81, https://doi.org/10.1037/a0029488.

175 *bothersome to the other person:* Sandstrom and Boothby, "Why Do People Avoid Talking to Strangers?," 47–71.

175 *surprisingly open to questions:* Michael Kardas, Amit Kumar, and Nicholas Epley, "Overly Shallow?: Miscalibrated Expectations Create a Barrier to Deeper Conversation," *Journal of Personality and Social Psychology* 122, no. 3 (2022): 367–98, https://doi.org/10.1037/pspa0000281.

175 *when he meets someone new:* David Brooks, "The Essential Skills for Being Human," *New York Times*, October 19, 2023, https://www.nytimes.com/2023/10/19/opinion/social-skills-connection.html.

175 *"30,000-foot questions":* Brooks, "Essential Skills."

176 *a card game:* The Skin Deep, accessed December 24, 2024, https://www.theskindeep.com.

176 *Researchers define passion:* Robert J. Vallerand, "On the Psychology of Passion:

In Search of What Makes People's Lives Most Worth Living," *Canadian Psychology* 49, no. 1 (2008): 1–13, https://doi.org/10.1037/0708-5591.49.1.1.

177 *feel about your conversation partner:* Gerben A. Van Kleef, "How Emotions Regulate Social Life: The Emotions as Social Information (EASI) Model," *Current Directions in Psychological Science* 18, no. 3 (2009): 184–88, https://doi .org/10.1111/j.1467-8721.2009.01633.x.

177 *divided college students into two groups:* Todd B. Kashdan and John E. Roberts, "Trait and State Curiosity in the Genesis of Intimacy: Differentiation from Related Constructs," *Journal of Social and Clinical Psychology* 23, no. 6 (2005): 792–816, https://doi.org/10.1521/jscp.23.6.792.54800.

178 *their lives and experiences:* Guy Itzchakov, personal communication, May 17, 2024.

178 *A recent study from Sonja's lab:* Madison A. C. Montemayor-Dominguez and Sonja Lyubomirsky, "Exploring the Impacts of a Week-Long Curiosity Intervention on Well-Being," in-review manuscript, 2025.

Chapter 8: Open-Heart Mindset

181 *"You are all here probably seeking something":* This wisdom was delivered by Harvard University professor and *Atlantic* columnist Arthur Brooks, the organizer of our visit to His Holiness the Dalai Lama in Dharamsala, India, April 7, 2024.

183 *our colleague Caryl Rusbult:* Caryl E. Rusbult, Eli J. Finkel, and Madoka Kumashiro, "The Michelangelo Phenomenon," *Current Directions in Psychological Science* 18, no. 6 (2009): 305–9, https://doi.org/10.1111/j.1467-8721.2009 .01657.x.

185 *both romantic and platonic love:* Kevin E. Hegi and Raymond M. Bergner, "What Is Love? An Empirically Based Essentialist Account," *Journal of Social and Personal Relationships* 27, no. 5 (2010): 620–36, https://doi .org/10.1177/0265407510369605.

186 *start-up called PolarBear:* Not its real name.

186 *potential to help people flourish:* Sonja Lyubomirsky, "Everything Everywhere All at Once," in *AI Anthology*, ed. Eric Horvitz (Microsoft, June 12, 2023), https://unlocked.microsoft.com/ai-anthology/sonja-lyubomirsky.

188 *"prosocial behavior," defined:* David R. Cregg and Jennifer S. Cheavens, "Healing Through Helping: An Experimental Investigation of Kindness, Social Activities, and Reappraisal as Well-Being Interventions," *Journal of Positive Psychology* 18, no. 6 (2023): 924–41, https://doi.org/10.1080/17439760.2022.2154695; and Annie Regan, Nina Radošić, and Sonja Lyubomirsky, "Experimental Effects of Social Behavior on Well-being," *Trends in Cognitive Sciences* 26, no. 11 (2022): 987–98, https://doi.org/10.1016/j.tics.2022.08.006.

188 *in both friends and potential mates:* Daniel Farrelly and Laura King, "Mutual Mate Choice Drives the Desirability of Altruism in Relationships," *Current Psychology* 38 (2019): 977–81, https://doi.org/10.1007/s12144-018-0059-4; and David Moore, Stuart Wigby, Sinead English, Sonny Wong, Tamás Székely, and Freya Harrison, "Selflessness Is Sexy: Reported Helping Behaviour Increases Desirability of Men and Women as Long-Term Sexual Partners," *BMC Ecology and Evolution* 13, no. 182 (2013), http://biomedcentral.com/1471-2148/13/182.

188 *prompted to recall recent kind acts:* Kellon Ko, Seth Margolis, Julia Revord, and Sonja Lyubomirsky, "Comparing the Effects of Performing and Recalling Acts of Kindness," *Journal of Positive Psychology* 16, no. 1 (2021): 73–81, https://doi .org/10.1080/17439760.2019.1663252; and Lilian J. Shin, Seth M. Margolis,

Lisa C. Walsh, Sylvia Y. C. L. Kwok, Xiaodong Yue, Chi-Keung Chan, et al., "Cultural Differences in the Hedonic Rewards of Recalling Kindness: Priming Cultural Identity with Language," *Affective Science* 2 (2021): 80–90, https://doi .org/10.1007/s42761-021-00013-7.

189 *above average in kindness:* Simon Usborne, "Why Do We Think We're Nicer Than We Actually Are?," *The Guardian*, March 13, 2017, https://www .theguardian.com/science/shortcuts/2017/mar/13/why-do-we-think-were-nicer -than-we-actually-are.

189 *meaningful kind gestures per week:* Chris Melore, "How Kind Are You? Average Person Performs 25,000 Thoughtful Acts in Their Life," *StudyFinds*, February 9, 2022, https://studyfinds.org/average-person-performs-25000-thoughtful-acts-of -kindness/.

189 *less than 10 percent of the time:* Letter.ly, "Negative News Statistics," accessed December 3, 2024, https://letter.ly/negative-news-statistics/.

189 *characters helping each other out:* Patrick Cooke, "TV Causes Violence? Says Who?," *New York Times*, August 14, 1993, 19, https://www.nytimes.com/1993 /08/14/opinion/tv-causes-violence-says-who.html.

189 *Sesame Workshop/Harris poll: Elmo's Just Checking In: How Are You Doing? The State of Well-Being Report* (Sesame Workshop, August 13, 2024), https:// sesameworkshop.org/wp-content/uploads/2024/08/The-State-of-Well-being -Report.pdf.

190 *Glassdoor/Harris poll:* Glassdoor Team, "Employers to Retain Half of Their Employees Longer If Bosses Showed More Appreciation; Glassdoor Survey," *Glassdoor*, November 13, 2013, https://www.glassdoor.com/blog/employers -to-retain-half-of-their-employees-longer-if-bosses-showed-more-appreciation -glassdoor-survey/.

190 *offering sincere compliments:* Xuan Zhao and Nicholas Epley, "Insufficiently Complimentary?: Underestimating the Positive Impact of Compliments Creates a Barrier to Expressing Them," *Journal of Personality and Social Psychology* 121, no. 2 (2021): 239–56, https://doi.org/10.1037/pspa0000277.

190 *"we're miscalibrated!":* Amit Kumar and Nicholas Epley, "A Little Good Goes an Unexpectedly Long Way: Underestimating the Positive Impact of Kindness on Recipients," *Journal of Experimental Psychology: General* 151, no. 8 (2022): 1934–46, https://doi.org/10.1037/xge0001271; and Nicholas Epley, Amit Kumar, James Dungan, and Margaret Echelbarger, "A Prosociality Paradox: How Miscalibrated Social Cognition Creates a Misplaced Barrier to Prosocial Action," *Current Directions in Psychological Science* 1, no. 1 (2023): 1–9, https:// doi.org/10.1177/09637214221128016.

191 *happy than the givers expect:* Kumar and Epley, "A Little Good Goes," 1934–46.

191 *greater benefits than do the recipients:* Oliver Scott Curry, Lee A. Rowland, Caspar J. Van Lissa, Sally Zlotowitz, John McAlaney, and Harvey White-house, "Happy to Help? A Systematic Review and Meta-Analysis of the Effects of Performing Acts of Kindness on the Well-Being of the Actor," *Journal of Experimental Social Psychology* 76 (2018): 320–29, https://doi.org/10.1016/j .jesp.2018.02.014.

191 *scriptural adage:* Acts 20:35 KJV.

191 *effects of doing kind actions on happiness:* Sonja Lyubomirsky, Kennon M. Sheldon, and David Schkade, "Pursuing Happiness: The Architecture of Sustainable Change," *Review of General Psychology* 9, no. 2 (2005): 111–31, https://doi.org/10.1037/1089-2680.9.2.111.

191 *one of three assignments:* S. Katherine Nelson, Kristin Layous, Steven W. Cole, and Sonja Lyubomirsky, "Do Unto Others or Treat Yourself? The Effects of

Prosocial and Self-Focused Behavior on Psychological Flourishing," *Emotion* 16, no. 6 (2016): 850–61, https://doi.org/10.1037/emo0000178.

192 *acts of kindness* for others: Oliver Scott Curry, Lee A. Rowland, Caspar J. Van Lissa, Sally Zlotowitz, John McAlaney, and Harvey Whitehouse, "Happy to Help? A Systematic Review and Meta-Analysis of the Effects of Performing Acts of Kindness on the Well-Being of the Actor," *Journal of Experimental Social Psychology* 76 (2018): 320–29, https://doi.org/10.1016/j.jesp.2018.02.014.

192 *adults to do more kind acts:* Annie Regan, Seth Margolis, Daniel J. Ozer, Eric Schwitzgebel, and Sonja Lyubomirsky, "What Is Unique About Kindness? Exploring the Proximal Experience of Prosocial Acts Relative to Other Positive Behaviors," *Affective Science* 4, no. 1 (2023): 92–100, https://doi.org/10.1007/s42761-022-00120-7.

192 *actually doing them:* Kellon Ko, Seth Margolis, Julia Revord, and Sonja Lyubomirsky, "Comparing the Effects of Performing and Recalling Acts of Kindness," *Journal of Positive Psychology* 16, no. 1 (2021): 73–81, https://doi.org/10.1080/17439760.2019.1663252.

192 *think kind thoughts about others:* Adam Waytz and Wilhelm Hofmann, "Nudging the Better Angels of Our Nature: A Field Experiment on Morality and Well-Being," *Emotion* 20, no. 5 (2019): 904–9, https://doi.org/10.1037/emo0000588.

193 *also tend to last longer:* Ed O'Brien and Samantha Kassirer, "People Are Slow to Adapt to the Warm Glow of Giving," *Psychological Science* 30, no. 2 (2019): 193–204, https://doi.org/10.1177/0956797618814145.

193 *region called the ventral striatum:* William T. Harbaugh, Ulrich Mayr, and Daniel R. Burghart, "Neural Responses to Taxation and Voluntary Giving Reveal Motives for Charitable Donations," *Science* 316, no. 5831 (2007): 1622–25, https://doi.org/10.1126/science.1140738.

193 *returned to school the next day:* Kristin Layous, S. Katherine Nelson, Eva Oberle, Kimberly A. Schonert-Reichl, and Sonja Lyubomirsky, "Kindness Counts: Prompting Prosocial Behavior in Preadolescents Boosts Peer Acceptance and Well-Being," *PLOS ONE* 7, no. 12 (2012): e51380, https://doi.org/10.1371/journal.pone.0051380.

193 *blood samples from participants:* S. Katherine Nelson-Coffey, Megan M. Fritz, Sonja Lyubomirsky, and Steve W. Cole, "Kindness in the Blood: A Randomized Controlled Trial of the Gene Regulatory Impact of Prosocial Behavior," *Psychoneuroendocrinology* 81 (2017): 8–13, https://doi.org/10.1016/j.psyneuen.2017.03.025; and Annie Regan, Megan M. Fritz, Lisa C. Walsh, Sonja Lyubomirsky, and Steven W. Cole, "The Genomic Impact of Kindness to Self vs. Others: A Randomized Controlled Trial," *Brain, Behavior, & Immunity* 106 (2022): 40–48, https://doi.org/10.1016/j.bbi.2022.04.013.

194 *reactivity to stressors:* Rachel L. Piferi and Kathleen A. Lawler, "Social Support and Ambulatory Blood Pressure: An Examination of Both Receiving and Giving," *International Journal of Psychophysiology* 62, no. 2 (2006): 328–36, https://doi.org/10.1016/j.ijpsycho.2006.06.002; Rodlescia S. Sneed and Sheldon Cohen, "A Prospective Study of Volunteerism and Hypertension Risk in Older Adults," *Psychology and Aging* 28, no. 2 (2013): 578–86, https://doi.org/10.1037/a0032718; and Sae Hwang Han, Kyungmin Kim, and Jeffrey A. Burr, "Stress-Buffering Effects of Volunteering on Salivary Cortisol: Results from a Daily Diary Study," *Social Science & Medicine* 201 (2018): 120–26, https://doi.org/10.1016/j.socscimed.2018.02.011.

194 *productivity, efficiency, cooperation, and customer satisfaction:* Philip M. Podsakoff, Scott B. MacKenzie, Julie Beth Paine, and Daniel G. Bachrach, "Organizational Citizenship Behaviors: A Critical Review of the Theoretical and Empirical

Literature and Suggestions for Future Research," *Journal of Management* 26, no. 3 (2000): 513–63, https://doi.org/10.1177/014920630002600307; and Adam Grant, *Give and Take: Why Helping Others Drives Our Success* (Viking, 2013).

194 *conducted at Coca-Cola's Madrid office:* Joseph Chancellor, Seth M. Margolis, Katherine Jacobs Bao, and Sonja Lyubomirsky, "Everyday Prosociality in the Workplace: The Benefits of Giving, Getting, and Glimpsing," *Emotion* 18, no. 4 (2018): 507–17, https://doi.org/10.1037/emo0000321.

194 *with the other's welfare in mind:* Peter A. Caprariello and Harry T. Reis, "'This One's on Me!': Differential Well-Being Effects of Self-Centered and Recipient-Centered Motives for Spending Money on Others," *Motivation and Emotion* 45, no. 6 (2021): 705–27, https://doi.org/10.1007/s11031-021-09907-0.

194 *feel like a good person:* Dylan Wiwad and Lara B. Aknin, "Motives Matter: The Emotional Consequences of Recalled Self- and Other-Focused Prosocial Acts," *Motivation and Emotion* 41 (2017): 730–40, https://doi.org/10.1007/s11031-017-9674-4.

195 *write letters of gratitude to others:* Tanya Vannoy, Ramona L. Martinez, and Sonja Lyubomirsky, "Self-Directed Positive Interventions," in *The Oxford Handbook of Well-Being in Higher Education*, ed. L. Tay and B. McCuskey (Oxford University Press, in press).

195 *more connected with the person:* Lisa C. Walsh, Annie Regan, Jean M. Twenge, and Sonja Lyubomirsky, "What Is the Optimal Way to Give Thanks? Comparing the Effects of Gratitude Expressed Privately, One-to-One via Text, or Publicly on Social Media," *Affective Science* 4 (2023): 82–91, https://doi.org/10.1007/s42761-022-00150-5.

195 *called "find-bind-and-remind":* Sara B. Algoe, "Find, Remind, and Bind: The Functions of Gratitude in Everyday Relationships," *Social and Personality Psychology Compass* 6 (2012): 455–69, https://doi.org/10.1111/j.1751-9004.2012.00439.x.

196 *how much they felt appreciated:* Allen W. Barton and Qiujie Gong, "A 'Thank You' Really Would Be Nice: Perceived Gratitude in Family Relationships," *Journal of Positive Psychology* (2024): 1–10, https://doi.org/10.1080/17439760.2024.2365472.

196 *things their partners did for them:* Sara B. Algoe, Shelly L. Gable, and Natalya C. Maisel, "It's the Little Things: Everyday Gratitude as a Booster Shot for Romantic Relationships," *Personal Relationships* 17, no. 2 (2010): 217–33, https://doi.org/10.1111/j.1475-6811.2010.01273.x.

196 *praising the other person's kindness:* Sara B. Algoe, Laura E. Kurtz, and Natalie M. Hilaire, "Putting the 'You' in 'Thank You': Examining Other-Praising Behavior as the Active Relational Ingredient in Expressed Gratitude," *Social Psychological and Personality Science* 7, no. 7 (2016): 658–66, https://doi.org/10.1177/1948550616651681.

196 *in The Book of Joy:* Dalai Lama, Desmond Tutu, and Douglas Carlton Abrams, *The Book of Joy: Lasting Happiness in a Changing World* (Avery, 2016).

197 *Mahayana Buddhism:* Lama Tsultrim Allione, *The Four Immeasurables: Practices and Commentary* (Machig, 2009), https://www.taramandala.org/wp-content/uploads/TFI_Booklet.pdf.

197 *"I wish for this person":* Douglas A. Gentile, Dawn M. Sweet, and Lanmiao He, "Caring for Others Cares for the Self: An Experimental Test of Brief Downward Social Comparison, Loving-Kindness, and Interconnectedness Contemplations," *Journal of Happiness Studies* 21 (2020): 765–78, https://doi.org/10.1007/s10902-019-00100-2.

197 *loving-kindness meditations:* Instructions for loving-kindness meditation were adapted and modified from a variety of sources, including Christopher Germer

and Kristin Neff, *Teaching the Mindful Self-Compassion Program: A Guide for Professionals* (Guilford, 2019); and Hopelab, *Hopelab Loneliness Intervention Content Card Deck*, https://hopelab.org.

198 *loving-kindness and compassion meditation interventions:* Barbara L. Fredrickson, Michael A. Cohn, Kimberly A. Coffey, Jolynn Pek, and Sandra M. Finkel, "Open Hearts Build Lives: Positive Emotions, Induced Through Loving-Kindness Meditation, Build Consequential Personal Resources," *Journal of Personality and Social Psychology* 95, no. 5 (2008): 1045–62, https://doi.org/10.1037/a0013262; and Stefan G. Hofmann, Paul Grossman, and Devon E. Hinton, "Loving-Kindness and Compassion Meditation: Potential for Psychological Interventions," *Clinical Psychology Review* 31, no. 7 (2011): 1126–32, https://doi.org/10.1016/j.cpr.2011.07.003.

198 *held at their workplace:* Michael A. Cohn and Barbara L. Fredrickson, "In Search of Durable Positive Psychology Interventions: Predictors and Consequences of Long-Term Positive Behavior Change," *Journal of Positive Psychology* 5, no. 5 (2010): 355–66, https://doi.org/10.1080/17439760.2010.508883.

199 *According to Sharon Salzberg:* Sharon Salzberg, *Real Love: The Art of Mindful Connection* (Flatiron Books, 2017).

200 *"radical friendliness":* D'Simone, *Spiritually, We.*

200 *enjoyable, natural, and meaningful to them:* Ramona L. Martinez, Annie Regan, Peter M. Gollwitzer, Gabriele Oettingen, and Sonja Lyubomirsky, "Increasing Extraversion via Intervention: Lay Insights, Person-Activity Fit, and Implications for Well-Being and Persistence," *Personality and Social Psychology Compass* 19, no. 2 (2025): e70043.

200 *speech by writer George Saunders:* Joel Lovell, "George Saunders's Advice to Graduates," *New York Times*, July 31, 2013, https://archive.nytimes.com/6thfloor.blogs.nytimes.com/2013/07/31/george-saunderss-advice-to-graduates/.

201 *convey love in their everyday lives:* Harry Reis, Michael R. Maniaci, and Ronald D. Rogge, "The Expression of Compassionate Love in Everyday Compassionate Acts," *Journal of Social and Personal Relationships* 31 (2014): 652–77, https://doi.org/10.1177/0265407513507214.

201 *what behaviors make them feel loved:* Saeideh Heshmati, Zita Oravecz, Sarah Pressman, William H. Batchelder, Chelsea Muth, and Joachim Vandekerckhove, "What Does It Mean to Feel Loved: Cultural Consensus and Individual Differences in Felt Love," *Journal of Social and Personal Relationships* 36, no. 1 (2019): 214–43, https://doi.org/10.1177/0265407517724600; and Zita Oravecz, Chelsea Muth, and Joachim Vandekerckhove, "Do People Agree on What Makes One Feel Loved? A Cognitive Psychometric Approach to the Consensus on Felt Love," *PLOS ONE* 11, no. 4 (2016): e0152803, https://doi.org/10.1371/journal.pone.0152803.

202 On Becoming a Person: Carl Rogers, *On Becoming a Person: A Therapist's View of Psychotherapy* (Houghton Mifflin, 1961).

202 *name for it is:* Caryl E. Rusbult, Eli J. Finkel, and Madoka Kumashiro, "The Michelangelo Phenomenon," *Current Directions in Psychological Science* 18, no. 6 (2009): 305–9, https://doi.org/10.1111/j.1467-8721.2009.01657.x.

203 *greater movement over two months:* Stephen M. Drigotas, Caryl E. Rusbult, Jennifer Wieselquist, and Sarah W. Whitton, "Close Partner as Sculptor of the Ideal Self: Behavioral Affirmation and the Michelangelo Phenomenon," *Journal of Personality and Social Psychology* 77, no. 2 (1999): 293–323, https://doi.org/10.1037//0022-3514.77.2.293.

203 *residents of Florida, Texas, California, and New York:* Thomas E. Trail and Benjamin R. Karney, "What's (Not) Wrong with Low-Income Marriages," *Journal*

of Marriage and Family 74, no. 3 (2012): 413–27, https://doi.org/10.1111/j.1741 -3737.2012.00977.x.

204 *branch of philosophy called* care ethics: Elissa Strauss, "The Branch of Philosophy All Parents Should Know," *Atlantic*, October 16, 2024, https://www.the atlantic.com/family/archive/2024/10/parents-care-ethics-philosophy/680263/.

205 *partner's kindness, affirmation, and endorsement:* Jennifer Wieselquist, Caryl E. Rusbult, Craig A. Foster, and Christopher R. Agnew, "Commitment, Pro-Relationship Behavior, and Trust in Close Relationships," *Journal of Personality and Social Psychology* 77, no. 5 (1999): 942–66, https://doi.org/10.1037/0022 -3514.77.5.942; and Caryl E. Rusbult, Eli J. Finkel, and Madoka Kumashiro, "The Michelangelo Phenomenon," *Current Directions in Psychological Science* 18, no. 6 (2009): 305–9, https://doi.org/10.1111/j.1467-8721.2009.01657.x.

206 *Mister Rogers:* Shea Tuttle, "The Deep Fear That Makes Us Turn to Mister Rogers: Why Do We Keep Summoning Mister Rogers? And Why Is Now the Time for a Feature Film About His Influence?" *Greater Good Magazine*, November 26, 2019, https://greatergood.berkeley.edu/article/item/deep_fear_that_makes_us _turn_to_mister_rogers.

207 *the science of self-compassion:* Kristin D. Neff, "Self-Compassion, Self-Esteem, and Well-Being," *Social & Personality Psychology Compass* 5 (2011): 1–12, https:// doi.org/10.1111/j.1751-9004.2010.00330.x.

207 *three main elements of self-compassion:* Neff, "Self-Compassion, Self-Esteem, and Well-Being," 1–12.

208 *Whole Self-Love Scale:* Katy Carol Sine, *Whole Self-Love Scale*, unpublished measurement instrument, January 2019.

208 *self-compassion interventions:* Madeleine Ferrari, Caroline Hunt, Ashish Harrysunker, Maree J. Abbott, Alissa P. Beath, and Danielle A. Einstein, "Self-Compassion Interventions and Psychosocial Outcomes: A Meta-Analysis of RCTs," *Mindfulness* 10, no. 8 (2019): 1455–73, https://doi.org/10.1007/s12671 -019-01134-6.

208 *markers of positive mental health:* Karen Bluth and Kristin D. Neff, "New Frontiers in Understanding the Benefits of Self-Compassion," *Self and Identity* 17, no. 6 (2018): 605–08, https://doi.org/10.1080/15298868.2018.1508494.

208 *brain-imaging study out of UCLA:* Michael H. Parrish, Tristen K. Inagaki, Keely A. Muscatell, Kate E. B. Haltom, Mark R. Leary, and Naomi I. Eisenberger, "Self-Compassion and Responses to Negative Social Feedback: The Role of Fronto-Amygdala Circuit Connectivity," *Self and Identity* 17, no. 6 (2018): 723–38, https://doi.org/10.1080/15298868.2018.1490344.

209 *self-compassionate people have been found:* Jia Wei Zhang, Serena Chen, and Teodora K. Tomova Shakur, "From Me to You: Self-Compassion Predicts Acceptance of Own and Others' Imperfections," *Personality and Social Psychology Bulletin* 46, no. 8 (2020): 1139–56, https://doi. org/10.1177/0146167220909954; Kristin D. Neff and Elizabeth Pommier, "The Relationship Between Self-Compassion and Other-Focused Concern Among College Undergraduates, Community Adults, and Practicing Meditators," *Self and Identity* 12, no. 2 (2013): 160–76, https://doi.org/10.1080/15298868.2011. 649546; Laura R. Welp and Christina M. Brown, "Self-Compassion, Empathy, and Helping Intentions," *Journal of Positive Psychology* 9, no. 1 (2014): 54–65, https://doi.org/10.1080/17439760.2013.831465; Kristin D. Neff and S. Natasha Beretvas, "The Role of Self-Compassion in Romantic Relationships," *Self and Identity* 12, no. 1 (2013): 78–98, https://doi.org/10.1080/15298868.2011.63954 8; and Christine R. Lathren, Sanjana S. Rao, Jinyoung Park, and Karen Bluth, "Self-Compassion and Current Close Interpersonal Relationships: A Scoping

Literature Review," *Mindfulness* 11, no. 8 (2020): 2085–102, https://doi.org
/10.1007/s12671-020-01566-5.

209 *in healthy repair behaviors:* Levi R. Baker and James K. McNulty, "Self-
Compassion and Relationship Maintenance: The Moderating Roles of Conscientiousness and Gender," *Journal of Personality and Social Psychology* 100, no. 5
(2011): 853–73, https://doi.org/10.1037/a0021884.

211 *many practical, research-backed strategies:* Instructions for the self-compassion
practices in this chapter were adapted and modified from a variety of sources,
including the following: Joanna J. Arch, Kirk Warren Brown, Derek J. Dean,
Lauren N. Landy, Kimberley D. Brown, and Mark L. Laudenslager, "Self-
Compassion Training Modulates Alpha-Amylase, Heart Rate Variability, and
Subjective Responses to Social Evaluative Threat in Women," *Psychoneuroendocrinology* 42 (2014): 49–58, https://doi.org/10.1016/j.psyneuen.2013.12.018;
Karen Bluth, Susan A. Gaylord, Rebecca A. Campo, Michael C. Mullarkey, and
Lorraine Hobbs, "Making Friends with Yourself: A Mixed Methods Pilot Study
of a Mindful Self-Compassion Program for Adolescents," *Mindfulness* 7, no.
2 (2016): 479–92, https://doi.org/10.1007/s12671-015-0476; James N. Kirby,
"Compassion Interventions: The Programmes, the Evidence, and Implications
for Research and Practice," *Psychology and Psychotherapy: Theory, Research and
Practice* 90, no. 3 (2017): 432–55, https://doi.org/10.1111/papt.12104; Kristin
D. Neff, "Self-Compassion: An Alternative Conceptualization of a Healthy
Attitude Toward Oneself," *Self and Identity* 2, no. 2 (2003): 85–101, https://
doi.org/10.1080/15298860309032; Christopher Germer and Kristin D. Neff,
"Mindful Self-Compassion (MSC)," in *The Handbook of Mindfulness-Based
Programs: Every Established Intervention, from Medicine to Education*, ed. Ioannis
Itvzan (Routledge, 2019), 357–67; and Hopelab, *Hopelab Loneliness Intervention
Content Card Deck.*

213 *less defensiveness and less distress:* Mark R. Leary, Eleanor B. Tate, Claire E. Adams, Ashley B. Allen, and Jessica Hancock, "Self-Compassion and Reactions to
Unpleasant Self-Relevant Events: The Implications of Treating Oneself Kindly,"
Journal of Personality and Social Psychology 92, no. 5 (2007): 887–904, https://
doi.org/10.1037/0022-3514.92.5.887.

213 *created a chatbot named Vincent:* Minha Lee, Sander Ackermans, Nena van As,
Hanwen Chang, Enzo Lucas, and Wijnand IJsselsteijn, "Caring for Vincent:
A Chatbot for Self-Compassion," in *Proceedings of the 2019 CHI Conference on
Human Factors in Computing Systems* (Paper no. 702, Association for Computing
Machinery, 2019), https://doi.org/10.1145/3290605.3300932.

213 *"I try to see my failings":* These are included in the Self-Compassion Scale: Kristin
D. Neff, "Development and Validation of a Scale to Measure Self-Compassion,"
Self and Identity 2 (2003): 223–50, https://doi.org/10.1080/15298860309027.

215 *writing about cherished values:* Gregory M. Walton and Geoffrey L. Cohen,
"A Brief Social-Belonging Intervention Improves Academic and Health Out-
comes of Minority Students," *Science* 331, no. 6023 (2011): 1447–51, https://
doi.org/10.1126/science.1198364; and S. Katherine Nelson, Joshua A. K. Fuller,
Incheol Choi, and Sonja Lyubomirsky, "Beyond Self-Protection: Self-Affirmation
Benefits Hedonic and Eudaimonic Well-Being," *Personality and Social Psychology
Bulletin* 40 (2014): 998–1011, https://doi.org/10.1177/0146167214533389.

216 *stop focusing on building their self-esteem:* Mark Leary, "Is It Time to Give Up on
Self-Esteem?" *Society for Personality and Social Psychology*, May 9, 2019, https://
spsp.org/news-center/character-context-blog/it-time-give-self-esteem.

217 *self-compassionate people are happier:* Kristin D. Neff, *Self-Compassion: The
Proven Power of Being Kind to Yourself* (William Morrow, 2015); Laura R. Welp

and Christina M. Brown, "Self-Compassion, Empathy, and Helping Intentions," *Journal of Positive Psychology* 9, no. 1 (2014): 54–65, https://doi.org/10.1080 /17439760.2013.831465; and Christine R. Lathren, Sanjana S. Rao, Jinyoung Park, and Karen Bluth, "Self-Compassion and Current Close Interpersonal Relationships: A Scoping Literature Review," *Mindfulness* 11, no. 8 (2020): 2085–102, https://doi.org/10.1007/s12671-020-01566-5.

218   *way that they see themselves:* Edward P. Lemay Jr., Margaret S. Clark, and Brooke C. Feeney, "Projection of Responsiveness to Needs and the Construction of Satisfying Communal Relationships," *Journal of Personality and Social Psychology* 92, no. 5 (2007): 834–53, https://doi.org/10.1037/0022-3514.92.5.834; and Edward P. Lemay Jr. and Margaret S. Clark, "How the Head Liberates the Heart: Projection of Communal Responsiveness Guides Relationship Promotion," *Journal of Personality and Social Psychology* 94, no. 4 (2008): 647–71, https://doi.org/10.1037/0022-3514.94.4.647.

218   *see through to their social deficiencies:* Xianmin Gong and Jana Nikitin, "When I Feel Lonely, I'm Not Nice (and Neither Are You): The Short- and Long-Term Relation Between Loneliness and Reports of Social Behaviour," *Cognition and Emotion* 35, no. 5 (2021): 1029–38, https://doi.org/10.1080 /02699931.2021.1905612.

219   *more acceptance of their limitations:* Jia Wei Zhang, Serena Chen, and Teodora K. Tomova Shakur, "From Me to You: Self-Compassion Predicts Acceptance of Own and Others' Imperfections," *Personality and Social Psychology Bulletin* 46, no. 2 (2020): 228–42, https://doi.org/10.1177/0146167219853.

219   *less likely to catastrophize problems:* Mark R. Leary, Eleanor B. Tate, Claire E. Adams, Ashley B. Allen, and Jessica Hancock, "Self-Compassion and Reactions to Unpleasant Self-Relevant Events: The Implications of Treating Oneself Kindly," *Journal of Personality and Social Psychology* 92, no. 5 (2007): 887–904, https://doi.org/10.1037/0022-3514.92.5.887.

219   *talk openly about problems:* Levi R. Baker and James K. McNulty, "Self-Compassion and Relationship Maintenance: The Moderating Roles of Conscientiousness and Gender," *Journal of Personality and Social Psychology* 100, no. 5 (2011): 853–73, https://doi.org/10.1037/a0021884https://doi.org /10.1037/a0021884.

Chapter 9: Multiplicity Mindset

223   *Whole Trait theory:* William Fleeson and Eranda Jayawickreme, "Whole Traits: Revealing the Social-Cognitive Mechanisms Constituting Personality's Central Variable," *Advances in Experimental Social Psychology* 63 (2021): 69–128, https:// doi.org/10.1016/bs.aesp.2020.11.002.

223   *Participants were randomly prompted:* William Fleeson, "Toward a Structure-and Process-Integrated View of Personality: Traits as Density Distributions of States," *Journal of Personality and Social Psychology* 80, no. 6 (2001): 1011–27, https://doi.org/10.1037/0022-3514.80.6.1011.

223   *work has been replicated many times:* A. Timothy Church, Marcia S. Katigbak, Charles M. Ching, Hengsheng Zhang, Jiliang Shen, Rina Mazuera Arias et al., "Within-Individual Variability and Personality States: Applying Density Distribution and Situation-Behavior Approaches Across Cultures," *Journal of Research in Personality* 47, no. 6 (2013): 922–35, https://doi.org/10.1016/j .jrp.2013.09.002; William Fleeson and Mary Kate Law, "Trait Enactments as Density Distributions: The Role of Actors, Situations, and Observers in Explaining Stability and Variability," *Journal of Personality and Social Psychology* 109, no.

6 (2015): 1090–1104, https://doi.org/10.1037/a0039517; Ashley Bell Jones, Nicolas A. Brown, David G. Serfass, and Ryne A. Sherman, "Personality and Density Distributions of Behavior, Emotions, and Situations," *Journal of Research in Personality* 69, no. 1 (2017): 225–36, https://doi.org/10.1016/j.jrp.2016.10.006; and William Fleeson and Eranda Jayawickreme, "Whole Traits: Revealing the Social-Cognitive Mechanisms Constituting Personality's Central Variable," *Advances in Experimental Social Psychology* 63 (2021): 69–128, https://doi.org/10.1016/bs.aesp.2020.11.002.

224 *may provide more insights:* Kira O. McCabe and William Fleeson, "What Is Extraversion For? Integrating Trait and Motivational Perspectives and Identifying the Purpose of Extraversion," *Psychological Science* 23, no. 12 (2012): 1498–1505, https://doi.org/10.1177/0956797612444490; and Andrew J. Elliot and James W. Fryer, "The Goal Construct in Psychology," in *Handbook of Motivation Science*, ed. James Y. Shah and Wendi L. Gardner (Guilford, 2008), 235–50.

225 *Kristin Kinkel grew up:* Jennifer Gonnerman, "What Happens to a School Shooter's Sister?" *New Yorker*, December 4, 2023, 38–47, https://www.newyorker.com/magazine/2023/12/04/what-happens-to-a-school-shooters-sister.

226 *Sah D'Simone:* D'Simone, *Spiritually, We.*

226 *early impressions can be modestly accurate:* Nalini Ambady, Mark Hallahan, and Robert Rosenthal, "On Judging and Being Judged Accurately in Zero-Acquaintance Situations," *Journal of Personality and Social Psychology* 69, no. 3 (1995): 518–29, https://doi.org/10.1037/0022-3514.69.3.518; and Maurice J. Levesque and David A. Kenny, "Accuracy of Behavioral Predictions at Zero Acquaintance: A Social Relations Analysis," *Journal of Personality and Social Psychology* 65, no. 6 (1993): 1178–87, https://doi.org/10.1037/0022-3514.65.6.1178.

226 *As you become better acquainted:* David C. Funder, David C. Kolar, and Melinda C. Blackman, "Agreement Among Judges of Personality: Interpersonal Relations, Similarity, and Acquaintanceship," *Journal of Personality and Social Psychology* 69, no. 4 (1995): 656–72, https://doi.org/10.1037/0022-3514.69.4.656.

227 *the way you probably see yourself:* Christina M. Brown, Steven G. Young, and Allen R. McConnell, "Seeing Close Others as We See Ourselves: One's Own Self-Complexity Is Predicted in Perceptions of Meaningful Others," *Journal of Experimental Social Psychology* 45, no. 3 (2009): 515–23, https://doi.org/10.1016/j.jesp.2009.02.005.

227 *view members of their in-group:* George A. Quattrone and Edward E. Jones, "The Perception of Variability Within In-groups and Out-groups: Implications for the Law of Small Numbers," *Journal of Personality and Social Psychology* 38, no. 1 (1980): 141–52, https://doi.org/10.1037/0022-3514.38.1.141; and Bernadette Park and Charles M. Judd, "Measures and Models of Perceived Group Variability," *Journal of Personality and Social Psychology* 59, no. 2 (1990): 173–91, https://doi.org/10.1037/0022-3514.59.2.173.

227 *"vitally necessary for the other":* Thich Nhat Hanh, *True Love: A Practice for Awakening the Heart* (Shambhala, 2011).

227 *one hundred percent good:* Sidney Piburn, *The Dalai Lama: A Policy of Kindness* (Snow Lion Books, 1990), 96.

228 *a "self-redemption narrative":* Dan P. McAdams, *The Redemptive Self: Stories Americans Live By* (Oxford University Press, 2006); William L. Dunlop, "The Cycle of Life and Story: Redemptive Autobiographical Narratives and Prosocial Behaviors," *Current Opinion in Psychology* 43 (2022): 213–18, https://doi

.org/10.1016/j.copsyc.2021.07.019; and Dan P. McAdams, "The Redemptive Self: Generativity and the Stories Americans Live By," *Research in Human Development* 3, no. 2–3 (2006): 81–100, https://doi.org/10.1080/15427609.2006 .9683363.

228 *a trait known as* attributional complexity: Lisa A. Fast, Heather M. Reimer, and David C. Funder, "The Social Behavior and Reputation of the Attributionally Complex," *Journal of Research in Personality* 42, no. 1 (2008): 208–22, https:// doi.org/10.1016/j.jrp.2007.05.009.

229 *William James's pioneering essays:* William James, *The Writings of William James: A Comprehensive Edition* (University of Chicago Press, 1978).

230 *self-complexity can confer resilience:* Patricia W. Linville, "Self-Complexity as a Cognitive Buffer Against Stress-Related Illness and Depression," *Journal of Personality and Social Psychology* 52, no. 4 (1987): 663–76, https:// doi.org/10.1037/0022-3514.52.4.663; and Eshkol Rafaeli and Atara Hiller, "Self-Complexity," in *Handbook of Adult Resilience*, ed. John W. Reich, Alex J. Zautra, and John Stuart Hall (Guilford, 2010), 171–92.

230 *story challenges the common tendency:* Christina Caron, "What 'Inside Out 2' Teaches Us About Anxiety," *New York Times*, June 14, 2024, https://www .nytimes.com/2024/06/14/well/mind/inside-out-2-anxiety.html.

231 *this individual difference as* emotion differentiation: Caron, "What 'Inside Out 2' Teaches."

231 *describe their emotions in highly differentiated ways:* Katharine E. Smidt and Michael K. Suvak, "A Brief, but Nuanced, Review of Emotional Granularity and Emotion Differentiation Research," *Current Opinion in Psychology* 3, no. 3 (2015): 48–51, https://doi.org/10.1016/j.copsyc.2015.02.007; and Renee J. Thompson, Tabea Springsteen, and Matt Boden, "Gaining Clarity About Emotion Differentiation," *Social and Personality Psychology Compass* 15, no. 3 (2021): e12584, https://doi.org/10.1111/spc3.12584.

231 *conversations between psychotherapists and patients:* Razia Sahi, Derrick Hull, Vera Vine, and Erik Nook, "Large Natural Emotion Vocabularies Are Linked with Better Mental Health in Psychotherapeutic Conversations," symposium presentation, Society for Personality and Social Psychology convention, Denver, CO, February 2025.

231 *the complexity in their own emotions:* Richard D. Lane and Ryan Smith, "Levels of Emotional Awareness: Theory and Measurement of a Socio-Emotional Skill," *Journal of Intelligence* 9, no. 3 (2021): 42, https://doi .org/10.3390/jintelligence9030042.

233 *relatively high levels of shame:* Brandon J. Griffin, Jaclyn M. Moloney, Jeffrey D. Green, Everett L. Worthington Jr., Brianne Cork, June P. Tangney et al., "Perpetrators' Reactions to Perceived Interpersonal Wrongdoing: The Associations of Guilt and Shame with Forgiving, Punishing, and Excusing Oneself," *Self and Identity* 15, no. 6 (2016): 650–61, https://doi.org/10.1080/15298868.2016.1187669; and June P. Tangney, *Shame and Guilt* (Guilford, 2003).

233 *crucial distinction between guilt and shame:* Tangney, *Shame and Guilt.*

233 *Brené Brown encourages:* "The Top 10 Brené Brown Quotes to Live By," *Medium*, September 10, 2021, https://medium.com/@podclips/the-top-10-brené -brown-quotes-to-live-by-e84572f5e92d.

234 *Integrative Behavioral Couple Therapy (IBCT):* Donald H. Baucom, Norman B. Epstein, and Susan Stanton, "The Treatment of Relationship Distress: Theoretical Perspectives and Empirical Findings," in *The Cambridge Handbook of Personal Relationships*, ed. Anita L. Vangelisti and Daniel Perlman (Cambridge

University Press, 2018), 745–65; and Andrew Christensen, Neil S. Jacobson, and Julia C. Babcock, "Integrative Behavioral Couple Therapy," in *Clinical Handbook of Couple Therapy*, ed. Neil S. Jacobson and Alan S. Gurman (Guilford, 1995), 31–64.

235 *Internal Family Systems (IFS):* Richard C. Schwartz, *Internal Family Systems Therapy* (Guilford, 1997); and IFS Institute, "What Is Internal Family Systems?," accessed January 25, 2025, https://ifs-institute.com/.

236 *Acceptance and Commitment Therapy (ACT):* Steven C. Hayes, Kirk D. Strosahl, and Kelly G. Wilson, *Acceptance and Commitment Therapy: An Experiential Approach to Behavior Change* (Guilford, 1999); and Steven C. Hayes, Jason B. Luoma, Frank W. Bond, Akihiko Masuda, and Jason Lillis, "Acceptance and Commitment Therapy: Model, Processes and Outcomes," *Behaviour Research and Therapy* 44, no. 1 (2006): 1–25, https://doi.org/10.1016/j.brat.2005.06.006.

237 *exercise developed by ACT trainers:* Russ Harris, *ACT with Love: Using Acceptance and Commitment Therapy to Improve Relationships* (New Harbinger, 2013).

239 *what researchers mean by forgiveness:* Michael E. McCullough, Kenneth I. Pargament, and Carl E. Thoresen, eds., *Forgiveness: Theory, Research, and Practice* (Guilford, 2001).

239 *supports the benefits of forgiveness:* Michael E. McCullough, "Forgiveness: Who Does It and How Do They Do It?" *Current Directions in Psychological Science* 10, no. 6 (2001): 194–97, https://doi.org/10.1111/1467-8721.00147; and Michael E. McCullough and Charlotte vanOyen Witvliet, "The Psychology of Forgiveness," in *Handbook of Positive Psychology*, ed. C. R. Snyder and Shane J. Lopez (Oxford University Press), 446–58.

240 *Randomized controlled intervention studies:* Alex H. S. Harris, Frederic Luskin, Sonya B. Norman, Sam Standard, Jennifer Bruning, Stephanie Evans, and Carl E. Thoresen, "Effects of a Group Forgiveness Intervention of Forgiveness, Perceived Stress, and Trait-Anger," *Journal of Clinical Psychology* 62, no. 6 (2006): 715–33, https://doi.org/10.1002/jclp.20264; and Everett L. Worthington, "REACH Forgiveness: A Narrative Analysis of Group Effectiveness," *International Journal of Group Psychotherapy* 74, no. 3 (2024): 330–64, https://doi.org/10.1080/00207284.2024.2340593.

240 *secrets in marriage involves infidelity:* Frank D. Fincham and Ross W. May, "Infidelity in Romantic Relationships," *Current Opinion in Psychology* 13, no. 1 (2017): 70–74, https://doi.org/10.1016/j.copsyc.2016.03.008; Paul R. Amato and Stacy J. Rogers, "A Longitudinal Study of Marital Problems and Subsequent Divorce," *Journal of Marriage and Family* 59, no. 3 (1997): 612–24, https://doi.org/10.2307/353949; and E. S. Allen, D. C. Atkins, D. H. Baucom, D.K. Snyder, K. C. Gordon, and S. P. Glass, "Intrapersonal, Interpersonal, and Contextual Factors in Engaging in and Responding to Extramarital Involvement," *Clinical Psychology: Science and Practice* 12, no. 2 (2005): 101–30, https://doi.org/10.1093/clipsy/bpi014.

Chapter 10: Feeling Loved in Different Kinds of Relationships

245 *between a parent and child:* We use the word *parent* as shorthand for anyone who has a caregiving (or "parental") role in a child's life. We similarly use the word *child* to refer to a role more than a status (biological, adopted, step, foster, etc.).

247 *men's well-being than to women's:* Iris V. Wahring, Jeffry A. Simpson, and Paul A. M. Van Lange, "Romantic Relationships Matter More to Men than to Women," *Behavioral and Brain Sciences* (Published online by Cambridge

University Press, December 26, 2024): 1–64, https://doi.org/10.1017
/S0140525X24001365.

251   *series of escalating personal questions:* Arthur Aron, Edward Melinat, Elaine N.
Aron, Robert D. Vallone, and Renee J. Bator, "The Experimental Generation of
Interpersonal Closeness: A Procedure and Some Preliminary Findings," *Personality and Social Psychology Bulletin* 23, no. 4 (1997): 363–77, https://doi.org/10
.1177/0146167297234003.

251   *David Schnarch:* Schnarch, *Passionate Marriage.*

253   *other craves deep conversation:* Chapman, *5 Love Languages.*

253   *see each other in a new light:* Amy Muise and Sophie Goss, "Does Too Much
Closeness Dampen Desire? On the Balance of Closeness and Otherness for the
Maintenance of Sexual Desire in Romantic Relationships," *Current Directions
in Psychological Science* 33, no. 1 (2023): 68–74, https://doi.org/10.1177
/09637214231211542.

253   *Research out of the University of Toronto:* Amy Muise and Emily A. Impett, "Applying Theories of Communal Motivation to Sexuality," *Social and Personality
Psychology Compass* 10, no. 8 (2016): 455–67, https://doi.org/10.1111/spc3.12261.

253   *when one partner consistently prioritizes:* Jenna V. Hogue, Natalie O. Rosen,
Alexandra Bockaj, Emily A. Impett, and Amy Muise, "Sexual Communal Motivation in Couples Coping with Low Sexual Interest/Arousal: Associations with
Sexual Well-Being and Sexual Goals," *PLOS ONE* 14, no. 7 (2019): e0219768,
https://doi.org/10.1371/journal.pone.0219768.

255   *with the right support:* Geoffrey L. Cohen, Julio Garcia, and J. Parker Goyer,
"Turning Point: Targeted, Tailored, and Timely Psychological Intervention,"
in *Handbook of Competence and Motivation,* 2nd ed., ed. Andrew Elliot, Carol
Dweck, and David Yeager (Guilford, 2017), 657–86.

255   *healthiest when they feel comfortable:* Judith G. Smetana, Aaron Metzer,
Denise C. Gettman, and Nicole Campione-Barr, "Disclosure and Secrecy in
Adolescent–Parent Relationships," *Child Development* 77, no. 1 (2006): 201–17,
https://doi.org/10.1111/j.1467-8624.2006.00865.x.

257   *psychologist Haim Ginott:* Haim Ginott, *Between Parent and Child: The Bestselling Classic That Revolutionized Parent-Child Communication* (Three Rivers
Press, 2003).

257   *parenting and couples' communication:* John Gottman and Nan Silver, *The Seven
Principles for Making Marriage Work: A Practical Guide from the Country's Foremost Relationship Expert* (Harmony, 1999).

258   *days when their parents expressed warmth:* John K. Coffey, Mengyao Xia, and
Gregory M. Fosco, "When Do Adolescents Feel Loved? A Daily Within-Person
Study of Parent–Adolescent Relations," *Emotion* 22, no. 5 (2022): 861–73,
https://doi.org/10.1037/emo0000767.

258   *how loved they felt also mattered:* Mengyao Xia, John K. Coffey, and Gregory
M. Fosco, "Daily Dynamics of Feeling Loved by Parents and Their Prospective
Implications for Adolescent Flourishing," *Developmental Science* 27 (2024):
e13495, https://doi.org/10.1111/desc.13495.

258   *friends, as well, can break your heart:* Jennifer Senior, "It's Your Friends Who
Break Your Heart," *Atlantic,* February 9, 2022, https://www.theatlantic.com
/magazine/archive/2022/03/why-we-lose-friends-aging-happiness/621305/.

261   *Robert Putnam:* Robert Putnam, *Bowling Alone: The Collapse and Revival of
American Community* (Touchstone Books, 2001).

262   *commuters on trains and public buses:* Nicholas Epley and Juliana Schroeder,
"Mistakenly Seeking Solitude. *Journal of Experimental Psychology: General* 143,
no. 5 (2014): 1980–99, https://doi.org/10.1037/a0037323.

262 *assigned to chat with their baristas:* Gillian M. Sandstrom and Elizabeth W. Dunn, "Social Interactions and Well-Being: The Surprising Power of Weak Ties," *Personality and Social Psychology Bulletin* 40, no. 7 (2014): 910–22, https://doi.org/10.1177/0146167214529799.

262 *encouraged to converse with their drivers:* Güven Günaydin, Veysel Kanten, and Elif N. Yavuz, "Minimal Social Interactions with Strangers Predict Greater Subjective Well-Being," *Journal of Happiness Studies* 22 (2021): 1839–53, https://doi.org/10.1007/s10902-020-00298-6.

262 *kindness and giving simple compliments:* Elizabeth W. Dunn, Lara B. Aknin, and Michael I. Norton, "Spending Money on Others Promotes Happiness," *Science* 319, no. 5870 (2008): 1687–88, https://doi.org/10.1126/science.1150952; Lara B. Aknin, Christopher P. Barrington-Leigh, Elizabeth W. Dunn, John F. Helliwell, Robert Biswas-Diener, Imed Haddad, and Michael I. Norton, "Does Spending Money on Others Promote Happiness? A Registered Replication Report," *Journal of Personality and Social Psychology* 119, no. 2 (2020): e15-e26, https://doi.org/10.1037/pspa0000191; Amit Kumar and Nicholas Epley, "A Little Good Goes an Unexpectedly Long Way: Underestimating the Positive Impact of Kindness on Recipients," *Journal of Experimental Psychology: General* 151, no. 9 (2022): 2130–45, https://doi.org/10.1037/xge0001271; Erica J. Boothby and Vanessa K. Bohns, "Why a Simple Act of Kindness Is Not as Simple as It Seems: Underestimating the Positive Impact of Our Compliments on Others," *Personality and Social Psychology Bulletin* 47, no. 5 (2021): 826–40, https://doi.org/10.1177/0146167220949003; and Xuan Zhao and Nicholas Epley, "Insufficiently Complimentary? Underestimating the Positive Impact of Compliments Creates a Barrier to Expressing Them," *Journal of Personality and Social Psychology* 121, no. 2 (2021): 239–56, https://doi.org/10.1037/pspa0000277.

265 *felt "love" during the previous hour:* Saurabh Bhargava, "Experienced Love: An Empirical Account," *Psychological Science* 35, no. 1 (2024): 7–20, https://doi.org/10.1177/09567976231211267.

266 *asking follow-up questions:* Karen Huang, Michael Yeomans, Alison Wood Brooks, Julia Minson, and Francesca Gino, "It Doesn't Hurt to Ask: Question-Asking Increases Liking," *Journal of Personality and Social Psychology* 113, no. 3 (2017): 430–52, https://doi.org/10.1037/pspi0000097.

269 *lower in status and power:* Sanaz Talaifar, Michael D. Buhrmester, and William B. Swann, "Asymmetries in Mutual Understanding: People with Low Status, Power, and Self-Esteem Understand Better Than They Are Understood," *Perspectives on Psychological Science* 15, no. 6 (2020): 1345–58, https://doi.org/10.1177/1745691620958003.

269 *high-quality listening predicts greater job satisfaction:* Kluger and Itzchakov, "Power of Listening at Work," 121–46.

269 *speakers who conversed with good listeners:* Guy Itzchakov, Dotan R. Castro, and Avraham N. Kluger, "If You Want People to Listen to You, Tell a Story," *International Journal of Listening* 29, no. 3 (2015): 120–33, https://doi.org/10.1080/10904018.2015.1037445.

270 *their principals as good listeners:* Roy Rave, Guy Itzchakov, Netta Weinstein, and Harry T. Reis. "How to Get Through Hard Times: Principals' Listening Buffers Teachers' Stress on Turnover Intention and Promotes Organizational Citizenship Behavior," *Current Psychology* 42, no. 28 (2023): 24233–48, https://doi.org/10.1007/s12144-021-02367-2.

270 *and less burned out:* Kluger and Itzchakov, "Power of Listening at Work," 121–46.

270 *doctors as attentive and curious:* Epstein and Beach, "'I Don't Need Your Pills,'" 101685.

270 *One such technique:* Niels Van Quaquebeke and Will Felps, "Respectful Inquiry: A Motivational Account of Leading Through Asking Questions and Listening," *Academy of Management Review* 43, no. 1 (2018): 5–27, https://doi .org/10.5465/amr.2014.0537.

270 *Another approach:* Michael Yeomans, Julia Minson, Hanne Collins, Frances Chen, and Francesca Gino, "Conversational Receptiveness: Improving Engagement with Opposing Views," *Organizational Behavior and Human Decision Processes* 160 (2020): 131–48, https://doi.org/10.1016/j.obhdp.2020.03.005.

270 *evidence-based techniques are closely aligned:* Guy Itzchakov, Netta Weinstein, Dvori Saluk, and Moty Amar, "Connection Heals Wounds: Feeling Listened to Reduces Speakers' Loneliness Following a Social Rejection Disclosure," *Personality and Social Psychology Bulletin* 49, no. 8 (2023): 1273–94, https://doi.org /10.1177/01461672221100369.

271 *Researchers at the Human Flourishing Program:* Dorota Weziak-Bialowolska, Matthew T. Lee, Richard G. Cowden, Piotr Bialowolski, Ying Chen, Tyler J. VanderWeele, and Eileen McNeely, "Psychological Caring Climate at Work, Mental Health, Well-Being, and Work-Related Outcomes: Evidence from a Longitudinal Study and Health Insurance Data," *Social Science & Medicine* 323 (2023): 115841, https://doi.org/10.1016/j.socscimed.2023.115841.

271 *when they experience good listening:* Avraham N. Kluger, Thomas E. Malloy, Sarit Pery, Guy Itzchakov, Dotan R. Castro, Liora Lipetz et al., "Dyadic Listening in Teams: Social Relations Model," *Applied Psychology* 70 (2021): 1045–99, https://doi.org/10.1111/apps.12263.

272 *everyone we choose to love:* bell hooks, *All About Love: New Visions* (William Morrow, 2000).

272 *proportion as high as 35 percent:* Kim Parker and Renee Stepler, "The Share of Americans Living Without a Partner Has Increased, Especially Among Young Adults," *Pew Research Center*, October 11, 2017, https://www.pewresearch.org /short-reads/2017/10/11/the-share-of-americans-living-without-a-partner-has -increased-especially-among-young-adults/.

272 *twice as likely to be sexually inactive:* Jessica Leahy, "Inside the Rise of 'Relationship Virgins,'" *Courier-Mail*, November 11, 2018, https://www.courier mail.com.au/lifestyle/relationships/inside-the-rise-of-relationship-virgins/news -story/571af481b450062ba2a9ed73e5c5ecea; and Kate Julian, "Why Are Young People Having So Little Sex? Despite the Easing of Taboos and the Rise of Hookup Apps, Americans Are in the Midst of a Sex Recession," *Atlantic*, December 2018, https://www.theatlantic.com/magazine/archive/2018/12/the -sex-recession/573949/.

272 *55 percent of high school seniors:* Jean M. Twenge, *iGen: Why Today's Super-Connected Kids Are Growing Up Less Rebellious, More Tolerant, Less Happy—and Completely Unprepared for Adulthood* (Atria Books, 2017).

272 *friendship, rather than romance, on-screen:* Ryan Faughnder, "A Lonely Generation Craves Friendship on Screen," *Los Angeles Times*, October 19, 2023.

272 *Millennials and Gen Zers are having fewer children:* US Census Bureau, *Aging United States Population and Fewer Children in 2020*, May 25, 2023, https:// www.census.gov/library/stories/2023/05/aging-united-states-population-fewer -children-in-2020.html.

272 *an average of 1.6 per couple:* Gideon Lewis-Kraus, "The End of Children," *New Yorker*, February 24, 2025, https://www.newyorker.com/magazine/2025/03/03 /the-population-implosion.

273 *you can be single:* Yuthika U. Girme, Yoobin Park, and Geoff MacDonald,

"Coping or Thriving? Reviewing Intrapersonal, Interpersonal, and Societal Factors Associated with Well-Being in Singlehood from a Within-Group Perspective," *Perspectives on Psychological Science* 18, no. 5 (2023): 1097–1120, https://doi.org/10.1177/17456916221136119.

Chapter 11: What If One Size Doesn't Fit All?
Diagnosing the Personal Qualities That Make Feeling Loved Easier or Harder

276 *openness to experience:* Christopher J. Soto and Oliver P. John, "The Next Big Five Inventory (BFI-2): Developing and Assessing a Hierarchical Model with 15 Facets to Enhance Bandwidth, Fidelity, and Predictive Power," *Journal of Personality and Social Psychology* 113, no. 1 (2017): 117–43, https://doi.org/10.1037/pspp0000096.pubmed.ncbi.nlm.nih.gov.

276 *share more about themselves:* Barbara Caci, Maurizio Cardaci, and Silvana Miceli, "Development and Maintenance of Self-Disclosure on Facebook: The Role of Personality Traits," *SAGE Open* 9, no. 2 (2019): 1–14, https://doi.org/10.1177/2158244019856948.

276 *difficulties in reading nonverbal cues:* Michael Alexander Pelzl, Gabrielle Travers-Podmaniczky, Carolin Brück, Heike Jacob, Jonatan Hoffmann, Anne Martinelli et al., "Reduced Impact of Nonverbal Cues During Integration of Verbal and Nonverbal Emotional Information in Adults with High-Functioning Autism," *Frontiers in Psychiatry* 13 (2023), https://doi.org/10.3389/fpsyt.2022.1069028.

277 *intensely curious about particular topics:* Mirko Uljarević, Gail A. Alvares, Morgan Steele, Jaelyn Edwards, Thomas W. Frazier, Antonio Y. Hardan, and Andrew Jo Whitehouse, "Toward Better Characterization of Restricted and Unusual Interests in Youth with Autism," *Autism* 26, no. 5 (2022): 12961304, https://doi.org/10.1177/13623613211056720.

278 *challenges in theory of mind:* Simon Baron-Cohen, "The Autistic Child's Theory of Mind: A Case of Specific Developmental Delay," *Journal of Child Psychology and Psychiatry* 30 (1989): 28597, https://doi.org/10.1111/j.1469-7610.1989.tb00241.x; and Atsushi Senju, Victoria Southgate, Sarah White, and Uta Frith, "Mindblind Eyes: An Absence of Spontaneous Theory of Mind in Asperger Syndrome," *Science* 325 (2009): 88385, https://doi.org/10.1126/science.1176170.

278 *insecure attachment styles:* Mario Mikulincer and Phillip R. Shaver, *Attachment in Adulthood: Structure, Dynamics, and Change* (Guilford, 2010); and Mario Mikulincer and Phillip R. Shaver, *Attachment Theory Expanded: Security Dynamics in Individuals, Dyads, Groups, and Societies* (Guilford, 2023).

279 *improve the most over time:* William J. Chopik, Rebekka Weidmann, and Jeewon Oh, "Attachment Security and How to Get It," *Social and Personality Psychology Compass* 18, no. 1 (2024): e12808, https://doi.org/10.1111/spc3.12808.

279 *"Some of us live with the fear":* This quote has been attributed to Esther Perel.

280 *anxious attachment may overdisclose:* Cindy Hazan and Phillip R. Shaver, "Romantic Love Conceptualized as an Attachment Process," *Journal of Personality and Social Psychology* 52, no. 3 (1987): 511–24, https://doi.org/10.1037/0022-3514.52.3.511; Kim Bartholomew and Leonard M. Horowitz, "Attachment Styles Among Young Adults: A Test of a Four-Category Model," *Journal of Personality and Social Psychology* 61, no. 2 (1991): 226–44, https://doi.org/10.1037/0022-3514.61.2.226; Jeffry A. Simpson and William S. Rholes, "Adult Attachment, Stress, and Romantic Relationships," *Current Opinion in Psychology* 13 (2017): 19–24, https://doi.org/10.1016/j.copsyc.2016.04.006; and Nancy L.

Collins and Brooke C. Feeney, "An Attachment Theory Perspective on Closeness and Intimacy," in *Handbook of Closeness and Intimacy*, ed. Debra J. Mashek and Arthur P. Aron (Psychology Press, 2004), 163–87.

280 *don't challenge their autonomy:* Ximena B. Arriaga, Madoka Kumashiro, Jeffry A. Simpson, and Nickola C. Overall, "Revising Working Models Across Time: Relationship Situations That Enhance Attachment Security," *Personality and Social Psychology Review* 22, no. 1 (2018): 71–96, https://doi.org/10.1177/1088868317705257.

280 *signs of disinterest:* Geraldine Downey, Antonio L. Freitas, Benjamin Michaelis, and Hala Khouri. "The Self-Fulfilling Prophecy in Close Relationships: Rejection Sensitivity and Rejection by Romantic Partners," *Journal of Personality and Social Psychology* 75, no. 2 (1998): 545–560, https://doi.org/10.1037/0022-3514.75.2.545.

282 *narcissism—which psychologists define:* American Psychiatric Association, *Diagnostic and Statistical Manual of Mental Disorders*, 5th ed. (American Psychiatric Association, 2013).

283 *listeners rather than speakers:* Hazel R. Markus and Shinobu Kitayama, "Culture and the Self: Implications for Cognition, Emotion, and Motivation," *Psychological Review* 98, no. 2 (1991): 224–53, https://doi.org/10.1037/0033-295X.98.2.224.

283 *everyday interactions than do Westerners:* Joanna Schug, Masaki Yuki, and William Maddux, "Relational Mobility Explains Between- and Within-Culture Differences in Self-Disclosure to Close Friends," *Psychological Science* 21, no. 10 (2010): 1471–77, https://doi.org/10.1177/0956797610382786.

283 *prioritize active verbal feedback:* Sheida White, "Backchannels Across Cultures: A Study of Americans and Japanese," *Language in Society* 18, no. 1 (1989): 59–76, https://doi.org/10.1017/S0047404500013270.

284 *attunement to others' emotional states:* Harry C. Triandis, *Individualism and Collectivism* (Westview, 1995); and Hazel R. Markus and Shinobu Kitayama, "Culture and the Self: Implications for Cognition, Emotion, and Motivation," *Psychological Review* 98, no. 2 (1991): 224–53, https://doi.org/10.1037/0033-295X.98.2.224.

285 *in her groundbreaking book:* Tannen, *You Just Don't Understand.*

285 *disclose personal details of their lives:* Kathryn Dindia and Mike Allen, "Sex Differences in Self-Disclosure: A Meta-Analysis," *Psychological Bulletin* 112, no. 1 (1992): 106–24, https://doi.org/10.1037/0033-2909.112.1.106; Bernard Rimé, Batja Mesquita, Pierre Philippot, and Stéphanie Boca, "Beyond the Emotional Event: Six Studies on the Social Sharing of Emotion," *Cognition & Emotion* 5, no. 5–6 (1991): 435–65, https://doi.org/10.1080/02699939108411052; Charles T. Hill and Donald E. Stull, "Gender and Self-Disclosure: Strategies for Exploring the Issues," in *Self-Disclosure: Theory, Research, and Therapy*, ed. Valerian J. Derlega and John H. Berg (Plenum, 1987), 81–100; and Elizabeth J. Aries and Fern L. Johnson, "Close Friendship in Adulthood: Conversational Content Between Same-Sex Friends," *Sex Roles* 9 (1983): 1183–96, https://doi.org/10.1007/BF00303101.

286 *higher risk of loneliness and isolation:* Frank J. Infurna, Nutifafa E. Y. Dey, Kevin J. Grimm, Tita Gonzalez Avilés, Denis Gerstorf, and Margie E. Lachman, "Loneliness in Midlife: Historical Increases and Elevated Levels in the United States Compared with Europe," *American Psychologist* (APA PsycNet advance online publication, 2024) https://doi.org/10.1037/amp0001322.

286 *both verbal* and *nonverbal affirmations:* Judith A. Hall, "Gender Effects in De-

coding Nonverbal Cues," *Psychological Bulletin* 85, no. 4 (1978): 845–57, https://
doi.org/10.1037/0033-2909.85.4.845.

286 *two men to display physical synchrony:* Ken Fujiwara, Masanori Kimura, and
Ikuo Daibo, "Gender Differences in Synchrony: Females in Sync During Un-
structured Dyadic Conversation," *European Journal of Social Psychology* 49, no. 5
(2019): 1042–54, https://doi.org/10.1002/ejsp.2587.

287 *When men interact with women:* Kathryn Dindia and Mike Allen, "Sex Differences in Self-Disclosure: A Meta-Analysis," *Psychological Bulletin* 112, no. 1
(1992): 106–24, https://doi.org/10.1037/0033-2909.112.1.106; and Harry T.
Reis, Marilyn Senchak, and Beth Solomon, "Sex Differences in the Intimacy of
Social Interaction: Further Examination of Potential Explanations," *Journal of
Personality and Social Psychology* 48, no. 5 (1985): 1204–17, https://doi.org
/10.1037/0022-3514.48.5.1204.

287 *Harry's research has repeatedly shown:* Harry T. Reis, "Gender Effects in Social
Participation: Intimacy, Loneliness, and the Conduct of Social Interaction," in
The Emerging Field of Personal Relationships, ed. Robin Gilmour and Steve Duck
(Erlbaum, 1986), 91–105.

287 *emotional well-being depends more:* Wahring, Simpson, and Van Lange, "Romantic Relationships Matter More to Men than to Women," 1–64.

287 *mindset easier to use than do older adults:* Nandita Vijayakumar and Jennifer H. Pfeifer, "Self-Disclosure During Adolescence: Exploring the Means,
Targets, and Types of Personal Exchanges," *Current Opinion in Psychology* 31
(2020): 135–40, https://doi.org/10.1016/j.copsyc.2019.08.005; Sidney M. Jourard, "Age Trends in Self-Disclosure," *Merrill-Palmer Quarterly of Behavior and
Development* 7, no. 3 (1961): 191–97, https://www.jstor.org/stable/23082726;
and Michel Walrave, Ini Vanwesenbeeck, and Wannes Heirman, "Connecting
and Protecting? Comparing Predictors of Self-Disclosure and Privacy Settings
Use Between Adolescents and Adults," *Cyberpsychology: Journal of Psychosocial
Research on Cyberspace* 6, no. 1 (2012): Article 3, https://doi.org/10.5817
/CP2012-1-3.

288 *show greater curiosity about others:* Michiko Sakaki, Ayano Yagi, and Kou Murayama, "Curiosity in Old Age: A Possible Key to Achieving Adaptive Aging,"
Neuroscience & Biobehavioral Reviews 88 (2018): 106–16, https://doi.org/10.1016
/j.neubiorev.2018.03.007.

288 *express interest in diverse perspectives:* Robert W. Blum, Joanna Lai, Michelle
Martinez, and Cassandra Jessee, "Adolescent Connectedness: Cornerstone for
Health and Wellbeing," *BMJ* 379 (2022): e069213, https://doi.org/10.1136/bmj
-2021-069213; Sevgi Bayram Özdemir, Metin Özdemir, and Katja Boersma,
"How Does Adolescents' Openness to Diversity Change Over Time? The Role of
Majority-Minority Friendship, Friends' Views, and Classroom Social Context,"
Journal of Youth and Adolescence 50, no. 1 (2021): 75–88, https://doi.org/10.1007
/s10964-020-01329-4; Paul T. Costa Jr., Jeffrey H. Herbst, Robert R. McCrae,
and Ilene C. Siegler, "Personality at Midlife: Stability, Intrinsic Maturation, and
Response to Life Events," *Assessment* 7, no. 4 (2000): 365–78, https://doi.org
/10.1177/107319110000700405; and Laura L. Carstensen, Derek M. Isaacowitz,
and Susan T. Charles, "Taking Time Seriously: A Theory of Socioemotional Selectivity," *American Psychologist* 54, no. 3 (1999): 165–81, https://doi.org/10.1037
/0003-066X.54.3.165.

288 *According to Socioemotional Selectivity theory:* Carstensen et al., "Taking Time
Seriously," 165–81.

288 *diverse identities, beliefs, and lifestyles:* Jean M. Twenge, Nathan T. Carter, and

W. Keith Campbell, "Time Period, Generational, and Age Differences in Tolerance for Controversial Beliefs and Lifestyles in the United States, 1972–2012,"
Social Forces 94, no. 1 (2015): 379–99, https://doi.org/10.1093/sf/sov050.
288 *nontraditional relationship structures:* Twenge, *iGen.*
289 *reinforcing the Multiplicity mindset:* Twenge et al., "Time Period," 379–99.

Chapter 12: Can You Feel Loved by an AI Chatbot? How About a Throuple? And Other Questions for the New Age

292 *"Some Random Person":* Some Random Person, "Replika: My Whirlwind
Relationship with My Imaginary Friend and the People Who Broke Her,"
Medium, February 14, 2023, https://medium.com/@mythinmask/replika-my
-whirlwind-relationship-with-my-imaginary-friend-and-the-people-who-broke
-her-dd37b5198c53.
292 *Ayrin created an AI companion on ChatGPT:* Kashmir Hill, "She Is in Love
with ChatGPT," *New York Times*, January 17, 2025, https://www.nytimes.
com/2025/01/15/technology/ai-chatgpt-boyfriend-companion.html.
293 *Joseph Weizenbaum:* David M. Berry and Mark C. Marino, "Reading ELIZA:
Critical Code Studies in Action," *Electronic Book Review*, November 3, 2024,
https://electronicbookreview.com/essay/reading-eliza-critical-code-studies-in
-action/.
293 *active users monthly:* Emma Hinchliffe and Joey Abrams, "AI Chatbots Are Ste-
reotyped as for Lonely Men. But Replika's CEO Says the Products Are 'Built by
Women,'" *Fortune*, June 17, 2024, https://fortune.com/2024/06/17/ai-chatbots
-dating-men-women-replika-ceo-eugenia-kuyda/.
294 *at the University of Southern California:* Yidan Yin, Nan Jia, and Cheryl
Wakslak, "AI Can Help People Feel Heard, but an AI Label Diminishes This
Impact," *Proceedings of the National Academy of Sciences* 121, no. 14 (2024):
e2319112121, https://doi.org/10.1073/pnas.2319112121.
294 *more compassionate and emotionally supportive:* Dariya Ovsyannikova, Victoria
Oldemburgo de Mello, and Michael Inzlicht, "Third-Party Evaluators Perceived
AI as More Compassionate Than Expert Humans," *Nature Communications
Psychology* 3, no. 4 (2025), https://doi.org/10.1038/s44271-024-00182-6.
294 *interacting with voice-based AI chatbots:* Cathy Mengying Fang, Auren R. Liu,
Valdemar Danry, Eunhae Lee, Samantha W. T. Chan, Pat Pataranutaporn et al.,
"How AI and Human Behaviors Shape Psychosocial Effects of Chatbot Use: A
Longitudinal Randomized Controlled Study" (MIT Media Lab preprint, 2025),
https://arxiv.org/html/2503.17473v1.
294 *in real-life marriage:* Jia-Lin Zhao, Ru Jia, John Shields, Yu-Jia Wu, and
Wei-Wei Huang, "Romantic Relationships with Virtual Agents and People's
Marriage Intention in Real Life: An Exploration of the Mediation Mechanisms,"
Archives of Sexual Behavior (2025), https://doi.org/10.1007/s10508-025-03143-0.
294 *relies on more than just words:* Molly G. Smith, Thomas Bradbury, and Benjamin R. Karney, "Can Generative AI Chatbots Emulate Human Connection?
A Relationship Science Perspective" (PsyArXiv Preprints, April 2025), https://
doi.org/10.31234/osf.io/vyfa4_v2; and Shir Genzer, Yonat Rum, Ulrike M.
Kramer, and Anat Perry, "I See You: Seeing One's Partners During Emotional
Communication Enhances the Affective Experience and Promotes Prosocial
Behavior," (PsyArXiv Preprints, November 11, 2024), https://osf.io/preprints
/psyarxiv/4j8w3_v1.
294 *neural synchrony between conversation partners:* Thalia Wheatley, Olivia Kang,
Carolyn Parkinson, and Christine E. Looser, "From Mind Perception to Mental

Connection: Synchrony as a Mechanism for Social Understanding," *Social and Personality Psychology Compass* 6, no. 8 (2012): 589–606, https://doi.org/10.1111 /j.1751-9004.2012.00450.x.

295 *an inevitable mismatch:* David A. Sbarra, Julia L. Briskin, and Richard B. Slatcher, "Smartphones and Close Relationships: The Case for an Evolutionary Mismatch," *Perspectives on Psychological Science* 14, no. 4 (2019): 596–618, https://doi.org/10.1177/1745691619826535.

295 *to be curious or empathic:* Anat Perry, "AI Will Never Convey the Essence of Human Empathy," *Nature Human Behaviour* 7 (2023): 1808–09, https://doi .org/10.1038/s41562-023-01675-w.

295 *communal relationships:* Clark and Aragón, "Communal (and Other) Relationships," 255–80.

295 *lifting the other "person" up:* Smith et al., "Can Generative AI Chatbots Emulate Authentic Human Connection?"

295 *generally prefer to interact with humans:* Dunigan Folk, Jessica Yu, and Elizabeth Dunn, "Can Chatbots Ever Provide More Social Connection Than Humans?" *Collabra: Psychology* 10, no. 1 (2024): 117083, https://doi.org/10.1525/ collabra.117083.

295 *and never disappoint:* Derek Thompson, "The Anti-Social Century," *Atlantic* 335, no. 2 (2025): 26–38, https://cdn.theatlantic.com/media/magazine/pdfs /202502.pdf.

296 *strengthen feelings of love and connection:* Philip Brickman, *Commitment, Conflict, and Caring* (Prentice-Hall, 1987); and Sandra L. Murray and John G. Holmes, "Seeing Virtues in Faults: Negativity and the Transformation of Interpersonal Narratives in Close Relationships," *Journal of Personality and Social Psychology* 65, no. 4 (1993): 707–22, https://doi.org/10.1037/0022-3514.65.4.707.

296 *A recent report charged:* Mark Zao-Sanders, "How People Are Really Using Generative AI Now," *Harvard Business Review*, April 9, 2025, https://hbr.org /2025/04/how-people-are-really-using-gen-ai-in-2025.

297 *the classic 1982 sci-fi film:* *Blade Runner*, directed by Ridley Scott (Warner Brothers, 1982), DVD.

297 *Turing test:* The *Stanford Encyclopedia of Philosophy*, "The Turing Test," by Graham Oppy and David Dowe, ed. Edward N. Zalta, last substantive revision October 4, 2021, https://plato.stanford.edu/archives/win2021/entries/turing -test/.

298 *"ethical (consensual) nonmonogamy (ENM)":* These types of relationships are also called "consensually nonmonogamous" or "open"; Daniel Cardoso, Patricia M. Pascoal, and Francisco Hertel Maiochi, "Defining Polyamory: A Thematic Analysis of Lay People's Definitions," *Archives of Sexual Behavior* 50 (2021): 1239–52, https://doi.org/10.1007/s10508-021-02002-y.

299 *ENM community often gets:* For a deep dive into ENM/polyamory, see Jessica Fern, *Polysecure: Attachment, Trauma, and Consensual Nonmonogamy* (Thorntree, 2020); and Dossie Easton and Janet W. Hardy, *The Ethical Slut: A Practical Guide to Polyamory, Open Relationships, and Other Adventures*, 3rd ed. (Ten Speed Press, 2017).

299 *jealousy over a partner's attention:* Amy C. Moors, Jennifer L. Matsick, Amy Ziegler, Justin D. Rubin, and Terri D. Conley, "Jealousy in Consensual Non-Monogamous and Monogamous Romantic Relationships," *Personal Relationships* 28, no. 1 (2021): 131–53, https://doi.org/10.1111/pere.12364.

299 *more similarities than people often assume:* Terri D. Conley, Jessica L. Matsick, Amy C. Moors, and Ali Ziegler, "Investigation of Consensually Nonmonogamous Relationships: Theories, Methods, and New Directions," *Perspectives on*

Psychological Science 12, no. 2 (2017): 205–32, https://doi.org/10.1177 /1745691616667925; Óscar Lecuona, Mar Suero, Tobias Wingen, and Sara de Rivas, "Does 'Open' Rhyme with 'Special'? Comparing Personality, Sexual Satisfaction, Dominance, and Jealousy of Monogamous and Non-Monogamous Practitioners," *Archives of Sexual Behavior* 50, no. 4 (2021): 1537–49, https:// doi.org/10.1007/s10508-020-01865-x; Melissa E. Mitchell, Kim Bartholomew, and Rebecca J. Cobb, "Need Fulfillment in Polyamorous Relationships," *Journal of Sex Research* 51, no. 3 (2014): 329–39, https://doi.org/10.1080/00224499.2 012.742998; and Ryan Scoats and Christine Campbell, "What Do We Know about Consensual Non-Monogamy?" *Current Opinion in Psychology* 48 (2022): 101468, https://doi.org/10.1016/j.copsyc.2022.101468.

300 *studies using data from the US Census:* M. L. Haupert, Amanda N. Gesselman, Amy C. Moors, Helen E. Fisher, and Justin R. Garcia, "Prevalence of Experiences with Consensual Nonmonogamous Relationships: Findings from Two National Samples of Single Americans," *Journal of Sex & Marital Therapy* 42, no. 5 (2016): 424–40, https://doi.org/10.1080/0092623X.2016.1178675.

300 *in a 2023 YouGov poll:* YouGov, "Monogamy in Relationships," February 1–6, 2023, https://d3nkl3psvxxpe9.cloudfront.net/documents/Monogamy_Non Monogamy_Relationships_Toplines_crosstabs.pdf.

300 *widely misunderstood and often stigmatized:* Amy C. Moors, "Five Misconceptions About Consensually Nonmonogamous Relationships," *Current Directions in Psychological Science* 32, no. 5 (2023): 355–61, https://doi.org/10.1177 /09637214231166853; and Katarzyna Grunt-Mejer and Christine Campbell, "Around Consensual Nonmonogamies: Assessing Attitudes Toward Nonexclusive Relationships," *Journal of Sex Research* 53, no. 1 (2016): 45–53, https://doi .org/10.1080/00224499.2015.1010193.

300 *they may even fare better:* Alicia N. Rubel and Anthony F. Bogaert, "Consensual Nonmonogamy: Psychological Well-Being and Relationship Quality Correlates," *Journal of Sex Research* 52, no. 9 (2015): 961–82, https://doi.org/10.1080 /00224499.2014.942722; Conley et al., "Investigation of Consensually Nonmonogamous Relationships," 205–32; Rhonda N. Balzarini, Christoffer Dharma, Taylor Kohut, Lorne Campbell, Justin J. Lehmiller, Jennifer J. Harman, and Bjarne M. Holmes, "Comparing Relationship Quality Across Different Types of Romantic Partners in Polyamorous and Monogamous Relationships," *Archives of Sexual Behavior* 48, no. 6 (2019): 1749–67, https://doi.org/10.1007/s10508-019 -1416-7; Justin K. Mogilski, Stacy L. Memering, Lisa L. M. Welling, and Todd K. Shackelford, "Monogamy Versus Consensual Non-Monogamy: Alternative Approaches to Pursuing a Strategically Pluralistic Mating Strategy," *Archives of Sexual Behavior* 46, no. 2 (2017): 407–417, https://doi.org/10.1007/s10508-015 -0658-2; Amy C. Moors, William S. Ryan, and William J. Chopik, "Multiple Loves: The Effects of Attachment with Multiple Concurrent Romantic Partners on Relational Functioning," *Personality and Individual Differences* 147 (2019): 102–10, https://doi.org/10.1016/j.paid.2019.04.023; and Forrest Hagen, Dev Crasta, and Ronald D. Rogge, "Delineating the Boundaries Between Nonmonogamy and Infidelity: Bringing Consent Back into Definitions of Consensual Nonmonogamy with Latent Profile Analysis," *Journal of Sex Research* 57, no. 4 (2019): 443–57, https://doi.org/10.1080/00224499.2019.1669133.

301 *call for complex communication skills:* Conley et al., "Investigation of Consensually Nonmonogamous Relationships," 205–32.

301 *primary than with secondary partners:* Rhonda N. Balzarini, Lorne Campbell, Taylor Kohut, Bjarne M. Holmes, Justin J. Lehmiller, Jennifer J. Harman, and Nicole Atkins, "Perceptions of Primary and Secondary Relationships in Poly-

amory," *PLOS ONE* 12, no. 5 (2017): e0177841, https://doi.org/10.1371/journal
.pone.0177841.

303 *reinforcing emotional bonds:* Klara Austeja Buczel, Paulina D. Szyszka, and
Izu Mara, "Exploring Compersion: A Study on Polish Consensually Non-
Monogamous Individuals and Adaptation of the COMPERSe Questionnaire,"
Archives of Sexual Behavior 53, no. 8 (2024): 3285–3307, https://doi.org/10.1007
/s10508-024-02930-5.

304 *nicknamed the "love drug":* Brian D. Earp and Julian Savulescu, *Love Drugs:
The Chemical Future of Relationships* (Redwood, 2020); Alana R. Pentney, "An
Exploration of the History and Controversies Surrounding MDMA and MDA,"
Journal of Psychoactive Drugs 33, no. 3 (2001): 213–21, https://doi.org/10.1080
/02791072.2001.10400568; and Sonja Lyubomirsky, "Toward a New Science of
Psychedelic Social Psychology: The Effects of MDMA (Ecstasy) on Social Con-
nection," *Perspectives on Psychological Science* 17, no. 5 (2022): 1234–57, https://
doi.org/10.1177/17456916211055369.

304 *a renaissance of psychedelic science:* Rachel Nuwer, *I Feel Love: MDMA and the
Quest for Connection in a Fractured World* (Bloomsbury, 2023).

305 *after just a single dose of MDMA:* Annie Regan, Seth Margolis, Harriet de
Wit, and Sonja Lyubomirsky, "Does ±3,4 Methylenedioxymethamphetamine
(Ecstasy) Induce Subjective Feelings of Social Connection in Humans? A
Multilevel Meta-Analysis," *PLOS ONE* 16, no. 10 (2021): e0258849, https://
doi.org/10.1371/journal.pone.0258849; Hanna Molla, Royce Lee, Sonja
Lyubomirsky, and Harriet de Wit, "Drug-Induced Social Connection: Both
MDMA and Methamphetamine Increase Feelings of Connectedness During
Controlled Dyadic Conversations," *Scientific Reports* 13, no. 1 (2023): 15846,
https://doi.org/10.1038/s41598-023-43156-0; Timon Elmer, Tanya K. Vannoy,
Erich Studerus, and Sonja Lyubomirsky. "Subjective Long-Term Emotional and
Social Effects of Recreational MDMA Use: The Role of Setting and Intentions,"
Scientific Reports 14, no. 1 (2024): 3434, https://doi.org/10.1038/s41598-024
-51355-6; and June McDaniel, "'Strengthening the Moral Compass': The Effects
of MDMA ('Ecstasy') Therapy on Moral and Spiritual Development," *Pastoral
Psychology* 66, no. 6 (2017): 721–41, https://doi.org/10.1007/s11089-017-0789-6.

305 *In his trailblazing book:* Michael Pollan, *How to Change Your Mind: What the
New Science of Psychedelics Teaches Us About Consciousness, Dying, Addiction,
Depression, and Transcendence* (Penguin, 2018), 237.

305 *A Benedictine monk echoed the same idea:* Brother David Steindl-Rast, as quoted
in Tom Shroder, *Acid Test: LSD, Ecstasy, and the Power to Heal* (Plume, 2015).

305 *every one of the five mindsets:* Regan et al., "±3,4-Methylenedioxymethamphet-
amine," e0258849; Anya K. Bershad, Melissa A. Miller, Matthew J. Baggott,
and Harriet de Wit, "The Effects of MDMA on Socio-Emotional Processing:
Does MDMA Differ from Other Stimulants?" *Journal of Psychopharmacology* 30,
no. 12 (2016): 1248–58, https://doi.org/10.1177/0269881116663120; and Philip
Kamilar-Britt and Gillinder Bedi, "The Prosocial Effects of 3,4-Methylenedioxy-
methamphetamine (MDMA): Controlled Studies in Humans and Laboratory
Animals," *Neuroscience and Biobehavioral Reviews* 57 (2015): 433–46, https://
doi.org/10.1016/j.neubiorev.2015.08.016.

305 *more interested in them:* Debra S. Harris, Matthew Baggott, Jack H. Mendelson,
John E. Mendelson, and Reese T. Jones, "Subjective and Hormonal Effects of
3,4-Methylenedioxymethamphetamine (MDMA) in Humans," *Psychopharmacology* 162, no. 4 (2002): 396–405, https://doi.org/10.1007/s00213-002-1131-1.

305 *psychological walls between you and other people:* Gillinder Bedi, Kinh Luan D.
Phan, Mike Angstadt, and Harriet de Wit, "Effects of MDMA on Sociability

and Neural Response to Social Threat and Social Reward," *Psychopharmacology* 207, no. 1 (2009): 73–83, https://doi.org/10.1007/s00213-009-1635-z; and Charles G. Frye, Margaret C. Wardle, Greg J. Norman, and Harriet de Wit, "MDMA Decreases the Effects of Simulated Social Rejection," *Pharmacology, Biochemistry, and Behavior* 117 (2014): 1–6, https://doi.org/10.1016/j.pbb .2013.11.030.

305 *communicate with greater honesty and intimacy:* Matthew J. Baggott, Jeremy R. Coyle, Jennifer D. Siegrist, Kathleen J. Garrison, Gantt P. Galloway, and John E. Mendelson, "Effects of 3,4-Methylenedioxymethamphetamine on Socio-emotional Feelings, Authenticity, and Autobiographical Disclosure in Healthy Volunteers in a Controlled Setting," *Journal of Psychopharmacology* 30, no. 4 (2016): 378–87, https://doi.org/10.1177/0269881115626348.

306 *Randomized controlled experiments:* Regan et al., "±3,4-Methylenedioxymeth-amphetamine," e0258849; and Bershad et al., "Effects of MDMA," 1248–58.

306 *authentic interest in others:* Kim P. C. Kuypers, Patrick C. Dolder, Johannes G. Ramaekers, and Matthias E. Liechti, "Multifaceted Empathy of Healthy Volunteers After Single Doses of MDMA: A Pooled Sample of Placebo-Controlled Studies," *Journal of Psychopharmacology* 31, no. 5 (2017): 589–98, https://doi .org/10.1177/0269881117699617.

306 *likely to engage in physical touch:* Anya K. Bershad, Leah M. Mayo, Kathryne Van Hedger, Francis McGlone, Susannah C. Walker, and Harriet de Wit, "Effects of MDMA on Attention to Positive Social Cues and Pleasantness of Affective Touch," *Neuropsychopharmacology* 44, no. 10 (2019): 1698–1705, https:// doi.org/10.1038/s41386-019-0402-z.

306 *increase self-compassion:* Sunjeev K. Kamboj, Emma J. Kilford, Stephanie Minchin, Abigail Moss, Will Lawn, Ravi K. Das et al., "Recreational 3,4-Methylenedioxy-N-Methylamphetamine (MDMA) or 'Ecstasy' and Self-Focused Compassion: Preliminary Steps in the Development of a Therapeutic Psychopharmacology of Contemplative Practices," *Journal of Psychopharmacology* 29, no. 9 (2015): 961–70, https://doi.org/10.1177/0269881115587143.

306 *tolerance and acceptance of others:* Harriet de Wit, Anya K. Bershad, William Hutchison, and Michael Bremmer, "Can MDMA Change Sociopolitical Values? Insights from a Research Participant," *Biological Psychiatry* 89, no. 11 (2021): e61–62, https://doi.org/10.1016/j.biopsych.2021.01.016.

306 *"places the critic and the judge aside": Peter Jennings Reporting: Ecstasy Rising,* directed by Peter Jennings, produced by Mark Obenhaus (ABC News, 2004).

306 *Harriet de Wit's team:* Hanna Molla et al., "Drug-Induced Social Connection," 15846.

307 *higher self-worth and greater global trust:* Ramona L. Martinez, Nina Radošić, Hanna Molla, Harriet de Wit, and Sonja Lyubomirsky, "Unique Social Effects of the Love Drug: MDMA, but Not Methamphetamine, Increases Feelings of Trust During Dyadic Conversations," *Journal of Psychopharmacology* (in press).

307 *This is the real me:* Matthew J. Baggott, Jeremy R. Coyle, Jennifer D. Siegrist, Kathleen J. Garrison, Gantt P. Galloway, and John E. Mendelson, "Effects of 3,4-Methylenedioxymethamphetamine on Socioemotional Feelings, Authenticity, and Autobiographical Disclosure in Healthy Volunteers in a Controlled Setting," *Journal of Psychopharmacology* 30, no. 4 (2016): 378–87, https://doi .org/10.1177/0269881115626348.

307 *unearthed something about themselves:* Jennifer M. Mitchell, Michael P. Bogen-schutz, Alicia Lilienstein, Claire Harrison, Sarah Kleiman, Katherine Parker-Guilbert et al., "MDMA-Assisted Therapy for Severe PTSD: A Randomized,

Double-Blind, Placebo-Controlled Phase 3 Study," *Nature Medicine* 27, no. 6 (2021): 1025–33, https://doi.org/10.1038/s41591-021-01336-3.

308 *studies on MDMA-assisted psychotherapy:* Alicia L. Danforth, Christopher M. Struble, Berra Yazar-Klosinski, and Charles S. Grob, "MDMA-Assisted Therapy: A New Treatment Model for Social Anxiety in Autistic Adults," *Progress in Neuro-Psychopharmacology and Biological Psychiatry* 64 (2016): 237–49, https:// doi.org/10.1016/j.pnpbp.2015.03.011; Ben Sessa, Chloe Sakal, Steve O'Brien, and David Nutt, "First Study of Safety and Tolerability of 3,4 Methylene-dioxymethamphetamine (MDMA)-Assisted Psychotherapy in Patients with Alcohol Use Disorder: Preliminary Data on the First Four Participants," *BMJ Case Reports* 12 (2019): e230109, https://doi.org/10.1136/bcr-2019-230109; and Jennifer M. Mitchell, Marcela Ot'alora G, Bessel van der Kolk, Scott Shannon, Michael Bogenschutz, Yevgeniy Gelfand et al., "MDMA-Assisted Therapy for Moderate to Severe PTSD: A Randomized, Placebo-Controlled Phase 3 Trial," *Nature Medicine* 29, no. 10 (2023): 2473–80, https://doi.org/10.1038/s41591 -023-02565-4.

309 *a small number of doses:* Mitchell et al., "MDMA-Assisted Therapy for Severe PTSD: A Randomized, Double-Blind, Placebo-Controlled Phase 3 Study," 1025–33; and Mitchell et al., "MDMA-Assisted Therapy for Moderate to Severe PTSD: A Randomized, Placebo-Controlled Phase 3 Trial," 2473–80.

309 *can be experienced as less traumatic:* A recent study conducted after the October 7 Hamas attacks at the Nova Music Festival in Israel found that survivors who had taken MDMA reported less trauma and mental distress, highlighting the complex and context-dependent nature of the drug's effects. The study's authors suggest that MDMA's effects on prosocial hormones, such as oxytocin, may have played a role in minimizing fear and enhancing feelings of camaraderie among the attendees during the traumatic event. Lucy Williamson, "Party Drug MDMA May Have Protected Nova Attack Survivors from Trauma, Study Suggests," *The Guardian*, March 7, 2025, https://www.bbc.com/news/articles /c9wpy14wyd0o.

309 *Neuroscientific research:* Boris D. Heifets and Robert C. Malenka, "MDMA as a Probe and Treatment for Social Behaviors," *Cell* 166, no. 2 (2016): 269–72, https://doi.org/10.1016/j.cell.2016.06.045; Matthias Liechti, "Novel Psychoac-tive Substances (Designer Drugs): Overview and Pharmacology of Modulators of Monoamine Signaling," *Swiss Medical Weekly* 145 (2015): w14043, https://doi .org/10.4414/smw.2015.14043.

310 *multiple systems in the brain:* Matthias Liechti, "Novel Psychoactive Substances (Designer Drugs): Overview and Pharmacology of Modulators of Monoamine Signaling," *Swiss Medical Weekly* 145 (2015): w14043, https://doi.org/10.4414 /smw.2015.14043.

310 *scientists and mental-health professionals:* Matthias Liechti, "Novel Psychoactive Substances (Designer Drugs): Overview and Pharmacology of Modulators of Monoamine Signaling," *Swiss Medical Weekly* 145 (2015): w14043, https://doi .org/10.4414/smw.2015.14043; Ben Sessa, Lauren Higbed, and David Nutt, "A Review of 3,4-Methylenedioxymethamphetamine (MDMA)-Assisted Psycho-therapy," *Frontiers in Psychiatry* 10 (2019): 138, https://doi.org/10.3389/fpsyt .2019.00138; Anne C. Wagner, Michael C. Mithoefer, Ann T. Mithoefer, and Candice M. Monson, "Combining Cognitive-Behavioral Conjoint Therapy for PTSD with 3,4-Methylenedioxymethamphetamine (MDMA): A Case Exam-ple," *Journal of Psychoactive Drugs* 51, no. 2 (2019): 166–73, https://doi.org/10.1 080/02791072.2019.1589028; Marta Zaraska, "Can Ecstasy Treat Loneliness?" *Scientific American*, October 15, 2023, https://www.scientificamerican.com

/article/can-ecstasy-treat-loneliness; Brian D. Earp and Julian Savulescu, *Love Drugs: The Chemical Future of Relationships* (Redwood, 2020); George Greer, "Using MDMA in Psychotherapy," *Advances* 2, no. 2 (1985): 57–59; Boris D. Heifets and Robert C. Malenka, "MDMA as a Probe and Treatment for Social Behaviors," *Cell* 166 (2016): 269–72, https://doi.org/10.1016/j.cell.2016.06.045; Franz Zublin, "When MDMA Was the Secret to a Happy Marriage," *OZY*, January 3, 2020, https://www.ozy.com/true-and-stories/when-mdma-was-the-secret-to-a-happy-marriage/258352; and Rachel Nuwer, *I Feel Love: MDMA and the Quest for Connection in a Fractured World* (Bloomsbury, 2023).

311   *at the University of Houston:* C. Raymond Knee, "Implicit Theories of Relationships: Assessment and Prediction of Romantic Relationship Initiation, Coping, and Longevity," *Journal of Personality and Social Psychology* 74, no. 2 (1998): 360–370, https://doi.org/10.1037/0022-3514.74.2.360.

Index

acceptance, 10, 13, 75, 78, 91, 164, 232, 238, 293, 306, 317

Acceptance and Commitment Therapy (ACT), 236–38

ACT. *See* Acceptance and Commitment Therapy

active listening, 125–30, 176–77

admiration, vs. feeling loved, 5, 59

affection, 26

affectionate communication, 147

age differences, 287–89

AI. *See* artificial intelligence

alexithymia, 277

Algoe, Sara, 195–96

All About Love (hooks), 272

all-or-nothing thinking, 228

ambivalence, 172

anxiety, 28, 51, 115

anxious attachment style, 280–81

Anxious Generation, The (Haidt), 44

apiculture, balance in, 91

appreciation, 195–96

Argyle, Michael, 170

Armchair Expert (podcast), 161

Aron, Arthur, 87, 155–56

Aron, Elaine, 87, 155–56

artificial intelligence (AI), 186–87, 291–97

Art of Communicating, The (Nhat Hanh), 142

attachment, 28, 70, 217, 275, 278–81

attention
in listening, 83–85, 126–27, 144
on the self, 62–63
showing with body language, 84, 144
turning outward, 62–63, 76

attraction, reciprocated, 164

attributional ambiguity, 56–57

attributional complexity, 228

Attributions, Mindful, 215

attunement, 256

authenticity, 64, 98, 109, 121–22, 179–80

avoidant attachment style, 280–281

balance, in nature, 91–92

Baumeister, Roy, 28

Beaches (film), 104
Beauvoir, Simone de, 300
being known, 60, 78–79
being yourself, 5–7
belonging, 27–29
Benedict, Nex, 141
Bergerac, Cyrano de, 65
Berne, Eric, 119
best friend relationships, 258–60
biobehavioral synchrony, 25
Blade Runner (film), 297
Blocker, Darrell, 129
body language, 84, 144,
    276–77
bonding social capital, 261
Book of Joy, The (Dalai Lama and
    Tutu), 196–97
boomerasking, 116
Boothby, Erica, 159
boundaries, 116
Bourdain, Anthony, 161
Breakfast Club, The (film), 76, 89
Brewer, Judson, 163
Brickman, Philip, 295–96
bridging social capital, 261–62
Brooks, David, 175
Brown, Brené, 232, 233
Buddhist traditions, 197, 199,
    207, 210

Cacioppo, John, 51
capitalization process, 170–73
care ethics, 204–5

caring
    about another's sharing of
        self, 7–8
    for others, 58
Carnegie, Dale, 128–29, 140,
    162
Carter, June, 221–22
Cash, Johnny, 221–22, 224
category-based generalizations,
    150–51
Chapman, Gary, 67
charismatic figures
    enthusiasm of, 166
    as good listeners, 131–33
chatbots, 186–87, 213, 291–97
ChatGPT, 292
chemistry, interpersonal,
    81–82
Chen, Serena, 101
Chesterton, G. K., 64
Cicero, 87
Clance, Pauline Rose, 120
Cleese, John, 277
Clinton, Bill, 131
Coan, James, 30
collectivist cultures, 283–85
commitment, 22, 89, 94, 170,
    204, 300, 302
common humanity, 207
communal relationships, 22, 39,
    147, 183, 295
communication
    affectionate, 147
    digital, 44–46

gender differences in style of,
116–17, 285–87
nonverbal, 84, 144, 276–77
video conversations, 47–48
community building, 35
companionate love, 22, 26–27
compassion, 197–99, 202, 236.
See also self-compassion
compersion, 303
compliments, 190, 258
conflict
feeling heard and, 137–38
listening vs. hearing in, 135
mutual understanding and,
101–2
polarization in, 140–41
connection
authentic, 179–80
curiosity and, 162–65
feeling understood and, 101
find-bind-and-remind,
195–96
improving with Listening-
to-Learn mindset,
150–54
interpersonal chemistry,
81–82
as an intrinsic goal, 58
MDMA and, 308
mutuality of, 76
neuroscience of, 42
practicing, 63
real-world social, 48–49
Relationship Sea-Saw and, 9

shared reality, 42–43
technology and, 43–49
See also disconnection
contemplative traditions,
kindness in, 197–99
conversation
bringing passion to, 176–77
focusing on the person, not
the topic, 178–80
gender differences in style of,
116–17, 285–87
kindness in, 195–97
mirroring in, 89–90
receiving responsiveness,
85–86
Relationship Sea-Saw as,
92–93
responsive listening, 83–85
showing curiosity, 82–83
staying present in, 281
video, 47–48
conversational receptiveness,
270
conversational self-focus, 62
Couples Therapy (TV series),
135
Covey, Steven, 125
cuddle hormone, 26
cultural differences, 282–85
curiosity
connection and, 162–65
defining, 157–61
enthusiastic, 165–68, 171,
173

curiosity (*continued*)
    HFASD and, 277–78
    showing, 82–83
    social, 159–61
    social interactions shaped by,
      180
    triggered by feeling loved,
      86–88
    See also Radical-Curiosity
      mindset

Dalai Lama, 181–82, 187,
    196–97, 216, 227
Damon, John William, 108–9
death, fear of, 28
depression, 41, 51, 239, 271
dialectical thinking, 227
digital interactions, 43–49,
    59–60. *See also* artificial
    intelligence; chatbots
disagreements, 137. *See also*
    conflict
disconnection
    social, 29–30
    technology and, 43–49
    understanding, 38–43
dopamine, 25–26
drive to disclose, 110
D'Simone, Sah, 55, 226

education differences, 287–89
ELIZA, 293
Emerson, Ralph Waldo, 167

emotional complexity, 230
emotional safety, 218–19
emotion(s)
    Acceptance and
      Commitment Therapy
      and, 236–38
    benefits of kindness on, 193
    differentiation, 231
    HFASD and understanding,
      277
    high-arousal, 166
    oxytocin and, 26
    shared positive, 24
    vocabularies, 231
engineering, balance in, 92
enthusiastic curiosity, 165–68,
    171, 173
Epley, Nick, 190
Eremocene era, 35
ethical nonmonogamy (ENM),
    298, 299, 304
evolution, 28–29
expressive writing, 110
external validation, 54–58
extraversion, 276
extrinsic goals, 54–58

facial expressions, 276–77
factor analysis, 67
family relationships, 258–60
Fast Friends procedure, 155–57,
    251
fears
    about sharing, 117–19

of being intrusive, 63
of death, 28
in insecure attachment style,
    279
of opening up, 64
feedback, validating, 139
feeling loved
by AI, 294–97
vs. being admired, 5
vs. being loved, 69–71, 316
common beliefs about,
    53–71
curiosity triggered by,
    86–88
deserving of, 14
difficulties of, 2–3
examples of, 19–21
garden metaphor, 93–94
Gen Z trends, 272–73
helping others to, 9
importance of in
    relationships, 2
lack of loneliness and, 38
mindsets and power to,
    13–14
need for, 29–30
paradox of, 317
requirements for, 7
as the secret to happiness, 2
self-compassion and,
    217–20
showing your full self and,
    5–7
survey responses on, 33–35,
    52–53, 80–81, 86, 265

what it's like, 3–4
what not to do, 4–5
why humans crave, 27–31
feeling unloved
loneliness and, 34–35,
    37–38
as motivation to seek bonds
    with others, 50–51
personal and societal costs of,
    49–50
find-bind-and-remind, 195–96
Fitzgerald, F. Scott, 109
flattery, 122
Flaubert, Gustave, 56
flaws, 65–66
focus
on the self, 62–63, 216
turning outward, 63–64, 76
forgiveness, 238–41. See also
    self-forgiveness
Forrest Gump (film), 163
Forster, E. M., 132
Four Christmases (film), 253
Fredrickson, Barbara, 24–25,
    168
Freud, Sigmund, 153
friendliness, radical, 200

Gandhi, Mahatma, 131
gender
concerns about feeling
    unloved and, 247
differences in conversation
    style, 116–17, 285–87

gender (*continued*)
  Listening-to-Learn mindset
    and, 286–87
  loneliness and, 286
  self-disclosure and, 116–17
  Sharing mindset and, 285–
    86, 287
gender fluidity, 288
generosity, 194–95, 204, 219. *See
  also* kindness
Gen Z trends, 272, 288–89,
  300
Gide, André, 7, 121
Ginnott, Haim, 257
Goethe, Johann Wolfgang von,
  202
Good Will Hunting (film), 126,
  127–28
Gordon, Amie, 101
gratitude, 195–97, 214–15
Great Gatsby, The (Fitzgerald),
  109
growth mindset, 215
guilt, 233

Haidt, Jonathan, 44
happiness
  capitalization of, 170–73
  feeling loved as secret to, 2
  invested in each other's, 25
  kindness and, 191–192
  romantic relationships and,
    247

undermined by pursuit of
  extrinsic goals, 57–58
hearing, vs. listening, 133–36
hedonic treadmill, 57
Hemingway, Ernest, 130
HFASD. *See* high-functioning
  autism
Hidden Brain (podcast), 133
high-arousal emotions, 166
high-functioning autism
  (HFASD), 276–78
honesty, 66, 75, 118, 215, 305
hooks, bell, 272
How to Change Your Mind
  (Pollan), 305
*How to Win Friends and
  Influence People*
  (Carnegie), 128–29, 140
How Would You Treat a Close
  Friend practice, 213–14
Human Face, The (documentary),
  277
Human Flourishing Program,
  271
humblebragging, 61

IBCT. *See* Integrative Behavioral
  Couple Therapy
if-only beliefs, 53–71
IFS. *See* Internal Family
  Systems
illusion of transparency, 82
Imes, Suzanne, 120

imperfections, 65–66

imposter syndrome, 120–23

impressing others, 58–64

impression management, 65–66

inclusion, 164

individualist cultures, 283–85

infidelity, 238–41

insecure attachment style,
    278–81

Inside Out 2 (film), 230

Integrative Behavioral Couple
    Therapy (IBCT), 234–35

interdependence, 248–50, 258,
    268

Internal Family Systems (IFS),
    235–36

interviewers, curiosity of,
    160–61

intimacy, 78, 79, 114, 248–50,
    259. *See also* sexual
    intimacy

intrinsic goals, 58

intrinsic motivation, 166–67

introversion, 276

intrusiveness, fear of, 63

Isaacson, Walter, 132–33

It's Great to Suck at Something
    (Rinaldi), 122

Itzchakov, Guy, 124, 128, 130,
    139, 140, 148, 149, 165

James, William, 229

Jones, Daniel, 155, 162

Jong, David de, 86

Jourard, Sidney, 97–98

journalists, as good listeners,
    132–33

joy, 196–97

Kashdan, Todd, 177

Keltner, Dacher, 230

kindness
    in contemplative traditions,
        197–99
    in conversation, 195–97
    extending, 188
    gap, 188–90
    media depictions of, 189
    prevalence of acts of,
        188–89
    recommendations for
        embracing, 199–200
    research on, 187–90, 190–95
    returning, 87–88

Kinkel, Kristin, 225–26, 228

Kluger, Avi, 124, 128, 136, 140,
    148, 149

Knee, Chip, 311

knowing, 78–79

Koch, Ed, 76

Krueger, William Kent, 111

Kumar, Amit, 118

laughter, 167–68

Leary, Mark, 28, 139, 216

Letter from a Kind Friend
  practice, 211–13
liking gap, 106
liking others, 163–64
limerence, 21–22
Linville, Patricia, 230
listening
  active, 125–30, 176–77
  attention, 83–85, 126–27,
    144
  with the body, 252–53
  comprehension and
    elaboration, 127, 145–46
  distracted, 130
  feeling heard, 137–38
  vs. hearing, 133–36
  listener's intent, 295
  mindset, 148–50
  paying attention, 83–85,
    126–27
  positive intent, 127–28,
    147–48
  responsive, 83–85, 141
  traps, 150–54
  when it matters, 128–30
  See also Listening-to-Learn
    mindset
listening attitude, 148–50
listening circles, 148
Listening-to-Learn mindset
  about, 11
  attachment style and, 280–81
  attention, 143, 144
  best friend/close family
    relationships and, 260

charismatic leaders and,
  131–33
comprehension and
  elaboration, 143, 145–46
consequences of, 140–42
cultural differences and, 283
elements of, 143–48
garden metaphor, 93
gender and, 286–87
goals accomplished by,
  136–39
HFASD and, 276–77
high-quality listening,
  125–30
improving connections with,
  150–54
learning to be a better
  listener, 148–50
in Letter from a Kind Friend
  practice, 212
vs. listening to respond, 125
listening vs. hearing,
  133–36
MDMA and, 306
multipartner relationships
  and, 302
narcissism and, 282
new(er) relationships and,
  266
Open-Heart mindset and,
  182–83, 184–87
parent-child relationships
  and, 256
positive intent, 143, 147–48
purpose of, 134

sexual intimacy and, 252–53
when it matters, 128–30
workplace relationships and,
    269–70
loneliness
    chronic, 51
    defined, 39
    disconnection and, 38–43
    feeling left out and, 164
    feeling unloved and, 34–35,
        37–38
    gender and, 286
    prevalence of, 35–36
    shifting perspective, 40–41
    trends in, 35–43
looks-money-status (LMS),
    55–56
love
    acting with, 201–6
    believing you are deserving
        of, 206–7
    companionate, 22, 26–27
    as a decision, 182, 187
    difficulties describing
        workplace feelings as,
        270–71
    felt for others, 23
    languages, 66–69, 83
    in a moment, 23–25, 245,
        264–65
    neurobiology of, 25–27
    passionate, 21–22, 24, 25–26
    reciprocal, 70
    romantic, 21–22, 25–26
    self-, 218

self-compassion and, 208–9
    showing, 185
    as a universal concept,
        271–72
    See also feeling loved
Love 2.0 (Fredrickson), 24
love-languages hypothesis,
    66–69
loving-kindness meditation,
    197–98, 214

Madame Bovary, 56
Mad Men (TV series), 109
Magee, Hailey, 82–83
Mahayana Buddhism, 197
Mandela, Nelson, 131
Markman, Howard, 135
Markoff, Morrie, 158–59
masking, 6, 109, 119, 120
maternal bonding, 26
MDMA (Ecstasy), 304–10
mental health
    feeling unloved and, 51
    loneliness and, 35
    self-compassion and, 208
    shame and, 233
metamours, 298
metaperception, 105
Michelangelo effect, 202–4,
    205
Michelangelo mindset, 12, 183
mimicry, 144
Mindful Attributions, 215
mindfulness, 207–8

Mindful Self-Care, 215
mindset of paradox, 226
mindsets
    about, 11–13
    age/education differences,
        287–89
    application of particular,
        275
    applying, 13–14
    cultural differences and,
        282–85
    Five Mindsets Diagnostic,
        321–22
    gender differences and,
        285–87
    growth, 215
    Michelangelo, 12, 183
    personality/socioemotional
        traits and, 275–82
    visibility metaphor, 315–16
    See also Listening-to-Learn
        mindset; Multiplicity
        mindset; Open-Heart
        mindset; Radical-
        Curiosity mindset;
        Sharing mindset
Ministers of Loneliness, 35
mirroring, 89–90, 217
misunderstanding, 45, 101, 155,
    162, 284, 285
Mizrahi, Moran, 136
modeling, 257
Modern Love (newspaper
    column), 155

mortality, 28
Mulan (film), 109
multi-partner relationships,
    297–304
Multiplicity mindset
    about, 12–13
    Acceptance and Commitment
        Therapy for, 236–38
    age differences and, 288–89
    applying to yourself, 229–32
    behavior experiment,
        237–38
    best friend/close family
        relationships and, 260
    education differences and,
        289
    forgiveness and, 238–41
    garden metaphor, 93
    HFASD and, 278
    Integrative Behavioral Couple
        Therapy for, 234–35
    Internal Family Systems for,
        235–36
    in Letter from a Kind Friend
        practice, 213
    MDMA and, 306
    multipartner relationships
        and, 303–4
    new(er) relationships and,
        266–67
    Open-Heart mindset and,
        205, 210
    parent-child relationships
        and, 256–57

romantic partners and,
249–50
self-regard and, 281
shame as an obstacle to,
232–33
Sharing mindset and, 240
strategies for integrating,
234–38
viewing others with, 225–29
Whole Trait theory and,
223–24
Murphy, Kate, 130
Murthy, Vivek, 36
music, balance in, 92
mutual care, 25, 78–79, 295
mutual cyclical growth, 89
myths, 53

Nagoski, Emily, 147
narcissism, 282
Need to Belong theory, 30
Neff, Kristin, 207
neural synchrony, 90–91, 294
neurodivergence, 276–78
neuroscience
connection, 42
feeling understood, 102
feeling unloved, 49–50
kindness, 193–94
loneliness, 41
love, 25–27
MDMA, 309–10
Relationship Sea-Saw, 90–91

self-compassion, 208–9
new(er) relationships, 266–67
Nhat Hanh, Thich, 142, 227
nonmonogamous relationships,
297–304
noticing another's sharing of self,
7–8

Oishi, Shige, 159
On Becoming a Person (Rogers),
202
Open-Heart mindset
about, 12
acting with love, 201–6
cultural differences and,
284–85
defined, 182–83
feeling loved, 204–6, 316–17
garden metaphor, 93
kindness and, 187–220
light metaphor, 186
Listening-to-Learn mindset
and, 182–83, 184–87
MDMA and, 306
multipartner relationships
and, 302–3
Multiplicity mindset and,
205, 210
necessity of, 183–87
new(er) relationships and,
266–67
Radical-Curiosity mindset
and, 182–83, 184–87

Open-Heart mindset (*continued*)
  self-compassion, 206–20
  sexual intimacy and,
    253–54
  workplace relationships and,
    270–71
opening up
  fear of, 64
  self-disclosure, 112–17
openness, 276
open relationships, 297–304
organizational citizenship
    behavior, 140
orgasm, 27
outgroup homogeneity effect,
    227
oversharing, 66, 110, 115
oxytocin, 26–27, 309

Pankseep, Jaak, 29
parent-child relationships
  as asymmetric, 254
  listening in, 129
  Listening-to-Learn mindset
    and, 256
  Multiplicity mindset and,
    256–57
  parental behaviors and
    child's feeling loved,
    257–58
  Radical-Curiosity mindset
    and, 256
  Sharing mindset and,
    254–55

partner affirmation, 202–3,
    204
Parton, Dolly, 83
Parts Unknown (TV series),
    161
passion, 176–77
passionate love, 21–22, 24,
    25–26
Passionate Marriage (Schnarch),
    251–52
Patch Adams (film), 125–26,
    127
Patrick, Brian, 167
Pennebaker, Jamie, 110
Perel, Esther, 28, 279
personal growth, 58
personality psychology, 275
personality traits, 222–24,
    275–282
perspective-taking, 278
physics, balance in, 91
pleasure, amplified by sharing,
    167–68
PolarBear chatbot, 186–87
polarization, 129, 140–41
Pollan, Michael, 305
polyamory and polyromance,
    297–304
positive caring intent, 127–28
positivity resonance, 24–25,
    168
Powell, John, 119
Pride and Prejudice (Austen), 6
projection trap, 151–53
prosocial behavior, 188

psychedelic science, 304
psychotherapy
    Acceptance and
        Commitment Therapy,
        236–38
    Integrative Behavioral Couple
        Therapy, 234–35
    Internal Family Systems,
        235–36
    MDMA-assisted, 308
public social reputation, 106
Putnam, Robert, 44, 261

questions
    asking big, 174–76
    asking for comprehension,
        146
    for choosing the right partner,
        311–12
    respectful inquiry, 270

Radical-Curiosity mindset
    about, 11–12
    active listening, 176–77
    age differences and, 288
    asking big questions,
        174–76
    best friend/close family
        relationships and, 260
    capitalization process,
        170–73
    curiosity detector, 162–65
    defining curiosity, 157–161

enacting, 173–80
enthusiasm and, 165–68, 171,
    173
Fast Friends procedure,
    155–57
focusing on the person, not
    the topic, 178–80
garden metaphor, 93
HFASD and, 277–78
MDMA and, 306
multipartner relationships
    and, 302
new(er) relationships and,
    266
Open-Heart mindset and,
    182–83, 184–87
parent-child relationships
    and, 256
relationship length and,
    251–52
sexual intimacy and, 253
workplace relationships and,
    269–70
radical friendliness, 200
Raitt, Bonnie, 70
rapport talk, 287
reciprocated attraction, 164
reciprocity, 64, 78–79, 87–88,
    114, 205, 316–18
Reik, Theodor, 134
relationships
    acting with love in, 201–6
    with AI chatbots, 292–97
    being yourself in, 5–7
    best friends, 258–60

relationships (*continued*)
  capitalization process,
      170–73
  close family, 258–60
  communal, 22–23, 39, 147,
      183, 295
  filtering vs. cultivating,
      311–12
  Gen Z trends, 272–73,
      300
  gratitude within, 195–96
  importance of feeling loved
      in, 2
  inner circle, 260–61
  listening to improve, 141
  long-term, 250–52
  new(er), 265–67
  nontraditional structures,
      288
  parent-child, 129, 254–58
  polyamorous, 297–304
  romantic partners,
      246–54
  shared reality, 42–43
  types of love in, 21–22
  workplace, 128, 140, 142,
      194, 237–71
Relationship Sea-Saw
  actions of, 7–8
  balance in, 91–92
  brain and, 90–91
  dance metaphor, 79–80, 90
  example, 76
  knowing side, 79–80

  mindsets for, 10–11, 92–94
  partner discernment and, 14
  perspectives, 10
  principles of, 77–80
  receiving responsiveness,
      85–86
  reciprocal, 8–9
  responsive listening, 83–85
  sharing side, 79–80
  showing curiosity, 82–83
  sparking curiosity, 86–88
  stages of, 82–88
  underwater see-saw
      metaphor, 76–77
  virtuous cycle, 88–90
Renner, Britta, 160
Replika chatbot, 292, 293
report talk, 286
reproduction, 28–29
resilience, 25, 30, 122, 208, 215,
      230, 255, 302
respectful inquiry, 270
responsiveness
  about, 81–82
  in actions, 84
  in listening, 83–85, 141
  receiving, 85–86
  virtuous cycle of, 89
Rinaldi, Karen, 122
risk-reward dilemmas, 111
River We Remember, The
      (Krueger), 111–12
Rogers, Carl, 127, 134, 202,
      293

Rogers, Fred, 131–32, 206–207
romantic love, 21–22, 25–26
romantic partners
  choosing well, 310–13
  feeling loved by, 246–48
  multipartner, 297–304
  Multiplicity mindset and,
    249–50
  Radical-Curiosity mindset
    and, 251–52
  relationship length, 250–52
  sexual intimacy, 252–54
  Sharing mindset and, 248–
    49, 250–51
Rusbult, Caryl, 89, 183, 202

safety, 29, 248–50, 259, 268
Salzberg, Sharon, 199
Sandstrom, Gillian, 159
Sartre, Jean-Paul, 300
Saunders, George, 57, 200
Schnarch, David, 79, 251
Schwartz, Richard, 235–36
secrets, 108–12, 232–33, 240,
  249
security, 8, 29, 152, 153, 219,
  249, 279
Seek (Shigeoka), 163
self
  being known vs. being
    noticed, 60
  caring about another's sharing
    of, 7–8

defining, 229–30
hiding the true, 65–66,
  77–78, 99, 120–23
masking, 6, 109, 119, 120
metaperception of, 105
noticing another's sharing of,
  7–8
overfocusing on, 62–63
sharing complexity of, 7
true, 5–7, 78–79
self-awareness, 186, 282
Self-Care, Mindful, 215
self-compassion
  Acceptance and
    Commitment Therapy
    and, 236–37
  building, 209–15
  How Would You Treat a
    Close Friend practice,
    213–14
  elements of, 207–8
  feeling loved and, 217–20
  Gratitude Letter to Self
    practice, 214–15
  how not to practice,
    215–16
  Letter from a Kind Friend
    practice, 211–13
  as loving yourself, 206–7
  MDMA and, 306
  Mindful Attributions
    practice, 215
  Mindful Self-Care practice,
    215

self-compassion (*continued*)
    practicing, 211–17,
        281–82
    Self-Compassion Break
        practice, 214
self-complexity, 230
self-disclosure, 98–99, 107,
    111, 112–17, 254–55,
    281, 283
self-doubt, 120
self-esteem, 216–17, 233,
    281–82
Self-Expansion theory, 87
self-focus, 62–63, 216
self-forgiveness, 237, 240
self-kindness, 207
self-love, 218
self-perception, 217–18
self-presentation, 58–64,
    65–66, 265
self-redemption narratives,
    228
self-regard, 281–82
separation, 29
serotonin, 309
*7 Habits of Highly
    Effective People, The*
    (Covey), 125
sexual communal strength,
    253
sexual intimacy, 252–54
shame, 232–34
shared reality, 42–43
sharing

balancing, 66
complexity of full self, 7
happy events, 170–73
pleasure amplified by,
    167–68
Sharing mindset
    about, 11
    age differences and,
        287–88
    in asymmetric relationships,
        246
    attachment style and,
        279–80
    best friend/close family
        relationships and, 259
    cultural differences and,
        283
    extraversion/openness and,
        276
    feeling understood, 100–3
    garden metaphor, 93
    gender and, 285–86, 287
    importance of, 107–8
    imposter syndrome and,
        120–23
    keeping secrets and,
        108–12
    in Letter from a Kind Friend
        practice, 212
    MDMA and, 305–6
    multipartner relationships
        and, 301
    Multiplicity mindset and,
        240

new(er) relationships and,
    266–67
opening up, 112–17
parent-child relationships
    and, 254–55
relationship length and,
    250–51
romantic partners and,
    248–49
self-disclosure, 98–99
self-regard and, 281
sexual intimacy and, 252
undersharing, 117–19
understanding how others see
    you, 103–8
workplace relationships and,
    268–69
Shepard, Dax, 161
Sherlock Holmes, 134
Shigeoka, Scott, 163
sibling relationships, 258–60
Significance-Quest Theory, 56
small talk, 175, 179–80
smartphones, 45
Social Baseline theory, 30
social bonds, 26–27, 28
social capital, bridging vs.
    bonding, 261–62
social cues, 106
social curiosity, 159–61
Social Curiosity Scale, 160
social disconnection, 29–30
social interactions
    curiosity and, 180

digital, 43–48
loneliness and, 39–41
real-world, 48–49
social media, 44, 59–60, 110
social norms, 288–89
social psychology, 274
social rejection, 142
social validation, 139
socioemotional traits,
    275–82
Southside Johnny, 30–31
Speaker-Listener technique,
    135–36, 148
Spiritually, We (D'Simone),
    226
stereotyping trap, 150–51
storytelling, 113, 257
strangers, feeling loved by,
    262–65
subjective experiences, 99
sucking at something, joy of,
    122
suffering, 214
Swann, William, 139
Swift, Taylor, 107–8
synchronization, 90–91

Talented Mr. Ripley, The (film),
    109
Tannen, Deborah, 116, 285
teacher enthusiasm, 166–68
technology, connection and,
    43–44

Ted Lasso (TV series), 6
Teresa, Mother, 38–39
Terkel, Studs, 160–61
{THE AND} card game,
    176
theory of mind, 103–4, 278
therapeutic alliance, 102–3
Theravada Buddhism, 199
Tomlin, Mike, 132
Tournier, Paul, 109
transference trap, 153–54
transparency, illusion of, 82
trauma dumping, 66, 115
trust, 9, 26, 47, 57, 75, 84,
    89, 98, 101, 119, 138,
    140–42, 239, 259, 285,
    298
Turing, Alan, 297
Tutu, Desmond, 196

ubuntu (finding worth in self
    and others), 92
UCLA Loneliness Scale, 37, 44
unconditional positive regard,
    127
undersharing, 117–19
understanding
    feeling understood, 86,
        100–3
    how others see you, 103–8
    making others feel
        understood, 178–80
unmitigated sexual communion,
    253–54

Unmoved Versus Over-the-Top,
    165
upward cycle, 79

validation, 139, 281
Vedantam, Shankar, 133
virtuous cycle, 79, 88–90
visibility, 59–61
vulnerability
    authenticity and, 109
    emotional safety and,
        218–19
    fear of, 64
    as an invitation, 66
    paradox of, 11, 99–100, 253
    sharing, 105, 121–23, 253

Walk the Line (film), 221–22
Wegner, Daniel, 110
Weizenbaum, Joseph, 293
well-being, 12, 22, 25, 48,
    110, 129, 142, 148, 179,
    192–94, 216–17, 254,
    309
Wheatley, Thalia, 85
Whitman, Walt, 224
Whole Self-Love Scale, 208–9
Whole Trait theory, 223–24
*Why Am I Afraid to Tell You
    Who I Am?* (Powell), 119
Wilson, E. O., 35
Winehouse, Amy, 101
Winfrey, Oprah, 132

Wit, Harriet de, 306
"Without Love" (song), 31
Wohltjen, Sophie, 85
workplace
    acts of kindness in, 194
    asymmetrical power
        dynamics in, 267–68
    listening in, 128, 140, 142,
        269–70
    Listening-to-Learn mindset
        and, 269–70
    Open-Heart mindset and,
        270–71

Radical-Curiosity mindset
    and, 269–70
Sharing mindset and, 268–69
World Happiness Report, 36

Yesterday (film), 121
you-in-their-eyes judgments,
    105–7
You Just Don't Understand
    (Tannen), 116, 285
You're Not Listening (Murphy),
    130

About the Authors

Sonja Lyubomirsky (AB, summa cum laude, Harvard University; PhD, experimental social psychology, Stanford University) is Distinguished Professor of Psychology at the University of California, Riverside, and the author of *The How of Happiness* and *The Myths of Happiness* (translated into thirty-nine languages). Lyubomirsky's teaching has been recognized with the Faculty of the Year (twice) and Faculty Mentor of the Year Awards. Her research—on the possibility of lastingly increasing happiness via gratitude, kindness, and connection interventions—has received many honors, including an honorary doctorate from the University of Basel, the Diener Award for Outstanding Midcareer Contributions in Personality Psychology, the Christopher J. Peterson Gold Medal, the Faculty Research Lecturer Award, and a Positive Psychology Prize. Lyubomirsky is an elected fellow of the American Association for the Advancement of Science (AAAS) and lectures all over the world, but makes her home in Santa Monica, California, with her family.

Harry Reis (BS, cum laude, City College of New York; PhD, social-personality psychology, New York University) is Dean's Professor in the department of psychology at the University of Rochester. The university has recognized his teaching with several awards, including the Goergen Award for Distinguished Achievement and Artistry in Undergraduate Teaching and a Lifetime Achievement in Graduate Education Award. Reis introduced the concept of responsiveness to relationship science and is noted for his studies of close relationships, with a particular interest in intimacy, attachment, and emotion regulation. He has contributed more than 250 papers to the scholarly literature and has received many honors, including distinguished career contribution awards for his research from the Society for Personality and Social Psychology and the International Association for Relationship Research. Reis was named to the Foundation for Personality and Social Psychology's Heritage Wall of Fame in 2019. His work is frequently featured in the media, including NPR's *Hidden Brain*, *Scientific American*, *Psychology Today*, and *The New York Times*. He lives in Rochester, New York, with his wife, a clinical psychologist, and their cats George and Sullivan, who are both delighted to participate in Zoom talks.